Henry Deane

Principles of conveyancing

An elementary work for the use of students

Henry Deane

Principles of conveyancing
An elementary work for the use of students

ISBN/EAN: 9783337280369

Printed in Europe, USA, Canada, Australia, Japan

Cover: Foto ©Paul-Georg Meister /pixelio.de

More available books at **www.hansebooks.com**

Principles of Conveyancing.

AN

ELEMENTARY WORK

FOR

THE USE OF STUDENTS,

BY

HENRY C. DEANE,

OF LINCOLN'S INN, BARRISTER-AT-LAW.

LONDON:
STEVENS & HAYNES,
Law Publishers,
BELL YARD, TEMPLE BAR.
1874.

JOHN CHILDS AND SON, PRINTERS.

PREFACE.

The plan of this book has not, it is believed, been adopted in any previous work, with the exception of Watkins' Principles of Conveyancing, the last edition of which, although published some thirty years ago, is still in considerable demand. So many changes have taken place since then in the law and practice of conveyancing that the Author has ventured to hope that there may be room for another treatise of a somewhat similar nature. The present work, however, is purely elementary; it contains nothing which is not familiar to the practitioner, and aims only at the assistance of students entering upon the difficulties of real property law. The second part comprises, in substance, some lectures delivered by the Author at the Law Institution in the years 1873 and 1874, and is inserted here by the kind permission of the Council of the Incorporated Law Society.

Lincoln's Inn,
October 1874.

CONTENTS.

	PAGE
INTRODUCTION,	1

PART I.

OF CORPOREAL HEREDITAMENTS.

CHAP.
I.	OF THE EARLIER TENURES OF LAND,	4
II.	OF AN ESTATE FOR YEARS,	31
III.	OF AN ESTATE FOR YEARS (*continued*),	59
IV.	OF AN ESTATE FOR LIFE,	81
V.	OF AN ESTATE TAIL,	110
VI.	OF AN ESTATE IN FEE SIMPLE,	125
VII.	OF COPYHOLDS,	153
VIII.	OF THE STATUTE OF USES,	182
IX.	OF A REVERSION AND OF A REMAINDER,	193
X.	OF AN EXECUTORY INTEREST,	207
XI.	OF ESTATES IN JOINT-TENANCY, TENANCY IN COMMON, AND CO-PARCENARY,	226
XII.	OF HUSBAND AND WIFE,	234
XIII.	OF AN EQUITY OF REDEMPTION,	239
XIV.	OF AN EQUITY OF REDEMPTION (*continued*),	265

PART II.

OF CONVEYANCING.

CHAP.		PAGE
I.	OF THE HISTORY OF CONVEYANCING,	283
II.	OF CONDITIONS OF SALE,	300
III.	OF PURCHASE DEEDS,	329
IV.	OF LEASES,	343
V.	OF MORTGAGE DEEDS,	365
VI.	OF SETTLEMENTS,	387
VII.	OF WILLS,	400

TABLE OF ABBREVIATIONS.

A. & E.	Adolphus and Ellis' Reports.
Amb.	Ambler's Reports.
Anstr.	Anstruther's Reports.
Atk.	Atkyn's Reports.
B. & Ad.	Barnewall and Adolphus' Reports.
B. & Ald.	Barnewall and Alderson's Reports.
B. & C.	Barnewall and Creswell's Reports.
B. & S.	Best and Smith's Reports.
Ba. & B.	Ball and Beatty's Reports (Irish).
Bac. Uses.	Bacon's Reading on the Statute of Uses.
Barnard.	Barnardiston's Reports.
Batty.	Batty's Reports (Irish).
Beat.	Beatty's Reports (Irish).
Beav.	Beavan's Reports.
Bing.	Bingham's Reports.
Bl. Com.	Blackstone's Commentaries.
Bli.	Bligh's Reports.
Bos. & P.	Bosanquet and Puller's Reports.
Bracton.	Bracton on the Laws and Customs of England.
Bright H. & W.	Bright on Husband and Wife.
Bro. C. C.	Brown's Chancery Cases.
Bro. P. C.	Brown's Parliamentary Cases.
Brod. & B.	Broderip and Bingham's Reports.
Burr.	Burrows' Reports.
C. B.	Common Bench Reports.
C. & P.	Carrington and Payne's Reports.
Ca. Ch.	Cases in Chancery.
Camp.	Campbell's Reports.
Ca. t. Talb.	Cases *tempore* Talbot.
Chanc. Rep.	Chancery Chamber Reports (Upper Canadian).
Cl. & F.	Clark and Finnelly's Reports.
Co. Cop.	Coke's Compleat Copyholder.
Co. Litt.	Coke upon Littleton.
Coll.	Collyer's Reports.
Colles' P. C.	Colles' Parliamentary Cases.
Cox.	Cox's Reports.
Cowp.	Cowper's Reports.

TABLE OF ABBREVIATIONS.

Cr. & Mee.	Crompton and Meeson's Reports.
Cr. Mee. & R.	Crompton, Meeson, and Roscoe's Reports.
Cro. Car.	Croke's Reports *tempore* Charles the First.
Cro. Eliz.	Croke's Reports *tempore* Elizabeth.
Cro. Jac.	Croke's Reports *tempore* James the First.
Curt.	Curteis' Reports.
D. & Sm.	Drewry and Smale's Reports.
Daniell C. P.	Daniell's Chancery Practice.
Dart V. & P.	Dart on Vendors and Purchasers.'
Dav. Con.	Davidson's Precedents in Conveyancing.
De G. F. & J.	De Gex, Fisher, and Jones' Reports.
De G. & J.	De Gex and Jones' Reports.
De G. J. & S.	De Gex, Jones, and Smith's Reports.
De G. & Sm.	De Gex and Smale's Reports.
Deac.	Deacon's Reports.
Doug.	Douglas' Reports.
Dow.	Dow's Reports.
Dow. & Ry.	Dowling and Ryland's Reports.
Drew.	Drewry's Reports.
Dru. & War.	Drury and Warren's Reports (Irish).
Dyer.	Dyer's Reports.
E. & B.	Ellis and Blackburn's Reports.
E. & E.	Ellis and Ellis' Reports.
East.	East's Reports.
Eden.	Eden's Reports.
Ellis Domesday.	Ellis' Introduction to Domesday Book.
Eq. Ca. Ab.	Equity Cases Abridged.
Esp.	Espinasse's Reports.
Exch.	Exchequer Reports.
Fearne C. R.	Fearne on Contingent Remainders.
Free.	Freeman's Reports.
G. Coop.	George Cooper's Reports.
Ga. & D.	Gale and Davidson's Reports.
Giff.	Giffard's Reports.
Gilb. Uses.	Gilbert on Uses, by Sugden.
Gould.	Gouldsborough's Reports.
Grant.	Grant's Reports (Upper Canadian).
Grant. Corp.	Grant on Corporations.
H. Bl.	Henry Blackstone's Reports.
H. L. C.	House of Lords Cases.
H. & N.	Hurlstone and Norman's Reports.
Ha.	Hare's Reports.
Hallam, Con. Hist.	Hallam's Constitutional History.
Hardres.	Hardres' Reports.
Hay. & Jar.	Hayes and Jarman's Concise Forms of Wills.
Hayes Con.	Hayes on Conveyancing.
Holt.	Holt's Reports.
Ir. Ch. Rep.	Irish Chancery Reports.
Ir. Eq. Rep.	Irish Equity Reports.
Ir. R.	The Irish Reports.
J. & H.	Johnson and Hemmings' Reports.
Jar. Wills.	Jarman on Wills.
Jo. & L.	Jones and Latouche's Reports (Irish).
John.	Johnson's Reports.

TABLE OF ABBREVIATIONS. xi

Jur.	Jurist Reports.
Jur. Arg.	Hargreave's Juridical Arguments.
K. & J.	Kay and Johnson's Reports.
Kay.	Kay's Reports.
Keb.	Keblo's Reports.
Keen.	Keen's Reports.
L. C.	White and Tudor's Leading Cases.
L. J.	Law Journal Reports.
L. R.	The Law Reports.
L. T.	Law Times Reports.
Lev.	Levinz's Reports.
M. D. & De G.	Montagu, Deacon, & De Gex's Reports.
M. & G.	Macnaghten and Gordon's Reports.
Mad. Exch.	Madox's History of the Exchequer.
Mad. Form. Ang.	Madox's Formulare Anglicanum.
Madd.	Maddock's Reports.
Man. & Gr.	Manning and Grainger's Reports.
Man. & Ry.	Manning and Ryland's Reports.
Mau. & Sel.	Maule and Selwyn's Reports.
Mee. & W.	Meeson and Welsby's Reports.
Mer.	Merivale's Reports.
Mod.	The Modern Reports.
Moo. P. C.	Moore's Privy Council Reports.
Moo. & R.	Moody and Robinson's Reports.
My. & C.	Mylne and Craig's Reports.
My. & K.	Mylne and Keen's Reports.
N. C.	New Cases.
N. R.	The New Reports.
N. S.	New Series.
Nev. & M.	Nevile and Manning's Reports.
No. Cas.	Notes of Cases in the Ecclesiastical and Maritime Courts.
P. Wms.	Peere Williams' Reports.
Ph.	Phillip's Reports.
Prec. Ch.	Precedents in Chancery.
Pri.	Price's Reports.
Q. B.	Queen's Bench Reports.
Reeves.	Reeves' History of the English Law.
Rep.	Coke's Reports.
Rob.	Robertson's Reports.
Russ.	Russell's Reports.
Russ. & My.	Russell and Mylne's Reports.
Ry. & Moo.	Ryan and Moody's Reports.
S. & S.	Simon and Stuart's Reports.
Salk.	Salkeld's Reports.
Sand. Uses.	Sanders on Uses and Trusts.
Sch. & L.	Schoales and Lefroy's Reports (Irish).
Scriv. Cop.	Scriven on Copyholds.
Seton.	Seton on Decrees.
Shelf. R. P. Statutes.	Shelford on the Real Property Statutes.
Sid.	Siderfin's Reports.
Sim.	Simon's Reports.
Sm. & Giff.	Smale and Giffard's Reports.
Smith, L. C.	Smith's Leading Cases.

Stark.	Starkie's Reports.
Story, Eq. Jur.	Story's Equity Jurisprudence.
Str.	Strange's Reports.
Sug. Law of Property.	Sugden on Law of Property.
Sug. Pow.	Sugden on Powers.
Sug. V. & P.	Sugden on Vendors and Purchasers.
Sug. Wills.	Sugden on Wills.
Sw. & Tr.	Swabey and Tristram's Reports.
Swan.	Swanston's Reports.
T. Jones.	T. Jones' Reports.
T. R.	Term Reports (Durnford and East).
Taunt.	Taunton's Reports.
Tu. R. P.	Tudor's Leading Cases on Real Property.
Turn.	Turner's Reports.
Turn. & Russ.	Turner and Russell's Reports.
Vent.	Ventris' Reports.
Ver.	Vernon's Reports.
Ves.	Vesey's Reports.
W. Bl.	William Blackstone's Reports.
W. N.	Weekly Notes.
W. R.	Weekly Reporter.
Wat. Cop.	Watkins on Copyholds.
Willes.	Willes' Reports.
Wil.	Wilson's Reports.
Wilmot.	Wilmot's Opinions and Judgments.
Wms. Exors.	Williams on Executors.
Wms. Saunders.	Saunders' Reports, by Williams.
Yo. & C.	Younge and Collyer's Reports in Chancery.
Yo. & C. (Ex.).	Younge and Collyer's Reports in the Exchequer.

TABLE OF CASES.

Ackroyd v. Mitchell, 246
Adams, Re, 403
Affleck v. Affleck, 221
Ainsworth, Re, 406
Alden v. Foster, 259
Alderson v. White, 243
Aldworth v. Robinson, 273
Allen v. Allen, 122, 126
Allen v. Knight, 278
Amfield v. Moore, 357
Amfield v. White, 348
Amiss, Re, 408
Anderson v. Anderson, 409
Anderson v. Pignet, 79
Andrew v. Hancock, 53, 54
Andrews v. Emmott, 415
Anon. (Dyer, 74b), 210
Anon. (3 Atk., 313), 256
Appleton v. Rowley, 83
Archbold v. Scully, 52
Archer's Case, 212
Archer, Re, 406
Archer v. Snatt, 268
Arlett v. Ellis, 171
Arthur, Re, 406
Ashmead v. Ranger, 169
Ashmore, Re, 408
Atkinson v. Smith, 373
Attenborough v. Attenborough, 218
Atter v. Atkinson, 407
Atterbury v. Walters, 269
Attree v. Scutt, 168
Att.-Genl. v. Day, 305
Att.-Genl. v. Fullerton, 54
Att.-Genl. v. Marlborough, 112
Att.-Genl. v. Stephens, 54
Audsley v. Horn, 274
Auworth v. Johnson, 54
Avery v. Cheslyn, 57
Ayling, Re, 407

Badger v. Ford, 171
Bagot v. Bagot, 94
Bailey, Re, 407
Baker v. Dewey, 333
Baker v. Holtzappfel, 52
Bandy v. Cartwright, 363
Bargent v. Thompson, 68
Barker v. Barker (2 Sim. 249), 87
Barker v. Barker (3 C. & P. 557), 359
Barlow v. Rhodes, 337
Burnett v. Weston, 208
Barnhart v. Greenshields, 269
Barroll v. Sabine, 243
Barrett v. Hartley, 253
Barwick's Case, 199
Baskett v. Skeel, 282
Bateman v. Allen, 39
Bateman v. Hotchkin, 94
Bates v. Johnson, 277
Bateson v. Green, 171
Baumann v. James, 304
Bayley v. Fitzmaurice, 304
Baylis v. Le Gros, 360
Bayne v. Walker, 53
Beale v. Sanders, 351
Beard v. Westcot, 214
Beardman v. Wilson, 361
Beckett v. Buckley, 136, 245
Beckett v. Howe, 407
Beevor v. Luck, 272
Begbie v. Fenwick, 371
Bell v. Chamberlain, 383
Bell v. Holtby, 120
Bellamy v. Cockle, 260
Bence v. Gilpin, 164
Bennet v. Davis, 87, 236
Bennett v. Womack, 348
Benson v. Scott, 172
Berkeley v. Hardy, 352
Berrey v. Lindley, 45

xiv   TABLE OF CASES.

Betts v. Thompson, 171
Bewick v. Whitfield, 95
Binks v. Rokeby, 323
Bennington v. Harwood, 255
Birch v. Stephenson, 354
Bird v. Boulter, 307
Biscoe v. Elliott, 58
Bishop v. Fountaine, 204
Black v. Jobling, 420
Blackford v. Davis, 252
Blagden v. Bradbear, 303
Blair v. Nugent, 250
Bochm v. Wood, 322
Bond v. Rosling, 350
Bonithon v. Hockmore, 253
Boraston's Case, 198
Borrows v. Ellison, 143
Botting v. Martin, 65
Bourdillon v. Collins, 303, 328
Bourne v. Taylor, 169
Bover v. Trueman, 163
Bovey v. Skipwith, 271
Boyce v. Greene, 302
Boyd v. Shorrock, 371
Boydell v. Drummond, 304
Bowles v. Stewart, 104
Bowles' Case, 94, 389
Bowman v. Taylor, 333
Brace v. Marlborough, 266, 267, 268, 276
Bradford v. Belfield, 378
Brandon v. Brandon, 252
Braybroke v. Inskip, 415
Brereton, Re, 421
Brereton v. Evans, 45
Brewster v. Kidgill, 357
Bridges v. Stephens, 95
Briggs v. Jones, 282
Bringloe v. Goodson, 223
Brown v. Cole, 247
Brown v. Quilter, 53
Brown's Case, 171
Browne v. Amyott, 144
Bruce v. Bruce, 220
Brudenell v. Elwes, 201
Brummell v. M'Pherson, 60
Brunt v. Brunt, 422
Bryan v. White, 408
Brydges v. Stevens, 97
Bubb v. Yelverton, 97
Buchanan v. Greenway, 259
Buckland v. Butterfield, 57

Buckland v. Hall, 64
Buckley v. Howell, 222
Buckmaster v. Harrop, 312
Bullock v. Dommitt, 359
Bulwer v. Astley, 243
Bunter v. Coke, 411
Burgess v. Wheate, 192
Burnell v. Martin, 248
Burrell v. Egremont, 98
Burt v. Haslett, 58
Butler v. Kynnersley, 95
Buxton v. Rust, 304
Byrd, Re, 407

CADELL v. Palmer, 214
Cadge, Re, 405
Caldecott v. Brown, 94
Caldwell v. Fellowes, 228
Callaghan v. Lismore, 69
Calisher v. Forbes, 270
Campbell v. Lewis, 62, 339
Campbell v. Sandys, 122
Canada Permanent Building Society v. Young, 319
Capron v. Capron, 145
Carey v. Doyne, 281 ,
Carr v. Erroll, 208
Carroll v. Robertson, 268
Carter v. Carter, 277
Carwardine v. Carwardine, 211
Casborne v. Scarfe, 241
Cassamajor v. Strode, 318
Casson v. Dade, 407
Castle v. Fox, 414
Caswall, Ex parte, 219
Caulfield v. Maguire, 97
Chadwick v. Doleman, 394
Chamberlayne v. Dummer, 96
Champernoon v. Gubbs, 391
Chaplin v. Chaplin, 113
Chetham v. Williamson, 50
Chichester v. Donegall, 383
Chisholm v. Sheldon, 252
Cholmley v. Oxford, 247
Church v. Brown, 63, 340, 347
Clark, Re, 407
Clarke, Re, 381
Clarkson v. Scarborough, 107
Clavering v. Clavering, 93
Clay v. Sharpe, 378
Clayton v. Blakey, 351

TABLE OF CASES.

Clayton r. Burtenshaw, 349
Cleare r. Cleare, 407
Clere's Case, 213, 415
Clifton r. Molineux, 173
Climie v. Wood, 371
Clinan r. Cooke, 303, 304
Cline, Re, 109, 145
Clove r. Awdry, 416
Clun's Case, 106
Cobb r. Stokes, 70
Cockell r. Bacon, 248
Cockerell v. Cholmeley, 221
Codrington v. Foley, 395
Coffin r. Coffin, 96
Cole v. Scott, 413
Cole r. Sewell, 201
Colograve r. Dias Santos, 131, 336
Coles v. Trecothick, 307
Coles r. Winch, 268
Collingwood v. Stanhope, 394
Colman, Re, 407
Colman v. St Alban's, 246
Colyer r. Finch, 282
Coming, Ex parte, 279
Constable r. Howick, 259
Coomber r. Howard, 355
Coombs, Re, 406
Coope v. Creswell, 251
Cooper r. Emery, 312
Coppinger v. Gubbins, 94
Corbet's Case, 213
Cordingley r. Cheeseborough, 320
Corder v. Morgan, 378
Coslake v. Till, 322
Cotterell v. Purchase, 244, 289
Cotteroll v. Stratton, 248
Cottrell r. Cottrell, 340
Cottrell v. Hughes, 80
Cowbridge, Ry. Co., Re, 136, 245
Cox r. Bennett, 414
Cox v. Dolman, 249
Cozens r. Crout, 410
Creaswell v. Creswell, 409
Croft v. Lumley, 68, 361
Crook v. Corporation of Seaford, 306
Crosse v. Raw, 358
Crusoe r. Bugby, 361
Cullick r. Swindell, 371
Cunningham v. Moody, 172
Cuninghame v. Thurlow, 225
Curling v. Mills, 46

DADDS, Re, 422
Daglish, Ex parte, 371
Danco v. Goldingham, 309
Daniel v. Gracie, 50
Daniels v. Davison, 34, 35
Dashwood r. Blythway, 260
Davey r. Durrant, 380
Davis v. Marlborough, 95
Davis r. Shepherd, 335
Davis r. Thomas, 243, 244
Davison v. Stanley, 73
Dean of Windsor's Case, 62
Dennett v. Atherton, 339
Denny r. Hancock, 309
De Vismo v. Do Visme, 323
D'Eyncourt v. Gregory, 104
Diaper, Re, 409
Digby v. Atkinson, 359
Digge's Case, 223
Dilkes, Re, 434
Dimmock v. Hallett, 308
Dinham v. Bradford, 304
Dixon v. Muckleston, 282
Dodd v. Acklom, 73
Dodds v. Thompson, 390
Doe v. Alexander, 362
Doe r. Aplin, 201
Doe v. Ashburner, 46
Doe r. Bartlo, 174, 402
Doe r. Batton, 71
Doe v. Bell, 351
Doe r. Bird, 361
Doe r. Cadwallader, 245
Doe v. Carter, 361
Doe r. Cavendish, 218
Doe v. Chaplin, 228
Doe v. Clark, 156
Doe r. Clarke (7 B. 211), 247
Doe r. Clarke (2 H. Bl. 399), 203
Doe r. Cole, 286
Doe r. Cox, 382
Doe v. Crick, 71
Doe v. Eyre, 263
Doe r. Gwinnelli, 172
Doe v. Halley, 201
Doe v. Hellier, 163
Doe r. Hogg, 361
Doe r. Howell, 212
Doe r. Huntingdon, 154
Doe r. Jones, 67
Doe r. Keeling, 361
Doe r. Lawes, 159, 295, 412

Doe r. Lewis, 92
Doe v. Lightfoot, 251
Doe v. Maisey, 246
Doe v. Massey, 263
Doe v. Masters, 362
Doe v. Mewx, 360, 363
Doe v. Morse, 45
Doe v. Olley, 382
Doe v. Ries, 47, 349
Doe v. Roe, 35
Doe v. Smaridge, 71
Doe v. Smith (1 Man. & Ry. 137), 45
Doe v. Smith (5 A. & E. 35), 71
Doe v. Steele, 338
Doe v. Strickland, 157, 158
Doe v. Tofield, 159
Doe v. Tom, 382
Doe v. Williams (7 C. & P. 322), 73
Doe v. Williams (5 A. & E. 291), 262
Doe v. Wilson, 362
Doe v. Wood, 33
Doe v. Wroot, 366
Dougall v. Foster, 230
Downshire v. Sandys, 107, 389
Drewe v. Corp, 309
Drowe v. Hauson, 318
Driscoll, Re, 282
Drury v. Buckingham, 83
Duddell v. Simpson, 327
Dudley v. Warde, 104
Dumergue v. Rumsey, 58
Dumpor's Case, 60
Duncombe v. Mayer, 104
Dungannon v. Smith, 214
Dunk v. Hunter, 349
Duppa v. Mayo, 107
Durance, Re, 420
Durham v. Legard, 320
Dyas v. Currie, 319
Dyer v. Hargrave, 318, 319
Dykes, Re, 221
Dykes v. Blake, 309
Dyne v. Nutley, 335

East v. Harding, 170, 173
East v. Twyford, 403
East London Waterworks Co. v. Bailey, 306
Easton v. Pratt, 359

Eaton v. Jacques, 366
Eckersley v. Platt, 422
Eddlestone v. Collins, 158, 373
Ede v. Knowles, 279
Edwards v. Champion, 174
Edwards v. Cunliffe, 259
Edmunds v. Povey, 276
Elliot, Re, 402
Ellis v. Griffiths, 259
Ellison v. Thomas, 394
Elwes v. Maw, 57
Emmerson v. Heelis, 307
Emuss v. Smith, 413
Ensworth v. Griffith, 243
Esdaile v. Stephenson, 324
Espley v. Wilkes, 353
Evans v. Bicknell, 282
Evans v. Jones, 244
Evans v. Upsher, 166
Everest v. Glyn, 166
Eyre v. Hanson, 259

Fane v. Spencer, 313
Farebrother v. Simmons, 307
Farewell v. Dickenson, 50
Farmer v. Curtis, 274
Farrar v. Winterton, 419
Farrer v. St Catherine's College, Cambridge, 423
Faulkner v. Bolton, 247
Fawcet v. Lowther, 241
Fell v. Brown, 274
Fenwick, Re, 418
Fettiplace v. Gorges, 237
Fildes v. Hooker, 246
Finch v. Finch, 422
Fisher v. Dixon, 130
Fisher v. Wigg, 227
Fitch v. Stuckley, 164
Flack v. Downing College, 367
Flattery v. Anderdon, 67
Fleetwood's Case, 132
Flight v. Booth, 320
Flower v. Hartopp, 317
Footner v. Sturgis, 280
Ford v. Chesterfield, 244
Ford v. Wastell, 259
Fordyce v. Ford, 309
Forth v. Norfolk, 132
Foster v. Harvey, 260
Fowler v. Fowler, 392

Fox r. Clarke, 385
Francis r. Minton, 367
Freeman v. Freeman, 420
Freke r. Carbery, 410
French r. Barow, 253
Frend v. Buckley, 314
Fry r. Noble, 87
Fuller v. Abbott, 54

GARDEN v. Ingram, 376
Gardiner v. Parker, 57
Gardner r. Rowe, 190, 296
Garland r. Jekyll, 168
Garland r. Mead, 175, 412
Garlick r. Jackson, 259
Garrard c. Tuck, 76
Garth r. Cotton, 389
Garthshore r. Chalie, 83, 390
Gateward's Case, 171
Gaze r. Gaze, 407
Gibbons r. Snape, 157
Gibson r. Holland, 304
Gibson v. Ingo, 269
Gilbert v. Lewis, 236
Gilbertson v. Richards, 50
Giles r. Warren, 422
Gilliatt v. Gilliatt, 311
Gisbourn r. Hurst, 51
Glass v. Richardson, 175, 412
Glenorchy r. Bosville, 191
Glover v. Lane, 155
Godfrey v. Watson, 253
Godwin v. Francis, 307
Godwin v. Winsmoro, 172
Goodlad v. Burnett, 413
Goodman r. Grierson, 243
Goodright r. Cator, 223
Goodright v. Cordwent, 71
Goodright v. Glazier, 423
Goodtitle r. Billington, 211
Goodtitle v. Morgan, 78
Gordon v. Eakins, 255
Gordon r. Lothian, 267
Goreley, *Ex parte*, 53, 376
Goring v. Bickerstaffe, 211
Gosling v. Gosling, 214
Goss v. Nugent, 304
Gossip v. Wright, 243
Graham v. Sime, 161
Grant r. Astle, 162, 164
Gravenor v. Watkins, 416
Gray v. Fowler, 326

c.

Greaves v. Mattison, 395
Greeno v. Cole, 94
Gregory v. Wilson, 68, 70
Griffith r. Pownall, 218
Griffiths r. Evan, 111
Griffiths v. Griffiths, 408
Griffiths v. Vere, 216
Grimwood v. Moss, 68, 73
Grissell v. Robinson, 346
Grute r. Locroft, 238
Grymes r. Boweren, 104
Gully r. Davis, 414
Gutteridge v. Munyard, 359, 361

HAINES v. Welch, 33
Halford v. Hatch, 366
Hale v. Pew, 202
Hale v. Tokelove, 424
Hall v. Betty, 314
Hall v. City of London Brewery Co., 363
Halsey r. Grant, 318
Hamilton v. Graham, 354
Hamilton v. Jackson, 390
Hampton v. Fellows, 381
Harding r. Crethorn, 72
Hardy v. Felton, 381
Hardy v. Reeve, 253
Hare r. Groves, 52
Harmer r. Priestley, 248
Harnett v. Maitland, 33, 54.
Harrington v. Harrington, 214
Harrison v. Good, 361
Harter r. Harter, 404
Hastilow v. Stobie, 407
Hastings v. Astley, 373
Hatton v. Haywood, 136, 245
Hawkes v. Hubback, 236
Hawkins r. Gardiner, 333
Hawtrey v. Butlen, 369, 371
Hearle v. Greenbank, 172
Hemming r. Griffith, 394
Henderson r. Squire, 72
Henfrey r. Henfrey, 419
Henkel v. Pape, 307
Herbert r. Salisbury Ry. Co., 374
Hervey r. Hervey, 389
Hewitt r. Nanson, 260
Heydon r. Smith, 168, 170
Heydon's Case, 156
Hewitt r. Loosomore, 282
Hiatt r. Hillman, 366

b

TABLE OF CASES.

Hibbert v. Cooke, 94
Higgins v. Frankis, 273
Hill v. Barclay, 68
Hill v. Buckley, 319
Hills v. Laming, 333
Hills v. Rowland, 68
Hindmarch, Re, 405
Hinds, Re, 405
Hitchin v. Groom, 305
Hobart v. Hammond, 164
Hodgson v. Johnson, 302
Hodle v. Healey, 256
Holder v. Preston, 175
Holford v. Hatch, 64
Holford v. Yate, 258
Holland, Ex parte, 328
Holland v. Hodgson, 371
Holliday v. Denison, 337
Holloway v. Berkeley, 168
Holtzappfel v. Baker, 52
Honywood v. Foster, 157
Honywood v. Honywood, 93
Hood v. Barrington, 303, 328
Hood v. Easton, 252
Hooke v. M'Queen, 308
Hopewell v. Ackland, 416
Hopkins v. Robinson, 171
Hopkins v. Rolt, 269
Horsefall v. Mather, 55
Horsefall v. Testar, 360
Horlock v. Smith, 254
Horner v. Swann, 225
Howard, Re, 420
Howard v. Digby, 392
Howard v. Harris, 242
Howard v. Norfolk, 211
Howard v. Shaw, 33
Howland v. Norris, 318
Hoy v. Smithies, 319
Hubert v. Treherne, 306
Hudson v. Temple, 322
Hughes v. Williams, 252
Hulme v. Tenant, 238
Humphreys v. Harrison, 246
Hungerford v. Clay, 253
Hunloke v. Gell, 218
Hunt v. Hunt, 406
Hunter v. Walters, 281, 282
Hurst v. Hurst, 223, 275
Hussey v. Hussey, 95
Hutchins v. Osborne, 416
Hyde v. Dallaway, 257

Innes v. Sayer, 220
Irby v. Irby, 268
Ireson v. Denn, 272
Isaacson v. Harwood, 368

Jackman v. Hoddesdon, 162
Jackson v. Innes, 373
James v. Dean, 34
James v. James, 280
James v. Plant, 337
James v. Williams, 304
Jefferies v. Alexander, 127
Jeffrey v. Neale, 358
Jenkins v. Gething, 57
Jenkins v. Jones, 379, 380
Jenner v. Clegg, 71
Jenner v. Morgan, 107
Jennings v. Major, 347
Jervis v. Bruton, 112
Jodrell v. Jodrell, 392
Jolland v. Stainbridge, 269
Jones, Re, 406
Jones v. Griffiths, 273
Jones v. Mudd, 323
Jones v. Newman, 305
Jones v. Reynolds, 46
Jones v. Smith, 268
Jones v. Thorne, 361
Jones v. Williams, 269
Jones v. Winwood, 218

Keech v. Hall, 246
Keigwin v. Keigwin, 407
Kemeys v. Proctor, 307
Kendall v. Micfield, 372
Kennard v. Futvoye, 280
Kennedy v. Green, 269
Kensington, Ex parte, 279
Kensy v. Richardson, 166
Kenworthy v. Schofield, 303
Kenworthy v. Ward, 227
Kerr's Policy, Re, 281
Kine v. Balfe, 344
King v. Smith, 246
Kinnersley v. Orpe, 361
Kirkewood v. Thompson, 380
Knapp v. Knapp, 391
Knight v. Crockford, 306

Lacon v. Allen, 280
Lacon v. Mertins, 377

TABLE OF CASES.   xix

Lainson v. Tremere, 333
Lake v. Currie, 416
Lampet's Case, 211
Lampon v. Corke, 333
Langdale v. Briggs, 413
Langley v. Hammond, 336
Langstaffe v. Fenwick, 253
Latch v. Furlong, 380
Lawton v. Lawton, 104
Lawton v. Salmon, 104
Layard v. Maud, 282
Leech v. Thomas, 54
Leader v. Homowood, 58
Lechford's Case, 163
Lechmere v. Clamp, 281
Lee v. Alston, 93
Lee v. Lancashire Ry. Co., 333
Lee v. Risdon, 57
Lee v. Smith, 46
Leech v. Schweder, 339, 363
Leeds v. Choetham, 53, 359
Legh v. Hewitt, 55
Lemage v. Goodban, 420
Le Neve v. Le Neve, 269
Leslie v. Thompson, 319
Lees v. Whiteley, 376
Lester v. Foxcroft, 191, 305
Lewis v. Branthwaithe, 169
Lewis v. Mattthews, 415
Lilford v. Powyskeck, 413
Line v. Stephenson, 363
Lingen, Re, 92
Llewellyn v. Jersey, 335
Llewellyn v. Rous, 108
Lloyd v. Carew, 208
Lock v. De Burgh, 108
Lockhart v. Hardy, 248, 257
Lofft v. Dennis, 52
Long v. Rankin, 224
Longbotham v. Berry, 371
Longstaffe v. Meagoe, 369
Love v. Windham, 210
Lowther v. Raw, 166
Lowthian v. Hasol, 268
Lushington v. Boldero, 94
Lyde v. Russell, 58
Lyle v. Richards, 335

Maas v. Sheffield, 402
Macher v. Foundling Hospital, 68, 361

Mackensie v. Robinson, 246
Mackreth v. Symmons, 277
Major v. Lansley, 237
Makin v. Wilkinson, 54
Manlovo v. Bale, 242
Manning's Case, 211
Mansfield, Re, 407
Mardiner v. Elcott, 169
Marsh v. Lee, 276, 277
Marshall, Ex parte, 415
Martin v. Cotter, 320
Martin v. Laverton, 415
Martin v. Smith, 351
Martinez v. Cooper, 282
Martyn v. Clue, 62
Massey v. Barton, 218
Massy v. Lloyd, 395
Massy v. Rowen, 236
Matthew v. Osborne, 159, 295, 412
Matthews v. Gooday, 280
Matthews v. Matthews, 414
Maundrell v. Maundrell, 77
Maxfield v. Burton, 281
Mawson v. Fletcher, 320, 326, 327
Mayhow v. Crickitt, 244
Mayor of Kidderminster v. Hardwick, 306
M'Farlane v. Dickson, 344
M'Murdo, Re, 401
M'Queen v. Farquhar, 319
M'Vicar, Re, 418
Melling v. Leak, 33
Melwitch v. Luter, 12
Menzies v. Lightfoot, 270
Meux v. Allen, 371
Midland Ry. Co., Re, 413
Mildred v. Austin, 245
Minshull v. Oakes, 62, 63
Miles v. Furbor, 51
Miles v. Miles, 414
Millett v. Davoy, 252
Mills v. Trumper, 107, 109
Mogg v. Mogg, 203
Moody v. Walters, 206
Moor v. Raisbeck, 419
Mooro v. Webster, 88
Morgan v. Bissell, 46, 349
Morgan v. Milman, 312
Morley v. Saunders, 98
Morris v. Morris, 97
Morritt v. Douglas, 407

xx   TABLE OF CASES.

Mortimer v. Bell, 310
Morton v. Woods, 382
Mosse v. Salt, 375
Moule v. Garrott, 64, 342

NANNY v. Edwards, 258
Natal Land &c. Co. v. Good, 269
National Bank of Australasia v. Cherry, 279
Naylor v. Collinge, 58
Neath New Gas Co. v. Gwyn, 322
Nelthorpe v. Holgate, 319
Nesham v. Selby, 303
Neve v. Pennell, 270, 271, 275
Newcomb v. Bonham, 243
Newlands v. Paynter, 236
Newman v. Selfe, 260
Newton v. Clarke, 407, 408
Newton v. Newton, 424
Nickells v. Atherstone, 73
Nicolls v. Sheffield, 208
Noble v. Willock, 402
Noke v. Awder, 287
Nokes' Case, 363
Norfolk v. Stanway, 154
Norfolk v. Worthy, 308
Northen v. Carnegie, 91
Norton v. Bazett, 408

OLDERSHAW v. Holt, 356
Oliver v. Richardson, 84
Olding, Re, 407
Ord v. Smith, 256
Orme's Case, 187
Ossulton v. Yarmouth, 374
Oswald, Re, 420
Otter v. Vaux, 278
O'Toole v. Browne, 413
Otway v. Sadleir, 417
Oxwith v. Plummer, 366

PAGET v. Foley, 249
Paggett v. Gee, 124
Paine v. Coombes, 344
Palmer v. Earith, 358
Palmer v. Hendrie, 251
Palmerston v. Turner, 323
Papillon v. Voice, 113
Parish v. Sleeman, 348
Parker v. Housefield, 281
Parker v. Taswell, 350

Parker v. Watkins, 252
Parkinson v. Hanbury (L. R. 2 H. L. 1), 252
Parkinson v. Hanbury (2 De G. J. & S. 450), 379, 380
Parteriche v. Powlett, 228, 231
Patch v. Ward, 383
Patch v. Wild, 254
Payne v. Burridge, 358
Payne v. Cave, 310
Payne v. Hayne, 359
Pawlett v. Att.-Gen., 240
Peachy v. Somerset, 166, 173
Peacock v. Burt, 277
Pearce v. Corf, 307
Pearce v. Morris, 244
Pears v. Laing, 250
Peers v. Lambert, 318
Pemberton v. Barnes, 232
Pendleton v. Rooth, 257
Penton v. Robart, 56, 58
Perkins v. Ede, 318
Perrott v. Perrott, 93
Perry v. Keane, 280
Perry v. Meddowcroft, 243
Perry v. Walker, 252
Petchell, Re, 420
Philipps v. Bridge, 362
Philipps v. Caldcleugh, 319
Philipps v. Sylvester, 324
Phillimore v. Barry, 306
Phillips v. Phillips, 174
Philpot v. Hoare, 66
Phipps v. Sculthorpe, 73
Pidgeley v. Rawlings, 93
Pilcher v. Rawlins, 298
Platt v. Ashbridge, 259
Playford v. Playford, 244
Plummer v. Whiteley, 108
Pollen v. Brewer, 32
Poole v. Shergold, 318
Poole's Case, 56
Pope v. Garland, 35
Porphyry v. Legingham, 166
Portman v. Mill, 318
Portington's Case, 116, 213
Portland v. Hill, 155
Potter v. Duffield, 328
Potts v. Thames Haven &c. Co., 312
Poulett v. Hood, 340
Powdrell v. Jones, 172
Powel v. Peacock, 169

TABLE OF CASES.

Powell v. Powell, 422
Powley v. Walker, 55
Prance v. Sympson, 257.
Press r. Coke, 259
Prescott v. Barker, 414
Price v. Bury, 279
Price v. Dyer, 47
Price v. North, 320
Prichard v. Prichard, 237
Propert v. Parker, 347
Prosser v. Rice, 277
Prosser v. Watts, 316
Proud v. Bates, 354
Purssglove, Re, 410
Purvis v. Rayer, 314
Pym v. Blackburn, 305

R. v. Baker, 246
R. v. Bettesworth, 402
R. v. Bonsall, 164
R. v. Ferrybridge, 93
R. v. Garland, 175
R. v. Hendon, 161
R. v. Hexham, 162
R. v. Wellesley, 161
R. v. Wilberton, 165
R. v. Wilson (11 W. R. 70), 175
R. v. Wilson (10 B. & C. 80), 175
Rackham v. Siddall, 415
Raffety r. King, 257
Rands r. Clark, 72
Reay v. Rawlinson, 417
Rees v. Parkinson, 248
Reeve v. Long, 202
Ren v. Bulkeley, 224
Reuss r. Picksley, 306
Rovel v. Watkinson, 97
Reynal, Ex parte, 369
Reynolds, Re, 424
Reynolds r. Pitt, 70
Reynolds v. Wright, 92
Richards v. Cooper, 274
Richardson r. Gifford, 351
Richardson v. Kensit, 46, 162
Richardson v. Langridge, 33
Richardson v. Younge, 257, 376
Richmond v. Evans, 380
Riddell v. Riddell, 339
Right v. Darby, 70
Rivet's Case, 172

Roberts v. Berry, 322
Roberts v. Croft, 280
Roberts v. Karr, 354
Robinson v. Musgrove, 320
Roddam v. Morley, 250
Roe r. Harrison, 67
Roe v. Hayley, 62
Roe v. Jones, 204
Roe v. Paine, 363
Rogers r. Goodenough, 424
Rolfe v. Chester, 268
Rolland v. Hart, 269
Rolt r. Somerville, 95
Rooke v. Kensington, 332
Rooke v. Langdon, 424
Rooper v. Harrison, 276
Rose r. Bartlett, 414
Roseingrave v. Burke, 145
Round v. Bell, 249
Rowden v. Malster, 156, 186
Rowe v. Wood, 253
Rufford v. Bishop, 375
Russel v. Russel, 279

SACHEVERAL v. Frogat, 355
Sale v. Lambert, 328
Samme's Case, 187, 291
Sandon v. Hooper, 252
Saunders r. Dehew, 278
Saunderson v. Jackson, 306
Savage, Re, 423
Savile r. Blackett, 224
Scholefield v. Lockwood, 254
Seagram r. Knight, 95
Seaward v. Willock, 202
Selby v. Pomfret, 271
Sergeson v. Sealey, 113
Seton v. Slade, 322
Skaife r. Jackson, 333
Shannon r. Bradstreet, 22
Sharman, Re, 410
Sherman v. Brandt, 307
Sharpnell v. Blake, 247
Shaw r. Bunny, 380
Shaw v. Johnson, 249
Shaw r. Neale, 269
Shaw r. Thompson, 172
Sheath v. York, 417
Shepherd v. Elliott, 254
Shepherd v. Keatloy, 315

TABLE OF CASES.

Shepherd v. Titley, 267
Shelley's Case, 112, 191, 227
Sherwin v. Shakspear, 323
Shirley v. Watts, 132
Shore v. Wilson, 305
Simon v. Motivos, 307
Simpson v. Clayton, 62
Simpson v. Hartopp, 51
Sinclair v. Sinclair, 420
Sloane v. Cadogan, 219
Smallman, Re, 269
Smart v. Harding, 302
Smart v. Hunt, 253
Smith v. Adams, 172
Smith v. Death, 225
Smith v. Harris, 407
Smith v. Robinson, 260
Smith v. Smith, 407
Smith v. Tombs, 302
Smyth, Ex parte, 107
Smyth v. Foley, 395
Smyth v. North, 66
Soane v. Ireland, 155
Souter v. Drake, 314
Spencer v. Marlborough, 201, 213, 218
Spencer v. Pearson, 268
Spencer's Case, 50
Spurgeon v. Collier, 242
St John v. Boughton, 250
St Paul v. Dudley, 113
Staines v. Morris, 63
Staines v. Rudlin, 260
Stanley v. Hayes, 363
Stanley v. Towgood, 359
Stansfield v. Hallum, 373
Stansfield v. Hobson, 257
Stanton v. Hall, 236
Stanton v. Hobson, 257
Stanton v. Tattersall, 308
Stead v. Nelson, 237
Stead v. Platt, 87
Stebbing v. Gosnall, 169
Steel v. Prickett, 171
Steele, Re, 424
Stephens v. Stephens, 214
Stephens v. Taprell, 421
Stephenson v. Hill, 155
Stockwell v. Ritherdon, 422
Stoddart v. Grant, 420
Strangways v. Bishop, 348
Stanhope v. Manners, 374

Stevens, Re, 415
Stranks v. St John, 346
Stratton v. Pettit, 350
Strodo v. Parker, 374
Sturgis v. Corp, 238
Suffield v. Brown, 336
Surplice v. Farnsworth, 52
Sutton's Case, 49
Swayne's Case, 158
Sweet v. Seager, 358
Sweetapple v. Bindon, 87, 172, 192
Swinfen v. Bacon, 72
Swire v. Leach, 51
Sym's Case, 235

TALBOT v. Braddill, 242
Tassell v. Smith, 273
Tavernor v. Cromwell, 157
Taylor v. Biddall, 214
Taylor v. Meads, 126, 237, 238, 402
Taylor v. Wheeler, 221
Tewart v. Lawson, 215
Teynham v. Webb, 394
Thelluson v. Woodford, 214
Thomas, Re, 408
Thomas v. Bennet, 392
Thomas v. Cook, 73
Thomas v. Jones, 401
Thomas v. Thomas, 268
Thompson v. Hudson, 255
Thompson v. Lapworth, 358
Thompson v. Lawley, 414
Thompson v. Mashiter, 51
Thomson v. Waterlow, 336
Thornborough v. Baker, 241, 372
Thorneycroft v. Crockett, 252
Thorpe v. Holdsworth, 276
Thresher v. East London Waterworks Co., 56
Thurlow v. Mackeson, 380
Tidey v. Mollett, 351
Tidswell v. Whitworth, 358
Tierney v. Wood, 190, 296
Tilley v. Thomas, 322
Timmins v. Rowlinson, 71, 72
Tindall, Re, 393
Tipping v. Power, 280
Toleman v. Portbury, 68
Tollet v. Tollet, 220
Tooker v. Annesley, 95
Torriano v. Young, 54

Townley v. Watson, 421
Townsend v. Wilson, 378
Townshend v. Windham, 392
Tracy v. Hereford, 97
Traherne v. Gardner, 166
Trappes v. Harter, 130
Trash v. Wood, 145
Trower v. Butts, 203
Tuckley v. Thompson, 280
Tuffnell v. Page, 174
Tullett v. Armstrong, 236
Turner, Re, 423
Turner v. Bennett, 35
Turner's Case, 234
Tutton v. Darke, 50
Tweedale v. Tweedale, 270, 271
Twynam v. Pickard, 60
Tyler v. Lake, 236
Tyrrell's Case, 188

UPPERTON v. Nickolson, 320, 326

VANE v. Barnard, 96, 389
Van v. Corpe, 347
Varley v. Coppard, 361
Venn v. Cattell, 326
Vernon v. Smith, 62
Vint v. Padget, 271, 272
Vizard v. Longdale, 83, 390
Vyvyan v. Arthur, 64

WADDELL v. M'Coll, 375
Waddell v. Wolffe, 315
Wade v. Coope, 244
Wadman v. Calcraft, 68
Wainewright v. Elwell, 294
Waldron v. Jacob, 303
Waldron v. Sloper, 282
Walker v. Barnett, 320
Walker v. Jones, 251
Walker v. Walker, 172, 390
Wall v. Bright, 415
Want v. Stallibrass, 325
Ward v. Ghrimes, 325
Warden, Re, 407
Warner v. Fleetwood, 130
Warner v. Willington, 303
Warrick v. Warrick, 269
Waterfall v. Penistone, 370

Watkins v. M'Kellar, 380
Watts v. Symes, 270, 271, 275
Waugh v. Land, 244
Wayne v. Lewis, 374
Webb v. Austin, 45
Webb v. Russell, 49
Weeton v. Woodcock, 58
Wellesley v. Wellesley, 94, 97
Wellesley v. Withers, 174
West v. Berney, 225
Westbrooke v. Blythe, 135
Western v. Russell, 306
Weston, Re, 422
Whitbred, Ex parte, 279
Whitbred v. Jordan, 280
Whitechurch v. Holworthy, 170
Whittemore v. Whittemore, 319
Wickham v. Hawker, 354
Wildgoose v. Wayland, 269
Wilkes v. Holmes, 221
Williams, Re, 406
Williams v. Ashton, 405
Williams v. Bosanquet, 366
Williams v. Bryant, 330
Williams v. Byrnes, 302, 328
Williams v. Chitty, 83
Williams v. Earle, 62
Williams v. Glenton, 323
Williams v. Lake, 302, 306
Williams v. Owen, 243
Willie v. Lugg, 271
Willowe's Case, 162
Wilson, Ex parte, 246
Wilson, Re (L. R. 1 P. & M. 269), 408.
Wilson, Re (L. R. 1 P. & M. 582), 424.
Wilson v. Clour, 254
Wilson v. Eden, 414
Wilson v. Hoare, 165, 174
Wilson v. Whatoley, 58
Winchester v. Knight, 164
Winchester v. Paine, 247
Windham v. Graham, 394
Wingrove, Re, 405
Winn v. Ingleby, 131
Winter v. Anson, 333
Winter v. Blades, 324
Winter's Case, 60
Wisden v. Wisdon, 417
Wood v. Smith, 130
Wood v. Wood, 420

Woodliff v. Drury, 208
Woollam v. Hearn, 305
Worley v. Frampton, 340
Worthington, Re, 418
Worthington v. Morgan, 281
Wortley v. Birkhead, 277
Wotton, Re, 406
Wright, Re, 406
Wright v. Dannah, 307
Wright v. Rose, 381

Wyllie v. Pollen, 269
Wynne v. Styan, 244, 263

YATES v. Aston, 368
Yates v. Boen, 125
Yellowly v. Gower, 54, 94
Yelverton v. Yelverton, 187

ZOUCH v. Parsons, 126.
Zouch v. Willingale, 71.

ADDENDA.

93, note (b), Honywood v. Honywood is now reported L. R. 18 Eq. 306.

315, note (r), Waddell v. Wolffe is now reported L. R. 9 Q. B. 515.

403, line 6, *after* enacts *insert* (s^1), *and add at foot as note* (s^1)—S. 9.

CORRIGENDA.

192, note (y), *for* 3 & 4 Will. IV., c. 104, *read* 3 & 4 Will. IV., c. 105.

305, note (x), *for* 5 B. & C. 520ⁿ, *read* 5 C. B. 520ⁿ.

PRINCIPLES OF CONVEYANCING.

INTRODUCTION.

THE object of this work is, first, to present to the student an elementary view of the various forms of ownership of land which exist at the present day; and, next, to examine the simpler forms of conveyance used in transferring land from one person to another.

<small>Object of the work.</small>

Land acquired, from an early date, the name of Real Property. For, since it is immovable, the owner of it could always recover the thing (*res*) itself from any person who had wrongfully deprived him of it; whilst in respect of movable property, such as furniture, or money, his only remedy was to bring an action for damages against the person (*persona*) who had done him the wrong, and such property was, accordingly, distinguished as personal property.

<small>Land known as Real Property.</small>

Land, again, and property connected with land, are said in legal phrase to consist of hereditaments; because when any owner of them dies without having disposed of them by his will, the law transfers his ownership (with an exception to be presently noticed) to a person, selected in accordance with certain fixed rules, who is known as the heir (*heres*) of the deceased. Hereditaments are of two kinds, Corporeal and Incorporeal. Corporeal hereditaments have been

<small>Hereditaments.</small>

<small>Corporeal hereditaments.</small>

C. A

INTRODUCTION.

Incorporeal hereditaments.

defined as those which affect the senses, and may be seen and handled bodily: incorporeal as those which are not the object of sensation, can neither be seen nor handled, are creatures of the mind, and exist only in contemplation (a). In other words, corporeal hereditaments comprise land, and tangible property annexed to, and forming part of, land; whilst incorporeal hereditaments consist of rights derived from the ownership of land; such, for example, as the right of presentation to an ecclesiastical benefice, a right of way, and many others. Of these incorporeal hereditaments some will be considered, incidentally, in various parts of this work; but we do not propose, except to that extent, to treat of this particular subject. And since the special way in which a man owns corporeal hereditaments is called (for a reason which will be explained hereafter) his estate in them, it follows that estates in corporeal hereditaments and modes of assurance relating to them are alone to be the direct object of our attention.

Corporeal hereditaments only to be treated of.

Term of years is personal property.

It was mentioned above that there is one form of estate in land which does not in the event of its owner's intestacy go to his heir. This is the limited ownership which arises when a person is entitled to the use of land for a term of years, and which is considered by the law as personal, and not as real, property. Such property is, however, so closely connected with land that it may, it is thought, be appropriately included amongst the subjects of a work which does not, otherwise, deal with personal property.

Necessity of an acquaintance with the earlier tenures of land.

A knowledge of the law relating to estates in land would be insufficient unless accompanied by a slight acquaintance with the circumstances under which their characteristics were gradually changed. These causes can only be ascertained by studying the history

---

(a) 2 Bl. Com. 17.

of the ownership of land, and of the gradual modifications which took place in it. The system which now obtains even yet bears marks of its ancient origin: indeed the old rules of real property law are still almost literally preserved in the case of copyholds. We will, consequently, devote our first chapter to a brief inquiry into the earlier modes of tenure, and the way in which they have been modified; by which means we shall also arrive at a knowledge of the different varieties of estates in corporeal hereditaments which exist in our own times.

PART I.

OF CORPOREAL HEREDITAMENTS.

CHAPTER I.

OF THE EARLIER TENURES OF LAND.

Difference between the present and former systems of land tenure. IT is well known that the system of land tenure which obtains in this country at the present day permits of land being, practically, the subject of absolute property; so that its owner may do as he pleases with it during his lifetime, and dispose of it unrestrictedly by a will to take effect after his death. But in the earlier systems from which our own is derived no such absolute proprietorship was recognised. If a *Tenure by the family.* tribe settled down on a tract of country, part of the land was distributed in lots amongst the families who composed the tribe, whilst the rest was allowed to remain uncultivated, and formed the common property of all. At first the portion allotted to each family did not belong to it absolutely, but might be taken from it with a view to a fresh distribution of the land amongst the various members of the State (a). In time, however, each family acquired a right to hold its land in perpetuity, the management of the estate, and its ostensible ownership, belonging to the head of the family. But his interest in it did not extend beyond his own lifetime, and he had no power to prevent it from devolving on his descendants after his death. He had, therefore, that which we now call an

---

(a) See the account of Irish Gavelkind, 3 Hallam, Con. Hist. 458.

estate for life, whilst the family, as a whole, had that kind of interest from which our present estate tail is derived.

As the tribe grew in importance, and became a nation, certain families (those usually who formed the original stock) acquired higher rank than the others; the head of the most important of these became, with varying title, chief of the State, whilst the principal members of the others composed his council. The whole of the public land was vested in the chief as representing the State, and he, when a fresh tract of country was acquired, by conquest or otherwise, would retain some of it for his own use, and distribute part of the remainder amongst the principal leaders of the people. By this means the great families came to have more land than they could cultivate themselves, and the heads of them would consequently, in their turn, allot some part of their estates amongst those military retainers by whom every chieftain was surrounded. These did not, at first, obtain any property in such lands: they were merely entitled to have the use of them to cultivate for their own benefit. From this plan of distributing land arose two new names: the chieftain being called the Lord, from the Teutonic word *Hláford*—a giver,—whilst the retainer was called the Vassal, a word signifying a servant. The vassal originally held his land during the pleasure of his lord, and was then said to have a *Munus* or Gift: later on, he was allowed to have an estate for life, and this was distinguished as a *Beneficium* or Benefice (*b*).

[margin: The heads of great families distribute part of their lands amongst their retainers. The Lord and the Vassal. Munus. Beneficium.]

When a nation was in its infancy it was a matter of course that every able-bodied man should, when required, take up arms against the public enemy, and when the great men received grants of public land,

[margin: Military service an incident of land tenure.]

(*b*) Wright Ten. 19.

each grant was invariably accompanied by a condition of performing military service for the State, not only personally, but attended by a certain number of armed followers. The lords, therefore, when they in turn bestowed lands upon their vassals, made it a condition that the latter should accompany them to battle whenever required to do so. Hence the liability to perform military service became a universal accompaniment of the possession of land.

We have said that the land which a vassal received was at first held by him either during his lord's pleasure or for his own lifetime, and in the latter case it returned to the lord on the vassal's death. If, however, some member of the vassal's family was capable of performing military service, the lord would generally be disposed to allow him to remain in possession of the same land. Thus the estate of the vassal grew to be much the same as that of the lord, and hence, after a while, it became customary for the vassal to receive an estate similar to that of the lord; one, that is, conferring on him an estate for life, and descending to his issue after his death. Such an estate was called a *Feudum*, or Fee (c), and the system of tenure under which it existed is known as the Feudal System. But although land so granted might go in the vassal's family from one generation to another, its ultimate ownership still remained with the lord and his successors; it still formed a part of his seigniory or lordship; the tenant still remained liable to perform various military and other services; and if these were not duly rendered, or if his issue became extinct, his fee formed again the property of that family from whom it had been originally derived. A similar rule applied to the estates held by the lords: for these also returned to the State if the owner's issue became extinct, and were, moreover, liable to forfeiture if the

Fee.

(c) Wright Ten. 19.

OF THE EARLIER TENURES OF LAND.

lord failed to perform his due services, or were convicted of any grievous crime. The system which has been thus briefly sketched out was that in vogue amongst the Normans in the beginning of the eleventh century, and we will proceed to notice how they put it into practice upon their arrival in this country.

After the Battle of Hastings, William the Conqueror seized upon all the former Boc' land, or private estates, of Edward the Confessor, as well as upon the lands of those Saxons who had fought on the side of Harold; and the large tracts of land thus placed at his disposal were subsequently increased by the forfeitures, consequent on the many rebellions of the Saxons, which took place during the years immediately following the Conquest. Of these lands the king, following the system already described, retained part as his own demesne (*d*), and out of the rest made large grants to the principal chieftains, or barons, who had accompanied him from Normandy. Each estate granted to a baron, and made up of adjoining lands, was called his manor, and the immense extent of land thus disposed of by William may be estimated from the fact that, as appears by Domesday Book, the Earl of Moreton (William's brother) received no less than seven hundred and ninety-three manors, whilst many other barons received from one hundred to four hundred apiece (*e*). These manors were also dealt with according to the feudal system, that is to say, each was divided into two parts. Of these the baron reserved one to form his own demesne; cultivating so much of it as he thought fit, and leaving some as forest and marsh land, some (known as the lord's waste) as common grazing ground for the cattle of himself, his vassals, and his dependents. The other he distributed into fees, which he gave to his vassals.

William the Conqueror seizes upon large tracts of land.

He retains part as his own demesne and grants fees to his barons.

The Manor.

(*d*) From the French *mesner*, to govern.
(*e*) 1 Ellis Domesday, 247.

OF CORPOREAL HEREDITAMENTS.

Tenure of Fees granted at the Conquest. Knight Service.

All fees granted at the Conquest, whether to the barons, or by them to their vassals, were held by the tenure of Knight Service; that is to say, on condition of performing military service, when required; this being considered the most honourable form of tenure. Its principal characteristics were that the services to be rendered were uncertain, and also free, that is, worthy of being performed by a free man. The principal incidents of the tenure were Fealty and Homage. Of these, fealty was the older, and existed before the introduction of fees: it consisted in an acknowledgment, publicly made, of the relative position of the lord and his tenant: thus furnishing evidence to which either could resort to show what were the lands granted to the tenant, and what the conditions on which he held them.

Fealty and Homage.

In taking the oath of fealty (fidelity) the tenant stood covered before his lord, and swore that he would be his faithful tenant and render his due services. Afterwards, when it became usual to grant fees (which, since they extended beyond the lifetime of the tenant and went to his heir, were said to be "estates of inheritance"), homage was added to fealty, in order, by having a ceremony distinct from fealty, and publicly performed, to make it a matter of notoriety that the tenant had a more durable grant than one for his life only (*f*). Homage thus became the characteristic mark of such grants, and could only be claimed or rendered by the owner of an estate of inheritance.

In doing homage, the tenant knelt, uncovered and ungirt, before his lord, professed himself to be his man (*homo*), and received a kiss from him in recognition of the close intimacy which was hence-

---

(*f*) 1 Co. Litt. (Thomas Ed.), 65ᵃ note (*e*).

forth to subsist between them; after which he took
the oath of fealty in the usual way (*g*).

Homage, besides expressing this personal relation
between lord and tenant, drew with it other important consequences. A lord who took homage from
his tenant thereby guaranteed him secure possession
of his lands; and, on the other hand, could not, until
he had received his tenant's homage, claim many of
the privileges incident to his position of lord. The
performance of homage was, therefore, a benefit for
both parties, and could, if necessary, be enforced by
process of law.

In addition to the tenure by Knight Service, which
the Normans had brought with them, they soon came
to recognise, in a modified form, another tenure already established in England. It has been previously
mentioned that many of the Saxons had lost their
lands after the Conquest and during the subsequent
rebellions, and this number comprised nearly all the
eorls and thanes who made up the Saxon nobility.
There remained, however, a large number of middle-
class landowners, or ceorls, who had taken no part in
the struggle between William and Harold. These
at first remained unmolested in their estates, but after
a time, when a strong personal hatred had sprung
up between the Saxons and the Normans, the lands
of all the ceorls were comprised indiscriminately in
the grants made by the king. The Saxons, therefore, complained to William, who, after consulting his
barons, decided that what the ceorls could obtain of
their lords should be their own by inviolable right.
The Norman lords, however, were not disposed to give
up their newly-acquired territories without some
equivalent, and thus the Saxons who received back
any part of their lands were bound thenceforth by

New forms of tenure adopted by the Nor- mans.

(*g*) Bracton, lib. 2, c. 35, ¶ 8.

constant serviceableness to purchase their lord's favour (*h*).

Socage Tenure. The tenure thus established was called Socage (*i*) tenure, and, although modified to fit in with the feudal system, retained many marks of its Saxon origin.

Its characteristics. The great characteristic of Socage tenure was that the tenant was not bound to render military service, but held on what were considered the less honourable terms of paying rent, or rendering services, as to which it was essential that they should be both certain and free. The rent might be paid either in money or in kind, and the services rendered usually consisted in giving assistance in cultivating the lord's demesne. So long as the tenant observed these conditions he had a tenure as secure as that of Knight Service, although less highly esteemed.

Normans, after a time, hold land by Socage tenure. At first this tenure was confined to the Saxon freemen, but it is probable that as the kingdom became more settled, and trade increased, many of the Normans held lands in this way (*j*), since we learn that tenants by Socage were numerous even before the reign of Edward the First (*k*). Every tenant by Socage was bound to take an oath of fealty to his lord, and later on, when the obligation of military service ceased to be personal, he appears to have occasionally done homage also (*l*).

Fealty an incident of this tenure.

Homage sometimes added.

Every tenant had to be publicly put in Besides the public ceremonies of homage and fealty, it was also necessary that every tenant, whether by

---

(*h*) Somner on Gavelkind, 128.
(*i*) The derivation of this word has been ascribed by some writers to the French *soc*, a ploughshare, because the tenants were originally bound to assist in ploughing their lord's lands—by others to the Saxon *soc*, which signifies a franchise or privilege.
(*j*) As early as the date of Domesday Book (1085) many of the burdens of tenures had been commuted into money payments. 1 Ellis, Domesday viii.
(*k*) 2 Hallam's Middle Ages, 483.
(*l*) 2 Bl. Com. 79.

Knight Service or by Socage, should be openly put in formal possession of the land which he was to hold. This was called "livery (delivery) of the seisin," and might be accomplished either by a delivery by the lord to the tenant of some fantastic symbol; or by a public acknowledgment of the grant made by both parties in one of the king's courts; or, on the land, by the lord's handing to the tenant, before witnesses, some symbol of the land itself, such as a sod or piece of turf. When the king made a grant he usually directed a writ to the sheriff of the county where the lands lay, commanding him to deliver seisin of them to the grantee (*m*). The vassal to whom livery of seisin had been made was deemed to be in full possession of his feud, and was therefore said to be "enfeoffed." In addition to this formal putting into possession, it was usual, as early as the Conquest, to have a charter or deed, evidencing the fact of feoffment having been made (*n*). *Possession of his land. Livery of Seisin. A deed also usual.*

Those barons who received their lands direct from the king were called tenants *in capite* (in chief), and these naturally did homage and fealty to him. Other tenants at first did so only to the lords from whom they had received their lands, but about twenty years after the Conquest a law was passed that all freemen should profess themselves to be vassals of William as king, and thus bound to do homage and fealty to him as well as to their lords. The king, from whom the lands were originally derived, was in consequence said to be the "lord paramount," whilst the intermediate donors were called "mesne" (middle) lords, and thus sprung up the theory, which still holds good, that all lands in this country are held from the sovereign, who (homage having been abolished) is still entitled to an oath of fealty from every owner of land, although the obligation is never enforced. And *Tenants in capite did homage to the king. But other tenants did not at first. A change introduced. King styled Lord Paramount. Other lords called Mesne Lords.*

(*m*) Mad. Form. Ang. x.
(*n*) Ibid. iii.

hence also it is that, as mentioned in our Introduction, it is more accurate to speak of a person as having an "estate" in land, or as being a tenant of land, than as being the owner of land.

<small>Court Baron an incident of every manor.</small> In addition to the various services which he was entitled to claim from his tenants, every baron who had received a manor from the Crown had, as an essential incident of his grant, the right to hold a Court Baron (*o*), to which all his free tenants were bound to come. It was at these courts that homage and fealty were publicly performed, and they also served the purpose of adjusting claims and differences between the lord and his tenants, or between the tenants themselves. In these matters the tenants were the judges, and the proceedings were recorded by the lord's steward or deputy on the manor roll. Courts Baron had, originally, a criminal, as well as a civil, jurisdiction, but their criminal jurisdiction was soon taken away from them, and since civil proceedings originated in them were liable, at any stage, to be transferred to the king's courts, the Court Baron soon fell into disuse.

<small>Villein Tenure.</small> Besides the tenures of Knight Service and Socage, by one of which every freeman held his lands, there gradually arose another of an inferior nature. There had existed amongst the Saxons, previously to the Conquest, a large number of serfs, or slaves, who were either the descendants of the ancient Celtic population, or else Saxons who, through extreme poverty (*p*), or the commission of some crime, had fallen into a state of slavery. These wretched creatures were but little affected by the Conquest beyond the change of masters which it entailed. Some of them were employed in the lowest menial offices, the others (called by the Normans "villeins,") were employed in cultivating

---

(*o*) *Melwich* v. *Luter*, 4 Rep. 26ᵃ.
(*p*) 2 Hallam's Middle Ages, 384.

the lords' demesne lands, and were allotted in return
a small plot of ground from which to extract subsistence for themselves and their families. These lands
they held entirely at the will of their lord, a natural
consequence of their being themselves his property.
This tenure (if indeed it can be said to have been
originally a tenure at all) was called "Villein tenure,"
and was said to be base, both on account of the
nature of the services rendered, and of the uncertainty
which accompanied them; the serf being also unable
to quit the manor without his lord's permission.

Thus the three great tenures established in this country soon after the Conquest were, Tenure by Knight Service, Socage Tenure, and Villein Tenure. *Three great tenures soon after the Conquest were Tenure by Knight Service, Socage Tenure, and Villein Tenure.*

There was also another variety of Socage tenure which deserves mention. We learn from Bracton (*q*) that there were in his time (about 1285) on the king's demesne, in addition to the serfs, free men (probably of the lowest class amongst the Saxons), who had formerly held their lands by services free and certain, and that after the Conquest these received their holdings back again to hold in villenage (that is, by Villein tenure) on condition of performing services base, but freely performed and certain. "These indeed," he says, "are said to be bound to the soil, but they are none the less free, and although they may do base services, they do them, not by reason of their personal condition, but by reason of their tenure; and they are said to be bound to the soil because they enjoy this privilege, that they cannot be removed so long as they perform their due services ; nor can they be compelled to remain unless they choose. And to these no deeds" (showing their title to their lands) "are given, but if wrongfully dispossessed of their lands *Villein Socage. Bracton's account of it.*

(*q*) Lib. i. c. 11, ¶ 1.

they can be restored, because they can show that they know the certainty of their services and works by the year."

Villein Socage called also tenure by ancient demesne.

This tenure was called "Villein Socage" because it partook of the nature of both free and base tenures. It is to be found only in lands of ancient demesne, that is, in lands belonging to the Crown immediately after the Conquest, or in manors originally granted by the Crown, from which cause it is sometimes called tenure by ancient demesne, and was probably the result of the policy of the Conqueror, who, in the earlier years of his reign, made many attempts to ingratiate himself with his new subjects.

Burgage Tenure.

There were, besides, some other varieties of Socage tenure which may be here briefly noticed. Of these was Burgage (or Borough) tenure, where houses, or lands formerly the sites of houses, were held of the king, or of some lord, by a certain established rent (*r*). These boroughs had often customs of their own, such as that of Borough English, by which a man's land descended to his youngest son, and the custom of the City of London, by which all sons succeeded in equal shares on the father's death. These customs are for the most part abolished, but one, namely, Gavelkind, still prevails in some parts of Kent: its principal characteristics are, that the possessor of lands thus held could always alienate them by will (a privilege not extended to other tenants until the time of Henry the Eighth), and that the course of descent is to all the sons equally.

Tenure in Frankalmoign.

There was also tenure in Frankalmoign, which was where the religious houses or corporations received land to hold in perpetuity, generally on condition of

---

(*r*) Boroughs held of the King were often let out to farm, 1 Mad. Exch. 330. They were also subject to the payment of "tallage," or tax, to the king, or to the lord of whom they were held.

praying for the donor and his heirs. No obligation of fealty attached to this tenure, the divine service rendered being considered of a higher nature. This form of tenure exists at the present day, and is that by which the parochial clergy, and many ecclesiastical and charitable foundations, hold their lands.

The original incidents of tenure by Knight Service were, as we have seen, Homage and Fealty. There soon, however, grow up many others of a more burdensome kind; some of which appear to have been borrowed from the pre-existing Saxon tenure, but all having reference to the fact that the earlier grants had been matters of bounty. Thus, when it first became customary to allow the child of a deceased tenant to succeed him in his feud, this was a matter of favour, not of right, and the successor or heir would therefore pay to the lord a sum of money called a Relief (s) in acknowledgment of the benefit conferred. Similarly, when later on the tenant attained to the privilege of transferring his feud during his lifetime (t) (a point to which we shall advert presently), he paid to the lord a Fine in order to obtain his permission for so doing, and the name of Fine thus came to be given to any sum or money paid to the lord on a transfer of the tenant's land, whether by sale or in consequence of his death. Again, the vassal, who owed everything to the bounty of his lord, might naturally be expected to assist him in any pressing emergency. Thus if the lord were taken a prisoner, the faithful vassal would be bound to assist in procuring his ransom. If his oldest son were knighted, or his daughter married (both matters involving considerable outlay), the vassal would be expected to contribute; and these payments or Aids, at first voluntary, soon grew to be regular incidents of his tenure. The favours conferred on the tenant

<small>New incidents of tenure by Knight Service.

Relief.

Fine.

Aids.</small>

(s) From the Latin *relevare*, to lift or take up.
(t) In ancient times alienation was accomplished by the tenant's surrendering his fee to the lord, who regranted to the tenant's nominee.

benefitted his family as well as himself. It was natural, therefore, that the children of a deceased tenant should seek the protection of their benefactor. If the heir was under age, and unable to render the services the performance of which had been the condition of his father's tenure, the lord would constitute himself his guardian, and take charge of his lands until the heir was fit to do so, receiving in the mean time the profits of the estate in lieu of the services to which he was entitled. This Wardship continued until the heir, if a male, had attained the age of twenty-one or, if a female, that of sixteen years. It then came to an end, and the heir was entitled to enter into possession of the land without paying any relief. In addition to wardship there was the incident of Marriage. The feudal barons were often engaged in small private wars, and it was therefore of importance to the lord that no tenant of his should wed one of his enemies. He claimed, in consequence, a right to forbid any proposed marriage, and if he were the guardian of a female ward he would naturally himself look out for a husband for her. Lastly, there were Escheat and Forfeiture. If the tenant died without heirs the land " escheated " (*u*) to the lord who had granted it; if he neglected to perform the services due from him, or if he were convicted of cowardice, or of some grievous crime, his feud was taken from him, and became forfeited to his lord.

Wardship.

Marriage.

Escheat and Forfeiture.

Burdens of tenure by Knight Service become very heavy.

But these incidents, not unreasonable in their origin, and so long as they were kept within due limits, came in time to assume formidable proportions, and the burdens which they imposed seemed the more grievous as the original principle on which feuds were conferred was lost sight of. For in time the transmission of a man's feud to his heir, or the alienation of it during his lifetime, originally matters of favour, grew to be

---

(*u*) From the French *eschoir*, to fall in.

looked upon as rights, whilst on the other hand the lords took every opportunity of enriching themselves at the expense of tenants who no longer recognised them as their benefactors. Thus a fine was still imposed on alienation or succession, whilst the amounts claimed were at first arbitrary, although afterwards regulated according to the value of the land. Aids too were claimed on various pretexts other than those originally contemplated. But it was chiefly in the matters of wardship and marriage that the rapacity of the lords was shown. For the lord, who formerly was the careful guardian of the heir's estate, now began to consider his charge as a mere opportunity for plunder. Timber was cut down, hedges and buildings allowed to fall into decay, and, in addition, the heir was now compelled to pay a sum equal to half a year's value of his land before the lord would grant him that livery of seisin necessary to perfect his title. As to marriage, the lord now claimed the right to dispose of his ward in matrimony, and to suggest a match which he considered suitable, having previously bargained to receive a sum of money from the relatives of the proposed husband or wife. The ward who refused to come into this arrangement was liable, if a male, to forfeit double the sum which the lord was to have received; or, if a female, could not sue out her livery until she attained the age of twenty-one: whilst even if the lord had not proposed any marriage, he was entitled, on the ward's coming of age, to such a sum as he might be expected to have received had he negotiated an alliance.

It must not be imagined that the lords themselves received any better treatment at the hands of the king. On the contrary, the burdens imposed on them were still more grievous, and formed some excuse for the pressure which they put on their own tenants. For in addition to those already mentioned, the tenants *in capite* were liable to that of Primer Seisin, or right which the king had to take the profits of an estate for a year and a half after the heir had attained full age; and besides this, every heir was bound to be made a knight, an occasion which served as a pretext for fresh extortions (v).

Another and more recent burden pressed heavily upon all tenants by Knight Service, whether from the king or from a mesne lord. The obligation of military service had been at first personal, but after a short time it became usual for the army to be made up of hired soldiery, the tenants by Knight Service paying a tax called Escuage in lieu of personal service (w). From the time of Henry the Third escuage became almost universal (so that the name of Tenure by Escuage replaced that of Tenure by Knight Service), and although knights and gentlemen might be found serving in the army, they did so for pay and not by virtue of their birth or the tenure of their land (x).

Advantages of Socage tenure over tenure by Knight Service.

From many of these burdens Socage tenure was free, whilst those which it did sustain pressed less heavily. Thus Relief was due from the heir of a tenant in Socage: but it consisted simply in the payment of a sum equivalent to one year's rental of the land. Fines were payable on alienation, and lands held in Socage were liable to Escheat and Forfeiture. The tenants were also bound to furnish Aids for knighting the lord's son and marrying his eldest daughter. And tenants in Socage became further liable to payment of Escuage, but the amount was always certain (y). But it was principally in respect of Wardship and Marriage that Socage tenure and that by Knight Service differed: for in the former the wardship

---

(v) For an illustration of the height to which these abuses had risen, see *Christie's Memoirs of Shaftesbury*, pp. 7—12.
(w) This tax still remained uncertain, being assessed by Parliament after the termination of a war. Litt. Ten. s. 98.
(x) 2 Hallam's Middle Ages, 479.
(y) Litt. Ten. s. 98.

of an infant heir did not belong to the lord (inasmuch as he was not entitled to claim military service) but to the infant's nearest relation, not being one capable of succeeding him by descent, who, on the infant's coming of age, was bound to account to him for all rents and profits of the land received during minority; and in like manner the guardian could gain no benefit by his ward's marriage.

Whilst the free tenures thus put on new burdens, the position of the tenants by base tenure gradually improved. The clergy of that day lost no opportunity of impressing upon the lords the sinfulness of keeping their Christian brethren in bondage, whilst the courts were quick to construe any dealings between the lord and his villein as the manumission of the latter (z). The consequence was that by the time of Edward the Sixth nearly all the villeins had become freemen, except a few belonging to the clergy (a). !!!

Improvement of Villein Tenure.

At the same time that the personal status of the villeins was thus changed for the better, their tenure also improved. For when it became usual to allow them and their children to enjoy their possessions without interruption, the courts began to decide that they had acquired, by their long-continued enjoyment, a right to hold their lands without reference to their lord's will, so long as they performed their accustomed services, which now included fealty. From this the next step was, as in the case of feuds, to make to them grants of land so worded as to entitle their issue, if they had any, to succeed them. Their lands were still granted to them to be held at the will of their lord, and their tenure was still conditional on the performance of their due services, and had as its incidents Relief (here called Heriots), Fines, Escheat, and

---

(z) Thus taking homage from a villein made him a freeman.
(a) 2 Bl. Com. 96.

Forfeiture; but gradually such grants came to express that the tenant was to hold, not only at the will of the lord, but "according to the custom of the manor;" and these words were laid hold of by the courts as a means of restricting the lord's privileges. For it was now said that the lord's will must not be arbitrary, but that the tenant who could show that it had been the custom that lands should be permitted to remain in the same family should not be turned out of his land so long as he performed the services due from him, and this rule held good even in the case of grants made only for a life, or lives, if it could be shown to be the invariable custom of the manor to renew them from time to time as became necessary. The tenants were also held entitled to any privileges which had been enjoyed by them time out of mind; and, in the same way, the heriots and fines to be paid were to be regulated by the custom of the manor, and even the custom was afterwards made subject to the condition that it must be reasonable.

Establishment of Customary Courts. When the villeins thus came to acquire a prescriptive right to their lands it was the interest both of the lords and of themselves to preserve an accurate record of the lands which they held, and of the various customary rents and services on which they held them. For this purpose Customary Courts were established, at which, by analogy to the Court Baron, all the customary tenants were bound to attend. But, unlike the freeholders at a Court Baron, the customary tenants were not judges, that office being held by the lord's steward. At each meeting of this court, which generally took place once in three weeks, the steward produced the roll of the manor containing the names of the tenants and their services, the tenants, who were said to form the Homage, proceeded to "present" for the information of the lord any matters affecting the manor which had taken place since the last sitting, and these were all duly entered by the steward on the court roll. Tenants of this kind received no deed or evidence of their title, which depended entirely upon the court roll and upon the copies of, or extracts from, it made by the steward. For this reason these tenants became known as tenants by Copy of Court Roll, or Copyholders, and their tenure as Copyhold (*b*), and thus their position was made much the same as that of the tenants by Villein Socage: the various services which they were bound to render being, as a rule, gradually converted into fixed money payments. Thus the copyholders practically acquired fees, but the tenure itself remained, in contemplation of law, one at the will of the lord, and is still spoken of as base in contradistinction to the free Socage tenure which exists at the present day. *Villein tenure gets the name Copyhold Tenure.*

Copyhold tenure is still base.

The heavy burdens of tenure by Knight Service were partly taken away by the Charter of Henry the First, and by the Great Charter of John, but still continued to exist, although in a lesser degree. As trade increased, and the middle classes obtained more influence, the grievance of military tenures became intolerable. Consequently, at the Restoration of Charles the Second, Parliament seized the opportunity of abolishing military tenures, and a law (*c*) was passed, enacting that all wardships, liveries, primer seisins, values and forfeitures of marriage, by reason of any tenure of the king or others, be totally taken away: that all fines for alienations, tenures by homage, knight service, and escuage, and also all aids for marrying the daughter and knighting the son, and all tenures of the king *in capite*, be likewise taken away: and that all sorts of tenures held of the king or others be turned into free and common Socage, save only tenures in frankalmoign, copyholds, and the honorary services of grand-serjeanty, which consisted in carrying the king's banner, *Tenure by Knight Service turned into Socage Tenure.*

(*b*) Co. Litt. 58ᵃ.
(*c*) 12 Car. II. c. 24.

or his sword, or in being his butler, champion, or other officer at his coronation.

We have now seen how tenure by Knight Service became merged in that of Socage, and also how copyhold tenure became gradually established amongst us; the result being that these two tenures, the one free, the other base, are the only kinds by which land is now held in England. We proceed next to inquire what estates may be held in land; and this will involve the necessity of first tracing the steps by which the present power of alienating real property was arrived at.

Earlier fees descended only to the tenant's issue.

It has been previously mentioned that one of the earliest forms of estates in land was that which conferred an estate for life upon the recipient, and at the same time gave his children, if he had any, a right to succeed him in the possession of the land after his death. These estates were, as we have seen, called Feuds or Fees, and the course of descent was usually to the eldest son and his issue, or if he had none, then to the next son and his issue, and so on; and failing these, to the daughters and their issue. But in the event of the tenant's having no issue, or of his issue failing, his estate escheated to his lord. When fees were first established, the deed which usually followed livery of

Fees were granted to the feoffee and his heirs.

"Heirs" originally meant issue.

seisin expressed that the land in question had been granted to the tenant or "feoffee" and his "heirs." The word "heirs" originally meant only a man's issue: they alone being the persons entitled to succeed him. Gradually, however, it became allowable, if a tenant died without issue, for, at first, a brother,

Heirs now include brothers and collateral relations capable of succession.

and finally, all collateral relations, provided they were descended from, and were of the blood of, the feoffee(d), to succeed him in his feud, and the word "heirs" thus came to include all such persons. The heir, whoever

---

(d) Wright. Ten. 18.

he might be, was entitled to succeed to a fee, not by reason of any favour of the tenant in possession of it, but because he had been designated for that purpose in the grant of the fee. He had thus a material interest in preserving the fee, and his consent was therefore, at first, necessary to allow of its alienation. So also was that of the lord, for he, having granted it to certain persons, had a right to insist that no one else should hold it; since otherwise the rents and services on condition of rendering which it had been granted might not be properly performed, and the lord would also have less chance of regaining the lands by escheat. But when the word "heirs" came to have a more comprehensive meaning, the lord's prospect of escheat was considerably diminished. He had therefore no great interest in preventing his tenant from alienating a part of his fee : on the contrary, if he could get an immediate payment or fine for giving his consent, alienation was to his advantage, for the old tenant still remained subject to the performance of all the services due to the lord, whilst the land acquired by the new tenant remained liable for the payment of all the rents in consideration of which it had been originally granted (e). Moreover, the lords took care, after a time, to guard themselves against risk of losing their tenant's services by inserting in the Great Charter of Henry the Third a proviso (f) that no freeman should, from thenceforth, give or sell any part of his land but so that, of the residue, the lord of the fee might have the services due to him which belonged to the fee. Since then, the tenant, who was anxious to sell his land, and the lord, who was the only person powerful enough to prevent him, had come to an understanding on the subject, it is not to be wondered at that the heir's right of succession was soon ignored, and his power of forbidding

Heir's consent at first necessary for alienation of a fee.

Lord's consent also necessary.

Lords permit alienation of fees.

Heir's consent became unnecessary.

(e) Perkins' Profitable Book, s. 674.
(f) 9 Hen. III. c. 32.

a transfer of the fee lost to him. These changes were not indeed effected all at once; for instance, the first law, which permitted the alienation (*g*) of fees, only applied to lands which a man had himself purchased, which must, moreover, have been expressed to be granted to him, his heirs, and "assigns"; and afterwards, when the alienation of inherited lands was permitted, its exercise was limited to one-fourth of such lands (*h*). But as early as the year 1290, the statute of *Quia Emptores* (*i*), to which we shall have occasion to refer again presently, allowed all persons except the king's tenants *in capite* to alienate all or any part of their lands at their discretion. And even these tenants *in capite* were not long afterwards (*j*) permitted to alienate their fees on paying a fine to the king.

Passing of the statute of *Quia Emptores*. The loss of the heir's right to prevent the alienation of a fee bid fair at one time to involve the loss to the lord of the feudal rights subject to which the fee was held. For when once the privilege of alienating fees without the heir's consent had obtained a firm footing, the tenants began to look upon them as their own; and taking advantage, probably, of the disordered state of the kingdom at the time of the crusades, began, without the consent of their lords, to "subinfeudate," that is, to grant parts of their fees to subtenants, between whom and themselves the relation of lord and vassal was to subsist, without any reference to the lord, whose signorial rights were thus infringed upon. But when the kingdom became more settled under Edward the First, the lords quickly resumed their former rights. It was too late to forbid the transfer of a fee without the lord's consent, but they put a stop to the practice of subinfeudation by causing

---

(*g*) 1.1. Hen. I. c. 70.
(*h*) 2 Bl. Com. 289.
(*i*) 18 Ed. I. stat. 1.
(*j*) 1 Ed. III. c. 12.

to be passed a statute (*k*), (known, from its opening words (*l*), as the statute of *Quia Emptores*), which enacted (*m*) that it should be lawful for every freeman to sell at his own pleasure his lands and tenements, or part of them, but so that the feoffee should hold the same of the chief lord of the same fee by such services and customs as his feoffor held before, and (*n*) that if he sold any part of such lands and tenements to any, the feoffee should immediately hold it of the chief lord, and should be forthwith charged with the services, for so much as pertained or ought to pertain to the same chief lord, for the same parcel, according to the quantity of the land or tenement so sold. The alienation of a fee which had been granted to a man and his heirs, or to him his heirs and assigns, was thus established, and involved the right to transfer an estate granted to the feoffor for life only, which, when it came into the hands of another person, was called an estate *pur autre vie*, one, that is, held for the lifetime of another. But during the period of time necessary to bring about these changes there had grown up another kind of fee, to which different rules applied, and which now claims our consideration.

It will be recollected that the earlier fees descended only to a man's issue, and that the word "heirs" denoted only persons answering to that description. It is probable that fees limited to the feoffee's issue were the only kind known at the time of the Conquest, since fees only began to be introduced into Europe about the year 1000 (*o*). It was immaterial, therefore, at that time whether a grant were made to a man and "his heirs," or to him and "the heirs of his body". But when the word "heirs" came to mean a great many people besides the feoffee's issue, there

Origin of the fee tail.

(*k*) 18 Ed. I. stat. 1.
(*l*) All the older statutes were in legal Latin.
(*m*) C. 1.
(*n*) C. 2.
(*o*) Somner on Gavelkind, 102.

arose a marked difference between the two forms of grant. For although the new construction put upon the word "heirs," by taking away to a great extent the lord's chances of escheat, rendered him indifferent to the alienation of a fee granted to a man and his heirs, it was far otherwise when the fee had been given to a man and the heirs of his body, since these words did not admit of any larger interpretation, and consequently the lord's chances of escheat were still of considerable value. Hence, although when fees began to be alienated those granted in such a manner were not left untouched, a certain amount of restriction was imposed with regard to them. For the courts held that such a fee only conferred an alienable interest provided that the grantee had issue born to him; and that until that event happened, he could not part with his fee. Such fees acquired, in consequence, the name of Conditional Fees, as being conferred on condition that the feoffee had issue, failing which they reverted to the lord. This view of the case did not, however, by any means please the lords, who saw their chances of escheat thus seriously diminished. Therefore in the reign of Edward the First, shortly before the passing of the statute of *Quia Emptores*, another act (*p*) was passed, known as the Statute *De Donis Conditionalibus*, which, first reciting that in cases of lands given upon condition, after issue begotten and born between them unto whom they were given upon such condition, heretofore such feoffees had power to aliene the land so given and to disinherit their issue of their land, contrary to the minds of the givers, and contrary to the form expressed in the gift, enacted that thenceforth the will of the donor should be observed according to the words expressed in the deed of gift, and that lands or tenements given to a man and the heirs of his body or the like should go to his issue, if any, or, if there were not such

---

(*p*) 13 Ed. I, st. 1.

issue, should revert to the donor and his heirs. Such
an estate in consequence lost its name of a Conditional *Conditional Fee*
Fee, and acquired that of Fee Tail, since it was said to *now called a Fee Tail.*
be cut out (*q*) of the entire fee (henceforth distin- *Other fees*
guished as a Fee Simple), and was to last only so long *called Fees Simple.*
as there remained heirs of the body of him on whom
it was bestowed. These fees remained inalienable
for about two hundred years after the statute *De
Donis;* after which time they became, as we shall
see hereafter, capable of being turned into Fees Simple, and therefore subject to alienation.

It will be observed that we have, hitherto, spoken *Alienation of*
only of the alienation of an estate during its owner's *land by Will.*
lifetime: alienation by will not having been estab-
lished until comparatively recent times. One reason
for this was that the feudal system only permitted
land to be transferred by public delivery of the immediate ownership of it, a rule evidently inconsistent
with a transfer by will. To a certain extent this difficulty was overcome, by making a feoffment and livery
of seisin to a person who was, after the death of the
feoffor, to hold it for the benefit of such persons as
the feoffor desired; and this transaction would be
upheld by the Court of Chancery. But the right of
alienation by will was not recognised by the Common
Law or by Statute until the time of Henry the Eighth.
In the reign of that king an act (*r*) was passed which
enacted that all and every person having, or who thereafter should have, any manors, lands, tenements, or
hereditaments holden in Socage, or of the nature of
Socage tenure, should have full and free liberty, power,
and authority, to give, dispose, will, and devise as well
by his last will and testament in writing, or otherwise
by any act or acts lawfully executed in his lifetime,
all his said manors, lands, tenements, and hereditaments, at his free will and pleasure; and when by the

---

(*q*) French *taillé.*
(*r*) 32 Hen. VIII. c. 1.

act of Charles the Second, previously mentioned (*s*), the greater part of the land in this country became held by Socage, the power of alienation by will became of great value. It did not, however, until recent times, enable a person to dispose of real property other than that which he had at the time of making his will. But by the present Wills Act (*t*) it is enacted (*u*) that the power of disposition by will shall extend to all real estate to which the testator may be entitled at the time of his death, notwithstanding that he may become entitled to the same subsequently to the execution of his will. The earlier Wills Act did not, moreover, extend to copyholds; but we shall see, when we come to the chapter specially devoted to estates in land of this tenure, that they also can now be disposed of both during lifetime and by will.

Estates for Years.

It remains to add a few words on the subject of Estates for Years. The Feudal System, as we have seen, dealt only with tenure by Military Service: it despised all others. In time, however, there grew up a system of allowing persons of inferior degree to cultivate lands belonging to the lords on condition of accounting for the produce, out of which they received a certain allowance for themselves. They were thus little more than bailiffs, removable at their lords' pleasure. In time, however, the custom of letting lands became general, and such a tenancy ceased to imply a necessary superiority on the part of the person who let the land (or "lessor") over the person to whom it was let (or "lessee"). The lessees consequently arrived at a more independent position, paying a fixed rent for their lands, and, provided they did this, and also complied with any other conditions on which they held, were entitled to undisturbed possession during their term.

(*s*) 12 Car. II. c. 24.
(*t*) 7 Wm. IV. & 1 Vict. c. 26.
(*u*) S. 3.

OF THE EARLIER TENURES OF LAND.

At first, however, they had this right as against their landlord only. For although a lessee, who had been wrongfully turned out of his holding by his lessor, was, after a time, permitted to bring an action of ejectment against him, and thus recover the land, besides obtaining damages for the wrong done, the case was different if the lessee had been turned out by some other person claiming by a title paramount to that of the lessor. For then the lessee could indeed bring an action against his lessor for not securing him undisturbed possession of the land, but could not recover the land itself. This was made a means of defrauding the tenant, for a lessor who wished to put an end to a lease, would get some friendly plaintiff to bring a preconcerted action against him for the land which he would take care not to defend; judgment would accordingly be given against him, and the plaintiff could then proceed to eject the lessee. An act, known as the Statute of Gloucester (*v*), was passed in the reign of Edward the First, with a view to put a stop to this practice, but with little effect: and the lessee still remained liable to be ejected by the process above mentioned, until the passing of the 21 Hen. VIII., c. 15, which enacted that lessees, whether holding by a parol or written lease, or by one by deed, might prove that the action was fictitious, and that in that case the lessees should, notwithstanding such actions, hold their terms according to their leases. But a lease was never recognised by the law as of equal dignity with estates for life, or in fee; it is still, therefore, only personal estate, and the feudal seisin remains in the person who has the first estate for life, or in fee, after the term comes to an end; and who is therefore distinguished as the freeholder, since it is he, and not the lessee, who holds from the lord paramount. One advantage indeed formerly gained by the low estimation in which terms of years are held

Estate for Years is not freehold.

Always alienable.

(*v*) 6 Ed. I. c. 11.

by the law was that they could be, unlike more honourable estates, freely disposed of either during the tenant's lifetime or by his will; but this advantage has now disappeared, being, as we have seen, no longer peculiar to personal estate.

Summary.
The estates, therefore, in corporeal hereditaments which we have to consider are, besides the minor estates conferred by a tenancy at will, or at sufferance (terms to be explained hereafter), Estates for Years, Estates *pur autre vie* and for Life, Estates in Fee Tail, and Estates in Fee Simple. We will go on to examine them separately, taking them in the order in which they have just been named. In so doing we shall, at first, treat of such estates as being held in land of freehold tenure only, reserving the subject of copyholds for special consideration in a subsequent chapter.

CHAPTER II.

OF AN ESTATE FOR YEARS.

WE saw in the previous chapter that one great distinction between estates for years and those for life or any greater interest is that the former are personal, and the latter real, property. There is also another way in which the difference between them is strongly marked. In early times no freeman would condescend to accept an estate in land to endure for a shorter time than his own life; and, on the other hand, no man not a freeman was, at first, allowed to hold land for so long a time. Hence, land held for life, or any longer term, was said to be "freehold" (that is, held by a freeman), and although in process of time it was thought that a freeman might hold land for a shorter term than his life without loss of dignity, the old distinction still remains in the name; hence the estates which may be held in land are divided into two great classes, namely, Estates of Freehold (which include life estates and estates of inheritance) and Estates less than Freehold. Of the latter kind estates for years are by far the most important, and the consideration of them will, consequently, occupy the greater part of this chapter; but before coming to them a few remarks are necessary on two minor varieties of estates less than freehold, which are, respectively, known as Estates by Sufferance, and Estates at Will. We shall, therefore, proceed to discuss these, and in doing so will follow the course proposed to be adopted with reference to all estates with which we are about to deal, by inquiring,—1st, What they are, and how they may be created; 2nd,

Estates of Freehold, and Estates less than Freehold.

The incidents attaching to them; and 3rd, How they may be alienated or put an end to.

Estate by sufferance.

An estate by sufferance is where one who comes in by right holds over without right (a). If, for instance, a tenant for years after the expiration of his tenancy continues to occupy the land of which he was tenant, without either the assent or dissent of his landlord, he is a tenant by sufferance, the law not considering him a trespasser, because, having been originally rightfully in possession, it will be assumed in his favour that he is so still. It will not be necessary to say any more about this estate, since it is obvious that it has the barest existence, and can only arise by implication of law, inasmuch as any recognition of it by the owner of the land would convert it into an estate at will.

Estate at will. How created.

An estate at will has been defined as the case of lands or tenements being let by one man to another to have and to hold to him at the will of the lessor, by force of which lease the lessee is in possession. In this case the lessee is called a tenant at will, because he has no certain or sure estate, for the lessor may put him out at what time pleaseth him (b). But every lease at will must, at law, be at the will of both parties, and therefore upon a lease to hold at the will of the lessor, the law implies it to be at the will of the lessee also (c), and consequently the lessee may leave whenever he pleases.

Such a tenancy seldom exists except in the few cases where it is implied by law. Thus, if a trustee of land, who is in the eye of the law the owner of the

---

(a) Co. Litt. 57^b.
(b) No notice is necessary—a statement of the lessor's will that the tenancy should terminate, at once puts an end to it. *Pollen v. Brewer*, 7 C. B. (N. S.) 371.
(c) Co. Litt. 55^a.

property confided to him, permits the person who has the beneficial interest (and who is called his *cestui que trust*) to remain in possession as actual occupant of the land, the law will imply a tenancy at will on the part of the *cestui que trust* (d). Again, an implied tenancy at will arises in the case of a person entering upon land under an agreement for a sale of it to him and remaining in possession after the contract has gone off (e). A tenancy at will may, however, exist by express agreement between the parties, where the money rent, or other compensation to be made to the lessor, is to accrue from day to day and is not referable to a year or any aliquot part of a year (f); or where there is no rent paid, or any proof of an agreement to pay rent (g).

The incidents of the estate of a tenant at will do not call for much notice, since both his responsibilities and his privileges are very limited. He is not bound to take any care of the property which he occupies, and is not therefore accountable for "permissive waste," that is, for allowing buildings or fences to get out of repair by mere neglect (h). But he is, notwithstanding, entitled, if his estate is summarily determined by his lessor, to have Emblements, that is, to come upon the land after the expiration of his tenancy in order to take away such crops (provided they produce an annual profit) as were sown by him during his occupation. He will, also, if paying a rent equal to the full value of the land (i), come within the provisions of the 14 & 15 Vict., c. 25. This statute enacts (j) that when the lease or tenancy of any farms or lands held by any tenant at rack rent shall determine (that is,

Incidents of an estate at will.

Emblements.

14 & 15 Vict. c. 25.

(d) *Melling* v. *Leak*, 16 C. B. 652.
(e) *Howard* v. *Shaw*, 8 Mee and W. 119.
(f) *Richardson* v. *Langridge*, 4 Taunt. 128.
(g) *Doe* v. *Wood*, 14 Mee and W. 682.
(h) *Harnett* v. *Maitland*, 16 Mee and W. 257.
(i) *Haines* v. *Welch*, L. R. 4 C. P. 91.
(j) S. 1.

c.   C

be put an end to) by the death or cesser of the estate of any landlord, entitled for his life or any other uncertain interest, the tenant shall, instead of claims to emblements, continue to hold until the expiration of the then current year of his tenancy, at which time he shall, without being required to give or receive notice, quit upon the terms of his lease or holding, in the same manner as if his tenancy were determined by effluxion of time, or other lawful means, during the continuance of his landlord's estate. The succeeding owner is to be entitled to recover (as the landlord could have done if his interest had continued) a fair proportion of the rent for the period elapsed from the termination of the landlord's interest to the time of quitting: and the succeeding owner and tenant respectively are to be entitled, as against each other, to all the benefits, and be subject to the terms, to which the landlord and tenant respectively would have been entitled or subject in case the tenancy had determined in manner aforesaid at the expiration of such current year.

How tenancy at will is determined.

A tenant at will cannot transfer his interest to another person, either during his lifetime, or by will, because that could only be done with the consent of his lessor, and this consent would, of itself, create a new lease. His estate is put an end to by the death of either himself or his lessor (*k*), or by any act of either party inconsistent with the existence of the tenancy. Thus an agreement by the lessor to sell his land (*l*), or his making a new lease to another person, although with a proviso that the new lessee shall not enter upon the land until some future period, at once puts an end to the tenancy at will: as does also any act by the lessor in regard to the land for which he

---

(*k*). *James* v. *Dean*, 11 Ves. 383, 391.
(*l*) *Daniels* v. *Davison*, 16 Ves. 249, 252.

would otherwise be liable to an action of trespass at the suit of the lessee (*m*).

The inconveniences which attach to tenancies at will are so many that these estates are not favoured by the courts, which always prefer, if possible, to construe them as leases from year to year (*n*); and any reservation of a yearly rent will be taken to imply a tenancy from year to year (*o*), which cannot be put an end to by either party without due notice. This last-mentioned estate is only a modified form of an estate for years, to which, accordingly, we will next turn our attention.

An estate for years is generally spoken of as a "term" (*p*) of years, because it is essential to its existence that both its commencement and its duration should be either certain or capable of being made certain. Littleton defines a tenant for a term of years thus :—" Tenant for a term of years is where a man letteth lands or tenements to another for a term of certain years at the number of years that is accorded between the lessor and the lessee, and the lessee entereth by force of the lease, then he is tenant for years (*q*)." The term for which the lease is made is called in every case a term of years; for although the lease may be made for only half a year, or a quarter, or any less time, this lessee is respected as a tenant for years, and is styled so in some legal proceedings, a year being the shortest term which the law in this case takes notice of (*r*), and therefore any tenancy of definite duration, as for instance one for three months certain, is a term (*s*). The grant of such a term is

Estate for years.
Is a "term."

(*m*) *Turner* v. *Bennett*, 9 Mee and W. 643.
(*n*) *Daniels* v. *Davison*, 16 Ves. 249, 252.
(*o*) *Pope* v. *Garland*, 4 Yo. and C. (Ex.) 394.
(*p*) Latin *terminus*, an end.
(*q*) Co. Litt. 43b.
(*r*) 2 Bl. Com. 140.
(*s*) *Doe* v. *Roe*, 5 B. and Ald. 766.

also called a "demise," and the term itself is distinguished as a " chattel real," a phrase which points, on the one hand, to the fact of its being personal property and, on the other, to its connection with land.

<small>By whom it may be created.</small> A term of years may, as a general rule, be created by any one having an estate greater than the term itself. Thus not only can a tenant in fee, or for life, create a term of years, but, moreover, one who is himself a tenant for years can carve a smaller estate out of his own. The grantor (that is, the person making the grant of the term) is also called the " reversioner," because after the expiration of the term the estate out of which it was granted reverts or returns to him (and is therefore called his " reversion "), unless he has, at the same time, parted with the rest or " remainder " of his estate to another person, who, in such a case, is called the " remainder-man." A lease made by a tenant for years out of his own term was always binding on his representatives after his death, but, with this exception, the rule at one time was that if the grantor had an estate less than a fee simple all leases made by him were put an end to by his dying, or by his forfeiting his estate, and did not bind the reversioner or <small>Tenant in tail.</small> remainder-man. Thus if a tenant in tail made a lease, and died before the expiration of the term, the lease was not binding even on his issue. This was <small>32 Hen. VIII. c. 28.</small> partly remedied by the 32 Hen. VIII., c. 28, under which tenants in tail were enabled, subject to certain restrictions, to make leases of such lands as had been accustomed to be let for the last twenty years past, for a period not exceeding twenty-one years or three lives. Such leases, however, only bound the issue of the tenant in tail, and not the remainder-man, or reversioner; but now, under the Statute for the Abo- <small>Abolition of Fines and Recoveries Act.</small> lition of Fines and Recoveries (*t*), a tenant in tail can make a lease for any term not exceeding twenty-one

---

(*t*) 3 & 4 Wm. IV. c. 74, ss. 15, 40, 41.

years, provided the lease is made by deed, and commences from the date of such lease, or from any time not exceeding twelve calendar months from the date of such lease, and that a rent is thereby reserved which, at the time of granting such lease, is a rack rent (*u*), or not less than five-sixth parts of a rack rent. He may also make a lease for any term, by deed inrolled according to the provisions of the act; and all such leases will be binding on the issue in tail, reversioner, and remainder-man.

The last-mentioned act rendered the 32 Hen. VIII. c. 28 unnecessary, and it has therefore been repealed (*v*), except so much of it as relates to leases made by persons in right of their churches.

A tenant for life also could not, until lately, make binding leases to endure beyond his own life; but it is now enacted, by the Leases and Sales of Settled Estates Act (*w*), that it shall be lawful for every person entitled to the possession, or to the receipt of the rents and profits, of any settled estates for an estate for life, or for a term of years determinable with his life, or for any greater estate, either in his own right or in right of his wife, and claiming under a settlement made since the 1st of November, 1856 (*z*), to make, from time to time, unless the settlement contains an express declaration to the contrary, leases of such estates, or any part thereof, except the principal mansion-house and the demesnes thereof, and other lands usually occupied therewith, for any term not exceeding twenty-one years to commence from the date of the lease, provided that the demise be made by deed, and the best rent that can reasonably be ob-

Tenant for life.

Leases and Sales of Settled Estates Act.

(*u*) A rack rent (from *racheter*, to buy back) is a rent equal to the full value of the land, or nearly so.
(*v*) By the 19 & 20 Vict. c. 120, s. 35.
(*w*) 19 & 20 Vict. c. 120, s. 32.
(*z*) ss. 44, 46.

tained be thereby reserved, without any fine or other benefit in the nature of a fine, which rent shall be incident to the immediate reversion; and provided that the lease contains certain clauses enumerated by the act. Tenants who have life estates by curtesy or by dower (terms which will be explained hereafter) (*y*), are also enabled by the same act (*z*) to make leases for twenty-one years, subject to the same conditions as ordinary tenants for life. The act makes (*a*) every demise thus authorized valid against the person granting the same, and against all other persons entitled to estates subsequent to the estate of such person, if the estate be settled; and in the case of unsettled estates, against all persons claiming through or under the wife or husband (as the case may be) of the person granting the same. The Leases and Sales of Settled Estates Amendment Act (*b*) makes such demises valid also against the wife of any husband making such demises of estates to which he is entitled in right of such wife.

Tenants by Curtesy and by Dower.
Leases and Sales of Settled Estates Act.

Leases and Sales of Settled Estates Amendment Act.

The Leases and Sales of Settled Estates Act (*c*), and the Leases and Sales of Settled Estates Amendment Act (*d*), also enable the Court of Chancery to authorize various other leases of any settled estates, and without reference to the date of the settlement, but subject to the conditions contained in the acts. The principal of these conditions are, that every lease shall be made to take effect in possession at, or within one year next after, the making thereof, and shall be for a term of years not exceeding, for an agricultural or occupation lease, twenty-one years; for a mining lease, or lease of water, water-mills, way leaves, water leaves, or other rights or easements, forty years;

(*y*) See Chaps. IV. and VI.
(*z*) 19 & 20 Vict. 120, s. 32.
(*a*) S. 33.
(*b*) 21 & 22 Vict. c. 77, s. 8.
(*c*) 19 & 20 Vict. 120.
(*d*) 21 & 22 Vict. c. 77.

for building leases ninety-nine years (*e*); and for repairing leases sixty years (*f*); and that the rent reserved shall be the best that can reasonably be obtained without taking any fine or other benefit in the nature of a fine (*g*). The acts contain provisions for the benefit of the remainder-man, where the lease is one of any earth, coal, or mineral; and no lease is to authorize the felling of trees, except so far as is necessary for clearing the ground for buildings, excavations, or other works authorized by the lease (*h*). The court is further empowered, if satisfied that it will be for the benefit of the inheritance, to extend the above terms, except in the case of agricultural leases (*i*).

Terms of years may, moreover, be created within certain limits by persons under disability; such as married women, infants, lunatics, bankrupts, and convicts. As to married women, the powers conferred by the Leases and Sales of Settled Estates Act (*j*) have been already noticed; it is also enacted by the Act for the Abolition of Fines and Recoveries (*k*) that it shall be lawful for every married woman, except where she is a tenant in tail, by deed to dispose of lands of any tenure as fully and effectually as she could do if she were unmarried, provided that she does so with the consent of her husband, and that the deed in question is publicly acknowledged by her in the manner prescribed by the act. And a lease made by a husband and wife, or by the husband alone, of a wife's freehold property, although without any special formalities, is binding on them during their joint lives (*l*). If the married woman is a tenant in tail

Persons under disability.

Married women. Leases and Sales of Settled Estates Act. Abolition of Fines and Recoveries Act.

(*e*) 19 & 20 Vict. c. 120, s. 2.
(*f*) 21 & 22 Vict. c. 77, s. 2.
(*g*) 19 & 20 Vict. c. 120, s. 2.
(*h*) Ibid.
(*i*) 21 & 22 Vict. c. 77, s. 4.
(*j*) 19 & 20 Vict. c. 120, s. 32.
(*k*) 3 & 4 Wm. IV. c. 74, s. 77.
(*l*) *Bateman* v. *Allen*, Cro. Eliz. 437, 438.

she can make a lease by the same process as if she were unmarried, but with the additional requisites of obtaining her husband's consent, and acknowledging the deed (*m*).

Infants.
11 Geo. IV. & 1 Wm. IV. c. 65.

Infants cannot of themselves make binding leases; it has therefore been enacted (*n*) that where any infant is seised or possessed of, or entitled to, any land in fee, or in tail, or to any leasehold land for an absolute interest, it shall be lawful for such infant, or his guardian in the name of such infant, by the direction of the Court of Chancery, to make such lease of the whole, or any part, of his land, for such terms of years, and subject to such rents and covenants as the court shall direct. But in no case is any fine or premium to be taken, and the best rent that can be obtained, regard being had to the nature of the lease, is to be reserved. And no lease is to be made of the capital mansion-house and the park and grounds respectively held therewith, for any period exceeding the minority of such infant.

Lunatics.
16 & 17 Vict. c. 70.

The principal enactments relating to leases being made of the estates of lunatics are contained in the 16 & 17 Vict., c. 70, which enacts (*o*) that where any lunatic shall be seised or possessed of, or entitled to, any land in fee, or in tail, or to leasehold land for an absolute interest, the committee of his estate may, in his name and on his behalf, under order of the Lord Chancellor, make such a lease of the land, or any part thereof, as the Lord Chancellor shall order. This includes (*p*) power to make leases of mines already opened, or (*q*) to be opened. A subsequent section (*r*) also enables committees, with the sanction

---

(*m*) 3 & 4 Wm. IV. c. 74, s. 40.
(*n*) By the 11 Geo. IV. & 1 Wm. IV. c. 65, s. 17.
(*o*) S. 129.
(*p*) S. 130.
(*q*) S. 131.
(*r*) S. 133.

of the Lord Chancellor, to execute any powers of leasing which have been given to lunatics who have only a limited interest in land. All leases made in pursuance of this act are, by the 18 and 19 Vict., c. 13, declared to be good and effectual against all persons claiming under any estate tail vested in any lunatic. 18 & 19 Vict. c. 13.

As to the other persons under disability, two recent acts have given to the trustees of bankrupts (*s*), and the administrators of convicts (*t*), powers of dealing with the property of the persons whom they represent as fully as those persons might themselves otherwise have done. Moreover, the Leases and Sales of Settled Estates Act enacts (*u*) that all powers given by the act may be exercised by guardians on behalf of infants, by committees on behalf of lunatics, and by assignees (now called trustees) of bankrupts or insolvents. Bankrupts and Convicts. 32 & 33 Vict. c. 71. 33 & 34 Vict. c. 23. Leases and Sales of Settled Estates Act.

The Crown is empowered (*v*), subject to certain conditions, to make leases for terms not exceeding, in ordinary cases, thirty-one years, or three lives, or some term of years determinable on three lives; and not exceeding, in the case of repairing leases, the term of fifty years. And the Commissioners of Woods and Forests may (*w*) grant leases of Crown land, vested in them, for thirty-one years, or, in the case of leases of buildings or of ground for building on or for making gardens, for any term not exceeding ninety-nine years, subject to the conditions of the enabling act as to the leases being made for a rent amounting to the full value of the land unless they are granted for building purposes. The Crown. 1 Anne, c. 1. 10 Geo. IV. c. 50.

(*s*) 32 & 33 Vict. c. 71, ss. 15, 17.
(*t*) 33 & 34 Vict. c. 23, s. 12.
(*u*) 19 & 20 Vict. c. 120, s. 36.
(*v*) 1 Anne, c. 1, s. 5.
(*w*) 10 Geo. IV. c. 50, ss. 22—33.

OF CORPOREAL HEREDITAMENTS.

Ecclesiastical Corporations.
5 & 6 Vict. c. 27.

As to Ecclesiastical Corporations, incumbents of livings may (*x*), under certain conditions, and subject to obtaining the consent of their patrons and bishops, make binding leases for fourteen, and in some cases for twenty-one years. And by the 5 & 6 Vict., c. 108, ecclesiastical corporations, including incumbents, may, with the consent of their patrons and bishops, and of the Ecclesiastical Commissioners, make, subject to certain restrictions, building leases for terms not exceeding ninety-nine years.

5 & 6 Vict. c. 108.

32 Hen. VIII. c. 28.
5 Geo. III. c. 17.

Other ecclesiastical corporations can of themselves make leases of lands or hereditaments commonly let for twenty years before such leases (*y*), and also of tithes, tolls, and other incorporeal hereditaments (*z*), for terms not exceeding twenty-one years or three lives from the making thereof, subject to the observance of certain conditions. They may also (*a*), with the consent of the Ecclesiastical Commissioners (*b*), make building leases for terms not exceeding ninety-nine years (*c*), and leases of way leaves or water leaves for any term not exceeding sixty years (*d*), subject to the restrictions contained in the enabling act. Moreover, they may (*e*), under special circumstances, with the consent of the Ecclesiastical Commissioners, make leases for such terms, and subject to such conditions, and generally in such manner, as the Commissioners think proper and advisable. Special powers of leasing have also been given by statute to the Universities of Oxford, Cambridge, and Durham, and the Colleges of Eton and Winchester (*f*).

5 & 6 Vict. c. 108.

Universities and Colleges.
21 & 22 Vict. c. 44.
23 & 24 Vict. c. 59.

(*x*) 5 & 6 Vict. c. 27.
(*y*) 32 Hen. VIII. c. 28, ss. 1, 2.
(*z*) 5 Geo. III. c. 17.
(*a*) 5 & 6 Vict. c. 108.
(*b*) S. 20.
(*c*) S. 1.
(*d*) S. 4.
(*e*) 21 & 22 Vict. c. 57, s. 1.
(*f*) See the 21 & 22 Vict. c. 44, and the 23 & 24 Vict. c. 59.

Municipal Corporations are enabled to make leases, **Municipal Corporations.** subject to certain restrictions (*g*). For they may **5 & 6 Wm. IV.** make leases for building purposes for any term not **c. 76.** exceeding seventy-five years, and for other purposes **6 & 7 Wm. IV.** for terms not exceeding thirty-one years. They **c. 104.** may also make leases for longer terms if they have previously obtained the consent of the Lords Commissioners of the Treasury.

There are also certain restrictions, imposed on the **Restrictions on** ground of public policy, on the holding of estates for **holding estates for years.** years. Thus, it is enacted by the 1 & 2 Vict., c. 106 (*h*), **Spiritual per-** that it shall not be lawful for any spiritual person who **sons.** shall be licensed, or otherwise allowed, to perform the **1 & 2 Vict. c. 106.** duties of any ecclesiastical office whatever, to take to farm, for occupation by himself, by lease, grant, words, or otherwise, for term of life, or of years, or at will, any lands exceeding eighty acres in extent, for the purpose of occupying or using or cultivating the same, without the permission in writing of the bishop of the diocese specially given for that purpose; and this licence, when given, is not to be for a term exceeding seven years. Neither can religious and charitable **Religious and** institutions hold land with the same freedom as private **other corporations.** individuals. Conveyances, leases, or other assurances, **31 & 32 Vic.** not made by will, to a trustee or trustees on behalf of **c. 44.** any society or body of persons associated together for religious purposes, or for the promotion of education, arts, literature, science, or other like purposes, of land for the erection of buildings, or whereon a building shall have been erected, are good, provided that the grant or lease does not comprise more than two acres of land, and is made for full and valuable consideration, actually paid before the making of the grant or lease, or reserved by way of rent, rent charge, or other annual payment, or partly paid and partly re-

---

(*g*) 5 & 6 Wm. IV. c. 76, ss. 94, 96; 6 & 7 Wm. IV. c. 104, s. 2.
(*h*) S. 28.

served as aforesaid (*i*). But with these exceptions all gifts or conveyances of any lands or hereditaments, for any estate or interest whatever, to any persons, bodies, politic, or corporate, or otherwise, or for the benefit of any charitable uses whatever, excepting those really and *bonâ fide* made for full and valuable consideration actually paid without fraud or collusion at the time of making them (*j*), are void unless they are made by deed, witnessed by two witnesses, twelve calendar months at least before the death of the donor or grantor, and are inrolled in the Court of Chancery within six calendar months from the time of their execution (*k*). Such deeds must moreover take effect in possession, or for the charitable use intended, immediately from the making thereof, and be without any power of revocation, reservation, trust, condition, or agreement for the benefit of the grantor, or those claiming under him (*l*), except a grant or reservation of a nominal rent, or of mines or minerals, or of easements; and except any condition as to the erection or repair of buildings, or laying out of streets for the benefit of the premises, with powers of revocation, re-entry, or distress if such conditions or rent are not duly observed or paid (*m*).

Leases by estoppel.

Besides those leases which are made binding by express legislation, there is another variety which owes its validity to a rule of law. For if a lease has been granted by a deed to which both the lessor and the lessee are parties, neither of them can afterwards put an end to it on the ground that the lessor had no estate in the subject of the demise at the time of making the lease, the execution of a deed being in the eye of the law a solemn act which a man cannot be afterwards heard to contradict. Such a lease is

---

(*i*) 31 & 32 Vict. c. 44.
(*j*) 9 Geo. II. c. 36, s. 2.
(*k*) 9 Geo. II. c. 36, s. 1.
(*l*) 9 Geo. II. c. 36, s. 1.
(*m*) 24 Vic. c. 9, s. 1.

said to "work by estoppel," because a man's act or acceptance estops, or closes, his mouth so that he cannot allege anything contrary to his deed. If the lessor should afterwards acquire an estate in the premises, the lease will become as good as if he had been entitled all along to make the demise (*n*). If however he had, from the first, some interest in the premises, the lease will not work by estoppel, but will be held to transmit such interest only, although it may be less than that which the lessor purports to grant; the reason given for this somewhat curious doctrine being the technical one that one deed cannot enure to two intents (*o*); and this rule will hold good although the lessor may subsequently acquire a greater estate.

Next as to the modes by which an estate for years may be created. This may be done by implication of law, by parol, by writing, or by deed. We have seen that the courts lean to considering the payment of rent as proof of an intention to create a yearly tenancy, and that a tenancy at will may thus be enlarged into the greater estate of a tenancy from year to year. A yearly tenancy may also arise by implication of law, although it was the intention of the parties to create a longer term. Thus where a man, having entered into an agreement for a lease, was let into possession of the premises, and paid rent according to the terms of the agreement, but no lease was executed; it was held that a tenancy from year to year had been created (*p*). And the receipt of rent in pursuance of a lease granted under a supposed power of leasing which did not, in fact, exist (*q*), or in pursuance of a lease void from not having fulfilled the requirements of the Statute of Frauds (*r*), or of the Real Property

<small>Modes of creating an Estate for Years.
By implication of law.</small>

(*n*) *Webb* v. *Austin*, 7 Man & Gr. 701, 724.
(*o*) *Brereton* v. *Evans*, Cro. Eliz. 700.
(*p*) *Doe* v. *Smith*, 1 Man. & Ry. 137.
(*q*) *Doe* v. *Morse*, 1 B. & Ad. 365.
(*r*) 29 Car. II. c. 3. *Berrey* v. *Lindley*, 3 Man. & Gr. 498.

Amendment Act (*s*) (both of which will be referred to presently), have been held to create tenancies from year to year.

By parol or by writing.

A lease for a term of years may, except in the case of leases under statutory powers, be granted by parol, or by writing, if the term is for less than three years, and if the rent reserved amounts to two-thirds of the full improved value of the land (*t*), but a tenancy for any longer term, or for a lower rent, would formerly, under the Statute of Frauds (*u*), have had the force and effect of a tenancy at will only, unless created by writing; and now it is enacted by the Real Property Amendment Act (*v*) that all leases formerly required by law to be in writing are to be made by deed, that is, by an instrument sealed as well as written.

By deed. Real Property Amendment Act.

Form of Words.

No formal words are necessary to create such a term, any words denoting an intention to give possession being sufficient (*w*); and hence before the passing of the Real Property Amendment Act (*x*) questions often arose as to whether certain writings were leases, or only agreements for leases. The general rule is, that in each case the answer depends upon the intention of the parties as collected from the instrument (*y*): therefore if the words are of themselves apt for creating a lease, but no intent appears, no lease will be created (*z*). Thus, where there was an agreement to lease a mine but the mode of working was to be determined by some competent person (*a*), and, again, where the lessee agreed to accept a lease

---

(*s*) 8 & 9 Vict. c. 106. *Lee* v. *Smith*, 9 Exch. 662.
(*t*) The full improved value is the rent which a tenant would pay who was bound to keep the premises in repair. *Richardson* v. *Kensit*, 5 Man. & Gr. 485, 497.
(*u*) 29 Car. II. c. 3, s. 1.
(*v*) 8 & 9 Vict. c. 106, s. 3.
(*w*) *Curling* v. *Mills*, 6 Man. & Gr. 173.
(*x*) 8 & 9 Vict. c. 106.
(*y*) *Morgan* v. *Bissell*, 3 Taunt. 65.
(*z*) *Doe* v. *Ashburner*, 5 T. R. 163.
(*a*) *Jones* v. *Reynolds*, 1 Q. B. 506.

on condition that the premises were put into repair (b), it was held that no lease had been created. But, on the other hand, the use of the words "agree to let," although with a stipulation that a lease and counterpart should be prepared, has been held to create a present demise (c). Since the passing of the act such questions cannot arise as to writings, except where the term does not exceed three years, but may still do so as to deeds in cases where the wording of the deed is very ambiguous. If the lease is for an alternative period, such as for seven, fourteen, or twenty-one years, the lessee alone has the option of putting an end to it at the expiration of either of these terms (d). It is necessary that a tenant under an ordinary lease should enter upon the property, otherwise he will not have a term but only an *interesse termini* or right to enter.

<small>Lessee must enter.</small>

It should be here noticed that terms of years may be created for purposes other than the existence of the ordinary relation of landlord and tenant. When estates for years received the same protection as other estates it was soon discovered that, besides answering the purpose of short leases, they might, from their peculiar nature, when extended in duration, be applied with advantage in the settlements and complicated arrangements of real property, which became necessary in the advancing state of civilization (e). The manner in which long terms of years are used for this purpose will be more fully considered at the end of this chapter; at present we will confine our attention to terms of years created for the benefit of an ordinary lessee, and observe the rights and obligations which they confer and impose in the absence of any stipulation between the parties: questions as to the

<small>Long terms of years.</small>

(b) *Doe* v. *Clarke*, 7 Q. B. 211.
(c) *Doe* v. *Ries*, 8 Bing. 178.
(d) *Price* v. *Dyer*, 17 Ves. 356, 363.
(e) Watkins' Principles of Conveyancing, 45.

ordinary form and effect of such stipulations being reserved for a subsequent part of our work.

<small>Incidents of an estate for years. Rent or Rent-Service.</small>
In considering the incidents of such an estate, the first to be noticed is the payment of rent to the lessor by the lessee. This rent, when it exists, is properly called a Rent-Service, and is an annual return made by the tenant in retribution for the land that passes to him (*f*). It may be paid either in labour, money, or provisions; but is, at the present day, almost universally paid in money.

<small>Rent Service incident to the reversion.</small>
There is always an implied obligation on the part of the lessee to render rent-service to the reversioner, and rent is, therefore, said to be "incident" to, or follow, the reversion. The amount payable is presumed, in the absence of stipulation, to be equivalent to the annual value of the premises occupied, but it is the almost universal practice for the parties themselves to agree upon the precise amount of rent to be paid. A consequence of the rule that rent is incident to the reversion was, formerly, that if the reversion were destroyed the rent incident to it was destroyed also. Now it is a rule of law when two estates immediately reversionary to each other meet in the same person, in the same right, that the one which gives the title to possession, unless it is an estate tail, will, if less in quantity than the reversion, be *merged* or drowned in the other, and become extinct (*g*). If, therefore, a tenant for life, or for years, of land makes a lease and afterwards acquires the fee simple of the same land, his tenancy for life, or for years, is merged in the fee simple, and before the passing of the act to be presently mentioned the rent reserved by the lease would have been extinguished, because the reversion to which it

<small>Former consequence of the rule.</small>

(*f*) Gilbert on Rents, 9.
(*g*) Watkins' Principles of Conveyancing, 54.

was incident had ceased to exist: the same fate would have also attended the covenants of the lease. Thus, it was held in one case (*h*) that a tenant for years, who had made a lease out of his estate for years, and subsequently taken a conveyance of the fee simple of the same lands, could not maintain an action against his lessee for breach of covenant to pay rent and to repair the premises, since the acquisition of the fee simple had merged his former reversion, and that being gone the covenants incident to it had also become extinguished. But, notwithstanding this, the lessee continued to be entitled to hold his land for the remainder of the term granted to him, since the merger of the reversion was no act of his, and it could not be permitted that a lessor should be able, by any voluntary acts, to defeat his own grant (*i*). Again, if a tenant for years made an under-lease, and afterwards surrendered his own lease to his lessor in order to have it renewed, either to himself or to another person, the benefit of the rent and covenants contained in the under-lease was lost.

This last hardship was remedied by the 4 Geo. II., c. 28, which enacted (*j*) that when a lease was surrendered in order to be renewed the new lessee should be in the same position as if the original lease had been kept on foot; and now it is provided by the 9th section of the Real Property Amendment Act (*k*) that when any reversion expectant on a lease, made either before or after the passing of the act, is surrendered, or merged in a greater, the next estate is to be deemed the reversion for the purpose of preserving such incidents and obligations as would have subsisted but for the surrender or merger.

4 Geo. II. c. 28.

Real Property Amendment Act.

(*h*) *Webb* v. *Russell*, 3 T. R. 393.
(*i*) *Sutton's Case*, 12 Mod. 557, 558.
(*j*) S. 6.
(*k*) 8 & 9 Vict. c. 106.

OF CORPOREAL HEREDITAMENTS.

How rent must be reserved.

Rent service must issue out of the thing demised, and must be reserved out of lands or tenements to which the lessor can have recourse, and therefore (except in a demise by the Crown) cannot be reserved out of any incorporeal inheritance (*l*), nor out of goods (*m*). Consequently if rent is reserved out of two things, only one of which is capable of supporting rent, it will be presumed that all the rent was reserved out of that (*n*). It must also be reserved to the lessor himself (*o*), and not to a third party. Moreover it must be certain, but will be considered certain if capable of being reduced to certainty (*p*).

Distress for rent.

If these precautions are not attended to, the lessor will lose his common law right of Distress, that is, a right to enter upon the demised premises between the hours of sunrise and sunset (*q*) and seize any corn, grass, or other product growing on any part of the land demised (*r*), and also (subject to the exceptions to be presently noticed) any personal chattels found on the premises. The lessee must then either pay all rent due, and the costs incurred in the seizure, or, if he disputes the lawfulness of the seizure, he must "replevy" (*s*) the goods, by giving a bond to prosecute an action to recover them within a limited time (*t*). If he fails to adopt either of these courses within five days after notice in writing has been given to him of the distress being made (*u*), the lessor may proceed to sell the goods, taking care not to include in the distress more than is reasonably likely to produce, when sold, a sum sufficient to pay the rent due and all

---

(*l*) Co. Litt. 47ᵃ.
(*m*) *Spencer's Case*, 5 Rep. 16ᵃ.
(*n*) *Farewell* v. *Dickenson*, 6 B. & C. 251.
(*o*) *Chetham* v. *Williamson*, 4 East, 469; *Gilbertson* v. *Richards*, 4 H. & N. 277.
(*p*) *Daniel* v. *Gracie*, 6 Q. B. 145.
(*q*) *Tutton* v. *Darke*, 5 H. & N. 647.
(*r*) 11 Geo. II. c. 19, s. 8.
(*s*) *Replagiare*, to take a pledge.
(*t*) See as to this 19 & 20 Vict. c. 108, ss. 63 to 76.
(*u*) 2 Wm. & M. c. 5, s. 1.

expenses incurred in making the seizure. Any balance
over belongs, of course, to the lessee.

The chattels privileged by common law from dis- *Chattels exempted from distress.*
tress are—(1) Fixtures or things annexed to the freehold; (2) goods delivered to any person exercising a
public trade or employment, to be carried, wrought,
or managed in the way of his trade or employ (v),
including goods left in a warehouse until sale (w), or
pledged with a pawnbroker (x), or left at a depository
warehouse to be taken care of (y); and (3) implements of trade, if in actual use at the time (z).
It is also provided, by a recent statute (a), that any *Lodgers' Goods*
lodger whose goods are seized for rent due by the *Protection Act.*
immediate tenant may serve the landlord, or any person employed by him to levy the distress, with a declaration in writing setting forth that the immediate
tenant has no interest in such goods, and that they
are the property, or in the lawful possession of, the
lodger; and thereupon, and upon payment of the rent
(if any) due by the lodger to the immediate tenant,
the landlord is prohibited from proceeding to levy a
distress upon the goods of such lodger. If the tenant *Distress under*
fraudulently removes his goods from the premises, the *the 11 Geo. II.*
landlord may, within thirty days, follow and distrain *c. 19.*
the goods of such tenant (but not those of any other
person), unless they have been previously sold to a
bonâ fide purchaser (b).

Under the Statute of Limitations, 3 & 4 Wm. IV., *Arrears of rent.*
c. 27 (c), no arrears of rent can be recovered but *3 & 4 Wm. IV.*
within six years next after the same have become due, *c. 27.*

(v) *Gisbourn v. Hurst*, Salk. 249.
(w) *Thompson v. Mashiter*, 1 Bing. 283.
(x) *Swire v. Leach*, 18 C. B. (N. S.) 479.
(y) *Miles v. Furber*, L. R. 8 Q. B. 77.
(z) *Simpson v. Hartopp*, Willes, 512.
(a) 34 & 35 Vict. c. 79.
(b) 11 Geo. II. c. 19, ss. 1, 2.
(c) S. 42.

or next after an acknowledgment of the same in writing given to the person entitled thereto, or his agent, signed by the person by whom the same was payable, or his agent. This statute applies to every case where the rent has been reserved by a parol, or by a written, lease. But if the lease has been made by deed, the lessor is, under another Statute of Limitations (*d*), passed in the same year, in a more favourable position, so far as regards the time within which he may bring his action. For this statute enacts (*e*) that all actions of debt for rent upon an indenture (that is, a deed) of demise shall be commenced within twenty years after the cause of such action, but not after; this time being, however, extended (*f*) if the person entitled to bring the action is an infant, a married woman, a lunatic, or beyond seas; or if (*g*) any acknowledgment has been made either by writing signed by the party liable by virtue of such indenture or his agent, or by payment or part satisfaction on account of any principal or interest then due (*h*). Notwithstanding the statutes of limitation, it is settled that so long as the relation of landlord and tenant exists as a legal relation, the right to rent is not barred by non-payment, for however long a period, although the amount to be recovered is, in every case, limited to six years' rent (*i*).

marginal: 3 & 4 Wm. IV. c. 42.

marginal: Lessee's liability to pay rent.

The lessee is bound to pay rent, although the lessor may have failed to do repairs which he has covenanted to do (*j*). This obligation continues, both at law and in equity, even if the premises are burnt down (*k*),

---

(*d*) 3 & 4 Wm. IV. c. 42. See *Paget* v. *Foley*, 2 Bing. N. C. 679.
(*e*) S. 3.
(*f*) S. 4.
(*g*) S. 5.
(*h*) As to the conflicting nature of these statutes, see Sug. R. P. Statutes, 142, note (I).
(*i*) *Archbold* v. *Scully*, 9 H. L. C. 360.
(*j*) *Surplice* v. *Farnsworth*, 7 Man. & Gr. 576.
(*k*) *Baker* v. *Holtzappfel*, 4 Taunt. 45; *Holtzappfel* v. *Baker*, 18 Ves. 115; *Hare* v. *Groves*, Anstr. 687; *Lofft* v. *Dennis*, 1 E. & E. 474.

OF AN ESTATE FOR YEARS.

unless there is some stipulation to the contrary, for in the absence of agreement the lessor is not bound to rebuild premises destroyed by fire, nor will such an agreement be implied from a covenant on his part that the lessee shall have quiet enjoyment of the premises (*l*). At one time it appears to have been doubted whether the lessor could claim payment of rent without rebuilding the premises, if he had insured them and received the insurance money (*m*); but it is now well settled that he can (*n*). But under S. 83 of the Metropolitan Building Act (*o*), any person interested in any house or premises which may have been burnt down can require the directors of the office in the which the same had been insured to lay out the insurance money in rebuilding them, and it has been decided that the application of this section of the act is general, and not limited to the metropolis (*p*).

<small>Metropolitan Building Act.</small>

By the 5 & 6 Vict., c. 35 (*q*) the lessee is bound in the first instance to pay income tax, and then to deduct it from his rent; and no bargain between the lessor and lessee to the contrary is to have any binding effect. As to other taxes, the lessee, in the absence of any agreement, is bound to pay all personal charges in respect of the land, but not taxes on the land itself. He is therefore, in general, bound to pay poor, watching, water, highway, and county rates, but not land tax, sewer's rates, paving rate, or tithe rent charge, and if he does pay them he is entitled to deduct them from his rent, but only to the amount which the lessor would be bound to pay on his rent reserved (*r*); and a tenant who has paid his full rent without deducting the amount which he has paid on account of taxes

<small>Payment of taxes and rates. 5 & 6 Vict. c. 35.</small>

(*l*) *Bayne* v. *Walker*, 3 Dow, 233; *Brown* v. *Quilter*, Amb. 619.
(*m*) *Brown* v. *Quilter*, Amb. 619.
(*n*) *Leeds* v. *Cheetham*, 1 Sim. 146.
(*o*) 14 Geo. III. c. 78.
(*p*) Exparte *Gorely*, 34 L. J. (Bankr.) 1.
(*q*) S. 73.
(*r*) *Andrew* v. *Hancock*, 1 Brod. & B. 37.

.which the landlord ought ultimately to bear cannot recover it back (s).

Repairs.

A tenant for years is, in the absence of covenant, bound to keep the premises which he occupies wind and water tight, but not to do substantial repairs (t), and it would seem to follow that if he chooses to do them he cannot recover the amount so spent from his landlord. He is also, it would seem (u), liable for permissive waste, and is consequently entitled, in the absence of any proviso to the contrary, to take reasonable "estovers" or "botes," that is, to cut wood for fuel and for repairs, and to cut underwood and lop pollards.

Estovers.

Keeping boundaries distinct.

If he has land of his own adjoining that of his lessor it is his duty to keep the boundaries between such lands distinct, and if he fails to do so he must either restore the lessor's land specifically or substitute land of equal value (v); or, if he has suffered the boundaries to become confused, so that the lessor cannot tell to what he is entitled, must make good the loss to the lessor out of what may be considered as the common fund (w). The lessor is not bound to keep the demised premises in repair unless he has expressly agreed to do so (x), but it is probable that, if he has, the lessee could recover from him any money which he (the lessee) has expended on repairs, even though he had previously paid his rent to the lessor without claiming any deduction on that account. But a lessor covenanting to repair must have had notice that repairs are necessary, in order to render him liable to an action for breach of his covenant (y).

(s) *Andrew* v. *Hancock*, 1 Brod. & B. 37. See *Fuller* v. *Abbott*, 4 Taunt. 105.
(t) *Auworth* v. *Johnson*, 5 C. & P. 239; *Leach* v. *Thomas*, 7 C. & P. 327.
(u) *Harnett* v. *Maitland*, 16 Mee & W. 257; *Yellowly* v. *Gower*, 11 Exch. 274, 294; but see *Torriano* v. *Young*, 6 C. & P. 8.
(v) *Atty-Genl.* v. *Fullerton*, 2 Ves. & B. 263.
(w) *Atty-Genl.* v. *Stephens*, 6 De G. M. & G. 111
(x) *Gott* v. *Gandy*, 2 E. & B. 845.
(y) *Makin* v. *Wilkinson*, L. R. 6 Ex. 25.

A lessee is under an implied covenant to cultivate Waste. his land in a husbandlike manner (z) and according to the custom of the country in which it is situate (a). He is not entitled to commit "waste," which has been defined as a spoil or destruction in houses, gardens, trees, or other corporeal hereditaments, to the disinheritance of him that has the reversion or remainder (b). He may not, therefore, pull down houses, cut timber, open mines, dig for minerals, or alter the nature of the property demised as by converting arable land into woodland, or meadow or pasture land into arable. A tenant for years who did any of these things might formerly, under the Statute of Gloucester (c), have a writ of waste brought against him by his lessor, the result being that the place wasted was forfeited, and the tenant liable moreover to pay treble the amount of the damage which he had committed. The writ of waste has now been abolished (d), but a lessor may bring an action at law and recover damages against a lessee committing waste. He may also obtain from the Court of Chancery, or from the Court of Law in which he has brought, or is bringing, an action for waste, an injunction restraining the lessee from any repetition or continuance of waste (e). On the other hand, the lessee has the benefit of the 14 & 15 Vict., c. 25, already referred to as having been substituted for the former law relating to emblements.

Questions occasionally arise between the lessor and Fixtures.] the lessee as to the right of the latter to remove fixtures put up by him during his term. Fixtures include anything annexed to the freehold, that is fastened to or connected with it; mere juxta-position

---

(z) *Horsefall* v. *Mather*, Holt, N. P. C. 7, 9; *Powley* v. *Walker*, 5 T. R. 373.
(a) *Legh* v. *Hewitt*, 4 East, 154.
(b) 1 Inst. s. 67.
(c) 6 Ed. 1. c. 5.
(d) 3 & 4 Wm. IV. c. 27, s. 36.
(e) 17 & 18 Vict. c. 125, ss. 79, 82.

or laying an object, however heavy, on the freehold not amounting to annexation (*f*). According to the older law anything once annexed to the soil became part of it, and could only be removed by the owner of the soil, but exceptions to this rule have been gradually established in favour of the persons who may have put up fixtures, or their representatives.

Trade fixtures. The first exception appears to have been made in the case of fixtures put up by a tenant for years for the purposes of his trade. Thus, it was held in an old case (*g*) that a soap boiler was entitled to remove vats, &c., which he had put up for the purposes of his trade, and in a later case (*h*), where a lessee had erected buildings during his term for the purposes of his trade, it was held that he might lawfully remove such parts of them as consisted of a wooden structure raised on a brick foundation. But it appears to be doubtful whether he could remove a building, such as a lime kiln, having its foundations let into the ground (*i*).

The general rule has been stated as follows:— "Things which a tenant has fixed to the freehold for purposes of trade or manufacture may be taken away by him, whenever their removal is not contrary to any prevailing practice, when it will not cause material injury to the estate, and when they were of themselves of a perfect chattel nature before being put up (*j*).

Domestic fixtures. Notwithstanding some former decisions to the contrary (*k*), it is now well settled that the tenant has

---

(*f*) 2 Smith, L. C. 170.
(*g*) *Poole's Case*, Salk. 367.
(*h*) *Penton* v. *Robart*, 2 East, 88
(*i*) *Thresher* v. *East London Waterworks Co.*, 2 B. & C. 608.
(*j*) Amos on Fixtures, 48.
(*k*) *Poole's Case*, Salk. 367.

also a right (though not to the same extent as in the case of trade fixtures) to remove fixtures put up inside a house for domestic use, or for ornament. Thus, it has been held that wainscots screwed to the wall, grates, and the like, may be removed (*l*), as may also an ornamental wooden chimney-piece (*m*); but that a tenant is not entitled to remove a conservatory on a brick foundation, attached to the walls of the house (*n*), or green-houses on frames fixed with mortar to a foundation of brickwork (*o*).

With regard to fixtures put up for agricultural purposes, it was formerly held that, farming not being a trade, a farmer tenant had not the same privileges as one who was a trader. Thus, in one case (*p*), it was decided that a tenant could not remove brick and mortar buildings which he had put up for agricultural purposes. Now, however, it is provided by the 14 & 15 Vict:, c. 25 (*q*), that if any tenant, after the passing of the act, with the consent of his landlord, erects any buildings, engine, or machinery, either for agricultural purposes, or for the purpose of trade and agriculture (which shall not have been erected or put up in pursuance of some obligation on that behalf), he may remove the same, notwithstanding that they may consist of separate buildings, or be permanently fixed in the soil, provided he does no damage to the estate in their removal, or makes good any damage which may be caused thereby. The tenant must also give a month's notice to the landlord of his intention to remove the fixtures, and the landlord has a right, if he pleases, to purchase them at a valuation.

Agricultural fixtures.

14 & 15 Vict. c. 25.

(*l*) *Lee* v. *Risdon*, 7 Taunt. 188.
(*m*) *Avery* v. *Cheslyn*, 3 A. & E. 75.
(*n*) *Buckland* v. *Butterfield*, 2 Brod. & B. 54.
(*o*) *Jenkins* v. *Gething*, 2 J. & H. 520; *Gardiner* v. *Parker*, 18 Grant, 26.
(*p*) *Elwes* v. *Maw*, 3 East, 38, and, with notes, 2 Smith, L. C. 153.
(*q*) S. 3.

When fixtures must be removed. The tenant's right to remove fixtures should be exercised during his term. For it has been decided that a yearly tenant, who had quitted the premises of which he was tenant, had no right to recover bells and other fixtures which had been subsequently removed by the landlord (r). But it appears to be doubtful whether a tenant may not remove fixtures, notwithstanding that his term has expired, if he remains on the premises as a tenant by sufferance (s).

Effect of covenant as to fixtures. The tenant may, of course, deprive himself of the right to remove fixtures by entering into a covenant to that effect with his landlord (t). If, however, the articles enumerated in the covenant are all "landlord's fixtures" (that is, fixtures which the tenant would not be entitled to remove even in the absence of such a covenant), any other general words in the covenant which would *primâ facie* include tenant's fixtures will be held to refer to the landlord's fixtures only (u).

(r) *Lyde* v. *Russell*, 1 B. & Ad. 394.
(s) *Fenton* v. *Robart*, 2 East, 88; *Weeton* v. *Woodcock*, 7 Mee & W. 14; *Leader* v. *Homewood*, 5 C. B. (N. S.) 546.
(t) For examples of such covenants see *Naylor* v. *Collinge*, 1 Taunt. 19; *Burt* v. *Haslett*, 25 L. J. (C. P.) 295; *Wilson* v. *Whateley*, 1 J. & H. 436; *Dumergue* v. *Rumsey*, 33 L. J. (Ex.) 88.
(u) *Bishop* v. *Elliott*, 11 Exch. 113.

CHAPTER III.

OF AN ESTATE FOR YEARS (*continued*).

WE have already said that the consideration of the form of the covenants which are ordinarily inserted in a lease will be reserved for a future chapter, but it will be more convenient to notice in the present some recent enactments as to covenants and conditions in leases generally, and for this purpose we must refer briefly to the former state of the law on these two points. At one time it was held that no stranger to any covenant or condition could take any advantage or benefit by it. Thus, if A made a lease to B, and there were in the lease covenants by B for payment of rent, and other purposes, with a proviso that if B failed to pay the rent, or to observe the covenants, A might re-enter on the demised premises and put an end to the lease; and then A sold his reversion to C : C, being originally a stranger to the covenants and condition, could not take any advantage of them.

To meet this, an act was passed in the reign of Henry the Eighth (*a*), which enacted that the grantees or assignees of any reversion or reversions should have the like advantages against the lessees, by entry for non-payment of rent or for doing waste or other forfeiture, and should also have all and like and the same advantage, benefit, and remedies by action only, for not performing of other conditions, covenants, or agreements contained or expressed in their leases or grants, as the lessors or grantors themselves might have had at any time. Similar provisions were also

Covenants and conditions.

32 Hen. VIII. c. 34.

(*a*) 32 Hen. VIII. c. 34.

contained in the act in favour of lessees, as against the assignees of reversions.

Under this statute C, in the case we supposed above, could now re-enter on the land, or sue B for breach of covenant. If, however, A had only granted part of the reversion to C, or had granted the whole, not to C only, but in part to C and the rest to D; either of the new lessees could under the statute bring an action against B for any breach of covenant (b), but the statute did not confer on either of them a right of re-entry, which was in many cases far more valuable than that of bringing an action. For the common law had another doctrine applying to conditions, although not to covenants, namely, that a condition was entire and indivisible, and, consequently, that none but an assignee of the reversion of all the premises could take advantage of it, unless the reversion had been severed by operation of law (c).

The doctrine that conditions were indivisible also gave rise to another difficulty. Leases often contain a covenant by the lessee not to assign or underlet the premises, with a condition that if he does so the lease *Dumpor's Case.* shall be forfeited. But in *Dumpor's case* (d), decided in the year 1603, it was held that a condition in a lease that neither the lessee nor his assigns should alien it without the licence of the lessor was determined by an alienation by licence, and that consequently no subsequent alienation was a breach of the condition.

The application of the general rule to the facts of this case seems to have been erroneous, and the correctness of the particular decision was afterwards questioned by Lord Eldon (e), but it was nevertheless

---

(b) *Twynam* v. *Pickard,* 2 B. & Ald. 105, 112.
(c) *Winter's Case,* Dyer, 308ᵇ.
(d) 4 Rep. 119ᵇ.
(e) *Brummell* v. *McPherson,* 14 Ves. 173.

OF AN ESTATE FOR YEARS.

law until the passing, in the year 1859, of the 22 & 23 Vict., c. 35, which in effect provides (*f*) that every licence to do an act which, without such licence, would create a forfeiture, or give a right to re-enter, under a condition in any lease granted before or after the passing of the act, shall, unless otherwise expressed, extend only to the permission actually given, but not so as to prevent any proceedings for a subsequent breach unless otherwise specified in such licence, and that (*g*) a licence so given to one of several lessees or co-owners to assign or underlet his share or interest, or to do any other act prohibited to be done without licence, or to any lessee or owner, or to any one of several lessees or owners, to assign or underlet part only of the property, or to do any such acts as aforesaid in respect of part only of such property, shall not operate to destroy or extinguish the right of re-entry in case of any breach of the covenant by the co-lessee or co-lessees or owner or owners of the other shares in the property, or by the lessee of the rest of the property (as the case may be) over or in respect of such shares or interests or remaining property.

At the same time, the act places the position of assignees of part of a reversion on a more satisfactory footing, by enacting (*h*) that where the reversion upon a lease is severed, and the rent or other reservation is legally apportioned, the assignee of each part of the reversion shall, in respect of the apportioned rent or other reservation allotted or belonging to him, have, and be entitled to, all conditions or powers of re-entry for non-payment of the original rent or other reservation, in like manner as if such conditions or powers had been reserved to him as incident to his part of the reversion in respect of the apportioned rent or other reservation allotted or belonging to him.

22 & 23 Vict. c. 35.

(*f*) S. 1.
(*g*) S. 2.
(*h*) S. 3.

When covenants run with the land.
Of the various covenants contained in leases, some are binding only on the persons actually making them, or on whose behalf they are made, others again are said to "run with the land," meaning that the liability to perform them, and the right to take advantage of them, passes to every assignee of the land, this reciprocity being essential to their existence.

Spencer's Case.
The leading case on this subject is *Spencer's Case* (i), in which it was held (1) that covenants run with the land and bind the assignees, whether mentioned or not, when they extend to things *in esse* parcel of the demise, such, for instance, as to repair an existing house; but (2) that covenants relating to things not *in esse* at the time of the demise do not bind assignees unless mentioned; and (3) that if the thing to which the covenant relates is merely collateral to the land, such as to build a house on land of the lessor not part of the land demised, the assignee is not bound although mentioned. Covenants of the first sort are—by the lessor, that the lessee shall have quiet enjoyment of the premises during his term (j), or for renewal of the lease if required (k): by the lessee, to repair the premises when required (l), or to put them in repair and leave them peaceably and in good repair (m), or to insure them (n), or not to assign them without licence (o).

The soundness of the second resolution in Spencer's Case has been questioned in a modern case (p), in which the judges of the Court of Exchequer gave it as their opinion that covenants of the second kind ought to bind the assignee whether mentioned or not,

---

(i) 5 Rep. 16ᵃ, and see notes, 1 Smith L. C. 45, et seq.
(j) *Campbell* v. *Lewis*, 3 B. & Ald. 392.
(k) *Roe* v. *Hayley*, 12 East, 464, 469; *Simpson* v. *Clayton*, 4 Bing. N. C. 758.
(l) *Dean of Windsor's Case*, 5 Rep. 24ᵇ.
(m) *Martyn* v. *Clue*, 18 Q. B. 661.
(n) *Vernon* v. *Smith*, 5 B. & Ald. 1.
(o) *Williams* v. *Earle*, L. R. 3 Q. B. 739.
(p) *Minshull* v. *Oakes*, 2 H. & N. 793.

and such would seem to be the preferable view, but it would appear that the resolution in *Spencer's Case* is too firmly established to be shaken (*q*).

We have seen that before the 32 Hen. VIII., c. 34, covenants did not run with the reversion, but since the passing of that statute all covenants running with the land will also run with the reversion, and be available for the assignees of the whole or part of the reversion of the demised premises.

We have now arrived at the third division of our subject, namely, the alienation or determination of an estate for years. We have already seen who may create and who may acquire terms of years; also that terms of years may be disposed of by will, provided, of course, that the person purporting to act thus is capable of making a will. A term may also be the subject of involuntary alienation by being taken from the owner, or from his representatives after his death, in order to pay his debts. But of this we propose to treat more fully when considering the alienation of estates in fee simple, and will for the present content ourselves with calling attention to the other ways in which a term may be alienated. *The alienation and determination of an estate for years. Alienation.*

In the absence of any covenant on his part to the contrary, every lessee of a term, whether from year to year, or for a longer term, may assign all or part of his estate, notwithstanding that the lease may not have been expressly granted to him and his "assigns" (*r*). The same privilege belongs to every subsequent assignee, but the original lessee still remains liable under the covenants contained in the lease (*s*), as does also his assignee so long as he does not himself *By assignment. Liability of lessee and assignees.*

(*q*) Dart V. & P. 701, note (*i*); see however the remarks on *Minshull* v. *Oakes* in 1 Smith, L. C. 57.
(*r*) *Church* v. *Brown*, 15 Ves. 258, 264.
(*s*) *Staines* v. *Morris*, 1 Ves. & B. 8, 11.

assign (*t*), although the lessee may not have covenanted for his assigns (*u*); but an under-tenant who is not an assignee of the whole term is not liable (*v*). Every lessee who assigns his lease is, therefore, entitled to a covenant by his assignee for indemnity against any breach by the assignee of the covenants contained in the original lease; but such a covenant would probably be in any case implied, since it has been held that even the assignee of a lease by mesne assignments, who has entered into no covenants with the lessee, is bound to indemnify him against breaches of covenants in the lease committed during such assignee's own tenancy; and this obligation is not affected by the covenants which the assignee may have made with his immediate assignor (*w*).

22 & 23 Vict. c. 35. *repealed*

In order to protect the assignee of a lease from any liability in respect of a breach of covenant to insure, such breach having been committed before the assignment to him, it is enacted by the 22 & 23 Vict., c. 35 (*x*), that where on the *bonâ fide* purchase, after the passing of the act, of a leasehold interest under a lease containing a covenant on the part of the lessee to insure against loss or damage by fire, the purchaser is furnished with the written receipt of the person entitled to receive the rent, or of his agent, for the last payment of rent accrued due before the completion of the purchase; and there is subsisting at the time of the completion of the purchase an insurance in conformity with the covenant, the purchaser, or any person claiming under him, shall not be subject to any liability by way of forfeiture, or damages, or otherwise, in respect of any breach of the covenant committed at any time before the completion of the

---

(*t*) *Buckland* v. *Hall*, 8 Ves. 91, 94.
(*u*) *Vyvyan* v. *Arthur*, 2 Dow & Ry. 670.
(*v*) *Holford* v. *Hatch*, 1 Doug. 183.
(*w*) *Moule* v. *Garrett*, L. R. 7 Ex. 101.
(*x*) S. 8.

purchase, of which the purchaser had not notice before the completion of the purchase. The lessor, under these circumstances, still retains a right of action for breach of covenant against the original lessee.

By the Statute of Frauds (*y*), no lease (except in copyholds) is to be assigned except by writing, and this includes leases originally made by parol (*z*), and now, under the Real Property Amendment Act (*a*), every surrender of a lease must be made by deed. *Assignment must be by deed.*

A lessee may also part with his estate by death or by bankruptcy. No restriction against assignment can now prevent the lease from vesting in his executors or administrators, or his trustee in bankruptcy, as the case may be. His executors and administrators have the same interest in the lands demised, and are subject to the same liabilities under the lease, as the lessee himself, although the latter may have been only a tenant from year to year. In order to protect executors and administrators from a continuing liability in respect of their testator's leasehold estate, it is enacted by the 22 & 23 Vict. c. 35 (*b*), that when an executor or administrator who has acquired a lease by virtue of his office shall have satisfied all claims under any such lease, which may be due and claimed up to the time of the assignment thereinafter mentioned, and shall have set apart a sum sufficient to meet any ascertained liability under the lease, and shall then have assigned such lease, he shall not be subject to any further personal liability to the lessor. *By death or bankruptcy. 22 & 23 Vict. c. 35.*

If the lessee becomes bankrupt the lease will vest in his trustee in bankruptcy, who could always assign it to another party, unless the lease contained a

---

(*y*) 29 Car. II. c. 3, s. 3.
(*z*) *Botting v. Martin,* 1 Camp. 317.
(*a*) 8 & 9 Vict. c. 106, s. 3.
(*b*) S. 27.

66   OF CORPOREAL HEREDITAMENTS.

covenant by which "assigns" were expressly restrained from assignment (c). Under the former Bankruptcy Acts (d), the trustees (who were at that time called assignees) of a bankrupt were to elect within a reasonable time whether they would take to any leases the property of the bankrupt. And now it
Bankruptcy is provided by the Bankruptcy Act 1869 (e) that the
Act 1869. trustee of any bankrupt may, by writing, disclaim any lease acquired by him under the bankruptcy, and the lease is thereupon to be deemed to have been surrendered on that day. But (f) the trustee is not entitled to disclaim in cases where an application in writing has been made to him by any person interested in the property, requiring him to decide whether he will disclaim or not, and he has, for a period of twenty-eight days, or such further time as may be allowed by the Court of Bankruptcy, declined or neglected to give notice whether he will disclaim or not. It has been held that the Act does not put an end to the lease if the bankrupt was only an assignee of the lease, and not the original lessee, notwithstanding that the word "surrender" means *primâ facie* a delivering up of the lease in order that it may be put an end to. If therefore the assignee of a lease becomes bankrupt, and his trustee disclaims it, the person who had assigned the lease becomes the unwilling owner of the property with which he imagined himself to have parted, and liable upon all the conditions and covenants of the lease (g).

Determination   A term of years may also be put an end to by
of a term of   (1) forfeiture; (2) by effluxion of time; (3) by notice
years.   properly given by a landlord or by a tenant; and (4) by surrender.

(e) *Philpot* v. *Hoare*, 2 Atk. 219, note (2).
(d) 12 & 13 Vict. c. 106, s. 145; 24 & 25 Vict. c. 134, s. 131.
(e) 32 & 33 Vict. c. 71, n. 23.
(f) S. 24.
(g) *Smyth* v. *North*, L. R. 7 Ex. 242.

Most leases contain various covenants by the lessee, By forfeiture. such as that he will pay rent, keep the premises in repair, or insure them; and to these is added a proviso that on his failing to observe the covenants of his lease, the lessor shall be at liberty to re-enter on the premises, and put an end to the term. It is evident that there are many cases in which the enforcement of this proviso by the lessor may work great hardship. Consequently there are various circumstances under which he will not be allowed to exercise this power.

In the first place, he will be presumed to have Presumption of waived his right to a forfeiture, and be prevented there- waiver of lessor's right to fore from enforcing it, if, after being aware of a breach a forfeiture. of covenant, he does any act which amounts to the recognition of a subsisting tenancy by his lessee. Thus, a waiver will be presumed in such a case by the lessor's acceptance of rent, or by his bringing an action for rent due, unless the breach of covenant is a continuing one (*h*), or unless the acceptance is that of rent due on a day before that on which the forfeiture was incurred. So also, if a breach of covenant is known to a lessor, and he afterwards deals with the lessee so as to lead him to suppose that a forfeiture will not be insisted on, it will be presumed that the right to a forfeiture has been waived (*i*). And a distress for rent in pursuance of the lessor's common law right, even though only for rent due before the covenant was broken, waives his claim to a forfeiture; since the privilege of distress only belongs to him on the assumption that the person on whom he distrains is his tenant (*j*). But acceptance of rent is not a waiver of a breach of covenant unknown to the lessor at the time of acceptance (*k*), although the rent received

---

(*h*) *Doe* v. *Jones*, 5 Exch. 498.
(*i*) *Flattery* v. *Anderdon*, 12 Ir. Eq. R. 219.
(*j*) Co. Litt. 211ʰ; *Price* v. *Worwood*, 4 H. & N. 512.
(*k*) *Roe* v. *Harrison*, 2 T. R. 425.

became due after the breach (*l*). And if he has brought an action of ejectment against the lessee for breach of covenant, he will not waive his right by making a demand for rent for the use and occupation of the premises after the date of the breach (*m*), or even by distraining for rent (*n*), since bringing ejectment is a declaration on his part that he considers the tenancy at an end, and a distress in such case, if not justified by a statute (*o*) to be presently noticed, is merely a trespass on his part, and does not involve a continuance of the tenancy.

Relief against forfeiture.

A lessee may also, occasionally, obtain relief from the Courts of Chancery or of Common Law against the consequences of his breach of covenant. The courts will not interfere in favour of lessees who choose to break their covenants, except where it is evident that full compensation can be made to the lessor; and they will not therefore, in general, relieve against forfeiture incurred by a breach of covenant to repair (*p*), or to cultivate land in an husband-like manner (*q*), or not to carry on a trade on the premises without licence from the lessor (*r*), or not to assign the premises without licence from him (*s*); but in cases where complete compensation can be made the Court of Chancery would to a certain extent formerly, and all Superior Courts may now, subject to certain conditions, relieve against forfeiture for breach of covenant. Thus, the Court of Chancery would always relieve against forfeiture for nonpayment of rent (*t*),

---

(*l*) *Croft* v. *Lumley*, 6 H. L. C. 672.
(*m*) *Toleman* v. *Portbury*, L. R. 7 Q. B. 344.
(*n*) *Grimwood* v. *Moss*, L. R. 7 C. P. 360.
(*o*) 8 Anne, c. 18.
(*p*) *Gregory* v. *Wilson*, 9 Ha. 683, 689; *Hill* v. *Barclay*, 18 Ves. 56. In *Bargent* v. *Thompson*, 4 Giff. 473, V.-C. Stuart gave relief against forfeiture for a breach of covenant to repair, but the circumstances of the case were peculiar.
(*q*) *Hills* v. *Rowland*, 4 De G. M. & G. 430.
(*r*) *Macher* v. *Foundling Hospital*, 1 Ves. & B. 188.
(*s*) *Hill* v. *Barclay*, 18 Ves. 56.
(*t*) *Wadman* v. *Calcraft*, 10 Ves. 66ª.

unless accompanied by a breach of other covenants, and that, without reference to the length of time which had elapsed since the forfeiture. Subsequently it was enacted by the 4 Geo. II., c. 28 (*u*), that every lessee might, before the trial of any action for ejectment brought for nonpayment of rent, pay to the lessor, or into court, all rent then due, and all costs incurred, and that thereupon all proceedings in the action should cease; and further, that every lessee ejected for nonpayment of rent might, if he applied within six calendar months, obtain relief from the Court of Chancery, on condition of paying, within forty days from the lessor's putting in an answer swearing to the amount due for rent, such sum, together with all expenses incurred; and that in either of these cases the lessee should be entitled to hold the demised lands according to the lease thereof made without any new lease. This was re-enacted by the Common Law Procedure Act 1852 (*v*), and now by the Common Law Procedure Act 1860 (*w*), in case of any ejectment for nonpayment of rent, any Superior Court of Common Law may relieve in the same manner as the Court of Chancery. If the lessee has been ejected, and is re-admitted under these statutes, the lessor is to be accountable only for so much as he shall *bonâ fide* have made of the premises from the time of entering into actual possession thereof. It has been held under an Irish Statute, containing similar provisions (*x*), that the lessor is bound only to account for such rents as he has actually received during possession; but if he omits to use due diligence in collecting the rent, or in letting the land, he will be charged with a fair occupation rent (*y*).

4 Geo. II. c. 28.

Common Law Procedure Act 1860.

A lessee could not, formerly, obtain any relief against

(*u*) S. 4.
(*v*) 15 & 16 Vict. c. 76, ss. 210, 211, 212.
(*w*) 23 & 24 Vict. c. 126, ss. 1, 2.
(*x*) 11 Anne, c. 2. (Ir.)
(*y*) *Callaghan* v. *Lismore*, Beat. 223.

forfeiture for a breach of covenant to insure (z). It has, however, been provided by the 22 & 23 Vict., c. 35 (a), that a Court of Equity shall have power to relieve against a forfeiture for a breach of a covenant or condition to insure against loss or damage by fire, where no loss or damage by fire has happened, and the breach has, in the opinion of the court, been committed through accident, or mistake, or otherwise without fraud, or gross negligence, and there is an insurance on foot at the time of the application to the court in conformity with the covenant to insure, upon such terms as to the court may seem fit; but (b) the same person is not to have such relief more than once in respect of the same covenant or condition, nor if a forfeiture under the covenant in respect of which relief is sought shall have been already waived out of court in favour of the person seeking the relief. And under the Common Law Procedure Act 1860 (c) a Superior Court of Common Law is empowered to give relief in all cases in which relief could be obtained in the Court of Chancery, and upon similar terms.

22 & 23 Vict. c. 35.

Common Law Procedure Act 1860.

If a term of years is made for a fixed period of time it comes to an end when that period has expired, and no notice either to leave, or of an intention to leave, the demised premises need be given by the lessor, or by the lessee (d), except in cases where the lessor desires to establish a claim, under a statute which will be presently referred to, against a lessee wrongfully remaining on the premises after the expiration of his term.

By effluxion of time.

If the tenancy is one from year to year it may exist as long as both parties please, but is determinable at

By notice.

(z) *Gregory* v. *Wilson*, 9 Ha. 683; *Reynolds* v. *Pitt*, 19 Ves. 134.
(a) S. 4.
(b) S. 6.
(c) 23 & 24 Vict. c. 126, s. 2.
(d) *Cobb* v. *Stokes*, 8 East, 358; *Right* v. *Darby*, 1 T. R. 159, 162.

the end of the first, as well as of any subsequent year, unless in creating it the parties use words showing that they contemplate a tenancy for two years at least (e). Such a tenancy cannot be put an end to, unless by agreement, without notice being given by the party wishing to determine it. A term created by parol may be terminated by a parol notice (f), and if there are several tenants of premises held in common, notice to any one of them is sufficient (g). The notice must be at least half a year's (not six lunar months') (h) notice, and must be given so as to complete a year, reckoning from the commencement of the tenancy. If the time of the commencement of the tenancy cannot be proved, notice to quit, regulated by the time of the payment of the rent, is *primâ facie* evidence of the commencement of the tenancy at that period, but such a notice must be served personally on the tenant(i). The receipt by the lessor of rent, as such, accrued due after the expiration of the time fixed by the notice for determining the tenancy, is a waiver of the notice (j), as is also distraining for rent due after the expiration of the notice (k), and such a waiver, if assented to by the tenant (l), creates a new tenancy taking effect on the expiration of the old one. But acceptance of payment for the use and occupation of the premises after the expiration of the time fixed by the notice, is not a waiver of the notice (m).

If the tenancy is determined by forfeiture, effluxion of time, or notice to quit, and the lessee refuses to give up the premises, the lessor can proceed against him by bringing an action of ejectment. In order to pun-

Penalty on tenant holding over.

(e) *Doe* v. *Smaridge*, 7 Q. B. 957.
(f) *Timmins* v. *Rowlinson*, Burr. 1603.
(g) *Doe* v. *Crick*, 5 Esp. 196.
(h) *Doe* v. *Smith*, 5 A. & E. 350, 351.
(i) *Doe* v. *Forster*, 13 East, 405.
(j) *Goodright* v. *Cordwent*, 6 T. R. 219.
(k) *Zouch* v. *Willingale*, 1 H. Bl. 311.
(l) *Jenner* v. *Clegg*, 1 Moo. & Rob. 213.
(m) *Doe* v. *Batten*, Cowp. 243.

ish lessees wrongfully retaining possession, it is enacted by the 4 Geo. II., c. 28 (*n*), that a tenant wilfully holding over after the determination of the term, and after demand of possession made and notice in writing properly given, shall pay for the time he detains the lands at the rate of double their yearly value; and by the 11 Geo. II., c. 19 (*o*), that any tenant who has given notice to quit and does not deliver up possession at the specified time, is to pay double his former rent for such time as he continues in possession. It will be observed that the latter statute does not require the tenant's notice to be in writing, and accordingly it has been held that a tenant holding over after a parol notice is liable to pay double rent (*p*). In order to entitle the lessor to double value under the first of these statutes, the holding over must be with a consciousness on the part of the tenant that he has no right to retain possession (*q*), and the landlord, therefore, is not entitled to recover double value unless he can show a wilful holding over by the tenant, it not being enough to show that the premises were held over by a sub-tenant of the lessee, unless it can also be shown that this was done with the lessee's assent or authority (*r*). But every tenant is bound to render up possession at the end of his term, and therefore if a sub-tenant holds over, the lessee, although he himself has given the sub-tenant notice to quit, is liable to pay to the lessor the single value of the premises for the whole time during which the latter has been kept out of possession, and also all costs incurred by him in ejecting the sub-tenant (*s*). Where a tenant remains in occupation of the premises after the expiration of his term, the landlord is empowered by

---

(*n*) S. 1.
(*o*) S. 18.
(*p*) *Timmins* v. *Rowlinson*, Burr. 1603.
(*q*) *Swinfen* v. *Bacon*, 30 L. J. (Ex.) 368.
(*r*) *Rands* v. *Clark*, 19 W. R. 48.
(*s*) *Henderson* v. *Squire*, L. R. 4 Q. B. 170; and see *Hardin;* v. *Crethorn*, 1 Esp. 57.

statute (*t*) to distrain for any arrears of rent in the same manner as he might have done had the tenancy not been determined; but (*u*) the distress must be made within six calendar months from the termination of the tenancy, during the continuance of the landlord's title, and during the possession of the tenant from whom the arrears are due. It would seem that this act does not give a lessor a right of distress where a tenancy has been determined by forfeiture, and not in the ordinary course (*v*). 8 Anne, c. 18.

A term may also be put an end to by being surrendered or given back by the lessee to the lessor. Under the Statute of Frauds, (*w*) every surrender of a lease, other than a lease of copyholds, must be in writing, except in cases where a surrender would be implied at law, and by the Real Property Amendment Act (*x*), every surrender formerly required by law to be in writing must now be made by deed. A surrender will be implied at law if the lessee accepts a new good lease (*y*); or if a new lessee is accepted by consent of all parties (*z*); and the receipt of the key of a house from a yearly tenant has been held to operate as a surrender (*a*), as has also the acceptance of rent by the lessor from an under-tenant (*b*). By surrender.
Statute of Frauds.
Real Property Amendment Act.

Provision has been made by statute for the surrender of leases belonging to persons under disability. By the 11 Geo. IV. & 1 Wm. IV., c. 65, it is enacted that (*c*) the guardian of an infant, or a married Surrender of lease in case of persons under disability.
11 Geo. IV. & 1 Wm. IV. c. 65.

(*t*) 8 Anne, c. 18, s. 6.
(*u*) S. 7.
(*v*) *Doe* v. *Williams*, 7 C. & P. 322; *Grimwood* v. *Moss*, L. R. 7 C. P. 360, 365.
(*w*) 29 Car. II. c. 3, s. 3.
(*x*) 8 & 9 Vict. c. 106, s. 3
(*y*) *Davison* v. *Stanley*, Burr. 2210.
(*z*) *Phipps* v. *Sculthorpe*, 1 B. & Ald. 50; *Nickells* v. *Atherstone*, 10 Q. B. 944.
(*a*) *Dodd* v. *Acklom*, 6 Man. & Gr. 672.
(*b*) *Thomas* v. *Cook*, 2 B. & Ald. 119.
(*c*) S. 12.

woman, may, on application to the Court of Chancery, obtain leave to surrender any lease and accept in its stead a new lease, which is to be for such a term, and subject to such conditions, as the court shall think fit. Also (*d*), that the same persons may, with the sanction of the court, accept a surrender of any lease in order to make a new lease to be approved of by the court. And similar clauses are contained in the 16 & 17 Vict., c. 70, with reference to the committees of lunatics. Moreover, the Leases and Sales of Settled Estates Act (*e*) provides (*f*) that any lease granted under the act may be surrendered, either for the purpose of obtaining a renewal of the same or not: and that the power to authorize leases conferred by the act shall extend to authorize new leases of the whole, or any part, of the hereditaments comprised in any surrendered lease. The power of surrendering leases granted under this act, is by the Leases and Sales of Settled Estates Amendment Act (*g*), to be deemed to extend to all leases, whether granted in pursuance of the said act or otherwise.

Marginal notes:
16 & 17 Vict. c. 70.
Leases and Sales of Settled Estates Act.
Leases and Sales of Settled Estates Amendment Act.

Long terms of years.

We now come to the consideration of long terms of years not intended for the purpose of establishing the ordinary relation of landlord and tenant.

The reader is probably aware that there exist in this country two distinct methods of administering the law, namely, that of the Courts of Common Law and that of the Court of Chancery (*h*). The former and older method sufficed for doing justice at a time when the ownership of property existed only in its simpler forms. In time, however, the progress of civilization gave rise to more

---

(*d*) S. 16.
(*e*) 19 & 20 Vict. c. 120.
(*f*) S. 5.
(*g*) 21 & 22 Vict. c. 77, s. 5.
(*h*) This state of things will, next year, be altered by the Supreme Court of Judicature Act 1873 (36 & 37 Vict. c. 66).

refined and complicated modes of dealing with property, especially with land. These methods the Courts of Common Law, in many cases, declined to countenance, and notably in the instance of land held in trust. In a subsequent part of this work there will be found an account of the way in which trusts were encouraged and established by the Court of Chancery. At this stage we will content ourselves with stating that, as a general rule, the Courts of Common Law did not recognise trusts. If A conveyed the fee-simple of land to B, with directions to hold it for the benefit of C, the Courts of Common Law refused to look beyond B, to whom the land had been legally conveyed, and treated him alone as owner of it. But the Court of Chancery did not stop short at this, and, therefore, whilst not refusing to recognise B as the legal owner, would nevertheless compel him to carry out the purposes for which the land was intrusted to him. B therefore, in such a case, was said to have the legal estate in the land, whilst C had the beneficial or equitable estate.

Supposing that the owner of a landed estate wishes to preserve it in his family, so as to go after his death to his eldest son in the course of primogeniture, but at the same time desires to make some provision for his widow and younger children: a long term of years offers him an effectual means of accomplishing this object. He has merely to grant the estate for any number of years (say a thousand) to trustees, upon trust to raise portions for his widow and younger children, giving them power for that purpose to sell or mortgage the estate if necessary, and then, subject to the term, to entail the property upon his eldest son, by giving him an estate in it for life, with a remainder after that son's death to his sons in tail. By this means the eldest son will, on his father's death, have the freehold of the estate, subject to the term, but at the same time the trustees will have a

Their advantages.

right to take the profits of the land, if necessary, during the term. If the widow or younger children are to have a yearly income only, it will be merely necessary for the trustees to see that that income is paid by the eldest son, and if he should fail to pay it they can, under their powers, take possession of the property in order to secure payment. If the portions are to be paid in a lump sum, the trustees can mortgage or sell the whole, or part, of the estate in order to raise such money as may be wanted, leaving the eldest son otherwise in undisturbed enjoyment of the property. There will be no difficulty in raising the money on mortgage, since possession of an estate for a thousand years offers as ample security as possession of the fee-simple. The same means will be available for any other case where it is desired to raise money on the security of the estate.

Next, let us suppose that the objects for which the term was created are either accomplished, or have failed. In that case the term is said to be "satisfied." Before the passing of the 8 & 9 Vict., c. 112, the deed creating a long term of years usually contained a proviso (known as a "proviso for cesser") that when the term was satisfied it should come to an end, or else a declaration that, after being satisfied, it should be held in trust for the person for the time being entitled to the inheritance of the estate; in which case the term was said to be "attendant on the inheritance." If the deed made no provision for the case of the term becoming satisfied, a Court of Law would sometimes presume it to have been surrendered or put an end to, but only under special circumstances (*i*); and as a general rule would consider the term as existing, and the Court of Chancery would always hold an existing satisfied term to be attendant on the inheritance, whether so declared or

Satisfied terms.

(*i*) *Garrard* v. *Tuck,* 8 C. B. 231.

not (j). The beneficial interests both in the term and in the reversion being thus united in one person, were, by analogy to the law of merger previously explained, considered to be united, and the equitable estate in the term was therefore merged in the equitable estate in the reversion. But although the equitable estate in the term became extinguished, the legal estate in it remained, with a distinct and separate existence of its own; and this separation, caused by the difference between legal and equitable estates, was formerly used with advantage for the protection of the person entitled to the inheritance, and of those claiming under him.

For supposing a reversioner, on coming into possession, to have found that the person creating the term had mortgaged or otherwise incumbered the property subsequently to the term: in that case the reversioner was able, through his trustees, to claim the benefit of the legal term of years—an estate prior to the date of the incumbrances—and thus, both at Law and in Equity, to exclude all persons claiming by virtue of these incumbrances until after the expiration of the term; since it was obviously just that the owner of a prior estate should not be affected by the acts of the owner of a subsequent estate. And not only so, but any purchaser for value (that is, every person who takes an estate or charge in consideration of marriage, money, or other equivalent) from the reversioner would be equally protected, provided he took the precaution to obtain from the trustees of the term a declaration of trust in his favour, or an assignment of the term to trustees of his own, and provided he had no notice of prior incumbrances before he took a conveyance (k).

Advantages of satisfied terms.

(j) *Maundrell* v. *Maundrell,* 10 Ves. 246, 269.
(k) There were two exceptions to this last rule. The purchaser was protected against a widow's claim to dower even though he had notice, and on the other hand debts due to the Crown were not barred by absence of notice.

These advantages however were found in practice to be more than balanced by the evils arising from the system of attendant terms.

Disadvantages of satisfied terms.

Thus a purchaser from a reversioner, if he neglected to get an assignment of the term, was liable to find himself at any time postponed to a subsequent purchaser of the same estate, who had bought without notice of such first purchase, and had got an assignment of the term (*l*). This was the case even though the subsequent purchaser, at the time of getting the assignment, had become aware of the first purchase, since he had now acquired a prior legal title, and a Court of Equity would not interfere in such a case between two innocent parties, for, it was said, "Where the Equities are equal the Law shall prevail."

Moreover the doctrine of Equity as to notice rendered the position of a purchaser precarious, even when he had got in the term; and since, in order to guard against the difficulties which frequently arose in establishing terms at law, it became customary to keep several terms on foot, it was often difficult for a purchaser to be sure that he had got the oldest term, and the system had thus a tendency in some cases to promote fraud.

The expense also of every conveyance was necessarily greater, for in every case where there was an outstanding term the title to the term had to be shown in the same manner as that to the freehold, and if there was more than one term the title to each had to be shown. If the term and the inheritance were assigned by one deed, the deed was necessarily longer and more expensive. If separate deeds were used the expense was still greater. Moreover expense was incurred in ascertaining the trustees of

---

(*l*) *Goodtitle* v. *Morgan*, 1 T. R. 755.

terms, and the terms themselves were occasionally found to have been lost by the trustees having subsequently acquired the reversion (*m*).

For these reasons it was enacted by the 8 & 9 Vict., c. 112 (*n*) that every satisfied term of years which, whether by declaration, or by construction of law, should upon the 31st day of December 1845 be attendant upon the inheritance or reversion of any lands, should on that day absolutely cease and determine, as to the land upon the inheritance or reversion whereof such term should be attendant as aforesaid; except that every such term of years which should be so attendant by express declaration, although thereby made to cease and determine, should afford to every person the same protection against every incumbrance, charge, estate, right, action, suit, claim, and demand, as it would have afforded to him had it continued to subsist, but had not been assigned or dealt with, after the 31st of December 1845; and should, for the purpose of such protection, be considered in every Court of Law and Equity as a subsisting term: it was also enacted (*o*) that every satisfied (*p*) term then subsisting, or thereafter to be created, and which, either by express declaration, or by construction of law, should after that day become attendant upon the inheritance or reversion of any lands, should, immediately upon the same becoming so attendant, cease and determine as to the land upon the inheritance or reversion whereof such term should become attendant as aforesaid.

8 & 9 Vict. c. 112.

It results from this act, (which does not extend to

(*m*) The remarks in this and the two preceding paragraphs are taken, in substance, from the Second Report of the Real Property Commissioners, pp. 7—14.
(*n*) S. 1.
(*o*) S. 2.
(*p*) As to the meaning of the word "satisfied," see *Anderson* v. *Pignet*, L. R. 8 Ch. 180.

copyholds, customary freeholds, or leaseholds (*q*),) (1) that a satisfied term created before the 31st of December 1845, and not attendant upon the inheritance by express declaration, is altogether put an end to on that day; (2) that a satisfied term created before the 31st of December 1845, and attendant on the inheritance by express declaration, can no longer be assigned after that date, but affords, both to the person entitled to the inheritance and to any subsequent purchaser from him, the same protection as if it remained for ever vested in the then trustee on the trusts on which he held it on the day when the act came into operation; that is, will render such a purchaser safe against subsequent purchasers from the reversioner, but not against prior purchasers although he had no notice of their claims; and (3) that no term created after the 31st of December 1845 can be made, by any means, attendant on the inheritance.

It only remains to add that a satisfied term created before the 31st of December 1845, and attendant upon the inheritance by express declaration, will be considered as subsisting, unless a Court of Equity would, before the passing of the act, have restrained the person interested in it from setting it up in a Court of Law (*r*).

(*q*) Dart, V. & P. 465.
(*r*) *Cottrell* v. *Hughes*, 15 C. B. 532.

CHAPTER IV.

OF AN ESTATE FOR LIFE.

Having thus discussed estates less than freehold, we will now ascend to the next stage, and consider those estates which are of a freehold nature, first pausing to remind the reader that there is a distinction between freehold estates and estates in land of freehold tenure. For there may be a freehold estate (i.e., one for life or in fee) in copyholds, which are estates of a base, and not of a freehold, tenure. Freehold estates may be classed under the two principal headings of, 1st, Freeholds of inheritance, or estates in fee simple and in fee tail; and 2nd, Freeholds not of inheritance, or estates for life. It is proposed in this chapter to notice the chief points relating to estates for life.

These are of two kinds, namely, those which are conventional, or expressly created by act of parties; and those which are legal, or created only by construction and operation of law (*a*). The former are the more usual, and exist when a man has an estate in land which is to last for the term of his own life, or for that of another, or for the lives of two or more persons, of whom he may or may not be one.

<small>Estate for life.</small>

Such an estate may be created by any person, not under disability, who has an estate of freehold. But a tenant for years, however long his term may be, cannot create an estate for life; because, having only a chattel interest, he cannot out of it create that which

<small>By whom it may be created.</small>

(*a*) 2 Bl. Com. 120.

c. F

Corporations.
Infants.

the law considers a greater interest than his own. We have already seen that corporations may, to a certain extent, create estates for life (*b*), and we have to add that an infant may also create such an estate under special circumstances.

18 & 19 Vict. c. 43.

For it is enacted by the 18 & 19 Vict., c. 43, that, from and after the passing of the act (*c*), it shall be lawful for every male infant not under the age of twenty years, and for every female infant not under the age of seventeen years (*d*), upon or in contemplation of his or her marriage, to make (*e*), with the sanction of the Court of Chancery, a valid settlement of all or any part of his or her property, or of property over which he or she has any power of appointment. By means of such a settlement, then, an infant may create an estate for life, but the act goes on to provide (*f*) that any appointment or disentailing assurance executed under the provisions of the act by an infant who is a tenant in tail, shall be void if the infant afterwards dies before attaining the age of twenty-one years.

Mode of creating an estate for life.
By operation of law.

An estate for life may be created (1) by operation of law, (2) by deed, or (3) by will. The estates for life which are created by the first-named process are—1st, Estates in Dower; 2nd, Estates by Curtesy; and 3rd, Tenancy in tail after possibility of issue extinct. An Estate in Dower is that which a widow may have, during her lifetime, in hereditaments, of which her husband was tenant for an estate of inheritance. It will be necessary to explain this subject somewhat fully, and since the former law relating to dower was materially altered by the Dower Act (*g*) now in force,

Estate in Dower.

(*b*) 32 Hen. VIII. c. 28; 5 Geo. III. c. 17; 5 & 6 Vict. c. 108.
(*c*) 2nd July, 1855.
(*d*) S. 4.
(*e*) S. 1.
(*f*) S. 2.
(*g*) 3 & 4 Wm. IV. c. 105.

(which applies only to women who were married after the 1st of January 1834), we will first explain how the law stood before the passing of that statute.

Under the old law, a widow was deemed to be entitled to an estate for life in one-third part of all hereditaments, corporeal or incorporeal, of which her husband, at any time during the coverture, had had the sole legal possession for an estate in fee simple or in fee tail, and which any of her issue, actual or possible, was capable of inheriting. Of the right to this estate she could not be deprived, after her marriage, by any alienation or disposition which her husband might make of the hereditaments in question, unless she formally assented thereto and expressly released her right to dower. If before her marriage she, or her guardian for her (*h*), if she were an infant, accepted a jointure (that is, a competent livelihood of freehold for her life of lands, to take effect in possession immediately on her husband's death (*i*),) then she was, under the Statute of Uses (*j*), deprived of her right to dower. She would also have been restrained by the Court of Chancery from claiming dower if the provision thus made for her were sufficient, although it might not have come out of property strictly within the terms of the statute (*k*). She could not be deprived of her dower by any jointure made for her after her marriage, but she would, in such a case, have been compelled to give up either her dower or her jointure. If, however, nothing had been done which barred her dower, her right to it was paramount to the claims of all purchasers, incumbrancers, or creditors, from, or of, her husband.

Former law of dower.

The widow herself was not entitled to take posses-

(*h*) *Drury* v. *Buckingham*, 3 Bro. P. C. 492.
(*i*) Co. Litt. 36ᵇ.
(*j*) 27 Hen. VIII. c. 10, s. 6.
(*k*) *Williams* v. *Chitty*, 3 Ves. 545; Co. Litt. 36ᵇ, note D.; *Vizard* v. *Longdale*, cited 3 Atk. 8; *Garthshore* v. *Chalie*, 10 Ves. 1.

sion of any land for her dower, but it was the duty of the heir to assign one-third of her husband's lands for that purpose; if he neglected to do so, or made an unfair assignment, she was entitled to a writ of dower, in pursuance of which the lands out of which her dower was to be derived would be marked out by the sheriff of the county in which they lay. If any dower was to come out of incorporeal hereditaments, she was entitled to receive one-third of the profits derived from them.

She could also claim arrears of dower which had become due, either from neglect in paying her or in consequence of no land having been assigned for her benefit. At one time there was no limit, either at law or in equity (*l*), to the amount which might be so claimed, but her rights in this respect were afterwards limited to six years' arrears of dower (*m*).

The former law of dower was not open to much objection in the days when the alienation of land was prohibited, but afterwards it became a source of very serious inconvenience. The Court of Chancery did indeed permit a purchaser of land to protect himself against the dower of the vendor's wife, if he could manage to procure the assignment, to a trustee for himself, of one of those long terms of which we spoke in the last chapter. He could also prevent his own wife's right to dower from fastening upon land which he purchased, by framing the conveyance of it to himself in a manner which need not be particularized here, further than to say that, by means of the intervention of a life estate, given to a trustee for the purchaser, the latter did not take a legal estate of inheritance in the lands, in the absence of which, as we have seen, his widow had no claim to dower. A man might also

---

(*l*) *Oliver* v. *Richardson*, 9 Ves. 222.
(*m*) 3 & 4 Wm. IV c. 27, s. 41.

coerce his widow into relinquishing her dower, by
making some provision for her in his will conditional
on her doing so. Practically, therefore, the widow's
claim to dower was in most instances evaded, though
not without considerable expense and some risk, and
the Legislature consequently decided to make a sweeping change in the law.

This was effected by the Dower Act (*n*), which Dower Act.
applies, as we said, to all women who were married
after the 1st of January 1834 (*o*). The act (*p*) gives
every widow to whom it applies a right to dower not
merely out of all legal, but also out of all equitable, or
partly equitable and partly legal, estates of inheritance
in possession (other than estates in joint tenancy) to
which her husband was beneficially entitled at the
time of his death, or which (*q*) he had a right to enter
upon. The act in this respect applies as well where
the parties were married before as after its passing (*r*).
It also affirmed by fresh enactment what had been the
law previously, namely, that (*s*) no gift made by a husband to his widow by will of personal estate or of any of
his land not liable to dower should defeat or prejudice
her right to dower, unless a contrary intention were
declared by the will. But the other sections of the
act render the widow's dower very precarious, and
entirely dependent upon the pleasure of her husband.
For it is enacted that (*t*) no widow shall be entitled
to dower out of any "land" (a term which in the act
extends to all hereditaments liable to dower, corporeal or incorporeal, and to any share thereof (*u*),)
which shall have been absolutely disposed of by her

(*n*) 3 & 4 Wm. IV. c. 105.
(*o*) S. 14.
(*p*) S. 2.
(*q*) S. 3.
(*r*) *McIntosh* v. *Wood*, 15 Grant, 92.
(*s*) S. 10.
(*t*) S. 4.
(*u*) S. 1.

husband in his lifetime or by will (*v*); that all partial estates and interests, and all charges created by any disposition, or will, of a husband, and all debts, incumbrances, contracts, and engagements to which his land shall be subject or liable, shall be valid and effectual as against the right of his widow to dower; that (*w*) a widow shall not be entitled to dower out of any land of her husband, when in the deed by which such land was conveyed to him, or by any deed executed by him, it shall be declared that his widow shall not be entitled to dower out of such land; that (*x*) a widow shall not be entitled to dower out of any land of which her husband shall die wholly or partially intestate, when by his will he shall declare that she shall not be entitled to dower out of such land, or out of any of his land; that (*y*) the right of a widow to dower shall be subject to any conditions, restrictions, or directions, which shall be declared by the will of her husband; and (*z*) that where a husband shall devise any land out of which his widow would be entitled to dower but for such devise, or any estate or interest therein, to, or for the benefit of, his widow, such widow shall not be entitled to dower out of, or in, any land of her said husband unless a contrary intention is declared by his will. But it is provided (*a*) that the Court of Chancery may enforce any covenant or agreement entered into by, or on the part of, any husband not to bar the right of his widow to dower out of his lands, or any of them; and (*b*) that the act shall not extend to the dower of any widow who shall have been, or shall be, married on or before the 1st of January 1834; and shall not give to any will, deed, contract, engagement, or charge executed, entered into, or created

---

(*v*) S. 5.
(*w*) S. 6.
(*x*) S. 7.
(*y*) S. 8.
(*z*) S. 9.
(*a*) S. 11.
(*b*) S. 14.

before the said 1st of January 1834, the effect of defeating or prejudicing any right to dower. It results from these enactments that a declaration against dower, contained in a deed executed before the 1st of January 1834, will not bar the dower of a woman who was married after that date (c); and that the old form of conveyance which was employed to bar dower is no longer effectual, since a widow can now claim dower out of land in which her husband had only an equitable estate of inheritance.

If a wife dies seised of an estate of inheritance, either legal or equitable (d), in any hereditaments, her husband, if he survives her and has had by her issue born alive and capable of inheriting her estate, is entitled to hold the lands for the remainder of his life (e). He is said in such a case to have an estate by the curtesy of England, or more shortly an estate by curtesy. The wife's estate must have been one of inheritance, consequently there can be no curtesy out of an estate granted for lives however numerous (f). It is also necessary that the husband's children by her might have been able to claim the estate as heirs; if it has been expressly given to them after their mother's death, they will take as purchasers, and their father's claim to curtesy will be excluded (g). The result will be the same if an instrument giving a life estate to the wife expressly declares that, upon her death, the inheritance shall descend to her heir, and that her husband shall not be tenant by the curtesy (h). Curtesy, unlike dower, could never be barred by getting in a prior attendant term, since it always took effect out of equitable, as well as out of legal, estates, but it would appear to be doubtful

Estate by curtesy.

(c) *Fry* v. *Noble*, 7 De G. M. & G. 687.
(d) *Sweetapple* v. *Bindon*, 2 Ver. 536.
(e) 2 Bl. Com. 126.
(f) *Stead* v. *Platt*, 18 Beav. 50, 56.
(g) *Barker* v. *Barker*, 2 Sim. 249.
(h) *Bennet* v. *Davis*, 2 P. Wms. 316.

whether the husband's curtesy is not barred by an estate being given to the wife with a declaration that the whole of the estate shall be held for her separate use independently of her husband (*i*).

Tenancy after possibility of issue extinct.

A tenancy after possibility of issue extinct may occur where land has been given in special tail, as for instance, to a man and the heirs of his body by his present wife (*j*). Here, if the wife dies without issue the man cannot have issue who can take the estate; his possibility of issue is therefore said to be extinct, and he himself, since he is prohibited by statute (*k*) from barring the estate tail after his issue have become extinct, has an estate in the land for his life only, but with the privilege of committing waste; a privilege which, as we shall see hereafter, is not incident to the estate of any other tenant for life.

By deed.

An estate for life can also be created by deed. Such an estate, if intended to take effect during the lifetime of the person creating it, might, before the passing of the Statute of Frauds (*l*), have been created either by means of a deed, or by feoffment and livery of seisin without any writing. The statute, however, enacted (*m*) that all estates of freehold in messuages, manors, lands, tenements, or hereditaments, made or created by livery of seisin only, and not put in writing and signed by the parties making or creating the same, or their agents thereunto lawfully authorized by writing, should have the force and effect of estates at will only, and no greater force and effect: any consideration for making such estates, or any former law or usage to the contrary, notwithstanding. Hence, before the passing of the statute next to be mentioned,

---

(*i*) Lewin on Trustees, 524; *Moore* v. *Webster*, L. R. 3 Eq. 267; but see *Appleton* v. *Rowley*, L. R. 8 Eq. 139.
(*j*) 2 Bl. Com. 124.
(*k*) 3 & 4 Wm. IV. c. 74, s. 18.
(*l*) 29 Car. II. c. 3.
(*m*) S. 1.

an estate for life might be created either by feoffment
and livery evidenced by writing, or by deed. But
now it is provided by the Real Property Amendment *Real Property Amendment Act.*
Act (n) that a feoffment made after the 1st day of
October 1845, other than a feoffment made under a
custom by an infant, shall be void at law unless
evidenced by deed.

An estate for life may moreover be created by will, *By will.*
which must be in writing, but need not be under
seal.

The words of a deed or will creating an estate for *Form of words.*
the recipient's own life do not, obviously, include any
person besides the tenant himself. It is not necessary that the estate should be expressly conferred on
him for life. A grant by deed " to A " is enough to
give A an estate for life in the land, and will not give
him any greater estate. It is a general rule of law
that a grant is to be construed most strongly against
the grantor, and hence, if in the case supposed the
grantor had an estate in fee simple in the land, it
would seem to follow that A ought to acquire that
estate and not one for his life only. But this case is
an exception to the general rule. The earlier fees,
as we know, were granted only for life, and thus a
grant " to A " would then have given him all that
the grantor was capable of bestowing, and would,
therefore, have complied with the rule. And afterwards, when it became possible to acquire a fee of
inheritance, it was made essential that every grant by
feoffment or by deed of such an estate should be made
to the grantee's " heirs " or the " heirs of his body "
as well as to himself, failing which he still takes an
estate for life only. As to wills, the rule is now different; for a devise of real estate " to A " gives him
the whole estate or interest which the testator had

(n) 8 & 9 Vict. c. 106, s. 3.

power to dispose of by will in such real estate, unless a contrary intention appears by the will (*o*).

<small>Limitation of an estate *pur autre vie*.</small>

An estate granted to one person, and which is to last so long as one, or more, other person, or persons, live, is called an estate *pur autre vie*, that is, for the life of another. In order to provide for the event of a tenant *pur autre vie* dying before the expiration of the life or lives for which his estate is granted, it is customary to " limit " or define the boundaries of it, by specifying the persons who are, if necessary, to take it after his death. Before the passing of the Statute of Frauds (*p*) this was a matter of importance, since an estate *pur autre vie* was not devisable. If, therefore, the estate had not been limited to any person after the tenant, and the latter died in the lifetime of a *cestui que vie* (or person for whose life it was granted), the estate became vacant ; for the heir could not claim it, since it was not an estate of inheritance ; and the executor could not claim it, since it was real estate, and an executor, as such, has only a right to receive the personal estate of his testator ; whilst at the same time the estate continued to exist so long as any *cestui que vie* was alive. The consequence of this, in the case of a corporeal hereditament, was that the first person who could get possession of the land, by actually entering upon it, might keep it during the rest of the term as " general occupant." And this person, even if he happened to be the heir of the tenant *pur autre vie*, was not liable, in respect of this estate, to pay any of the tenant's debts, since the estate had not come to him by descent. But an estate *pur autre vie* in a corporeal hereditament may be limited either to the tenant and his heirs, or to him and his executors or administrators (in which latter case it becomes personal estate), and the persons so named will take

<small>Estate *pur autre vie* not, at one time, devisable.</small>

(*o*) 7 Wm. IV. & 1 Vict. c. 26, s. 28.
(*p*) 29 Car. II. c. 3.

the estate as "special occupants," and would at any time have prevented general occupancy.

If the estate *pur autre vie* was in an incorporeal hereditament there could be no general occupancy, because there could be no entry, but such an estate, if no person was named to succeed the tenant *pur autre vie*, was put an end to by the death of the latter. If, however, the estate had been limited to the tenant and his heirs, the heir could take as special occupant. It is doubtful whether an estate *pur autre vie* in an incorporeal hereditament can be limited to the tenant and his executors or administrators (*q*), but this point is not at present of much importance. For it was enacted by the Statute of Frauds (*r*), that, from thenceforth, the owner of an estate *pur autre vie* might dispose thereof by his will, and by that act and the 14 Geo. II., c. 20, general occupancy was put an end to. The sections of these statutes relating to estates *pur autre vie* were repealed, but substantially re-enacted, by the Wills Act (*s*), which provides (*t*) that all estates *pur autre vie* shall be devisable whether there shall, or shall not, be any special occupant thereof, and also (*u*) that if no disposition be made by will of any estate *pur autre vie* of a freehold nature, the same shall be chargeable in the hands of the heir, if it shall come to him by reason of special occupancy, as assets by descent, as in the case of freehold land held in fee simple: and in case there shall be no special occupant of any estate *pur autre vie*, whether freehold or customary freehold, tenant-right, customary or copyhold, or of any other tenure, and whether a corporeal or incorporeal hereditament, it shall go to the executor or administrator of the party that had the estate there-

Statute of Frauds.

14 Geo. II. c. 20.

Wills Act.

(*q*) Bacon's Abridgemen', Title Estate for life, B. S. 3; Sug. Pow. 197ª, but see *contrd, Northen v. Carnegie*, 4 Drew. 587.
(*r*) 29 Car. II. c. 3.
(*s*) 7 Wm. IV. & 1 Vict. c. 26.
(*t*) S. 3.
(*u*) S. 6.

of by virtue of the grant: and that if the same shall come to the executor or administrator by reason of special occupancy, or by virtue of the act, it shall be assets in his hands, and shall be applied and distributed in the same manner as the personal estate of the testator or intestate. The result of these acts is that there can no longer be any general occupancy, and that if there are no special occupants of an estate *pùr autre vie*, or if those named cannot take, the estate will go to the tenant's executors or administrators as personal estate (*v*).

In order to prevent any person, having an estate *pur autre vie*, from keeping possession of it wrongfully after the death of the *cestui que vie*, it was enacted by the 6 Anne, c. 72 (*w*), that any person having a claim to any estate after the death of any other person, upon making an affidavit that he has reason to believe that such person is dead, and that his death is concealed, may, once a year, obtain from the Lord Chancellor, or Keeper of the Great Seal, an order to the person suspected of the concealment, directing him to produce the *cestui que vie*, and if the person so ordered refuse or neglect to produce the *cestui que vie*, the latter shall be taken to be dead, and the person claiming may enter upon such lands, tenements, or hereditaments as if the *cestui que vie* were actually dead (*x*); and it is also provided that any persons having an estate determinable upon any life or lives who, after the determination of such estate, without the express consent of the person next entitled, shall remain in possession of such lands or hereditaments, shall be adjudged to be trespassers (*y*).

(*v*) *Doe* v. *Lewis*, 9 Mee and W. 662; *Reynolds* v. *Wright*, 25 Beav. 100, and 2 De G. F. & J. 590.
(*w*) S. 1.
(*x*) For the course of procedure to obtain the benefit of the Act, see *Re Lingen*, 12 Sim. 104.
(*y*) S. 5.

Inasmuch as an estate for life, even when it extends beyond the lifetime of the grantee, gives the tenant but a limited interest in the property, he cannot, without permission, do any act which will change the nature of the thing demised, by either diminishing the value of the inheritance, or increasing the burdens already imposed upon it. Thus, he is entitled to *estovers*, but only for the purposes of the estate from which they are taken (z). He may get stone, for the purpose of doing repairs on the property of which he is tenant, from any existing quarries on the estate; and has a right to cut underwood when fit for cutting, and to have for his own benefit the thinnings of trees, such as fir-trees, which are planted for the protection of other trees rather than for profit (a), and of timber cut for the necessary purpose of preserving, or allowing the growth of, other trees (b). He may also work mines lawfully opened by a preceding tenant, although such opening may have been made subsequently to the settlement under which he himself claims (c); and may fell timber for repairs.

_{Incidents of an Estate for life.}
_{Estovers.}
_{Stone for repairs.}
_{Underwood.}
_{Thinnings of trees.}
_{Mines.}
_{Timber for repairs.}

But he may not, under ordinary circumstances, commit any act of waste on the property. He cannot, therefore, cut down timber, although decayed, for any other purpose than that of doing repairs on the estate (d); neither may he convert one species of land into another, nor dig for gravel or stone in new quarries, nor pull down old buildings. He is not even entitled to erect new buildings, since his doing so would impose additional burdens on the inheritance. Hence, if he lays out money in building, or in making improvements, on the property, he cannot charge the

_{Tenant may not, ordinarily, commit waste.}

(z) *Lee* v. *Alston*, 1 Bro. C. C. 194.
(a) *Pidgeley* v. *Rawling*, 2 Coll. 275; *R.* v. *Ferrybridge*, 1 B. & C. 375.
(b) *Honywood* v. *Honywood*, W. N. (1874) 131.
(c) *Clavering* v. *Clavering*, 2 P. Wms. 388.
(d) *Perrott* v. *Perrott*, 3 Atk. 94.

expense on the inheritance (*e*). He cannot, in short, do any act which would immediately occasion any damage to, or impose fresh burdens on, the inheritance; even though such act would, ultimately, lead to the improvement of the estate (*f*).

We have already seen, in the previous chapter, that a tenant for years may be restrained by injunction by the Court of Chancery or by a superior Court of Common Law from committing waste, and the same remarks apply to the case of a tenant for life who wrongfully commits waste. A tenant for life is also liable to an action for permissive waste (*g*), although a Court of Equity will not interfere in such a case.

Rule when timber is blown down.

If buildings are blown down by the force of the wind, a tenant for life has a special property in the timber of such buildings for the purpose of rebuilding them (*h*). Subject to this right, the proper course, when timber is blown down, appears to be to sell it, invest the proceeds, and pay the interest to the successive tenants for life; the fund itself becoming ultimately the property of the first owner of an estate of inheritance who succeeds to the possession of the land (*i*).

When wrongfully severed.

If timber or other things are wrongfully severed from the inheritance by the tenant for life, then, according to recent decisions, it would seem that the same course is to be adopted, but that the wrongdoer himself is to be excluded from receiving any benefit from the fund (*j*).

(*e*) *Caldecott* v. *Brown*, 2 Ha. 144; *Hibbert* v. *Cooke*, 1 S. & S. 552.
(*f*) *Coppinger* v. *Gubbins*, 9 Ir. Eq. R. 304.
(*g*) *Yellowly* v. *Gower*, 11 Exch. 274, 294; *Greene* v. *Cole*, 2 Wms. Saunders, 644, 646 note (*c*).
(*h*) *Bowles' Case*, 11 Rep. 79[b].
(*i*) *Bateman* v. *Hotchkin*, 31 Beav. 486.
(*j*) *Wellesley* v. *Wellesley*, 6 Sim. 497; *Lushington* v. *Bolders*, 15 Beav. 1; *Bateman* v. *Hotchkin*, 31 Beav. 486; *Bagot* v. *Bagot*,

If timber is in a decaying state, and it is for the benefit of the inheritance that it should be cut down, the Court of Chancery will sanction the cutting of such timber, provided that it is decaying or is injuring the growth of other trees (k). But the timber must be actually decaying, not merely ripe for cutting (l). If timber is cut thus under the sanction and direction of the court it will be sold, and the proceeds of the sale will belong to the first owner of an estate of inheritance who succeeds to the possession; and in the mean time the income of the fund will be paid to the tenant for life for the time being in possession of the estate (m).

_{Cutting timber under order of the Court of Chancery.}

[marginal note: See left. Estates 1877.]

If it is desired that the tenant for life shall have power to commit waste, the instrument creating his estate must contain a declaration that he is to be tenant for life "without impeachment of waste," or some other words to that effect. It is clearly settled that, since the Statutes of Marlebridge (n), and of Gloucester (o), a tenant unimpeachable of waste is not merely protected from the penalties which those statutes impose, but is authorized to convert to his own use timber, minerals, &c., severed from the estate (p). A tenant for life however, although unimpeachable for waste, has no property in such timber, or minerals, until he has actually severed them from the estate. Forgetfulness of this fact gave rise to very serious hardship in the well-known case of *Cockerell v. Cholmeley* (q). There, the trustees of a settled

_{"Without impeachment of waste."}

_{Tenant has no property in timber, &c., until severed.}

_{Cockerell v. Cholmeley.}

---

32 Beav. 509. But see *contrà, Rolt v. Lord Somerville*, 2 Eq. Ca. Ab. 759; *Butler v. Kynnersley*, 8 L. J. (Ch.) 67, in which it was held that in such a case the timber, &c., belonged at once to the owner of the first estate of inheritance *in esse* at the time.
(k) *Bewick v. Whitfield*, 3 P. Wms. 267; *Hussey v. Hussey*, 5 Madd. 44.
(l) *Seagram v. Knight*, L. R. 2 Ch. 628.
(m) *Tooker v. Annesley*, 5 Sim. 235.
(n) 52 Hen. III. c. 23.
(o) 6 Ed. I. c. 5.
(p) Note to *Davis v. Marlborough*, 2 Swan, 145; *Bridges v. Stephens*, 2 Swan, 150ª.
(q) 1 Russ. & My. 418, 1 Cl. & F. 60.

estate which they were authorized to sell, sold it with the growing timber on it, and allowed the tenant for life to receive the value of the timber: the consequence was that the sale was set aside some forty years afterwards, although the mistake had been discovered in the mean time, and the tenant for life had repaid to the trustees the amount which he had received for the timber.

22 & 23 Vict. c. 35.

In order to meet any future case of this kind it is enacted by the 22 & 23 Vict., c. 35 (*r*), that where, under a power of sale, a *bonâ fide* sale shall be made of an estate with the timber thereon, or any other articles attached thereto, and the tenant for life, or any other party to the transaction, shall by mistake be allowed to receive for his own benefit a portion of the purchase-money, as the value of the timber or other articles, the Court of Chancery may remedy the mistake, upon payment by the purchaser of the full value of the timber or other articles at the time of the sale, and interest.

Equitable Waste.

A tenant for life, although without impeachment of waste, will be prevented by the Court of Chancery from committing what is known as "equitable waste," that is, capricious, or extravagant, waste. A case is reported as early as the year 1717, in which the Court restrained a tenant for life from committing equitable waste, and since that time it has restrained, as being equitable waste, the pulling down a mansion-house on the estate (*s*); cutting down ornamental timber planted near the mansion-house (*t*), even if planted by the tenant for life himself (*u*); cutting down timber, although at some distance from the mansion-house, if

---

(*r*) S. 13.
(*s*) *Vane* v. *Barnard*, 2 Ver. 738.
(*t*) *Chamberlayne* v. *Dummer*, 1 Bro. C. C. 166; 3 Bro. C. C. 549.
(*u*) *Coffin* v. *Coffin*, Jac. 70, 71.

planted for ornament (*v*); cutting down ornamental timber, even though the mansion-house had been lawfully pulled down (*w*); and cutting saplings not ready to be felled (*x*), or underwood not fit for cutting (*y*). The court has also decided that under no circumstances can the words "impeachable for waste," or any others of like nature, have the effect of permitting a tenant for life to commit equitable waste. "The principle on which the court proceeds in these cases is, that the tenant for life of an estate is liable to account in equity for an improper use of his legal powers in committing equitable waste (*z*)." On this principle, a tenant for life unimpeachable for waste was held not liable to account for the materials of an old mansion-house which he had pulled down, he having employed the same materials in building a new mansion-house on the estate (*a*). If ornamental timber has been actually severed, the amount of damage which the tenant for life can be made to pay can only be measured by the damage actually done to the inheritance (*b*).

A tenant for life in possession is bound to keep down the interest on any charges, carrying interest, which may have been properly imposed on the land, even though the whole rent derived from the estate may be required for this purpose (*c*); but he is not bound to pay more than the amount of the rent, nor is he bound to pay off interest allowed to fall into arrear during the possession of the estate by a previous tenant for life (*d*); nor, if he allows the interest to fall into arrear, is he directly liable to the incum-

Keeping down interest.

(*v*) *Downshire* v. *Sandys*, 6 Ves. 107.
(*w*) *Wellesley* v. *Wellesley*, 6 Sim. 497.
(*x*) *Downshire* v. *Sandys*, 6 Ves. 107.
(*y*) *Brydges* v. *Stevens*, 6 Madd. 279.
(*z*) *Per* L. J. Turner, 3 De G. & J. 328.
(*a*) *Morris* v. *Morris*, 3 De G. & J. 323.
(*b*) *Bubb* v. *Yelverton*, L. R. 10 Eq. 465.
(*c*) *Tracy* v. *Hereford*, 2 Bro. C. C. 128; *Revel* v. *Watkinson*, 1 Ves. 93.
(*d*) *Caulfield* v. *Maguire*, 2 Jo. & L. 141.

brancers, since the obligation to keep down interest exists only as between himself and the remainder-man, and not as between himself and the incumbrancers on the estate (*e*). If the tenant for life pays off a charge on the estate, he is *primâ facie* entitled to keep it up for his own benefit, it not being assumed, in the absence of evidence to the contrary, that he intended the payment to be for the benefit of the inheritance (*f*).

Power to grant leases. We have already seen that a tenant for life may grant leases, in some cases on his own authority, in others by leave of the Court of Chancery. The Leases and Sales of Settled Estates Act (*g*), the same which authorizes the court to sanction the granting of leases, provides (*h*) also that it may authorize a sale of the whole, or any parts, of any settled estates, or of any timber (not being ornamental timber) growing on any settled estates; that (*i*) on any sale of land, any earth, coal, stone, or minerals may be excepted; and (*j*) that the court may direct that any part of any settled estates be laid out for streets, roads, paths, squares, gardens, or other open spaces, sewers, drains, or water-courses, either to be dedicated to the public or not.

Sales under order of the Court of Chancery.

Making improvements on the property.

Several acts have been passed with the object of enabling tenants for life to improve the property of which they are in possession. Thus by the 8 & 9 Vict., c. 56 (*k*), it is enacted (*l*) that any person entitled in possession to any land, either as tenant by curtesy, or for his own life, or for any other life or lives, or an

8 & 9 Vict. c. 56.

(*e*) *Morley* v. *Saunders*, L. R. 8 Eq. 594.
(*f*) *Burrell* v. *Egremont*, 7 Beav. 205, 227
(*g*) 19 & 20 Vict. c. 120.
(*h*) S. 11.
(*i*) S. 13.
(*j*) S. 14.
(*k*) Repealing the 3 & 4 Vict. c. 55.
(*l*) S. 3.

infant entitled as aforesaid, by his guardian or next friend, or a lunatic entitled as aforesaid, by his committee, or any married woman entitled as aforesaid, by her next friend, or the husband of any married woman entitled as aforesaid in her right, may apply to the Court of Chancery for leave to make any permanent improvements in the land to which such person shall be so entitled, by draining the same, or by warping, irrigation, or embankment in a permanent manner, or by erecting any buildings thereon of a permanent kind, in connection with such improvements, and shall be at liberty to pray that such permanent improvement may be made a charge on the inheritance of the land, under the provisions of the act. The court may (*m*), after proper inquiry (*n*), authorize or permit such permanent improvements to be made, and thereupon (*o*) the inheritance of the land shall be charged with the sum expended and interest not exceeding the rate of £5 per cent. per annum, payable half-yearly (*p*). The principal so advanced is to be repaid by instalments, which, in the case of improvements by draining, warpage, irrigation, or embankment, are not to be less than twelve nor more than eighteen in number, and, in the case of improvements by the erection of buildings, not less than fifteen, nor more than twenty-five, in number (*q*). The person on whose application such charge is made, and every succeeding tenant for life, or other person having only a limited interest in the land charged, is to pay the interest and instalments which become from time to time due and payable during the continuance of his title to the land, and on the termination of such title, by death or otherwise, the inheritance is to remain chargeable with no more than six

---

(*m*) S. 5.
(*n*) S. 4.
(*o*) S. 6.
(*p*) S. 8.
(*q*) S. 9.

months' arrears of interest then due, and one half of the last instalment then due, and the interest and instalments thereafter to become due (*r*). Every tenant for life, or other person having a limited interest, is bound also to keep in repair any buildings erected or built, or embankments or works for irrigation constructed or made, under the provisions of the act, as if he were tenant for life subject to impeachment for waste (*s*).

Private Money Drainage Act.

By the Private Money Drainage Act 1849 (*t*) provision was made for enabling tenants for life to borrow money from private persons, for the purpose of improving the lands occupied by such tenants. This act is repealed, except so far as regards proceedings and charges under it then in existence, by the Improvement of Land Act 1864 (*u*).

Improvement of Land Act.

Under this latter act, a landowner (who is defined (*v*) to mean any person in actual possession of, or in receipt of the rents and profits of any land of any tenure, except where such person is tenant for life or lives holding under a lease for life or lives not renewable, or tenant for years holding under a lease or agreement for a lease not renewable whereof less than twenty-five years shall be unexpired at the time of making such application), who is desirous of borrowing or advancing money under the act for the improvement of his land, is to make an application on the subject to the Inclosure Commissioners. The improvements contemplated by the act are (*w*) the drainage, the irrigation and warping, the embanking, and the reclamation of land; the making of permanent farm roads, and permanent tramways and railways, and navigable canals, for all purposes connected with the improve-

(*r*) S. 10.
(*s*) S. 11.
(*t*) 12 & 13 Vict. c. 100.
(*u*) 27 & 28 Vict. c. 114.
(*v*) S. 8.
(*w*) S. 9.

ment of the estate; the clearing of land; the erection of labourers' cottages, farm-houses, and other buildings, and the improvement of those already existing; planting for shelter; the constructing or erecting any engine-houses, mills, kilns, shafts, wells, ponds, tanks, reservoirs, dams, leads, pipes, conduits, water-courses, bridges, weirs, sluices, floodgates or hatches, which will increase the value of any lands for agricultural purposes; the construction or improvement of jetties or landing-places on the sea coast, or on the banks of navigable rivers, or lakes, for the transport of stock or things for agricultural purposes, provided that the Commissioners approve thereof: and, finally, the execution of all such works, as in the judgment of the Commissioners, may be necessary for carrying into effect any of the above improvements, or for deriving the full benefit thereof. The Commissioners may (x) sanction any of the proposed improvements, or any part of them, and fix a rate of interest, not exceeding £5 per cent. per annum, to be allowed on their cost. They may (y) from time to time, as such improvements are executed, charge the inheritance of the land with the sum thus expended, and interest. Every charge created under the act is (z) to be by way of rent-charge, payable half-yearly, extending over the term of years fixed by the order of the Commissioners. Every landowner on whose land a charge has been made under the act, and every succeeding person having a limited interest in the land so charged, is (a), as between himself and the persons in reversion or remainder, bound to pay the periodical payments of such charge which become payable during the continuance of his interest, and if in actual occupation or entitled to an apportioned part of the rents and profits of the land up to the time of the termination

---

(x) S. 25.
(y) S. 49.
(z) S. 51.
(a) S. 66.

of his interest, is to pay an apportioned part of the rent-charge which becomes due next after the termination of his interest. But he is not to be liable, as between himself and the persons entitled to the rent-charge, to pay any arrears of the charge which were due at the time of his becoming entitled in possession, beyond the amount of two years' payment of such charge. The landowner is bound (*b*), so long as the land continues charged under the act, to uphold all the improvements and works in respect of which the charge is made, unless expressly relieved from this responsibility by the Commissioners (*c*). The act also contains similar provisions (*d*) enabling a landowner to subscribe for shares or stock in any railway company whose works are upon, or near to, and will improve or benefit his lands, and to charge the amount of such subscription, or any part of it, on the lands.

Limited Owners' Residence Acts.

The Limited Owners' Residence Act 1870 (*e*), which is to be construed as one with the Improvement of Land Act 1864 (*f*), enacts (*g*) that the erection, completion, and improvement of mansion-houses, with their usual and necessary buildings and offices, are to be included under the definition of improvements, but it is provided (*h*) that the sum expended on erecting any mansion-house is not to exceed the amount of two years' clear rental of the estate, to be calculated as therein provided. By the Limited Owners' Residence Amendment Act 1871 (*i*), part of the act of 1870 was repealed, in order to remove doubts as to its meaning, but the repealed sections were substantially re-enacted by the act of 1871, which is to be (*j*) construed as one with the former act.

(*b*) S. 72.
(*c*) S. 76.
(*d*) SS. 78—89.
(*e*) 33 & 34 Vict. c. 56.
(*f*) S. 2.
(*g*) S. 3.
(*h*) S. 4.
(*i*) 34 & 35 Vict. c. 84.
(*j*) S. 4.

OF AN ESTATE FOR LIFE.

Under the Public Money Drainage Acts (*k*), the Commissioners of the Treasury are empowered to advance money to any owner (which term by reference to the Tithe Commutation Act (*l*) includes any person in actual possession or receipt of the rents or profits of any land, except any tenant for life or lives, or for years, holding under a lease or agreement for a lease on which a rent of not less than two-thirds of the clear yearly value of the premises comprised therein shall have been reserved, and except any tenant for years whatever holding under a lease or agreement for a term which shall not have exceeded fourteen years from the commencement thereof) who desires to make improvements on his land by drainage, and who has obtained the sanction of the Inclosure Commissioners to such advance. The land is thereupon (*m*) to be charged with a rent charge at the rate of six pounds ten shillings for every hundred pounds so advanced; the rent charge to last for twenty-two years. The owner, and every person having a limited interest in the land, is (*n*) to pay the instalments of rent charge which become due during his possession, with provisions similar to those contained in the Improvement of Land Act 1864. He is (*o*), so long as the land continues charged with the rent charge, to uphold the works on account of which the lands have been charged, and he is (*p*) to have power to redeem the rent charge on making certain specified payments.

Public Money Drainage Acts.

Persons having a life estate in lands may also sell them under certain circumstances, it being provided by the Lands Clauses Consolidation Act 1845 (*q*) that

Sale under Lands Clauses Consolidation Act.

(*k*) 9 & 10 Vict. c. 101; 10 & 11 Vict. c. 11; 11 & 12 Vict. c. 119; 13 & 14 Vict. c. 31, and 19 & 20 Vict. c. 9.
(*l*) 6 & 7 Wm. IV. c. 71, s. 12.
(*m*) 9 & 10 Vict. c. 101, s. 34.
(*n*) Ibid. s. 38.
(*o*) Ibid. s. 39.
(*p*) Ibid. s. 45.
(*q*) 8 & 9 Vict. c. 18, ss. 7, 69, 74.

when lands are required for undertakings of a public nature, any tenant for life in possession may sell them to the promoters of such an undertaking, and that the money thus obtained is either to be applied in the purchase of other lands, or, when derived from the sale of an estate less than one in fee simple, is to be applied in such manner as will, in the opinion of the Court of Chancery, give the parties interested in such money the same benefit therefrom as they might lawfully have had from the estate in respect of which such money shall have been paid, or as near thereto as may be.

Custody of title-deeds.

A tenant for life is entitled to the custody of the title-deeds of land of which he is in possession (r).

Fixtures.

Rule as between tenant for life and remainder-man.

With regard to Fixtures, the rules stated in the previous chapter as affecting the case of landlord and tenant apply also, but in a modified form, to that of tenant for life, or his representatives, and the remainder-man or reversioner; the rule not being so favourable to tenants for life as to those for years. Thus, a tenant for life, or his representatives, may remove articles put up for the purpose of trade, such as a fire-engine erected to work a colliery (s), or salt pans (t), put up by him; and he has also been allowed to remove fixtures, put up by him, of a domestic (u) or ornamental character, in cases where they have been very slightly affixed to the freehold. In a modern case (v) a tenant for life had put up, in and about the mansion-house of the estate, (1) tapestry, pictures in panels, frames fitted with satin attached to the walls, statues, figures, vases and stone garden-seats, and (2) glasses and pictures not in panels. It was held that the glasses

---

(r) *Duncombe* v. *Mayer*, 8 Ves. 320; *Bowles* v. *Stewart*, 1 Sch. & L. 209, 223.
(s) *Lawton* v. *Lawton*, 3 Atk. 12; *Dudley* v. *Warde*, Amb. 112.
(t) *Lawton* v. *Salmon*, 1 H. Bl. 259ⁿ.
(u) *Grymes* v. *Boweren*, 6 Bing. 437.
(v) *D'Eyncourt* v. *Gregory*, L. R. 3 Eq. 382.

and pictures not in panels were alone removable; although it was proved that the tapestry, other pictures, and frames, could be removed without doing any damage to the house, and that the statues, figures, vases, and garden-seats only rested on the soil, and therefore according to the definition of fixtures previously given were not fixtures at all.

If a tenant for life dies, leaving fixtures which he would himself have had a right to remove, his executors may remove them, provided they do so within a reasonable time. The decision as to what is a "reasonable time" would probably vary with the circumstances of each case. *Time for removing fixtures.*

A tenant for life of lands may, if he pleases, assign his estate, during his lifetime, to some other person. Such an assignment must be made or evidenced (*w*) by deed, and his assignee will thereupon have the same rights, and be subject to the same liabilities in respect of the estate, as his assignor, except where the latter is tenant after possibility of issue extinct. For although such a tenant is unimpeachable of waste, this privilege is personal to himself, and does not pass to his assignee. A tenant for life may, moreover, surrender his estate to the remainder-man or reversioner, whereupon it will become merged. This also must be done by deed (*x*). An estate for the tenant's own life cannot, of course, be disposed of by will, but an estate *pur autre vie* may be, whether there is, or is not, any special occupant of it, and whatever its tenure may be, and whether the same is a corporeal or an incorporeal hereditament (*y*). We have already seen what are the provisions of the Wills Act when there is no disposition made of an estate *pur autre vie* of a freehold nature (*z*). *Alienation of an estate for life. Assignment. Surrender. By will.*

(*w*) 8 & 9 Vict. c. 106, s. 3.
(*x*) Ibid.
(*y*) 7 Wm. IV. & 1 Vict. c. 26, s. 3.
(*z*) 7 Wm. IV. & 1 Vict. c. 26, s. 6.

106   OF CORPOREAL HEREDITAMENTS.

Involuntary alienation. An estate for life may also be the subject of involuntary alienation, either by being taken under the statutes relating to judgments (a point to be explained in a subsequent chapter), or, if the tenant becomes bankrupt, by vesting in the trustee under his bankruptcy, who may dispose of it for the benefit of the tenant's creditors (a).

Determination. Old law of forfeiture. An estate for life might formerly have been put an end to by forfeiture. This occurred if the tenant endeavoured, by means of a feoffment, to grant a greater estate in the land than that which he himself possessed. But now, under the Real Property Amendment Act (b), such a feoffment made by a tenant for life will merely convey his life interest, and will not work a forfeiture.

By death of tenant. Rent not formerly apportionable. The tenant's estate may also come to an end by his death. Until the year 1738, lessees from a tenant for life whose leases were put an end to by his death were not bound to pay any rent accrued due between the last day when the rent fell due and the date of the death of the tenant for life. This rule was founded on the Common Law doctrine that an entire contract cannot be apportioned, and that under a lease with a periodical reservation of rent, the contract for the payment of each portion is distinct and entire (c). Rent is not due until the last day fixed for payment, because it is to be rendered out of the issues and profits of the land (d), and differs in this respect from interest, which accrues from day to day. From this it followed that on the determination of a lease by the death of the lessor before the day appointed for the payment of the rent, the event on the completion of which that payment was stipulated (namely, the occu-

---

(a) 32 & 33 Vict. c. 71, ss. 17, 25.
(b) 8 & 9 Vict. c. 106, s. 4.
(c) 1 Swan. 338ᵃ.
(d) *Clun's Case*, 10 Rep. 127ᵃ.

pation of the lands during the period specified) never occurring, no rent became payable at law, nor would the Courts of Equity afford any assistance (e).

This state of things was partly remedied by the 11 Geo. II., c. 19, which enacts (f) that where any tenant for life shall happen to die before, or on, the day on which any rent was reserved, or made payable, upon any demise or lease of any lands, tenements, or hereditaments, which determined on the death of such tenant for life, the executors or administrators of such tenant for life shall, and may, recover of and from such under-tenant or under-tenants of such lands, tenements, and hereditaments—if such tenant for life shall die on the day on which the same was made payable, the whole of—or if before such day, then a proportion of—such rent, according to the time such tenant for life lived, of the last year or quarter of a year or other time in which the said rent was growing due as aforesaid, making all just allowances, or a proportionate part thereof, respectively. This act included the case of a lease made by a tenant for life, professedly under a power given to him for that purpose, but determined by his death from not having been exercised in conformity with his power (g); but it did not apply to cases where a tenant for life had made a lease which was binding on the remainder-man (h), and which did not therefore come to an end on the death of the tenant for life. In that case, the under-tenant had to pay his rent, on the day next fixed for its payment, to the remainder-man or reversioner, because his obligation to do so was incident to the reversion, but no part of it could be claimed by the representatives of the tenant for life. In order

---

(e) *Jenner* v. *Morgan*, 1 P. Wms. 392.
(f) S. 15.
(g) *Ex parte Smyth*, 1 Swan, 337; *Clarkson* v. *Scarborough*, ib. 354*.
(h) See *Duppa* v. *Mayo*, 1 Wms. Saunders, 380, 455; *Mills* v. *Trumper*, L. R. 4 Ch. 320.

to remedy this, the 4 & 5 Wm. IV., c. 22 (*i*) provides that, from and after the passing of the act, all rents service reserved on any lease shall be apportioned so and in such manner that on the death of any person interested in any such rents, or on the determination by any other means whatever of the interest of any such person, he or she, and his or her executors, administrators, or assigns shall be entitled to a proportion of such rents, according to the time which shall have elapsed from the commencement or last period of payment thereof (as the case may be), including the day of the death of such person or of the determination of his or her interest, all just allowances being made; and that every such person, his or her executors, administrators, and assigns, shall have such and the same remedies at law and in equity for recovering such apportioned parts of the said rents as he, she, or they would have had for recovering and obtaining such entire rents if entitled thereto; but so that persons liable to pay rents reserved by any lease or demise, and the lands, tenements, and hereditaments comprised therein, shall not be resorted to for such apportioned parts specifically as aforesaid, but the entire rent of which such portions shall form part shall be received and recovered by the person or persons who, if the act had not been passed, would have been entitled to such entire rents: and such portion shall be recoverable from such person or persons by the persons entitled to the same under the act, in any action or suit at law or in equity; but the act (*j*) is not to apply to cases where it has been expressly stipulated that no apportionment shall be made. This act applies to all cases where either the lease reserving the rent, or the instrument creating the life estate, has been executed since the passing of the act (*k*). The act of William the Fourth had re-

---

(*i*) S. 2.
(*j*) S. 3.
(*k*) *Lock* v. *De Burgh*, 4 De G. & Sm. 470; *Plummer* v. *Whiteley*, John. 585; *Llewellyn* v. *Rous*, L. R. 2 Eq. 27.

ference to leases in writing only (*l*), and since the act of George the Second only applied to leases which were put an end to by the death of the tenant for life, the rent reserved by a parol lease not determined by the tenant's death was not apportionable (*m*). Moreover, the act did not include tithes.

These omissions have been supplied by the Apportionment Act 1870 (*n*), which enacts that (*o*) after the passing of the act (*p*) all rents and other periodical payments in the nature of income (whether reserved or made payable under an instrument in writing or otherwise) shall, like interest on money lent, be considered as accruing from day to day, and shall be apportionable in respect of time accordingly; and (*q*) that in the construction of the act, the word "rent" shall include rent service, rent charge, and rent seck, and also all tithes and periodical payments or renderings in lieu of, or in the nature of, rent or tithe. This act applies to all instruments, whether coming into operation before, or not until after, the passing of the act (*r*).

Apportionment Act, 1870.

We conclude this chapter by remarking that on the death of a tenant for life whose estate is determined by his death, his executors or administrators are entitled to emblements, the 14 & 15 Vict., c. 25, only applying to cases where terms of years are determined by the death of a lessor who is tenant for life.

Emblements.

(*l*) *Re Markby*, 4 My. & C. 484.
(*m*) *Mills* v. *Trumper*, L. R. 4 Ch. 320.
(*n*) 33 & 34 Vict. c. 35.
(*o*) S. 2.
(*p*) 1st August, 1870.
(*q*) S. 5.
(*r*) *Re Cline*, L. R. 18 Eq. 213.

CHAPTER V.

OF AN ESTATE TAIL.

We come next to the consideration of freehold estates of inheritance, and will take first estates in fee tail, or, as they are commonly called, Estates Tail.

<small>Different kinds of estates tail.</small>
We spoke of estates tail generally, in our introduction, as being those estates which are given to a man and the heirs of his (*a*) body: but we must now point out that there are various classes into which estates tail may be divided. Thus, such an estate <small>General.</small> may be "general," that is given to a man and the <small>Special.</small> heirs of his body generally; or it may be "special," that is, given to a man and the heirs of his body by some specified person. Again, an estate tail, whether general or special, may be given to a man and his sons exclusively, or to him and his daughters exclusively; <small>Tail male and tail female general.</small> whence we get the four sub-divisions of estates tail male general, estates tail female general, estates tail <small>Tail male and tail female special.</small> male special, and estates tail female special. The course of descent of an estate tail general is to the first tenant's eldest son, and such son's eldest sons and grandsons in succession. If the eldest son leaves no issue, the estate goes to the second and other sons in succession, and their issue, according to the same rule. If there are no sons, or if their issue fails, the daughters take the estate, but in equal shares, and are succeeded by their eldest or other sons and their issue, in a course of primogeniture. The same rule applies to

---

(*a*) It is to be understood that the words "man" and "his" when used with reference to estates include females except where otherwise stated.

the other kinds of estates tail, but with such modifications as are necessary to suit their particular form.

Besides the above varieties of estates tail there is that which is known as a *quasi* estate tail. This occurs when lands held *pur autre vie* are limited in one of the ways by which a regular estate tail may be created. *Quasi estate tail.*

An estate tail can only be created by a person who has an estate in fee simple, and such person must not, as a rule, be under any disability; but, as we saw in the last chapter, an infant may, under the 18 & 19 Vict., c. 43, create such an estate in contemplation of marriage (*b*); subject however (*c*) to the estate being defeated if the infant does not live to attain full age. *By whom an estate tail can be created.*

An estate tail may be created by deed or by will. As to the form of words necessary to create it, it has been already mentioned that the words of an instrument purporting to confer an estate were formerly always construed strictly. Thus, a gift to a man "for ever," or to him "in fee simple," whether made by deed or will, would have conferred an estate for life only, notwithstanding that the intention to give a fee simple might be very apparent. For it was said that an estate of inheritance could not be conferred except by words of inheritance, such as "heirs." On the same principle, it was necessary in giving an estate tail to use words, such as "heirs of the body," clearly limiting the estate to the offspring of the grantee, and although this rule is not now strictly enforced in construing gifts by will (*d*), it still holds good as to deeds. If an estate, then, is given to a man and the heirs of his body, he will take an estate tail; and the result *Mode of creating. Form of words.*

(*b*) S. 1.
(*c*) S. 2.
(*d*) *Griffiths* v. *Evan*, 5 Beav. 241.

Rule in Shelley's Case.

will be the same if the gift is to him for life, and after his death to the heirs of his body: for in *Shelley's Case* (e) it was decided that the words "heirs" or "heirs of the body" only serve, in such a case, to limit, or define, the extent of the estate which the first grantee is to take. If, however, land is limited to a man for life, and after his death either to "his sons," or to "his daughters," in tail, the sons or daughters will be said to take by purchase (f), and not by inheritance; because they are entitled as being the persons named in the deed of gift, and not as heirs of the body of their father. The result therefore of such a limitation will be that the father will take an estate for life only, whilst the persons to whom the estate is limited after his death will have an estate tail, which will not commence until after the death of the tenant for life.

Incidents of an estate tail.

We shall see, before we conclude this chapter, that a tenant in tail can, at the present day, by a very simple process, convert his estate into one in fee simple. Both for this reason, and on account of the superior nature of his estate, he can deal with the property in a manner forbidden to a tenant for life or for years.

May commit any kind of waste.

Thus, he cannot be restrained from committing waste, even though it be equitable waste, and no distinction is made in this respect between an ordinary tenant in tail and one who is restrained by Act of Parliament from barring the estate tail (g); although the reason given for the general rule, namely, that a tenant in tail has it in his power, at any time, to convert his estate into one in fee simple, does not seem to apply to this latter case. Moreover a tenant in tail cannot be bound by any covenant not to commit waste (h).

(e) 1 Rep. 93^b.
(f) Any person taking an estate otherwise than by descent is said in law to be a purchaser.
(g) *Atty.-Genl.* v. *Marlborough*, 3 Madd. 498, 532.
(h) *Jervis* v. *Bruton*, 2 Ver. 251.

On account also of the power which a tenant in tail *Not bound to keep down interest on* has over his estate, he cannot be compelled to keep *charges.* down the interest of incumbrances affecting it, unless he is an infant and therefore incapable of barring it (*i*). Should he, however, pay off any charges on the estate, it will be presumed, in the absence of evidence to the contrary, that he has done so for the benefit of the inheritance, and not for that of his personal representatives (*j*).

A tenant in tail in possession is entitled to the custody of the title-deeds of the entailed lands (*k*). *Custody of title-deeds.*

Since a tenant in tail has, as an inseparable incident *Fixtures.* of his estate, the right to commit every kind of waste, he may, whilst in possession of the property, remove any fixtures put by a previous tenant or by himself, and that without reference to the object, or to the mode, of their annexation. But this right ceases with his death. If he has himself put up fixtures during his possession, and the estate tail comes to an end on his death, his executor or administrator has, as against the remainder-man or reversioner, the same right in respect of fixtures as the executor or administrator of a tenant for life has, as against the person entitled to an estate after the expiration of that for life. But if the tenant in tail is succeeded by another person claiming under the entail, questions as to fixtures are decided as if they arose between the heir and the executor of a tenant in fee simple; a point which will be gone into in the next chapter.

We have already seen that a tenant in tail can, by *Making leases.* deed, make leases for terms not exceeding twenty-one years; or for longer terms, provided that the deed is

---

(*i*) *Sergeson* v. *Sealey*, 2 Atk. 411, 416; *Chaplin* v. *Chaplin*, 3 P. Wms. 234.
(*j*) *St Paul* v. *Dudley*, 15 Ves. 167, 172.
(*k*) *Papillon* v. *Voice*, 2 P. Wms. 470.

C. H

inrolled in manner required (*l*) by the Fines and Recoveries Abolition Act.

Barring estates tail.
An estate tail, as such, cannot be the subject of alienation. A tenant in tail, it is true, can dispose of his estate by deed, but the very fact of his doing so converts it into either a fee simple or some lesser estate, according to the form of disposition made. And if he wishes to dispose of his estate by will, he must first convert it into an estate in fee simple, in which case it will be subject to the rules governing the alienation of such estates. We proceed therefore to show how the power of barring estates tail arose, and the means by which it can now be exercised.

Statute De Donis.
It will be recollected that the statute *De Donis*, passed in the year 1285, put a stop to the alienation of estates in fee simple conditional, in lands of freehold tenure, and converted those fees into fees tail which could not be alienated. The statute remained in force until about the year 1473, at which date means were found to bar estates tail, by converting them into estates in fee simple, and thus to render the statute a dead letter.

Suffering a Recovery.
This might be effected by a process known as " suffering a recovery," which was, in fact, a legal fiction countenanced by the courts, in order to evade the statute. The process was usually as follows—A preconcerted action was brought in the Court of Common Pleas, against the tenant for life who was in possession of the property entailed. This was either a tenant who had a life estate in the land prior to the estate tail, by virtue of the grant creating the entail, and whose consent was necessary in order to admit of the recovery being suffered, or, if there were no existing life estate prior to the estate tail, some person who had had a life

---

(*l*) 3 & 4 Wm. IV. c. 74, s. 41.

estate conveyed to him by the tenant in tail, for the
purpose of enabling the action to be brought.

The tenant for life was called the tenant to the
præcipe, or writ by which the proceedings were commenced. The plaintiff or "demandant" began by
alleging to the court that the tenant to the *præcipe*
had no right to the possession of the land, but that
it belonged to him (the demandant) in fee simple.
Thereupon the tenant to the *præcipe* stated that his
title had been warranted as good by the tenant in tail,
and asked that the latter might be allowed to appear
and defend it. This was called "vouching" (*m*) the Vouching to
tenant in tail to warranty. The tenant in tail, in his warranty.
turn, vouched to warranty a third person, who really
knew nothing at all about the matter, but who had
agreed to be one of the actors in this solemn farce.
This person, who was called the "common vouchee,"
accordingly appeared, and proceeded to defend the
title: whereupon the demandant asked leave from the
court to "imparl," or speak in private with, the common vouchee. This was granted as a matter of course;
the demandant and common vouchee left the court
together for that purpose, and after a short time the
demandant returned alone, the common vouchee
having meanwhile disappeared. On this, the court
assumed that the common vouchee was unable to defend the title, and proceeded to give judgment that
the demandant should recover the land which he
claimed from the tenant for life, and that the latter
should be recompensed by the tenant in tail, who in
his turn was to be indemnified by the common vouchee.
Thus the demandant obtained the fee simple of the
land, and having done so might re-convey it in fee
simple to the tenant in tail, or otherwise dispose of it
as the latter thought fit.

This form of recovery was said to be with double

(*m*) From the French *voucher*—to call.

voucher, and had the effect of barring not only the issue claiming in virtue of the estate tail, but also all remainders or reversions expectant on the determination of that estate. After this process of defeating the expectation of those claiming after the tenant in tail had been invented, the courts, in order to make it effectual, held that the right to suffer a recovery was inseparable from every estate tail (*n*).

Levying a Fine.

Another, but less efficacious, way of barring an estate tail, was "levying a fine." A fine (*o*) was an amicable composition of a suit, with the consent of the court in which it was commenced; the terms agreed upon being preserved in the records of the court. It was originally made use of in order to secure doubtful titles, by giving public notice that the possession of the estate was in dispute, after which all claims not asserted within a specified time were absolutely barred. The idea was taken from the Roman law: it appears to have been unknown to the Normans before the Conquest, but was commonly in use in Normandy in the sixteenth century (*p*). A fine was, like a recovery, a fictitious proceeding, but it was necessary that the suit to be compromised should be actually commenced in the usual way (*q*), by a friendly plaintiff bringing, against the person intending to levy the fine (who must have had some interest in the lands in question), an action for the breach of a supposed covenant to convey the lands to him. The defendant at once admitted himself to be in the wrong, and was supposed to make overtures to the plaintiff, who thereupon obtained leave from the court to make up the matter with him.

In pursuance of this supposed compromise, the de-

(*n*) *Portington's Case*, 10 Rep. 36ᵃ.
(*o*) From the Latin *finis*—an end.
(*p*) 1 Cruise on Fines and Recoveries, 10.
(*q*) 18 Ed. I. st. 4.

fendant appeared in open court, and acknowledged the right of the plaintiff; a note was made of this acknowledgment and of the other proceedings, and proclaimed in court on successive occasions, and all persons not asserting their claims to the land within a fixed time were thereafter deprived of all right to do so. A fine duly levied barred the issue in tail, but not persons in remainder or reversion, unless the tenant himself had the immediate reversion, in which case he did, indeed, acquire a fee simple estate in the lands, but became liable for all incumbrances created by any of the persons through whom the reversionary fee had descended to him.

The process of barring an estate tail by means of a fine was afterwards recognised by the 32 Hen. VIII., c. 36, which enacted that fines levied by any person of full age to whom, or to whose ancestors, land had been entailed, should be a perpetual bar to them and their heirs claiming by force of such entail. 32 Hen. VIII. c. 36.

The reader may here be reminded that an estate tail does not merge in an estate in fee simple in the same land, even though the two estates happen to be united in the same person, without any other intervening estate; for if they did, a tenant in tail might easily have destroyed the estate tail by purchasing the reversion, and thus, from the first, have frustrated the object of the statute *De Donis*.

If a tenant in tail who barred his estate had not the immediate reversion, he, and any person to whom he transferred his estate, had only a qualified fee simple, which lasted so long as the tenant had heirs of his body who could have claimed the estate if the entail had not been barred: but on the failure of such issue, the land went to the remainder-man or reversioner; and such an estate was therefore called a base fee, as being inferior to an ordinary fee simple. Base fee.

Neither of the above-described modes of barring estates tail were satisfactory. The proceedings in both were complicated, and if in a recovery any mistake were made in selecting the tenant to the *præcipe*, the whole proceedings might be reversed, whilst a fine did not as a rule entirely bar the estate tail; it was therefore generally necessary first to levy a fine, and then to make the plaintiff in that proceeding tenant to the *præcipe* in a suit commenced in order to suffer a recovery: for this tenant, having been declared entitled to the freehold in a court of law, could not be objected to as not having the freehold in possession.

Abolition of Fines and Recoveries Act.

Fines and recoveries abolished.

This expensive and complicated process was at length abolished by the Act for the Abolition of Fines and Recoveries (*r*). By this statute it is enacted that (*s*) no fines or recoveries shall be levied or suffered after the 31st of December 1833; that any fine or recovery levied or suffered contrary to this provision shall be absolutely void; and (*t*) that all warranties of lands which, after the 31st of December 1833, shall be made, or entered into, by any tenant in tail thereof, shall be absolutely void against the issue in tail, and against all persons whose estates are to take effect after the determination of the estate tail.

Every tenant in tail to have power to dispose of his estate.

But on the other hand (*u*), every actual tenant in tail has given to him full power to dispose of, for an estate in fee simple absolute, or for any less estate, the lands entailed, as against all persons claiming them by force of any estate tail which shall be vested in, or might be claimed by, or which but for some previous act would have vested in, or might have been claimed by, the person making the disposition at the time of his making the same : and also as against all persons,

---

(*r*) 3 & 4 Wm. IV. c. 74.
(*s*) S. 2.
(*t*) S. 14.
(*u*) S. 15.

- including the Crown, whose estates are to take effect after the determination of the estate tail. He (v) can also convert into a fee simple absolute any base fee, whether created before or after the passing of the act. But (w) a widow who is tenant in tail of lands which have been inherited or purchased by her husband, or which were conveyed to her and her husband in tail by any of the ancestors of the husband, or by any trustee for the husband, or for his ancestors, cannot bar the estate tail without the consent of the persons next entitled to the inheritance (x).

The statute puts a certain amount of restriction on the power of a tenant in tail to dispose of his estate, by enacting (y) that if, at the time when there shall be a tenant in tail of lands under a settlement, there shall be subsisting, in the same lands, or any of them, any estate for years determinable on the dropping of a life or lives, or any greater estate (not being an estate for years) prior to the estate tail, then the person who shall be owner of the prior estate, or the first of such prior estates if more than one, then subsisting under the same settlement, or who would have been so if no absolute disposition thereof had been made, shall, subject to a provision to be presently mentioned, be the protector of the settlement so far as regards the lands in which such prior estate shall be subsisting. The term "owner of a prior estate" includes a tenant by curtesy (z); two or more owners of a prior estate (a); and a husband and wife where the prior estate belongs to the wife (b). But it does not include lessees at a rent (c); nor a woman in respect

Protector of the settlement.

(v) S. 19.
(w) S. 16.
(x) 11 Hen. VII. c. 20; 32 Hen. VIII. c. 36, s. 2; Shelf. R. P. Statutes, 322, note (g).
(y) S. 22.
(z) S. 22.
(a) S. 23.
(b) S. 24.
(c) S. 26.

of her dower, or a bare trustee, heir, executor, administrator, or assign (*d*): for where these persons have the first existing estate, then the person entitled to the next estate (if any) prior to the estate tail is to be the protector of the settlement (*e*).

<small>Settlor may appoint a protector.</small>

The owner of the prior estate will not, however, necessarily be the protector of the settlement; for the act further provides (*f*) that it shall be lawful for any settlor entailing lands to appoint, by the settlement by which the lands are entailed, any number of existing persons, not exceeding three, and not being aliens, to be protector of the settlement in lieu of the person who would otherwise have been protector. Such person or persons may be protector of the settlement for any part, or for the whole, of the period for which the person whose substitutes they are might have continued protector, but not, it will be observed, for any greater period of time. The settlement appointing a protector may contain a power to perpetuate, during the whole, or any part, of such period, the protectorship of the settlement, by filling up vacancies caused by the retirement or death of any person appointed protector. It has also been recently decided that where this power is omitted, and one of the persons named as protector dies, the survivors or survivor may execute the office (*g*).

<small>Powers of protector.</small>

The protector's consent is necessary (*h*) to enable a tenant in tail, if not entitled to the remainder or reversion in fee simple immediately expectant on the determination of his estate tail, to create an estate larger than a base fee. Moreover (*i*), so long as

---

(*d*) S. 27.
(*e*) S. 28.
(*f*) S. 32.
(*g*) *Bell* v. *Holtby*, L. R. 15 Eq. 178.
(*h*) S. 34.
(*i*) S. 35.

there is a protector of the settlement, his consent is necessary in order to enable the owner of a base fee to convert it into a fee simple absolute.

No protector is (*j*) to be subject to any control in the exercise of his power of consenting, but (*k*) he may not revoke a consent formally given. If a base fee (*l*) and a remainder or reversion in the same lands become united in the same person, and there is no intermediate estate, then the base fee is not to be merged in the remainder or reversion, but to be enlarged into a fee simple absolute; thus avoiding letting in any incumbrances of an ancestor. A base fee not to be merged.

Every disposition of lands made by a tenant in tail may be made (*m*) by any assurance, other than a will, by which such tenant could have made the disposition if his estate were an estate at law in fee simple absolute; but if the tenant in tail making the disposition is a married woman, she must obtain the concurrence of her husband, and the deed effecting the disposition must be acknowledged by her before a judge of one of the superior courts at Westminster, or before two of the commissioners appointed for the purpose (*n*); and the person taking the acknowledgment (*o*) must have previously examined her, apart from her husband, touching her knowledge of such deed, and ascertained that she freely and voluntarily consents to the same. The Court of Common Pleas may, however, in certain cases, dispense with the husband's concurrence (*p*). How estate tail may be disposed of under the act
Married woman.

Moreover, no assurance by which any disposition of lands is effected under the act by a tenant in tail Inrolment.

(*j*) S. 36.
(*k*) S. 44.
(*l*) S. 39.
(*m*) S. 40.
(*n*) S. 79.
(*o*) S. 80.
(*p*) S. 91.

(except a lease for a term not exceeding twenty-one years, made in accordance with the provisions of the act) is to have any operation under the act, unless inrolled in the Court of Chancery within six months after its execution (*q*). And the deed by which a protector gives his consent to any disposition by a tenant in tail under the act, which deed may be either the same assurance by which the disposition is effected or one distinct from the assurance, is to be void unless executed on or before the day on which the assurance is made (*r*); and unless, if a distinct deed, it is inrolled either at or before the time when the assurance is inrolled (*s*).

Barring quasi estate tail.

A *quasi* estate tail cannot, any more than a regular estate tail, be barred by will (*t*), but it may be barred by deed, by any disposition of the land made by a tenant in tail in actual possession. But a tenant in tail not in actual possession must obtain the consent of the owner of the prior estate, in order to bar the reversions or remainders which are limited after the estate tail. A deed barring a *quasi* estate tail need not be inrolled (*u*).

Involuntary alienation. Bankruptcy.

An estate tail may be also the subject of involuntary alienation. Thus the Abolition of Fines and Recoveries Act (*v*) contains (*w*) provisions for the event of a tenant in tail becoming bankrupt, and these are confirmed by the Bankruptcy Act, 1869 (*x*), which enacts (*y*) that the trustee of any bankrupt is to have power to deal with any property to which the bank-

---

(*q*) S. 41.
(*r*) S. 42.
(*s*) S. 46.
(*t*) *Campbell* v. *Sandys*, 1 Sch. & L. 281; *Allen* v. *Allen*, 2 Dru. & War. 307, 326.
(*u*) *Allen* v. *Allen*, 2 Dru. & War. 307.
(*v*) 3 & 4 Wm. IV. c. 74.
(*w*) SS. 56—72.
(*x*) 32 & 33 Vict. c. 71.
(*y*) S. 25.

rupt is beneficially entitled as tenant in tail, in the same manner as the bankrupt himself might have done, and that the sections of the Abolition of Fines and Recoveries Act relating to the bankruptcy of a tenant in tail are to apply to any proceedings under the Bankruptcy Act.

Under the 1 & 2 Vict., c. 110, the creditor of any tenant in tail can, after obtaining a judgment (z) against him, sue out a writ of *elegit*, in pursuance of which he is entitled to retain possession of his debtor's land, and repay himself his debt; and the land will be bound by the judgment as against any person whose estate the debtor might himself have barred. Under that act a registration of the judgment in the Court of Common Pleas would, alone, have bound the land against the same persons, and also against any purchaser for value who had notice of the registration. Now, however, the 27 & 28 Vict., c. 112, renders it necessary, for that purpose, that the land should be actually taken in execution. *Judgments. 1 & 2 Vict. c. 110. 27 & 28 Vict. c. 112.*

The 33 Hen. VIII., c. 39, made estates tail liable for debts due to the Crown, and by the 2 & 3 Vict., c. 11, and the 22 & 23 Vict., c. 35, judgments obtained by the Crown are put on the same footing as other judgments; but under the 28 & 29 Vict., c. 104, writs of execution obtained by the Crown may be registered immediately on being obtained, and thereupon bind the debtor's land, without the necessity of taking it in execution. *Crown Debts. 33 Hen. VIII. c. 39; 2 & 3 Vict. c. 11; 22 & 23 Vict. c. 35. 28 & 29 Vict. c. 104.*

Lastly, the estate of a tenant in tail may be put an end to by his death. In that case the Apportionment Acts (a) will apply to any leases which he has made, since although he might, if he pleased, have turned *Determination of tenant's estate by his death. Apportionment.*

(z) The law relating to judgments will be more fully explained in the next chapter.
(a) 11 Geo. II. c. 19; 4 & 5 Wm. IV. c. 22; 33 & 34 Vict. c. 35.

Emblements. his estate into a fee simple, yet, not having done so, he was at the moment of his death merely a tenant for life (b). For the same reason, his executor or administrator is entitled to emblements, as against the heir in tail, remainder-man, or reversioner.

(b) *Pagget* v. *Gee*, 9 Mod. 482.

CHAPTER VI.

OF AN ESTATE IN FEE SIMPLE.

WE have now arrived at the consideration of an estate in fee simple — the greatest which the law recognises in a subject, and that out of which all other estates in land are derived.

This estate may be either "absolute," which is the more ordinary form, or "qualified." An instance of the latter kind occurs if an estate is given to A and his heirs "tenants of the manor of Dale:" here, whenever the heirs of A cease to be tenants of that manor the grant is entirely defeated (a). Is absolute or qualified.

No person can create an estate in fee simple, unless he has himself that estate in the lands with which he professes to deal. There are also certain persons who are, more or less, unable to create such an estate, from the fact of their having only a limited power of alienation. Thus any conveyance, or will of land, made by an idiot or lunatic (unless made in a lucid interval) is absolutely void (b). A married woman, too, is unable to dispose by deed of her real estate, unless it is settled to her separate use (a point to be adverted to hereafter), or unless the previous owner has given her a power to appoint that it shall go to certain persons (in which case she is merely acting as agent of the person who conferred the power), except with her husband's consent, and by a deed acknowledged in manner provided by the Fines and Recoveries Creation of a fee simple. By whom it may be created. Idiots and Lunatics. Married women.

(a) 2 Bl. Com. 109.
(b) *Yates* v. *Boen*, Str. 1104.

Infants.

Abolition Act (c). She cannot dispose by will of any land other than that over which she has a power of appointment (d), or which is settled to her separate use (e). And an infant cannot, as a rule, make a conveyance, by deed, of land, which will be binding upon him if he chooses to repudiate it at, or before, coming of age, although it will be binding upon a purchaser from him (f). But we have already seen, in previous chapters, that an infant may, under the 18 & 19 Vict., c. 43, make a binding settlement of land, and thus create an estate in fee simple, in contemplation of his marriage. An infant cannot dispose of land by will, being incapable of making a valid will (g).

Who may have an estate in fee simple.

Corporations.

Magna Charta.

Statute De Religiosis.

At Common Law all persons are capable of acquiring lands, but various restrictions have been imposed on this capacity by statute. We must notice these, in order to understand the difficulties which they oppose to the creation of estates in fee simple. From an early period, the feudal lords objected to lands being acquired by the monasteries and other religious houses who made up the greater number of the earlier corporations; for the fact that these bodies were perpetual, made it impossible that their lands should ever escheat as in ordinary cases, and lands held by them were consequently said to be in *mortmain* (*in mortuâ manu*). Hence we find a provision in Magna Charta (h), forbidding gifts to them, and afterwards it was enacted by the statute *De Religiosis* (i) that no persons, religious or other ecclesiastical corporation, body politic ecclesiastical or lay, sole or aggregate, should buy or sell lands, whereby the same should come into mortmain, under pain of forfeiture. This was extended by

---

(c) 3 & 4 Wm. IV c. 74, ss. 77, 79, 91.
(d) Sug. Pow. 153; 7 Wm. IV. & 1 Vict. c. 26, s. 8.
(e) *Taylor* v. *Meads*, 13 W. R. 394.
(f) *Zouch* v. *Parsons*, Burr. 1794; *Allen* v. *Allen*, 2 Dru. & War. 307.
(g) 7 Wm. IV. & 1 Vict. c. 26, s. 7.
(h) 9 Hen. III. c. 36.
(i) 7 Ed. I. c. 1.

the 15 Ric. II., c. 5, to all lands purchased by guilds or fraternities, on the ground that mayors, bailiffs, and commons of cities, boroughs, and other towns, were as perpetual as people of religion. Consequently, it became customary, on the foundation of a lay corporation, to insert in its charter a licence from the Crown to hold lands, and the validity of these licences was recognised by the 7 & 8 Wm. III., c. 37, which permits the Crown, when it thinks fit, to grant to any persons, or bodies politic or corporate, licence to alien in mortmain, and also to purchase, acquire, take, and hold, in perpetuity or otherwise, any hereditaments whatever.

15 Ric. II. c. 5.

Licence from Crown.

7 & 8 Wm. III. c. 37.

With respect to religious corporations, the old law still obtains to a great extent; the principal act relating to this subject being that generally known as the Mortmain Act (*j*), passed in the reign of George the Second. This act only applies to gifts of land, or any interest in land, or of money to be invested in land, although it would appear from the preamble that it was the intention of its framers to give it a wider application (*k*). It enacts (*l*) that no manors, lands, tenements, rents, advowsons, or other hereditaments, corporeal or incorporeal, or any sum or sums of money, or personal estate whatever, to be laid out or disposed of in the purchase of any lands or hereditaments, shall be given, granted, or in any ways conveyed to any persons, bodies politic or corporate, or otherwise, for any estate or interest whatever, in trust for, or for the benefit of any charitable uses whatsoever, unless made by a deed executed in the presence of two or more credible witnesses, twelve calendar months at least before the death of the donor or grantor, and inrolled in Chancery within six calendar months after its execution. The deed must also be intended to take effect in possession for the charitable use, immediately from the making thereof, and be

Charitable Corporations.

Mortmain Act

(*j*) 9 Geo. II. c. 36.
(*k*) See the judgments in *Jefferies* v. *Alexander*, 8 H. L. C. 594.
(*l*) S. 1.

without any power of revocation, reservation, trust condition, clause, or agreement whatever, for the benefit of the donor or of any person claiming under him. But these provisions are not (*m*) to extend to any purchase made *bonâ fide* for valuable consideration, or (*n*) to prejudice the Universities of Oxford and Cambridge, or the Colleges of Eton, Winchester, and Westminster.

29 & 30 Vict. c. 57. The time allowed for inrolling conveyances under the Mortmain Act was enlarged by subsequent statutes (*o*), and now it is provided by the 29 & 30 Vict., c. 57, that (*p*) any trustee of a charity may, at any time, apply to the Court of Chancery for an order authorizing the inrolment of any deed, or other instrument, whereby any hereditaments have been conveyed for charitable uses, or any deed connected with any charitable trust, which deed ought to have been inrolled, but has not been inrolled within the time limited by law.

31 & 32 Vict. c. 44. By a subsequent act (*q*), grants of lands made to a trustee or trustees on behalf of any society or body of persons associated together for religious purposes, or for the promotion of education, arts, literature, science, or other like purposes, in order to erect a building thereon, or whereon a building used, or intended to be used, for such purposes, or any of them, shall have been erected, are to be exempted from the necessity of inrolment, provided they are made *bonâ fide* and for valuable consideration, and provided that each such piece of land shall not exceed two acres in extent or area in each case. In addition to the above, the Charitable Trusts Acts. ritable Trusts Act, 1853 (*r*), and the Charitable Trusts

---

(*m*) S. 2.
(*n*) S. 3.
(*o*) 24 & 25 Vict. c. 9 ; 25 & 26 Vict. c. 17 ; 27 & 28 Vict. c. 13.
(*p*) S. 1.
(*q*) 31 & 32 Vict. c. 44.
(*r*) 16 & 17 Vict. c. 137.

Amendment Act, 1855 (s), enable trustees of charities to purchase lands for building purposes, and the 33 & 34 Vict., c. 34, permits (t) corporations and trustees holding monies in trust for any public or charitable purposes to invest the same in any mortgages or charges of lands and hereditaments of any tenure (u).

<small>33 & 34 Vict. c. 34.</small>

With respect to corporations formed for purposes not strictly charitable, the law of mortmain has been of late considerably relaxed. Thus, highway boards are now empowered to take lands without a licence from the Crown (v), as are also joint-stock companies formed under the Companies' Act 1862 (w), it being, however, provided by this act (x) that no company formed for the purpose of promoting art, science, religion, charity, or any other like object, not involving the acquisition of gain by the company, shall hold more than two acres of land without the sanction of the Board of Trade. Aliens were also, until recently, forbidden to hold land in this country, except for business purposes, and then only for terms not exceeding twenty-one years, but now the Naturalization Act 1870 (y) provides that real and personal property of every description may be taken, acquired, held, and disposed of by an alien, in the same manner in all respects as by a natural-born British subject; and that a title to real or personal property of every description may be derived through, from, or in succession to an alien, in the same manner, in all respects, as through a British subject.

<small>Corporations not charitable. Highway boards. Joint-stock companies. Aliens. Naturalization Act 1870.</small>

An estate in fee simple may be granted or given, by deed or by will, by any competent person. We

<small>How a fee simple may be created.</small>

(s) 18 & 19 Vict. c. 124.
(t) S. 1.
(u) S. 3.
(v) 25 & 26 Vict. c. 61, s. 9.
(w) 25 & 26 Vict. c. 89.
(x) S. 21.
(y) 33 Vict. c. 14, s. 2.

Form of words.

have already seen that the use of the word "heirs" is essential in order to confer such an estate by deed, although not so where a disposition is made of it by will.

Incidents of an estate in fee simple.

The incidents of an estate in fee simple do not require any lengthy notice, since the absolute powers which its possessor has over it enable him to commit any kind of waste on the property, or to sell, lease, or incumber it at his pleasure, and free him from any obligation, as between himself and his successors, to keep down the interest on any charges which may exist on the land. But a few remarks may be made on the subject of fixtures. During his lifetime, a tenant in fee simple has uncontrolled power over any fixtures put up by a previous owner of the property, or by himself. He may also, if he pleases, dispose of them by his will. But if he dies, having neither removed them nor specifically bequeathed them, the right of his executor, or administrator, to claim them is less than in the case of any other deceased tenant. The old rule appears to have been that the executor or administrator of a tenant in fee simple was not entitled to any kind of fixtures (z). And even in modern times, it has been laid down by the House of Lords that the decisions in other cases in favour of trade fixtures do not apply as between the heir and executor, or administrator, of a tenant in fee; and hence, that machinery put up by such a tenant for the purpose of better using his land went, in the absence of any disposition of it having been made by him, to his heir, and not to his executor (a). And as to undisposed of ornamental or domestic fixtures, such as kitchen ranges, stoves, grates, or blinds, it has been

Fixtures.

(z) Amos on Fixtures, 152; *Warner* v. *Fleetwood*, cited 4 Rep. 64ª; *Wood* v. *Smith*, Cro. Jac. 129.

(a) *Fisher* v. *Dixon*, 12 Cl. & F. 312, 331; and see *Trappes* v. *Harter*, 2 Cr. & Mee, 153, 180.

hold that they also belong to the heir (*b*). It would seem therefore that the executor, or administrator, has no right to undisposed of fixtures of any kind, except where they have been merely loosely affixed to the freehold, in a manner which showed a clear intention that they should be removable.

Our previous remarks on the creation of a fee simple apply equally to its voluntary alienation by the tenant. We have next, therefore, to see how this estate can be the subject of involuntary alienation. Forfeitures of land, on account of its owner having committed some crime, having been recently abolished (*c*), the two principal grounds on which a tenant in fee simple may now be deprived of his estate are, his having failed to pay debts declared to be due from him by the judgment of a court of justice, or his having become bankrupt. *Alienation of an estate in fee simple. Voluntary. Involuntary.*

It will be recollected that the question of the effect of judgments on the various estates in land which we have discussed in previous chapters, was purposely deferred until we should have reached the stage at which we have now arrived. We will proceed, therefore, to state briefly the law of judgments, with reference to such estates generally. *Judgments.*

Before the passing of the Statute of Westminster (*d*), freehold and copyhold estates could not be taken in execution for debt, but under that act (the provisions of which relating to judgments were somewhat extended by the Statute of Frauds (*e*)) a creditor who had recovered a judgment in one of the King's courts might, at his option, have either a writ of *fieri facias* *Statute of Westminster.*

(*b*) See *Winn* v. *Ingilby*, 5 B. & Ald. 625; *Colegrave* v. *Dias Santos*, 2 B. & C. 76.
(*c*) 33 & 34 Vict. c. 23, s. 1.
(*d*) 13 Ed. I. c. 18.
(*e*) 29 Car. II. c. 3, ss. 10, 14, 15.

Writ of elegit.

directing the sheriff, or other officer, to sell the debtor's chattels, including his leaseholds, in order, out of the proceeds, to satisfy the debt; or he might have a writ of *elegit*, under which the sheriff might deliver to him the chattels of the debtor at an appraised value, without having been sold, and also, if these were not sufficient to pay the debt, one half of the debtor's land, again including leaseholds (*f*); which the creditor might hold until he had repaid himself out of the rents and profits.

Judgment a general lien on all the debtor's lands.

These statutes did not apply to an estate by the curtesy, or to an estate tail as against the issue in tail, or to copyholds, or to some forms of incorporeal hereditaments. Neither did they include an equitable estate in leaseholds, nor an equitable estate in freeholds if the trustee parted with it at any time before the writ of *elegit* was sued out. But where they did apply, a judgment became, under the Statute of Westminster (*g*), a general charge upon all the lands which the debtor had at the time of entering up (*h*) the judgment, and upon all those which he subsequently acquired; and no act of his, not even a sale to a *bonâ fide* purchaser who had no notice of the existence of the judgment, could get rid of this lien (*i*). This was remedied, as to estates for years, by the Statute of Frauds (*j*), which enacted (*k*) that no writ of execution should bind the " goods " (a term which in the statute included leaseholds) of the person against whom such writ was sued forth, but from the time that such writ had been delivered to the sheriff to be executed. The result was that as against an estate for years a judgment alone had no effect (*l*). And as regards

Statute of Frauds.
Leaseholds not to be bound until delivery of writ of execution.

(*f*) *Fleetwood's Case*, 8 Rep. 171a.
(*g*) 13 Ed. I. c. 18.
(*h*) A judgment is "entered up" by inscribing the fact of its having been obtained on the records of the Court.
(*i*) Prid. Judgments, 9.
(*j*) 29 Car. II. c. 3.
(*k*) S. 16.
(*l*) *Shirley* v. *Watts*, 3 Atk. 200; *Forth* v. *Norfolk*, 4 Madd. 503, 506.

OF AN ESTATE IN FEE SIMPLE.

other estates in land it was enacted by the 4 & 5 Wm. and M., c. 20 (*m*), that no judgment should affect any lands or tenements of the debtor's, as, against *bonâ fide* purchasers or mortgagees of the lands, unless it had been previously docketed in a book belonging to the court in which such judgment had been obtained. 4 & 5 Wm. & M. c. 20. Freeholds not to be bound unless judgment docketed.

Next came various statutes passed in the present reign in order to give a more complete remedy to creditors. The first of these, the 1 & 2 Vict., c. 110, enacts (*n*) that it shall be lawful for the sheriff or other officer to whom any writ of *elegit* shall be directed at the suit of any person, upon any judgment which at the time of the commencement of the act (*o*) shall have been recovered, or thereafter shall be recovered, in any of the superior courts at Westminster, to take and deliver execution, unto the party in that behalf suing, of *all* such lands, tenements, rectories, tithes, rents, and hereditaments, including lands and hereditaments of copyhold or customary tenure, as the person against whom execution is so sued or any person in trust for him shall have been seised or possessed of at the time of entering up the said judgment, or at any time afterwards, or over which such person shall, at the time of entering up such judgment, or at any time afterwards, have any disposing power which he might, without the assent of any other person, exercise for his own benefit, in like manner as the sheriff or other officer might at the time when the act was passed have made and delivered execution of one moiety of the lands and tenements of any person against whom a writ of *elegit* was sued out. Lands and hereditaments thus taken in execution are to be held and enjoyed by the person to whom such execution is delivered, subject to his being liable to account in a Court of Equity for the 1 & 2 Vict. c. 110.
Sheriff may take all debtor's lands under writ of *elegit*.

(*m*) S. 3.
(*n*) S. 11.
(*o*) 1st of October, 1838.

rents and profits received. Under this act (*p*) a judgment entered up against any person in any of the superior courts at Westminster, and also all orders of courts of equity, and all rules of courts of common law, or of the Lord Chancellor in matters of bankruptcy or of lunacy (*q*), were to operate as a charge upon all lands and hereditaments in which such person had, or should have, a legal or an equitable estate, or over which he had a disposing power which he might exercise for his own benefit without the assent of any other person, and were to be binding not only as against him, but also as against all persons claiming under him after such judgment, and also as against the issue of his body, and all other persons whom he might, without the assent of any other person, cut off and debar from any remainder, reversion, or other interest, in or out of any of the said lands and hereditaments. But (*r*) no judgment of any of the superior courts, nor any decree or order in any court of equity, nor any rule of a court of common law, nor any order in bankruptcy or lunacy, was, by virtue of the act, to affect any lands, tenements, or hereditaments, as to purchasers, mortgagees, or creditors, unless and until a memorandum of the judgment was registered in a book to be kept by the senior master of the Court of Common Pleas.

Entered up judgment to bind lands as against debtor and persons claiming under him.

But not against purchasers, mortgagees, and creditors unless registered.

The effect of this act was to make a registered judgment a charge on the debtor's lands generally, even as against purchasers and mortgagees, since they had now an opportunity of finding out for themselves that such a judgment existed. But the 2 & 3 Vict., c. 11, passed in the following year, enacted (*s*) that, as against purchasers and mortgagees without notice of such judgments, such judgments should not bind any

2 & 3 Vict. c. 11.

(*p*) S. 13.
(*q*) S. 18.
(*r*) S. 19.
(*s*) S. 5.

lands, tenements, or hereditaments, or any interest therein, although duly registered, further than they would have done had the 1 & 2 Vict., c. 110, never been passed. Hence, as against purchasers and mortgagees without notice, leaseholds again become unaffected by judgments, although duly registered, until a writ of execution had been delivered to the sheriff (*t*); whilst freehold and copyhold estates were, as to one moiety, bound by the fact of the judgment being registered. The 2 & 3 Vict., c. 11, and subsequent statutes (*u*) also improved the system of registration, and required judgments to be re-registered every five years. They were followed by the 23 & 24 Vict., c. 38, which, after reciting that it was desirable to place freehold, copyhold, and customary estates on the same footing with leasehold estates in respect of judgments, as against purchasers and mortgagees, enacted (*v*) that no judgment to be entered up after the passing of the act (*w*) should affect any land of any tenure as to a *bonâ fide* purchaser or mortgagee, (whether with notice or not), unless a writ of execution of such judgment should have been issued and registered before the conveyance to him, nor even then, unless the writ of execution were put in force within three months from the time when it was registered.

23 & 24 Vict. c. 38.

Meanwhile the Mercantile Law Amendment Act 1856 (*x*) had enacted (*y*) that no writ of execution against the goods of a debtor should prejudice the title of a *bonâ fide* purchaser of the goods before their actual seizure by virtue of such writ, unless the purchaser had notice, at the time of his purchase, of the writ having been issued.

(*t*) *Westbrooke* v. *Blythe*, 3 E. & B. 737.
(*u*) 3 & 4 Vict. c. 82; 18 & 19 Vict. c. 15.
(*v*) S. 1.
(*w*) 23rd July, 1860.
(*x*) 19 & 20 Vict. c. 97.
(*y*) S. 1.

27 & 28 Vict. c. 112.

It would appear that the word "goods" in this act did not include terms of years, for the next act relating to judgments which we have to notice, the 27 & 28 Vict., c. 112, recites that it is desirable to assimilate the law affecting freehold, copyhold, and leasehold estates to that affecting purely personal estates, in respect of future judgments; and proceeds to enact (z) that no judgment to be entered up after the passing of the act (a) shall affect any land, of whatever tenure, until such land shall have been actually delivered in execution by virtue of a writ of *elegit*, or other lawful authority, in pursuance of such judgment. In the construction of this act, land is (b) to include all hereditaments, corporeal or incorporeal, or any interest therein. And a creditor to whom any land of his debtor has been actually delivered in execution by virtue of any such judgment, and whose writ or other process of execution has been duly registered, may (c) obtain from the Court of Chancery an order for the sale of his debtor's interest in such land. The result is that judgments entered up after the 28th of July 1864 do not operate at all as a charge on land, as to any interest therein, until it has been actually delivered in execution; but when this is done, the creditor has a speedy means of obtaining payment of his debt, by a sale of the land under the order of the Court of Chancery. As to equitable interests of the debtor, and property which cannot be taken in execution from any cause, it has been lately decided that a creditor who has obtained a judgment and sued out a writ of *elegit* must apply to the Court of Chancery, whose order with reference to the matter will be a delivery of execution within the statute (d).

(z) S. 1.
(a) 28th July, 1864.
(b) S. 2.
(c) S. 4.
(d) *Hatton* v. *Haywood*, L. R. 9 Ch. 229; and see re *Cowbridge, Ry. Co.*, L. R. 5 Eq. 413; *Beckett* v. *Buckley*, L. R. 17 Eq. 435.

The above remarks apply to debts due from one Crown Debts. subject to another. The law relating to judgments obtained by the Crown against a subject is very similar. For every such judgment must be registered (*e*), and periodically re-registered (*f*), in order to bind land as against purchasers, mortgagees, and creditors, and, if obtained after the 5th July, 1865, must have been followed up by the issue of a writ of execution, which must also have been duly registered (*g*), but the land itself need not have been taken in execution.

Various statutes have also been passed, which have Bankruptcy. the effect of depriving a man of his land if he becomes bankrupt.

The Bankruptcy Act 1869 (*h*), which is the latest Bankruptcy enactment on this subject, enables (*i*) a creditor or two Act, 1869. or more creditors whose claims amount singly or in the aggregate to fifty pounds, to present a petition to the Court of Bankruptcy, asking that the debtor be adjudged bankrupt on one or more of the grounds mentioned in the act. On the adjudication being made, there (*j*) is to vest in the trustee appointed under the bankruptcy, for the purpose of division amongst the bankrupt's creditors, all such property as may belong to or be vested in the bankrupt at the commencement of the bankruptcy, or which may be acquired by or devolve on him during its continuance: and also the capacity to exercise, and to take proceedings for exercising, all such powers in, or over, or in respect of property, as might have been exercised by the bankrupt for his own benefit at the commencement of his bankruptcy, or during its continuance, except the right of nomination to an ecclesiastical benefice; and the

---

(*e*) 2 & 3 Vict. c. 11, s. 8.
(*f*) 22 & 23 Vict. c. 35, s. 22.
(*g*) 28 & 29 Vict. c. 104, s. 48.
(*h*) 32 & 33 Vict. c. 71.
(*i*) S. 6.
(*j*) S. 14.

bankrupt (k) is to be entitled only to any surplus remaining after payment of his debts, and of the costs, charges, and expenses of the bankruptcy.

Payment of debts out of real estate.

A man's real estate is also liable to be taken, after his death, in order to satisfy debts and obligations incurred by him during his lifetime (l). For a long time, the common law doctrine was that debts were payable out of personalty only, the one exception to this rule being that lands which had not been disposed of by will were subject to the payment of the owner's debts by specialty in which the heirs were bound, that is, debts for which some bond or covenant had been given, in which the heirs were specially named as undertaking to pay. If, however, the land had been devised, the devisee was not liable to pay his testator's debts. The first statute which struck a blow at this doctrine was the 3 Wm. and Mary, c. 14, known as the Statute of Fraudulent Devises, which, after reciting that it often happened that persons, who by bonds and other specialties had bound themselves and their heirs, had, to the defrauding of their creditors, devised or disposed of their lands, in such manner that such creditors had lost their debts, enacted that all wills of lands should (only as against such creditors) be deemed fraudulent and void.

Statute of Fraudulent Devises.

Real estate made liable to payment of specialty debts.

Thus the real estate of all persons became liable for payment of their specialty debts. The next step was the passing of the 47 Geo. III., c. 74, which enacted that the real estate of any person who was at the time of his death a trader, should be "assets" (m) to be administered in the Court of Chancery for payment of all the just debts of such person, as well debts due by

47 Geo. III. c. 74.

Real estate of a trader to be liable for payment of all his debts.

(k) S. 45.
(l) No reference is made in the following remarks to the order in which personalty and realty are respectively applied in payment of debts: that subject not being considered as within the scope of this work.
(m) From the French *assez*, enough.

simple contract as by specialty: provided that creditors by specialty in which the heirs were bound should be paid the full amount of their debts before any of the creditors by simple contract, or by specialty in which the heirs were not bound, were paid any part of their demands.

These two acts were repealed, as to the wills of persons who died after the 16th of July 1830, by the 11 Geo. IV. and 1 Wm. IV., c. 47, but were, in substance, re-enacted by the latter act. Next came the 3 & 4 Wm. IV., c. 104, which at length made the real estate of all persons, traders or not, liable for the payment of all their debts; reserving however the privileges previously given to specialty creditors. But now it is enacted by the 32 & 33 Vict., c. 46, that in the administration of the estate of every person who shall die on or after the 1st of January, 1870, no debt or liability of such person shall be entitled to any priority or preference, by reason merely that the same is secured by, or arises under, a bond, deed, or other instrument under seal, or is otherwise made or constituted a specialty debt: but that all the creditors of such deceased person shall be treated as standing in equal degree, and be paid accordingly out of the assets of such deceased person. *11 Geo. IV. & 1 Wm. IV. c. 47. 3 & 4 Wm. c. 104. Real estate of all persons made liable for payment of all their debts. 32 & 33 Vict. c. 46. No preference to specialty creditors.*

An estate in land may also be lost, if the owner allows some other person to take and keep possession of it, in a manner inconsistent with its being the property of such owner. For it is enacted by the 3 & 4 Wm. IV., c. 27, that (n) after the 31st day of December, 1833, no person shall make an entry or distress, or bring an action to recover any land or rent, but within twenty years next after the time at which a right to make such entry or distress, or to bring such action, shall have first accrued to him or, *Estate lost under Statute of Limitation. 3 & 4 Wm. IV. c. 27. No action to be brought but within twenty years from time when right first accrued.*

if he claims through some other person, to the person through whom he claims. "Land" in this act means every kind of corporeal hereditament, and every share, estate, or interest therein, whatever the tenure may be; whilst the word "rent" includes all services and suits for which a distress may be made (*o*). The right to make an entry or distress, or to bring an action, is to be deemed to have first accrued in manner following. If the person claiming, or the person through whom he claims, shall, in respect of the estate or interest claimed, have been in possession, or in the receipt of the profits, of such land, or in the receipt of such rent, and shall, while entitled thereto, have been dispossessed, or have discontinued such possession or receipt, then such right is to be deemed to have first accrued at the time of such dispossession or discontinuance of possession, or at the last time at which any such profits or rent were or was so received. If the person claiming claims the estate or interest of some deceased person who continued in such possession or receipt, in respect of the same estate or interest, until his death, and who was the last person entitled who was in such receipt or possession, then such right shall be deemed to have first accrued at the time of such death. If the person claiming claims an estate in possession assured by some instrument, other than a will, to him, or some person through whom he claims, by a person being, in respect of the same estate or interest, in possession of the land or rent, and no person entitled under such instrument shall have been in such possession or receipt, then such right shall be deemed to have first accrued at the time at which the person claiming, or the person through whom he claims, became entitled to such possession or receipt by virtue of such instrument. If the estate or interest claimed shall have been one in reversion or remainder, and no person shall have

When right to be deemed to have first accrued.
Person in possession.

Person claiming estate of deceased person in possession.

Person claiming under a conveyance of an estate in possession.

Person claiming under a conveyance of an estate in reversion.

(*o*) S. 1.

obtained the possession or receipt of the profits of such land, or the receipt of such rent, in respect of such estate or interest, then such right shall have been deemed to have first accrued at the time at which such estate or interest became an estate or interest in possession. And when the person claiming, or the person through whom he claims, shall have become entitled by reason of any forfeiture or breach of condition, then such right shall be deemed to have first accrued when such forfeiture was incurred or such condition was broken. But if the right to take advantage of a forfeiture has first accrued in respect of any estate or interest in reversion or remainder, and the land or rent has not been recovered by virtue of such right, then the right is to be deemed to have first accrued, in respect of such estate or interest, at the time when the same became an estate or interest in possession (*p*). The statute goes on to provide for the case of the land or rent being in the possession of tenants of the owner. It enacts (*q*) that when any person shall be in possession as tenant at will, the right of the person entitled subject thereto, or of the person through whom he claims, shall be deemed to have first accrued either at the determination of such tenancy, or at the expiration of one year after the commencement of such tenancy. That (*r*) where any person shall be in possession as tenant from year to year or other period, without any lease in writing, the right of the person entitled subject thereto, or of the person through whom he claims, shall be deemed to have first accrued at the determination of the first of such years or other periods, or at the last time when any rent payable in respect of such tenancy shall have been received (which shall last happen). And that (*s*) when any person shall be in possession by virtue of a lease in writing, by which a

<small>Person claiming under a forfeiture.</small>

<small>Where land in possession of tenant at will.</small>

<small>Of tenant from year to year by parol.</small>

<small>Of tenant under a written lease.</small>

(*p*) SS. 3, 4.
(*q*) S. 7.
(*r*) S. 8.
(*s*) S. 9

rent amounting to a yearly sum of twenty shillings or upwards shall be reserved, and the rent reserved by such lease shall have been received by some person wrongfully claiming to be entitled in reversion expectant on the lease, and no payment in respect of the rent reserved by such lease shall have been afterwards made to the person rightfully entitled thereto, the right of the person entitled, or of the person through whom he claims, shall be deemed to have first accrued at the time at which the rent reserved by such lease was first so received by the person wrongfully claiming as aforesaid. But the mere fact of a tenant under a written lease not paying any rent at all for any number of years will not, provided the lease is still running, affect the right of his lessor to the reversion or remainder expectant on the determination of the lease.

Written acknowledgment. The act also provides (*t*) that when any acknowledgment of the title of the person entitled to any land or rent shall have been given to him or his agent, in writing, signed by the person in possession, then such possession shall be deemed to have been the possession of the person to whom, or to whose agent, such acknowledgment shall have been given at the time of giving the same, and the right of such last-mentioned person, or any person claiming through him, to make an entry or distress, or bring an action, shall be deemed to have first accrued at, and not before, the time at which such acknowledgment, or the last of such acknowledgments, if more than one, was given.

Extension of time in cases of disability. The period for recovering land or rent is also enlarged if at the time when the right of any person first accrued, such person was an infant, a married woman, a lunatic, or absent beyond seas (*u*). In any of these cases, such person, or the person claiming through him, may, subject to a proviso to be pre-

(*t*) S. 14.
(*u*) S. 16.

OF AN ESTATE IN FEE SIMPLE.

sently noticed, make a distress or entry, or bring an action, at any time within ~~ten~~ years next after the time at which the person to whom such right first accrued ceased to be under any such disability, or died, whichever first happened. It has been held, with reference to this clause, that when the person to whom the right to bring an action accrues is under a disability, as by being an infant, and before the removal of that disability falls under another, as in the case of a woman by being married, the act preserves the right to bring an action until ~~ten~~ years after the removal of the latter disability (v). But in no case does the act permit an action to be brought but within ~~forty~~ years next after the time at which such right first accrued, although the person entitled may have been under disability for the whole of such forty years, or although the term of ~~ten~~ years from the time at which he shall have ceased to be under any such disability, or have died, shall not have expired (w). The act also provides (x) that where the right of a tenant in tail has been barred by lapse of time, no entry, distress, or action shall be made, or brought, by any person claiming any estate, interest, or right which such tenant in tail might lawfully have barred. But in all cases where land or rent has been vested in a trustee upon an express trust, the right of the *cestui que trust*, or any person claiming through him, to recover such land or rent is not to be deemed to have first accrued until the land or rent has been conveyed to a purchaser for a valuable consideration (y). And in every case of a concealed fraud, the right of any person to bring a suit in equity for the recovery of land or rent of which he, or any person through whom he claims, may have been deprived by such fraud, shall be deemed to have first accrued at, and not before, the

No extension beyond forty years.

Tenant in tail.

Express trust.

Fraud.

(v) *Borrows v. Ellison*, L. R. 6 Ex. 128.
(w) S. 17.
(x) S. 21.
(y) S. 25.

time at which such fraud shall be, or with reasonable diligence might have been, first known or discovered (z). This, however, is not to prejudice a *bonâ fide* purchaser who has not assisted in the commission of such fraud, and who, at the time when he made the purchase, did not know, and had no reason to believe, that any such fraud had been committed.

Real Property Limitation Act 1874.

The provisions of the 3 & 4 Wm. IV., c. 27, will, in course of time, be materially altered by the Real Property Limitation Act 1874 (a), which is to be read as one with it. For under this act, which will come into force on the 1st of January, 1879, no land or rent will be recoverable by persons not under disability but within twelve years after the time when the right of action has first accrued. In cases of infancy, coverture, or lunacy, a further time of six years will be allowed, but so that no action can, under any circumstances, be brought but within thirty years from the time when the right of action first accrued. And no extension of time will be allowed on the ground of absence beyond seas.

Results of death of tenant in fee simple.

We have already seen how an estate by curtesy, or in dower, may arise on the death of a tenant in fee simple. There was not, formerly, on the happening of such an event, any apportionment, between the tenant's real and personal representatives, of any rents which he had reserved to himself; but such rents all went to the heir or, if the tenant had made a will, to the devisee of the lands out of which the rent issued (b). Now however, under the Apportionment Act 1870 (c), the executor or administrator is entitled to a proportion of such rents, and it would seem that, as between the executor and a devisee the act applies,

Apportionment.

Apportionment Act 1870.

(z) S. 26.
(a) 37 & 38 Vict. c. 57.
(b) *Browne v. Amyot*, 3 Ha. 173.
(c) 33 & 34 Vict. c. 35.

although the devisee claims under a will executed before the passing of the act (*d*).

We will conclude this chapter with some remarks on the devolution of an estate in fee simple, when the owner of it has died intestate. In such a case, it descends to his heir—a person who can only be ascertained after the owner's death, since it is a maxim of law that no one can be the heir of a living man; although he may be his heir-apparent, or heir-presumptive. The law as to the inheritance of real estate, both legal and equitable (*e*), so far as regards the descent of any land the owner of which has died since the 1st January 1834, is regulated by the 3 & 4 Wm. IV., c. 106. But as this statute is founded upon a pre-existing law, and has no retrospective operation, it will be necessary to refer to the former law, in order to state the new law grafted on it by the statute (*f*). For this purpose, we will take the old canons or rules of descent as laid down by Blackstone (*g*), observing the changes made in them by the statute.

Descent of an estate in fee simple.

3 & 4 Wm. IV. c. 106.

Blackstone's canons of descent.

The first rule stated by Blackstone is, that inheritances shall descend lineally (that is, in a direct line) to the issue of the person who last died actually seised, *in infinitum*; but shall never lineally ascend. These two propositions, namely, that the person from whom the inheritance is traced must have died seised, and that an inheritance can never lineally ascend, were based on feudal principles. As to the first proposition, we know that every transfer of a corporeal hereditament had formerly to be accomplished by a public and solemn delivery of possession, known as

Blackstone's 1st Canon.

(*d*) *Roseingrave* v. *Burke*, Ir. R. 7 Eq. 186; *Capron* v. *Capron*, L. R. 17 Eq. 288; *Re Cline*, L. R. 18 Eq. 213.
(*e*) *Trash* v. *Wood*, 4 My. & C. 324.
(*f*) Tables illustrating the rules of descent before, and after, the 1st Jan. 1834, are to be found in 1 Stephens' Commentaries (6 ed.) at pages 402 and 439.
(*g*) 2 Bl. Com. 200, *et seq.*

c.   K

making livery of the seisin : the person thus invested with the possession of the land being said to be seised of it. In those times, our present complex system of owning land was unknown. Hence, the possession of land was the most convincing proof of a right to it, and therefore no one was held to have a transmissible title unless he had been seised of the land in question. The second proposition was derived as follows—A feud given to a man and his heirs was, as we also know, at first held to include him and his issue only; the first grantee of a feud being said to have a *feudum novum*, or new feud, whilst he who inherited a feud conferred on an ancestor had a *feudum antiquum*, or ancient feud. No one could succeed to a new feud but the direct issue of the grantee, that is, of the person last seised; but a man might inherit an ancient feud, although not the direct issue of the person last seised, provided he were of the issue of the original grantee. Thus, if a feud were given to A and his heirs, and A died, leaving two sons, B and C, of whom C died in his father's lifetime, leaving a son, D; if B, after succeeding his father, died without issue, D, although not of the direct issue of B, could succeed to the feud (now become an ancient feud), since he claimed as issue of A; and in like manner D's son could have succeeded his great-uncle B. In order therefore to enable collateral relations (that is, those neither ancestors nor issue) of the grantee of a new feud to succeed him, it became customary, on granting a new feud, to provide that it should be held *ut feudum antiquum*, *i.e.*, in the same manner as if it had been an ancient feud. Descent being thus traced from an imaginary ancestor, a collateral relation of the person last seised could inherit, since he was supposed to trace his descent from the remote common ancestor, and thus an uncle could succeed his nephew. But this fiction was untenable as regarded a father and his son, for it is obvious that an inheritance claimed by the father as descending from an ancestor common to him and the son, could only have reached the son after the father's death; and therefore, if a man died without issue, he might be succeeded by his uncle or great-uncle, but could not be succeeded by his father or grandfather. Leaving for a short time any further reference to this point, let us now turn to the changes made by the statute in the first proposition contained in the old rule stated above, namely, that an inheritance shall descend lineally to the issue of the last person who died seised of it.

The act first (*h*) attaches a meaning to the word "purchaser," defining such an one in substance as being the person who last acquired the land otherwise than by descent, (this latter word again being defined as the title to inherit land by reason of consanguinity, as well where the heir is an ancestor or collateral relation as where he is a child or other issue). It then proceeds to enact (*i*) that in every case descent shall be traced from the purchaser, and in order to simplify the evidence required to establish the fact of any person's being the purchaser, provides that the person last entitled to the land shall be considered to have been the purchaser, unless it shall be proved that he inherited the same, in which case the person from whom he inherited shall be considered to have been the purchaser, unless it shall be proved that he inherited; and in like manner, the last person from whom the land shall be proved to have been inherited shall in every case be considered to have been the purchaser, unless he shall be proved to have inherited. And by a section of a subsequent act (*j*), which section is to be incorporated with the act now under consideration, it is provided that where there shall be a total failure of heirs of the purchaser, or where any

Alteration made by the act.

(*h*) S. 1.
(*i*) S. 2.
(*j*) S. 19 of the 22 & 23 Vict. c. 35.

lands shall be descendible as if an ancestor had been the purchaser thereof, and there shall be a total failure of heirs of such ancestor, the land is to descend, and the descent to be traced, from the person last entitled to the land as if he had been the purchaser.

Turning then the first proposition of Blackstone's canon into a rule in conformity with the statute, we may state it thus—

New First Canon.
I. Inheritances shall descend lineally to the issue of the last purchaser *in infinitum*.

Blackstone's 2nd, 3rd, and 4th Canons unaltered.
The second, third, and fourth canons as laid down by Blackstone remain unaltered. They are as follows—

Second Canon.
II. The male issue shall be admitted before the female.

Third Canon
III. Where there are two or more males in equal degree, the oldest only shall inherit: but the females all together.

Fourth Canon.
IV. The lineal descendants *in infinitum* of any person deceased shall represent their ancestor: that is, shall stand in the same place as the person himself would have done had he been living. Thus, the child, grandchild, or great-grandchild (either male or female) of the eldest son succeeds before the younger son, and so *in infinitum* (*k*).

Rule where tenant dies without issue. Blackstone's Fifth Canon.
We now come to the rules which govern the descent of an inheritance, if the person last in possession dies without issue. Blackstone's canon is, that on failure of lineal descendants or issue of the person last seised, the inheritance shall descend to his collateral relations,

---

(*k*) 2 Bl. Com. 217.

being of the blood of the first purchaser; and he adds that the collateral heir of the person last seised must be his next collateral kinsman of the whole blood. Under the old law, a relation of the half blood (that is, one not descended from a common pair of ancestors, male and female,) could not inherit: a man's half brother, for instance, could not inherit from him. The original feudal rule had been that no one could succeed to an inheritance unless he could show that he was descended from the first grantee of the feud. When collateral relations were allowed to inherit, it often became difficult to comply with this requirement, and a new rule was therefore introduced, namely, that no collateral relations could succeed unless they were of the whole blood of the person from whom descent was to be traced, that is, of the person last seised. Thus, if A had two sons, B and C, by different wives, and died, leaving B, the elder son, to succeed him: on B's death without issue, C could not inherit, not being of the whole blood of B, the person last seised: although if B had not lived to inherit, C could have taken as heir of A. Blackstone (*l*) goes into an elaborate defence of the rule, although he admits that it sometimes produced hardship, but it is now almost entirely done away with by the act, which provides (*m*) that any relation of the half blood of the person from whom descent is to be traced may be his heir, and is to be entitled next after any relations, in the same degree, of the whole blood, and their issue, where the common ancestor is a male, and next after the common ancestor, where the common ancestor is a female. The act also puts aside the feudal rule which prevented a father from succeeding his son, for it enacts (*n*) that every lineal ancestor is to be capable of being heir to any of his issue, and that in every case where there is no issue of the purchaser, his nearest lineal ancestor is to be

Alteration made by the act.

(*l*) 2 Bl. Com. 227.
(*m*) S. 9.
(*n*) S. 6.

his heir, in preference to any person tracing his descent through such lineal ancestor or in consequence of there being no descendant of such lineal ancestor. The reader will also recollect that, by canon IV.; the lineal descendants *in infinitum* of any person deceased are to represent their ancestor. We thus arrive at the following rules—

New Fifth Canon.

V. On failure of lineal descendants or issue of the purchaser, the inheritance shall descend to his nearest lineal ancestor, and the issue of such ancestor *in infinitum*.

New Sixth Canon.

VI. Every relation of the half blood of the purchaser is to be entitled next after any relations in the same degree of the whole blood, and their issue, where the common ancestor is a male; and next after the common ancestor, where the common ancestor is a female.

The next question is, how the nearest lineal ancestor is to be chosen—whether preference is to be given to ancestors on the father's side or on the mother's? and further, what is to be the order of inheritance amongst the favoured class—whether, for instance, an aunt is to inherit before a grandfather? The act supplies an answer to these questions, by enacting (*o*) what we may take as the next rule, viz.—

New Seventh Canon.

VII. None of the maternal ancestors of the person from whom the descent is to be traced, nor any of their descendants, shall be capable of inheriting until all his paternal ancestors and their descendants shall have failed; no female paternal ancestor of such person, nor any of her descendants, shall be capable of inheriting until all his male paternal ancestors and their descendants shall have failed; and no female maternal ancestor of such person, nor any of her descendants,

(*o*) S. 7.

OF AN ESTATE IN FEE SIMPLE.

shall be capable of inheriting until all his male maternal ancestors and their descendants shall have failed.

Thus we see, that on the death of the purchaser without issue, his father is the next heir, and after the father his issue, that is, the purchaser's brothers and sisters; the brothers taking singly in order of seniority, and being represented by their issue, if any: and on failure of these, the purchaser's sisters will be his coheiresses, and be in their turn represented by their issue. Failing issue of the purchaser's father, the inheritance will next go to his grandfather and his issue, and so on until the whole line of male paternal ancestors and their issue is exhausted.

After this, the female line on the father's side is to be admitted. It was formerly greatly disputed whether preference should, in such a case, be given to the nearer, or more remote, female ancestor; for instance, whether the purchaser's paternal grandmother, or his paternal great-grandmother, had the best claim to be taken as the root of descent, and similarly in tracing descents on the mother's side. This question is now settled by the act, which has decided (p) in favour of the more remote female ancestor, whether on the paternal or maternal side, and thus we arrive at our last rule.

VIII. Where there shall be a failure of male paternal ancestors of the person from whom the descent is to be traced, and their descendants, the mother of his more remote male paternal ancestor, or her descendants, shall be the heir or heirs of such person, in preference to the mother of a less remote male paternal ancestor, and her descendants: and where there shall be a failure of male maternal ancestors of such person, and their descendants, the mother

New Eighth Canon.

(p) S. 8.

of his more remote male maternal ancestor, and her descendants, shall be the heir or heirs of such person, in preference to the mother of a less remote male maternal ancestor, and her descendants. If, therefore, there is a failure of the purchaser's male paternal ancestors, ~~and~~ his heirs must be sought for amongst his female paternal ancestors, and his father's mother, or her descendants, will come last in order of selection. Next, if all the paternal ancestors, male and female, of the purchaser, and their heirs, have failed, recourse must be had to his maternal ancestors. In that case, his mother will first be his heir, and then descent must be traced through her ancestors, by the same process as has been followed in tracing descent through the purchaser's father, and thus, supposing all the intervening heirs to have failed, the inheritance will at last devolve upon his maternal grandmother and her heirs. If these fail, there will be no more heirs of the purchaser: in that case, the person last entitled must be sought for, and the process gone through again with him. Finally, if it is utterly impossible to find any person entitled to the inheritance, it will escheat to the Crown as lord of the fee.

CHAPTER VII.

OF COPYHOLDS.

THE origin of copyholds has been treated of in an earlier part of this work. It is, therefore, only necessary, as to that point, to add that no copyholds can be created at the present day. The existing form of copyhold tenure is the result of a number of very gradual changes, each of which, being an encroachment upon the rights of the lords of manors, was not recognised by the law until it had been impressed with the stamp of long-continued custom. Hence arose the saying, that "time is the nurse of manors (a)." And since it is manifestly impossible to create a custom, it follows that it is impossible to create a copyhold to be held according to that custom. Nor is it possible to create a copyhold, by providing for land being held according to the custom of some existing manor. For in every copyhold there must be "perfect tenure between very lord and very tenant (b);" in other words, all the services due from the tenant must be centred in one lord. But it has been for a long time impossible to originate such a tenure, inasmuch as the Statute of *Quia Emptores* (c), passed in the year 1290, enacted that every feoffee of lands should hold them of the same chief lord, and by the same services and customs, as his feoffor had done. If, then, a feoffor does not reserve any new services to himself the land is held by its former tenure; if he does, the services due from the tenant are not cen-

No copyhold tenure can be created now.

(a) Co. Cop. s. 31.
(b) Ibid.
(c) 18 Ed. I. c. 1.

tred in one lord, and there is not therefore a perfect tenure. "Upon the reason of this it is, that if the lord of a manor purchase foreign land, lying without the precincts and bounds of the manor, he cannot annex this to the manor, though the tenants be willing to do their services; for this amounteth to the creation of a new tenure, which cannot be effected at this day (*d*)." A *quasi* manor may however be created by act of parliament, as was done by the 37 Hen. VIII., c. 2, which enacted that certain parts of Hounslow Heath should be of the nature of copyholds. There is also an apparent exception to the general rule, in the case of the waste lands of a manor, for, in manors where there is a custom to that effect, part of the waste may, although never granted before, be granted by the lord to a tenant, to be held according to the custom of the manor. But this is not really an exception, for land of this description, having been granted by virtue of an immemorial custom, is considered to be as much a copyhold tenement as if it had been held from time immemorial by copy of court roll (*e*).

But quasi manor may be created by statute.

Case of grant of waste lands.

Ordinary manors may be divided into two kinds, namely, freehold and copyhold. Freehold manors are those which have freehold tenants; copyhold manors are those which have only tenants by base tenure, and it is to this latter kind that we shall, in general, refer in the following pages. There is, however, another variety of manor which should be briefly noticed, that, namely, which is distinguished as a customary manor. Manors of this kind are to be found principally on the border counties between England and Scotland, and were granted originally on condition of performing military service against the Scotch when required (*f*). They are held, in general, for lives, the lord being bound to renew the

---

(*d*) Co. Cop. s. 31.
(*e*) *Northwick* v. *Stanway*, 3 Bos. & P. 346, 347.
(*f*) *Doe* v. *Huntingdon*, 4 East, 271, 288.

terms when necessary, and are expressed to be held "according to the custom of the manor" only, and not "at the will of the lord;" but they are, in fact, merely a superior kind of copyholds, the freehold remaining in the lord, as in the case of ordinary copyholds (g).

It has been already mentioned that to every manor, as originally created, a court baron was an essential incident. The fact, however, that a court baron cannot be held in the manor (as happens, for instance, when there are not at least two freehold tenants holding of the manor and subject to escheat), although it puts an end to the manor in point of law (h), does not altogether extinguish it. Such a manor is said to be a "reputed" manor, and the lord may still exercise his prescriptive rights in it (i). Nor does the absence of a court baron prevent the holding of a customary court for the manor, and such a court may now be held by the lord of the manor, or by his steward or deputy, although there may not be any tenant present at it (j). *Reputed manors.*

Inasmuch as copyhold tenure depends upon custom, all dealings in copyholds must be regulated by the customs of the manor, the best evidence of which are the various entries made from time to time in the manor roll. Any one setting up a custom of a manor must show that it has been immemorial, uninterrupted, peaceably acquiesced in, reasonable, certain, and compulsory (k). *All dealings in manors regulated by custom.*

New estates in copyholds can only be granted by the lord of the manor, or his steward or deputy, and must be evidenced by entries in the manor roll. In *Estates in copyholds.*

(g) *Stephenson* v. *Hill*, Burr. 1273, 1278; *Portland* v. *Hill*, L. R. 2 Eq. 765.
(h) *Glover* v. *Lane*, 3 T. R. 445, 447.
(i) *Soane* v. *Ireland*, 10 East, 259.
(j) 4 & 5 Vict. c. 35, s. 86.
(k) 2 Wat. Cop. 46.

this, as in all other matters relating to copyholds, custom plays an important part. Thus, the tenant must hold according to the custom of the manor, and the grant itself must not be for an estate greater than that recognised by the custom; but if it is the custom to make grants in fee simple, lesser estates may, as a rule, be granted, since the power to grant a fee simple includes, ordinarily, a power to grant a lesser estate.

Estates tail. To this rule, however, there is one exception, for although an estate tail may be granted in copyholds where there is a custom to that effect, it is otherwise where there is no such custom (*l*). The reason for this is, that the Statute *De Donis* (*m*) only mentions hereditaments which can be given by charter or deed, and does not, therefore, apply to copyholds (*n*). Consequently, in the absence of a custom permitting lands in a manor to be entailed, the old rule of law still applies to lands of this tenure, and hence, a grant of them to a man and the heirs of his body would give him a fee simple conditional on his having issue born to him, and disposable by him immediately on the happening of that event (*o*). In order to prove that the custom of a manor authorizes entails, it must be shown not only that it is customary to limit estates in the manor to a grantee and the heirs of his body, but also that persons claiming in remainder under such a limitation have been admitted on the manor rolls.

Barring estates tail. If estates tail are permitted in any manor, they must be barred by a process analogous to that employed in the case of estates tail in lands of free tenure, and with the same formalities; for the 41st section of the Fines and Recoveries Abolition Act (*p*) enacts that no assurance by which any disposition of lands shall be effected

---

(*l*) *Heydon's Case,* 3 Rep. 7ᵃ.
(*m*) 13 Ed. I. c. 1.
(*n*) *Rowden* v. *Malster,* Cro. Car. 42.
(*o*) *Doe* v. *Clark,* 5 B. & Ald. 458.
(*p*) 3 & 4 Wm. IV. c. 74.

under the act by a tenant in tail thereof, shall, with certain exceptions, have any operation under the act, unless it be inrolled in the Court of Chancery within six calendar months after the execution thereof. And a subsequent section (*q*) of the same act provides, that all the previous clauses of the act, so far as circumstances and the different tenures will admit, shall apply to lands held by copy of court roll, except that a disposition of any such lands under the act by a tenant in tail thereof, whose estate shall be an estate at law, shall be made by surrender, and except that a disposition of any such lands under the act by a tenant in tail thereof whose estate shall be merely an estate in equity, may be made either by surrender, or by a deed as is afterwards provided by the act. It has been also decided that the surrender, or deed, whichever it may be, is invalid unless entered on the court rolls within six calendar months from the time of its being made or executed (*r*); and that if there is a previous tenant for life, he must give his consent to the entail being barred, and the deed by which he does so must be inrolled within the same time.

All grants of copyholds must be made under the usual services and returns, for in these matters the lord is only an instrument carrying out dealings warranted by the custom (*s*). Therefore even when copyhold lands have escheated to the lord, although he may change their nature if he pleases, yet if he still continues to dispose of them as copyhold, he is bound to observe the ancient customs precisely in every point (*t*). *Grants must conform to the custom of the manor.*

On the same principle, namely, that the lord is only an instrument, is founded the rule that the lord of a *Fitness of lord or his steward is immaterial.*

(*q*) S. 50.
(*r*) *Honywood* v. *Foster*, 30 Beav. 1; *Gibbons* v. *Snape*, 1 De G. J. & S. 621.
(*s*) See *Taverner* v. *Cromwell*, 4 Rep. 27ᵃ.
(*t*) 2 Bl. Com. 370; and see *Doe* v. *Strickland*, 2 Q. B. 792.

manor may, although only a tenant for life, make grants which will stand good after his decease, for the grantee's estate is not derived out of the lord's only, but stands on the custom (*u*); all such grants must, however, conform to the custom of the manor, otherwise they will be void (*v*). And the fact of the lord's being only an instrument causes the fitness of him or his agent to make a grant to be immaterial (*w*). In conferring estates in copyholds, the same technical words are necessary as in making grants of lands of freehold tenure.

Same technical words are used as in grants of freehold land.

Surrender and admittance. Every new tenant of a manor must be "admitted," and if he is a purchaser from any existing tenant, the latter must have previously "surrendered" his estate to the lord or his steward in order to allow of the admittance of the new tenant.

Surrender, followed by admittance, is founded on the theory that the copyholder is a tenant at the will of the lord, and was formerly essential to the validity of every transfer of copyholds, whether made during the tenant's lifetime or by his will. Consequently, no devise of copyholds was good at law, unless the testator had, during his lifetime, formally surrendered them to the use of his will, but the Court of Chancery would sometimes supply the want of surrender, in order to make provision for the tenant's wife, or children, or in favour of a creditor, or of a purchaser for value, or of a charity.

Enactments relative to surrender and admittance. 55 Geo. III. c. 192. The necessity for a surrender to the use of a will was partly taken away by the 55 Geo. III., c. 192, s. 1, which enacted that in all cases where by the custom of any manor any copyhold tenant of such manor might, by his or her last will and testament, dispose of or

---

(*u*) See *Swayne's Case*, 8 Rep. 63ᵃ.
(*v*) *Doe* v. *Strickland*, 2 Q. B. 792, 810.
(*w*) *Eddleston* v. *Collins*, 3 De G. M. & G. 1.

appoint his or her copyhold tenements, the same
having been surrendered to such uses as should be
declared by such last will and testament, every disposition or charge made, or to be made, by any such
last will and testament, by any person who should die
after the passing of the act, of any such copyhold
tenements, should be as valid and effectual to all intents and purposes, although no surrender should have
been made to the use of the last will and testament of
such person, as the same would have been if a surrender had been made to the use of such will. But
since the act only professed to supply the want of a
surrender by a person competent to make one, and
since a surrender, even when made, did not pass the
legal estate in copyholds to a devisee or a surrenderee
until their admittance, the act did not enable an unadmitted devisee (*x*), or surrenderee (*y*), of copyholds to
devise them. Neither could copyholds pass by will,
where the surrender to the use of a will had preceded
the admittance of the testator (*z*). Now, however,
the Wills Act enables every person to dispose by
will of all his real estate which, if not so disposed of,
would devolve upon his heir at law, or customary
heir (*a*): and this power is to extend to all real estate
of the nature of customary freehold, or tenant right,
or customary, or copyhold, notwithstanding that the
testator may not have surrendered the same to the
use of his will, or notwithstanding that, being entitled
as heir, devisee, or otherwise to be admitted thereto,
he shall not have been admitted thereto (*b*).

7 Wm. IV. &
1 Vict. c. 26.

A surrender could, formerly, only be effected by the
tenant's coming to the steward in court, or (if the

4 & 5 Vict. c.
35.

(*x*) *Doe* v. *Lates*, 7 A. & E. 195.
(*y*) *Matthews* v. *Osborne*, 13 C. B. 919.
(*z*) *Doe* v. *Tofield*, 11 East, 246.
(*a*) A customary heir is the person entitled as heir by the custom of manor.
(*b*) 7 Wm. IV. & 1 Vict. c. 26, s. 3.

custom allowed) out of court (*c*), and then, by the delivery of some customary symbol (*d*), resigning into the hands of the lord, all his title and interest to the estate, in trust to be again granted out by the lord, to such persons, and on such trusts, as were named in the surrender, and the custom of the manor would warrant (*e*) : but now, by the Copyhold Act 1841 (*f*), the lord or his steward may (*g*), either in or out of the manor, make grants of land in the usual way, and may also (*h*) admit new tenants, either within or without the manor, and without holding any court for the purpose. No special words are necessary to make a good surrender : any words signifying a clear intention to that effect being sufficient.

Presentment formerly necessary.

Before the passing of the act lastly referred to, the surrender, if made in court, was immediately inrolled, and the new tenant became thereupon entitled to admittance : if it had been made out of court, it was necessary that this fact should be "presented," and the surrender inrolled, at a customary court. If this was not done within the time prescribed by the custom of the manor, which was generally at the next meeting of the court, the surrender was void at law (*i*), and the surrenderee therefore no longer able to claim admittance. Now, however, all difficulties of this kind have been removed by the act which enacts (*j*)

Change made by the Copyhold Act 1841.

that every surrender, made either at any court at which the homage are assembled, or out of court, and also every grant and admission, are to be forthwith entered on the roll of the manor, and then

---

(*c*) In some manors the custom allowed the tenant to surrender his estate into the hands of two other tenants.
(*d*) This symbol was often a rod or twig, from which cause copyholders are sometimes spoken of as tenants *by the verge* (Lat. *virga*, a twig).
(*e*) 2 Bl. Com. 366; 4 & 5 Vict. c. 35.
(*f*) 4 & 5 Vict. c. 35.
(*g*) S. 87.
(*h*) S. 88.
(*i*) Co. Litt. 62ᵃ.
(*j*) S. 89.

to have the force of a presentment, which (k) is no longer essential to the validity of the admission of any person.

The lord is bound to observe the confidence on which the estate was surrendered to him, and can, if necessary, be compelled to do so, by a writ of *mandamus* from the Court of Queen's Bench.

It follows, from the above, that a surrender has become practically a mode of conveyance, of which an admittance is only the formal completion, and consequently admittance, when made, dates back to the time of the surrender. The admittance follows the form of the surrender as to the estate conferred, the formal part consisting in the delivery, by the steward to the tenant, of the customary symbol of admittance. The tenant is also, in strictness, bound to take an oath of fealty on admittance, but this is now invariably respited, an entry to that effect being, at the same time, made on the court roll.

The statute of Charles the Second which abolished military tenures (l) having expressly excepted copyholds from its operation, the lord is still entitled to a fine on the admittance of every new tenant; but since the fine only becomes due by reason of admittance, he is not entitled to it until after admittance (m), except in manors where there is a special custom to the contrary. He is, moreover, bound to admit the person entitled, although the amount of the fine may be in dispute (n); that being a matter which can be properly settled afterwards, and if there is any doubt as to the proper person to be admitted, the lord is bound to admit all persons who claim; as otherwise he would

<small>Incidents of copyhold estates.</small>

<small>Fines on alienation.</small>

(k) S. 90.
(l) 12 Car. II. c. 24.
(m) R. v. *Hendon*, 2 T. R. 484; *Graham* v. *Sime*, 1 East, 632.
(n) R. v. *Wellesley*, 2 E. & B. 924.

be taking upon himself the decision of the conflicting claims (o).

<small>Amount of fine depends on custom.</small> The amount of the fine to be paid is *primâ facie* uncertain, and must, partly, depend upon the custom of the manor. Until the time of Elizabeth, the courts do not appear to have imposed any restriction on a <small>But custom must be reasonable.</small> custom as to the amount of the fine. In that reign, however, it was decided that the amount of the fine <small>Rule as to amount of fine on admission of one tenant to a single tenement.</small> must be reasonable (*p*). And it appears to have been gradually assumed that no fine for the admission of a single tenant to one tenement should exceed the amount of two years' improved value of the land, that is, the value of the land after making a deduction of the annual amount necessary to keep the premises in repair (*q*). This rule, after some little fluctuation of opinion, is now firmly established (*r*), but it applies only to cases where the lord is bound to admit, and where he is entitled to a fine on the admittance of every new tenant. If the admittance is voluntary, the lord may make any bargain he pleases.

<small>The lord cannot compel the admittance of a purchaser.</small> If a copyhold tenement is surrendered by a tenant in favour of a purchaser, the lord has no right, except by virtue of a special custom, to compel the purchaser to be admitted and thus make himself liable to the payment of a fine. For the lord's right to a fine on alienation only arises upon an actual transfer of his tenant's land, and not upon a mere agreement to transfer, to which alone a surrender without admittance <small>Rule where a copyholder dies.</small> amounts in law. But if the tenant dies, the case is different. For in that event, the lord is entitled to have on the manor roll a new tenant, capable of performing the services due in respect of the tenement in question, and he has also a right to a fine when that tenant is admitted. As a general rule, the heir or

---

(*o*) *R.* v. *Hexham*, 5 A. & E. 559.
(*p*) *Jackman* v. *Hoddesdon*, Cro. Eliz. 351.
(*q*) *Richardson* v. *Kensit*, 5 Man. & Gr. 485.
(*r*) *Willowe's Case*, 13 Rep. 1; *Grant* v. *Astle*, 2 Doug. 722, 724ª.

devisee of a copyholder cannot be compelled to be admitted to the estate of his ancestor or testator, but may, if he prefers, forfeit the estate instead. The lord is, however, permitted to take measures in order to force him to decide which course he will adopt. With this object the lord may, on the decease of any tenant, make proclamation for the person entitled to his estate to come in and be admitted to it. This proclamation must be made at three consecutive courts, and all the customary ceremonies must be strictly observed (s). If, after due proclamation, no one appears in order to be admitted, the lord is entitled to seize the lands, either absolutely, if there is a custom to that effect (t), or else *quousque*, that is, until some person comes to be admitted. Proclamation.

Seizure, absolute or *quousque*.

A custom to seize absolutely was never good as against an heir beyond seas, nor against married women, infants, or lunatics, who from their position are incapable of being admitted.(u). As to them, it is now enacted by the 11 Geo. IV. & 1 Wm. IV., c. 65 (following the 9 Geo. I., c. 29), that infants, married women, or lunatics may be represented, for the purpose of admittance to copyhold estates, by their guardians, attorneys, or committees, and (v) that the lord may, if necessary, appoint such persons for the purpose of admittance: after their admittance, the lord's fines may (w) be demanded by a notice in writing, and if they are not paid he may seize until payment, but he must, upon demand, render quarterly accounts of his receipts, and (x) when the amount due for the fines is satisfied, he is to deliver up possession; moreover (y), the estates of the above persons are not to be liable Protection given by statute to persons under disability.

(s) *Bover* v. *Trueman*, 1 B. & Ad. 736.
(t) *Doe* v. *Hellier*, 3 T. R. 162.
(u) *Lechford's Case*, 8 Rep. 99$_a$.
(v) S. 5.
(w) S. 6.
(x) S. 7.
(y) S. 9.

to forfeiture for non-payment of fines or refusal to appear and be admitted.

Admittance compulsory where there is a special custom.
In some manors there is a custom by which the heir of a copyholder who has died intestate can be compelled to come in and be admitted, and such a custom is good, and in that case the heir must pay the proper fine: the same rule would probably apply also to a devisee, if there were any custom compelling him to be admitted (z).

Amount of fine payable in special cases. On admittance to several tenements.
The rule as to the amount of the fine payable on the admission of a single tenant to one tenement has been already stated. If there are more tenements than one, held by different services, the lord is entitled to a fine for each, and it is his duty to assess the amount of each fine separately (a), but if undivided tenements forming separate fees are afterwards re-united in one person, the lord is entitled to one fine only.

On admittance of more than one tenant.
If there is more than one tenant to be admitted, the lord is entitled to a fine in respect of each, but if the tenants only make up one fee, as in the case of a tenant for life and remainder-man, or of joint-tenants, or co-parceners (b), only one admission is necessary, although the amount of the fine may be greater than on the admission of a single tenant (c). If one of several joint-tenants is admitted, his admittance is that of all the other joint-tenants, who become, consequently, thereupon bound to pay the customary fine (d).

Tenant for life and remainder-man.
It does not appear to be certain what fine the lord is entitled to, in the absence of custom, on the admission of a tenant for life and remainder-man (e).

(z) 1 Wat. Cop. 290ⁿ.
(a) *Hobart* v. *Hammond*, 4 Rep. 27ᵇ; *Grant* v. *Astle*, 2 Doug. 722.
(b) *R.* v. *Bonsall*, 3 B. & C. 173.
(c) *Fitch* v. *Stuckley*, 4 Rep. 22ᵇ.
(d) See *Bence* v. *Gilpin*, L. R. 3 Ex. 76.
(e) Scriv. Cop. 227, note (y).

Where there is a custom, the fine payable by the remainder-man is usually one half of that payable by the tenant for life (*f*). In the case of joint-tenants, the rule is that the lord is entitled to a single fine for the first tenant, one half of that for the second, one fourth for the third, and so on, by which means the total amount of the fine can never quite amount to four years' value of the land (*g*). *Joint-tenants.*

It was formerly necessary for a copyholder who wished to dispose of his estate by will, first to surrender it to the lord to the uses of his (the copyholder's) will, and then to make his will, naming the devisee, or the person who was to carry out the intentions expressed in the will. A surrender to the use of the copyholder's will was a matter of right, without any special custom, but unless it were done, no devise of his estate could be effectual. We have already seen that the law on this point has been altered by the 55 Geo. III., c. 192 and the 7 Wm. IV. and 1 Vict., c. 26, but the latter act, in order to prevent the power of devising copyholds without a previous surrender from operating to the prejudice of lords of manors, further provides (*h*) that when the devisee of an unadmitted testator is admitted to copyholds, the same fines shall be paid as would have been payable if the testator himself had previously been admitted. Consequently, on such an admission, the lord is entitled to a double fine, and in this case half at least, if not the whole, of the fine must be paid before the new tenant can claim admittance (*i*). *Heir or devisee of an unadmitted copyholder.*

A tenant is liable, in some manors, to pay a fine on every change of the lord, and also on obtaining a licence to demise any part of his lands. The former *Fines on change of lord, and on licence to demise.*

(*f*) 1 Wat. Cop. 374.
(*g*) *Wilson* v. *Hoare*, 10 A. & E. 236.
(*h*) S. 4.
(*i*) *R.* v. *Wilberton*, 29 L. T. 126.

custom is good where the change takes place by the death of the lord (*j*), but not otherwise. With regard to the latter, the rule is that, in the absence of custom, a copyholder cannot demise his land for more than a year, unless he first obtain a licence from his lord (*k*); otherwise he will forfeit his estate, and cannot obtain any relief, even in equity (*l*). There is no rule of law as to the reasonableness of the amount of fine payable on a licence to demise, but where there is a custom in the manor regulating that amount, both the lord and the tenant are bound by it (*m*). If, however, there is no custom, the lord may make any demand he pleases; but a tendency to claim exorbitant fines, and thus prevent improvements from being made on the land, is, as we shall see hereafter, checked by various acts of parliament, under which a copyholder can compel the lord to enfranchise the land altogether.

Steward's fees. In addition to the payment of fines to the lord, the copyholder is liable to pay fees to the lord's steward, whenever the services of this officer are called into requisition,—a case which occurs most often on the admittance of a new tenant. The amount of the steward's fees is, like that of the lord's fines, determined by the custom of each manor, and it seems that the courts will not interfere to regulate the occasions on which a steward is entitled to fees, that point depending entirely on the custom (*n*). But they will not allow him to demand an unreasonable amount for any fee (*o*), and where there is no special custom on the subject, he can only claim a sum proportionate to the amount of work done by him (*p*).

(*j*) *Lowther* v. *Raw*, 2 Bro. P. C. 451.
(*k*) See *Kensy* v. *Richardson*, Cro. Eliz. 728.
(*l*) *Peachy* v. *Somerset*, Str. 447, and, with notes, 2 L. C. 1082.
(*m*) See *Porphyry* v. *Legingham*, 2 Keb. 344.
(*n*) *Evans* v. *Upsher*, 16 Mee & W. 675.
(*o*) See *Traherne* v. *Gardner*, 5 E. & B. 913, 940.
(*p*) *Everest* v. *Glyn*, 6 Taunt, 425; *Traherne* v. *Gardner*, 5 E. & B. 913.

We have already seen why it is that the payment of fines is still one of the incidents of copyhold tenure. The same reason makes a copyholder liable to those other burdens which we are about to enumerate.

The first to be mentioned consists of those pay- *Quit Rents.* ments, generally known as Quit Rents, which represent either small rents originally payable by the tenants of a manor according to agreement, but the amount of which has become settled, or else sums which have been fixed upon by the lord and the tenant as a compensation for those personal, and other, services to which the former was anciently entitled. Quit rents cannot be claimed by the lord unless he can show that they have been paid immemorially and without variation (*q*). Another relic of the old system *Heriot custom.* of tenures is the right which the lord has, in certain manors, to receive Heriots from his tenants. This is a custom whereby the lord is entitled, on the death of a tenant, to claim some personal chattel belonging to the deceased, or, occasionally, a fixed sum of money instead. This custom would seem, in the case of free *Origin of the* tenants, to have been substituted for a still older *custom.* custom, whereby the lord was entitled, on the death of a tenant, to claim the military weapons of the latter; and in the case of villein tenants, to have grown out of a favour accorded to them by the lord, who contented himself with taking their best chattel instead of seizing all their goods, as he might lawfully have done, seeing that the villeins themselves were his property: and as the villeins became gradually emancipated, this custom grew to be a fixed right.

This form of heriot was called Heriot Custom, in *Distinguished* order to distinguish it from Heriot Service, which *from heriot service.* was in fact only a reservation, in favour of the lord,

---

(*q*) Scriv. Cop. 248.

of a chattel, instead of money, by way of rent. A heriot by custom can only be claimed where the lord can show an immemorial usage for its payment, and is only due on the death of a tenant who is solely seised of his fee. Consequently, when a number of persons make up one tenant, as in the case of joint-tenants, or co-parceners, no heriot is payable until the death of the last survivor of them. And although if land held by one tenant is given by him to several persons, to take as tenants in common, each of them must pay a separate heriot, yet if the same property is afterwards re-united in one person, the lord becomes again entitled to one heriot only (*r*). But even where there is one tenant, a heriot is payable in respect of every distinct tenement, except in manors where there is a special custom to the contrary (*s*).

When heriot can be claimed.

Rights of lord and tenant as to timber and minerals.

The distinction between freehold and copyhold tenure is also strongly marked in questions as to the relative rights of the lord and of his tenants, with respect to the timber or minerals which are on, or under, the tenant's land. For whereas in freeholds a tenant in fee has an absolute dominion over such property, the contrary rule prevails in copyholds. We know that a copyholder is, in contemplation of law, only a tenant at will of his lands, which are supposed to belong to his lord. He is, therefore, in the absence of custom, in a position similar to that of a tenant at will of freeholds, being unable to do any act which amounts to a committal of waste, such as cutting down timber, or opening mines. On the other hand, the lord cannot, without a custom, do any of these acts. For his entry on the tenant's land for such a purpose would, if lawful, have the effect of determining the tenancy at will (*t*), and, as has been

---

(*r*) *Garland* v. *Jekyll*, 2 Bing. 273; *Holloway* v. *Berkeley*, 9 Dow & Ry. 83, overruling *Attree* v. *Scutt*, 6 East, 476.
(*s*) See Scriv. Cop. 264, note (*s*).
(*t*) See *Heydon & Smith's Case*, 13 Rep. 67.

already explained, the copyholder's tenancy, although nominally at will, cannot be determined at the arbitrary pleasure of his lord. If then, there is a custom author- *In the absence* izing either the lord or the tenant to cut timber or *of custom neither can cut* open mines on the land of the latter, that custom is *timber or open* good (*u*), except where the tenant's estate is merely *mines.* one for life (*v*), or *pour autre vie* (*w*); but failing its existence, neither party can exercise such rights without the consent of the other. This point was first settled with reference to the opening of mines. In an early case (*x*), the lord of a manor applied to the Court of Chancery for an injunction to restrain one of his tenants from continuing to work a copper mine, newly opened by the tenant. The court sent the case to a court of law for trial before a jury, who found that the tenant's acts had not been authorized by any custom of the manor. The Court of Chancery therefore decided that neither the tenant without the consent of the lord, nor the lord without the consent of the tenant, could dig in a new mine. This rule was subsequently extended to a case where the lord sought to abstract minerals from under his tenant's land, by driving a shaft from adjoining land of his own (*y*). A decision consistent with the above was afterwards arrived at in the Court of King's Bench, on an action by a copyholder, against his lord, for entering upon the lands in the tenant's possession and there digging for coal (*z*).

A distinction was, at one time, sought to be made between the cutting of trees and the opening of mines, on the ground that minerals need not be worked at any particular time, whereas timber, if not cut when ripe, would rot away and be wasted (*a*). But

---

(*u*) *Stebbing* v. *Gosnal*, Cro. Eliz. 629.
(*v*) *Powel* v. *Peacock*, Cro. Jac. 30.
(*w*) *Mardiner* v. *Ellcott*, 2 T. R. 746.
(*x*) *Winchester* v. *Knight*, 1 P. W. 406, 407.
(*y*) *Lewis* v. *Branthwaithe*, 2 B. & Ad. 437.
(*z*) *Bourne* v. *Taylor*, 10 East, 189.
(*a*) See *Ashmead* v. *Ranger*, Salk. 638.

it is now clearly settled that the courts will not attend to any consideration of this kind (b). A copyholder may, however, without being authorized by any custom, work mines or quarries which have been already lawfully opened upon his land. He is also entitled by the custom of most manors to estovers, and would seem to be entitled to them of common right, apart from any custom, since he, unlike an ordinary tenant at will, is bound to keep his premises in repair (c).

Rights of Common.

In the first chapter of this work, it was stated that the lord who obtained the grant of a manor from the Crown ordinarily allowed part of it to remain unenclosed, in order that it might serve as grazing ground for the cattle of himself, or of his tenants, or as wood or marsh land, wherein his tenants were permitted to cut turf, or to take timber for repairs. Long-continued custom has, in most manors, turned these privileges of the tenants into rights, subject however to such modifications as have also become customary; and these rights, being shared by all the tenants together with the lord, have acquired the name of Rights of Common.

Ordinary meaning of term.
Common of Piscary.
Common of Turbary.
Common of Estovers.

A right of common, in its most usual acceptation, signifies a right of pasture for cattle, but the term is also applied to rights of fishing (common of piscary), of cutting turf (common of turbary), and of taking timber for repairs (common of estovers). In addition to the above, the tenants may have a customary right to dig on the lord's waste, and to remove thence soil or gravel.

Rights of common are founded on prescription.

These customs are founded on prescription, that is, on the presumption of law that a right which has been exercised from time immemorial was originally ac-

---

(b) *Whitechurch* v. *Holworthy*, 19 Ves. 212, and 4 Mau. & Sel. 340.
(c) See *Heydon & Smith's Case*, 13 Rep. 67; *East* v. *Harding*, Cro. Eliz. 498.

quired by means of a grant from the then lord of the manor to his tenants (*d*). But the courts will not support any alleged right which is unreasonable, for they will decline to believe that it could ever have been granted. For instance, they have refused to presume a grant under which the tenants of a manor claimed to exclude the lord altogether from the waste (*e*), and, conversely, have held customs to be bad under which the lord claimed to make long leases of the whole of the waste (*f*), or to enclose it entirely at his pleasure (*g*), since such privileges on his part would be inconsistent with the existence of commonable rights in his tenants. The lord of a manor is, however, empowered by the Statute of Merton (*h*) to enclose the waste, provided he leaves sufficient for the tenant's pasture (*i*), and a custom for him to grant part of it with the consent of his tenants (*j*) is good, as is also one enabling him to dig for clay or minerals in the waste, even though he may thereby not leave sufficient pasturage for the tenant's cattle (*k*).

Hence must be reasonable.

We come next to the consideration of the copyholder's estate, apart from any rights of the lord. It will be recollected that an estate of inheritance in freehold land is, in certain cases, subject to the incidents of curtesy and dower. These are reproduced, with some variations, in copyholds, but both their existence and their peculiar form depend upon, and are regulated by, the custom of each manor (*l*). Thus, there can be no curtesy in such an estate except

Curtesy and Freebench.

No curtesy except by custom.

(*d*) See *Gateward's Case*, 6 Rep. 59ᵇ.
(*e*) Co. Litt. 122ᵃ; *Hopkins* v. *Robinson*, 1 Mod. 74.
(*f*) *Badger* v. *Ford*, 3 B. & Ald. 153.
(*g*) *Arlett* v. *Ellis*, 7 B. & C. 346, 365.
(*h*) 20 Hen. III. c. 4.
(*i*) See *Betts* v. *Thompson*, L. R. 6 Ch. 732.
(*j*) *Steel* v. *Prickett*, 2 Stark, 463, 470.
(*k*) *Bateson* v. *Green*, 5 T. R. 411.
(*l*) See *Brown's Case*, 4 Rep. 21ᵃ.

by custom (*m*), but, on the other hand, where there is a custom, it is not always necessary that the husband should have had issue born to him, and it would even seem to be doubtful whether the birth of issue is in any case essential (*n*). A husband may also have an estate by curtesy, where his wife has had an equitable estate of inheritance in copyholds (*o*), except in cases where the wife's estate has been given to her entirely for her separate use (*p*).

Birth of issue not always necessary.

Curtesy in equitable estates.

Freebench depends upon custom.

Dower is more generally known in copyholds as Freebench. It only exists when sanctioned by custom (*q*), by which also it is regulated. The widow's right to freebench does not, except in some special cases (*r*), attach to any land other than that of which her husband died seised (*s*). Hence, any surrender made by him will bar her right to freebench, although the surrenderee may not be admitted until after the husband's death (*t*), since, as previously mentioned, admittance, when it takes place, dates back to the time of the corresponding surrender. Neither is she entitled to dower out of copyholds to which her husband had not been admitted, although they had been surrendered to his use (*u*). It would seem that the Dower Act (*v*) does not apply to copyholds (*w*). But a widow who has had any other provision made for her out of her husband's lands, will be compelled to choose between that and her dower (*x*).

May be defeated by husband's surrender.

(*m*) *Rivet's Case*, 4 Rep. 22ᵇ. The word "cannot" is evidently omitted in the report.
(*n*) See 2 Wat. Cop. 74; Scriv. Cop. 64.
(*o*) See *Sweetapple* v. *Bindon*, 2 Ver. 536; *Cunningham* v. *Moody*, 1 Ves. 174.
(*p*) *Hearle* v. *Greenbank*, 1 Ves. 298, 306.
(*q*) *Shaw* v. *Thompson*, 4 Rep. 30ᵇ.
(*r*) See *Doe* v. *Gwinnell*, 1 Q. B. 682.
(*s*) *Benson* v. *Scott*, 4 Mod. 251; *Godwin* v. *Winsmore*, 2 Atk. 525, 526.
(*t*) *Powdrell* v. *Jones*, 18 Jur. 1111.
(*u*) *Smith* v. *Adams*, 18 Jur. 968.
(*v*) 3 & 4 Wm. IV. c. 105.
(*w*) *Powdrell* v. *Jones*, 18 Jur. 1111, 1112.
(*x*) *Walker* v. *Walker*, 1 Ves. 54.

We come next to the alienation of the copyholder's *Alienation of* estate, which may be either involuntary, as where it is *the copy-holder's estate.* taken for payment of his debts, or is forfeited to his lord, or voluntary, as when he disposes of it during his lifetime, or by his will.

Copyholds could not formerly be extended under a writ of *elegit*, for non-payment of the tenant's debts. Now, however, the 1 & 2 Vict., c. 110, has (*y*) ex- *Judgments.* pressly included lands and hereditaments of copyhold or customary tenure amongst those which may be taken in execution under such a writ, but provides that the party to whom any copyhold or customary lands shall be delivered in execution shall be liable, and is thereby required, to make, perform, and render to the lord of the manor, or other person entitled, all such and the like payments and services as the person against whom such execution shall be issued would have been bound to make, perform, and render, in case such execution had not issued; and that the party so suing out such execution, and to whom any such copyhold or customary lands shall have been so delivered in execution, shall be entitled to hold the same until the amount of such payments and the value of such services, as well as the amount of the judgment, shall have been levied.

Forfeiture of a copyholder's land is incurred if he, *Forfeiture.* without licence from his lord, and unauthorized by custom, commits on his land any act of waste, either voluntary or permissive (*z*), or if he, under similar circumstances, demise his land for more than one year (*a*); but a copyholder may safely make a lease for one year, with a condition to renew it the next year, and so on, for this passes no interest greater than that for one year.

We have already seen that a voluntary alienation *Wills of copy-holds.*

(*y*) S. 11.
(*z*) *Clifton* v. *Molineux*, 4 Rep. 27ᵃ.
(*a*) *East* v. *Harding*, Cro. Eliz. 498; *Peachy* v. *Somerset*, Str. 447.

of his land by a copyholder requires, if made by some instrument other than a will, a previous surrender to the lord of the manor, and that the same formalities were formerly essential to the devise of a legal interest in copyholds. An equitable interest in copyholds cannot be the subject of a surrender, excepting an equitable estate tail, and the equitable estate of a married woman, for which special provisions have been made by the Fines and Recoveries Abolition Act (*b*). Hence an equitable interest in an estate which can be disposed of by will, always passed by will, without a previous surrender (*c*), and it followed that the devisee of such an interest could also devise it without a surrender (*d*). And now the Wills Act (*e*) has made a surrender to the use of a will unnecessary, in all cases where it was only a matter of form (*f*). From this it will be seen that a will of copyholds is now similar to one of freeholds, but a remark may be made here as to the best form of devise, where it is desired that such property should be sold immediately after the testator's death.

Devise on trust for sale.

A devise to trustees on trust for sale will give them an estate in joint-tenancy, and we have seen that a larger fine is payable on the admittance of joint-tenants than on that of a single tenant (*g*). It is true that this difficulty may be partly overcome by making all the trustees except one disclaim, for in such a case the lord is bound to admit that one on payment of a single fine (*h*). But it will still be necessary to pay a second fine on the admittance of the purchaser. The better plan, therefore, in the case supposed, is for the testator to devise the estate to such uses as the trus-

---

(*b*) 3 & 4 Wm. IV. c. 74, ss. 50, 90.
(*c*) *Tuffnell* v. *Page*, 2 Atk. 37.
(*d*) *Phillips* v. *Phillips*, 1 My. & K. 649.
(*e*) 7 Wm. IV. & 1 Vict. c. 26, s. 3.
(*f*) See *Doe* v. *Bartle*, 5 B. & Ald. 492; *Edwards* v. *Champion*, 3 De G. M. & G. 202.
(*g*) *Wilson* v. *Hoare*, 10 A. & E. 236.
(*h*) *Wellesley* v. *Withers*, 4 E. & B. 750.

~~ees of his will shall appoint; they may then sell without being admitted, and the lord must admit their vendee on payment of a single fine (i). It is to be noticed that this~~ plan cannot be adopted where the estate is not to be sold. It is well settled that the will of a copyholder is nothing more than a direction to the lord as to the person who is to be admitted into the tenancy (j), and that on his death his estate descends to his heir, subject to the right of his devisees to be admitted. Consequently, if his devisees are not trustees, and choose to disclaim the benefits conferred on them by the will, the heir has a right to be admitted on payment of a single fine (k). But if the devisees are trustees the case is different. For under such circumstances, unless the trustees disclaim their trust altogether, the lord cannot be compelled to admit the heir (l), although he will not be allowed to seize *quousque* if the heir is willing to be admitted (m).

It remains to add, with reference to this part of our subject, that the descent of copyholds is, in the absence of custom, the same as that of freeholds, but there is often some custom under which they descend in a different way (n), and such customs, when established, are good.

<small>Descent of copyholds.</small>

The foregoing remarks will have made it apparent that copyhold tenure is by no means so advantageous to a tenant as freehold, whilst the lord is often much hampered by the difficulties which lie in the way of his establishing such rights as he has. Various statutes have accordingly been passed with the object of giving facilities for the conversion of copyhold,

<small>Enfranchisement.</small>

<small>Statutes relating to enfranchisement.</small>

(i) *Holder* v. *Preston*, 2 Wils. 400 ; *R.* v. *Wilson*, 11 W. R. 70.
(j) *Glass* v. *Richardson*, 9 Ha. 698, 701, 2 De G. M. & G. 658 ;. *Garland* v. *Mead*, L. R. 6 Q. B. 441, 447.
k) *R.* v. *Wilson*, 10 B. & C. 80.
(l) *R.* v. *Garland*, L. R. 5 Q. B. 269.
(m) *Garland* v. *Mead*, L. R. 6 Q. B. 441.
(n) See *Garland* v. *Mead*, L. R. 6 Q. B. 441.

into freehold, tenure; and a brief notice of them will form the concluding part of this chapter. The first *Copyhold Act 1841.* to be noticed is the Copyhold Act 1841 (*o*). This act commences by reciting (*p*) that it is expedient to provide the means for an adequate compensation for the rents, fines, and heriots payable to the lords of manors in respect of lands of copyhold and customary tenure, and in respect of other lands subject to such payments, or any of them, and for facilitating the voluntary enfranchisement of such lands, and for improving such tenure. It then proceeds (*q*) to appoint *Appoints copyhold Commissioners.* Copyhold Commissioners for carrying out the provisions of the act, and enacts (*r*) that any lord or *Lord and tenants may agree on commutation of rents, fines, and heriots, and of lord's rights in timber.* lords of any manor, whose interest shall not be less than one-fourth of the whole annual value of such manor, or any tenant or tenants of any manor to the number of ten, or where there shall not be so many tenants as ten, then one-half of the tenants of such manor, may call a meeting of the lords and tenants of the manor, for the purpose of making an agreement for the general commutation of the rents, fines, and heriots thereafter to become due in respect of lands holden of such manor, and of the lord's rights in timber. The lords and tenants present at this meeting may, provided the tenants are not less in number than three-fourths of the tenants of the manor, and that the interest of the lord and the interest of the tenants in the manor are not less than three-fourths of the total value of the manor, proceed to execute such an agreement. And the commutation may also, by express agreement, extend to rights in mines and *Considerations for enfranchisement.* minerals. The agreement for the commutation of the rights of the lord may (*s*) be for the payment of an annual sum by way of rent-charge, and of a small

---

(*o*) 4 & 5 Vict. c. 35.
(*p*) S. 1.
(*q*) S. 2.
(*r*) S. 13.
(*s*) S. 14.

fixed fine, in no case exceeding five shillings, on death or alienation, or for the payment of a fine only, on death or alienation or at any fixed period or periods, to be agreed upon by the parties (*t*). It is to be (*u*) confirmed by the copyhold commissioners, and is then to be binding on all persons interested in the manor. The act also enables any individual tenant to free his land from the various burdens before enumerated, by providing (*v*) that it shall be lawful for the lord of any manor, or for any tenant of such manor (whatever may be their respective interests), to enter into an agreement, with the consent of the commissioners, for the commutation of the lord's rights to rents, fines, and heriots, or of any of such rights respectively, and any other of the lord's rights affecting the land which shall be included in such agreement: the commutation being made in consideration of a rent-charge and of a fine, or of a fine alone.

Commutation to be confirmed by copyhold commissioners, and to be binding on all persons interested in the manor. Individual tenant may enter into an agreement with his lord.

Besides thus alleviating the principal inconveniences of copyhold tenure, the act provides for their total abolition. For it further enacts (*w*) that it shall be lawful for the lord of any manor, whatever may be his estate or interest therein, with the consent of the commissioners, at any time after the passing of the act, to enfranchise all, or any, of the lands holden of his manor, in consideration of such sums of money as shall be agreed to be paid by the tenant or tenants whose lands shall be enfranchised; and that it shall be lawful for any tenant, whatever may be his estate or interest, with the consent of the commissioners, to accept such enfranchisement on the terms agreed upon. This is followed by a proviso that whenever the estate of any party to such enfranchisement shall be less than an estate in fee simple in possession, or

Voluntary enfranchisement under the act.

Notice to be given in certain cases.

(*t*) SS. 14, 15.
(*u*) S. 23.
(*v*) S. 52.
(*w*) S. 56.

C.   M

corresponding copyhold or customary estate, notice shall be given to the other parties interested in the estate, and if they dissent from the proposed arrangement, the commissioners are to withhold their consent to it until, upon further inquiry, they shall be satisfied that it is not fairly open to objection. Provision is also made (*x*) for the distribution of the enfranchisement money, or of the liability to pay it, amongst the successive lords or tenants between whom the agreement is made, when such persons have, respectively, limited interests in the enfranchised lands. After a commutation of the lord's rights under the act, the lands included in such commutation are to be held and conveyed in the same way as before the commutation (*y*), but they are to cease to be subject to any customary mode of descent, or to any custom relating to freebench, or curtesy, and are, instead, to become subject to the laws relating to descents, dower, and curtesy, which are, for the time being, applicable to lands held in free and common socage. Lands which have been enfranchised under the act are (*z*) to become freehold, subject to the payment of the enfranchisement consideration; but nothing contained in the act is to operate to deprive any tenant of any commonable rights to which he may be entitled in respect of such lands, and such right is to continue notwithstanding that the lands have become freehold.

Distribution of enfranchisement money, and of liability to pay it.

Commuted lands to be subject to same laws as to descent, curtesy, and dower, as freeholds.

Enfranchised lands to become freehold.

Tenants not to be deprived of commonable rights.

Copyhold Act 1843.

The Copyhold Act 1841 was (*a*) supplemented by the Copyhold Act 1843, which is (*b*) to be taken and construed as a part of it. This act says that, in addition to the provisions contained in the previous act, any enfranchisement made under the same may be made, either wholly or in part, for the consideration

Consideration for enfranchisement.

(*x*) SS. 73—78.
(*y*) S. 79.
(*z*) S. 81.
(*a*) 6 & 7 Vict. c. 23.
(*b*) S. 16.

of an annual rent in fee charged on the lands enfranchised; also that, in addition to the provisions of the previous act, any commutation or enfranchisement, made under the same, may be made either wholly, or in part, for the consideration of a conveyance of lands parcel of the same manor as the lands commuted or enfranchised, and subject to the same uses and trusts as the lands commuted or enfranchised shall be subject to at the time of such commutation or enfranchisement; or any right to mines or minerals in, or under, such land, or any right to waste in lands belonging to such manor. The act (c) also dispenses with notice of an intended enfranchisement being given to any other persons, where the tenant has a limited interest, provided that such tenant pays the whole cost of the enfranchisement. Notice unnecessary in certain cases.

Another act (d) extends the means of obtaining commutation or enfranchisement, by enacting (e) that, in addition to the provisions of the acts already referred to, any commutation or enfranchisement may be made wholly, or in part, for the consideration of a conveyance of lands, or of any rights to mines or minerals, although the said lands or the said rights to mines or minerals, so to be conveyed, shall not be parcel of, or situate in, or under, the lands of the same manor as the lands so to be commuted or enfranchised; provided the commissioners approve of the arrangement. Copyhold Act 1844. Consideration for enfranchisement.

These three statutes only contemplate commutation or enfranchisement taking place by the mutual agreement of the lord and his tenants, but the next act which we have to notice enables either party to compel the other to enter into such arrangement.

(c) S. 13.
(d) 7 & 8 Vict. c. 55.
(e) S. 5.

OF CORPOREAL HEREDITAMENTS.

Copyhold Act 1852 provides for compulsory enfranchisement.

This is the Copyhold Act 1852 (*f*), which enacts (*g*) that, at any time after the next admittance to any lands which shall take place on or after the 1st of July 1853, in consequence of any surrender, bargain and sale or assurance thereof (except upon a mortgage, in cases where the mortgagee is not in possession), or in consequence of any descent, gift, or devise, it shall be lawful for the tenant so admitted, or for the lord, to require and compel enfranchisement, in manner mentioned in the act, of the lands to which there shall have been such admittance as aforesaid; provided, however, that no such tenant shall be entitled to require such enfranchisement, until after payment, or tender, of the fine or fines, and of the fees, consequent on such admittance.

Notice to be given by party desiring enfranchisement. Consideration to be ascertained, and proceedings approved of by the commissioners. Extinguishment of heriots.

The act then (*h*) provides for notice being given by the party desiring enfranchisement, and the way in which the consideration payable to the lord is to be ascertained; and for the confirmation of the proceedings by the commissioners (*i*). It also enacted (*j*) that, at any time after a heriot had become payable with respect to any freehold, or customary freehold lands holden of manors, on or after the 1st of July 1853, it should be lawful for the lord, or the tenant, to require, and compel the extinguishment of all such claim to heriots, and the enfranchisement of the lands subject thereto, in the same way as if such lands were copyhold. This section of the act is however repealed, and a more comprehensive rule introduced, by a subsequent act (*k*). Nothing in the act is to deprive any tenant of any commonable rights to which he shall be entitled in respect of any enfranchised lands (*l*), and the act is not to extend to

---

(*f*) 15 & 16 Vict. c. 51.
(*g*) S. 1.
(*h*) SS. 2—8.
(*i*) S. 9.
(*j*) S. 27.
(*k*) 21 & 22 Vict. c. 94, s. 7.
(*l*) S. 45.

any estate or rights of any lord or tenant in any mines or minerals within or under the lands enfranchised, or to any rights of way or other easement, or to any rights of the lord in respect of holding fairs, or his rights of sporting, unless with the express consent in writing of such lord or tenant (*m*). Not to extend to mines or minerals without express agreement. Or to easements, or rights of fairs, or of sporting.

This act was amended by the Copyhold Act 1858 (*n*), which empowers any tenant or lord of any copyhold lands to which the last admittance shall have taken place before the 1st of July 1853, or of any freehold or customary freehold lands in respect of which the last heriot shall have become due or payable before the same date, to require and compel enfranchisement, in the manner provided by the Copyhold Act 1852 (*o*). It also provides for the compulsory extinguishment of heriots in freehold, or customary freehold, lands holden of any manor (*p*), without reference to the time when the last heriot was payable. Copyhold Act 1858. Extends powers of compulsory enfranchisement.

The effect of these acts has been to diminish, to a certain extent, the amount of land held by copyhold tenure, but the process is, as might be expected, very gradual, and, unless the legislature should pass some new enactment on the subject, copyhold tenure seems likely to endure for many years to come.

(*m*) S. 48.
(*n*) 21 & 22 Vict. c. 94.
(*o*) S. 6.
(*p*) S. 7.

CHAPTER VIII.

OF THE STATUTE OF USES.

THE estates to which our attention has hitherto been directed are those which give their owner a right to the present possession of land. There are, however, others, which, although existing as estates, and thus giving a present interest in land, do not confer a right to its present possession, and these also will require our consideration.

But since much of the law relating to them has reference to the Statute of Uses (a), we will first of all devote a short chapter to an attempt at explaining this famous enactment.

Introduction of Uses.

In the earlier times of our legal history, the person who had the seisin of land was the only one known, or thought of, as having any immediate estate in it. The first persons to introduce a distinction between a right to the benefit of land and its legal ownership, appear to have been the foreign ecclesiastics who wished to elude the statutes against mortmain. These, as we know, prohibited the religious corporations from holding land. They consequently endeavoured to evade the law, by having conveyances of land made to some third person who was to hold it for their benefit or "use." This stratagem was very

15 Ric. II. c. 5. soon frustrated by the 15 Ric. II., c. 5, which enacted, in effect, that all lands held by, or in trust for religious houses, without licence from the Crown,

---

(a) 27 Hen. VIII. c. 10.

should be forfeited. But the idea of secret trusts had taken root, and the numerous forfeitures for treason occasioned by the Wars of the Roses caused it to flourish. So that, from the beginning of the 15th century, the plan of conveying land to uses was generally adopted. A use, as it existed before the Statute of Uses, was a right to receive the profits of land of which the legal ownership was vested in some other person. For example, if A had conveyed land to B, in order that the latter might hold it for the benefit of C, C had the use in the land thus held in trust for him. The Common Law Courts refused to recognise uses, and consequently left a person who had a use or, as he was called, a *cestui que use*, entirely dependent upon the good faith of his trustee. But besides the Common Law Courts, there had existed from an early period the Court of Chancery, which, professing especially to administer equity, was disposed to enforce rights which were clearly just, although they might not be legal. Thus there came to be two kinds of estates, the legal estate of which the ostensible owner was alone recognised by the law, and the equitable estate of the *cestui que use*, which was the peculiar favourite of equity.

Definition of a use before the Statute of Uses.

Uses not recognised by the Common Law.

But enforced by the Court of Chancery.

At first, the decisions of the Court of Chancery, in respect of uses, were not free from the scruples of the common law, and from the considerations arising from the laws and principles of tenure (*b*); but, by degrees, these gave way to more liberal views. One consequence was that land held to uses was allowed to be, indirectly, disposed of by will, although a devise of lands (except under some special custom) was not, at the time we are speaking of, permitted by law. For the use in it might be devised, and the Court of Chancery would then compel the legal owner to convey the land to the devisee. Uses were, more-

Uses not subject to the rules of law.

(*b*) 1 Sand. Uses, 5.

over, freed from the restrictions by which legal estates were hampered, and allowed to be dealt with in many ways not countenanced by the law. The most important of these was the employment of "conditional limitations," by means of which an estate of freehold might be made to come into existence, conditionally on the happening of some future event; a form of limitation which, as we shall see hereafter, was not, at that time, possible in the case of legal estates.

Resulting use.   Besides this, the Court of Chancery not only recognised a use which had been expressly created, but would, in some cases, allow a use to be raised by implication. Thus, if a man had covenanted by deed that he would, in consideration of natural affection, stand seised of land in trust for some near relative, named in the deed; or if he had agreed to sell his estate, and had received the purchase-money, the court would hold that a use had been raised in favour of the relative or purchaser, as the case might be.

Objections to system of uses.   This system of secret trusts was not only repugnant to the policy of the law, which favoured notoriety in the transfer of land, but also gave many opportunities to the owner of an equitable estate to avoid just claims upon him. In order to prevent this, several statutes,
Statutes of Pernors.   known as the Statutes of Pernors (*c*), were passed in the reigns of Henry the Sixth and Henry the Seventh; the object of which was to put the *cestui que use* in the same position as if seised of the actual possession at law (*d*); but since they did not suffice for the purpose, the legislature determined to strike a decisive blow, by abolishing trusts of land altogether. With
Statute of Uses.   this view it passed the famous Statute of Uses, the 27 Hen. VIII., c. 10.

(*c*) From *prendre*, to take.
(*d*) 3 Reeves, 364.

OF THE STATUTE OF USES. 185

This act began by declaring that, by the common laws of the realm, lands, tenements, and hereditaments were not devisable by will; nor ought to be transferred from one to another, but by solemn livery of seisin, matter of record, or writing sufficient, made *bonâ fide* without covin or fraud; yet that nevertheless divers and sundry imaginations, subtle inventions and practices, had been used, whereby the hereditaments of the realm had been conveyed from one to another by fraudulent feoffments, fines, recoveries, and other assurances, craftily made to secret uses, intents, and trusts. It then recited the various evils which this practice had introduced, and " to the extirping and extinguishment " of it, enacted(*e*) that where any person, or persons, should stand or be seised, or at any time thereafter should happen to be seised, of and in any hereditaments, to the use, confidence, or trust of any other person, or persons, by reason of any of the modes of assurance mentioned in the act, or by any other manner of means, every such person that had, or should have, any such use, confidence, or trust, in fee simple, fee tail, for term of life, or for years or otherwise, or any use, confidence, or trust, in remainder or reversion, should from thenceforth stand, be seised, deemed, and adjudged, in lawful seisin, estate, and possession of and in the same hereditaments, to all intents, constructions, and purposes in the law, of and in such like estates as they had, or should have, in use, trust, or confidence, of or in the same; and that the estate, title, right, and possession that was in such person that was, or should be, seised of any hereditaments to the use, confidence, or trust, of any person, should from thenceforth be deemed to be in him, or them, that had, or should have, such use, confidence, or trust, after such quality, manner, form, and condition as the person seised had before, in or to the use, confidence, or trust, that was in him.

―――――――――――――――――――――――――――
(*e*) S. 1.

The effect of this enactment was that, from thenceforth, the estate of the person who had the seisin was merged in that of the *cestui que use,* who now took an estate, both legal and equitable, commensurate with that which he formerly had in equity only. For example, if a fee simple were now granted to A to the use of B, this would operate as a two-fold conveyance. For A would still take, momentarily, an estate in fee simple, because he would have a grant good under the common law, but immediately afterwards, the estate would, by virtue of the statute, pass on to, and remain with, B. In other words, uses were now turned into legal possession. It resulted that uses were henceforth recognised by the common law, and a direct conveyance to a purchaser for value would, therefore, even at law, raise a use in his favour.

Uses now recognised by the law.

Various rules were also framed in respect to uses taking effect under the statute, these being founded on the wording of the act. Thus, the statute speaks of any person being *seised* of land to the use of another; consequently it was held that there could not be a use of an estate of which a person cannot be seised. Now we know that terms of years do not give a seisin. Hence, although a man may stand seised of a fee simple to the use of another for a term of years, there cannot be a use of a term which has been already created: so that if an existing term were assigned to A to the use of B, this would not have the effect of conferring any legal estate upon B.

Rules of law relating to uses.

1st Rule. No use of a term.

Nor does the statute apply to copyholds. For if uses were permitted to be limited of such estates, there would be a transmutation of possession by the sole operation of the law, which would be contrary to the nature of copyhold tenure; it being a principle of that tenure that the lands cannot be aliened without the consent of the lord (*f*).

Nor of copyholds.

Again, the statute speaks of being seised to the

2nd Rule. A man cannot be

(*f*) 1 Sand. Uses, 249-50; *Rowden v. Malster,* Cro. Car. 42, 44.

use *of any other person.* Therefore, the person seised seised to the to the use must not be also the *cestui que use;* for use of himself. in that case he does not take anything, except there be a direct impossibility for the use to take effect at common law (*g*). Consequently, if there were a grant to A and his heirs, to the use of A and his heirs, he would take the legal estate by force of the common law, without any need of the statute, and the use would not therefore be "executed," or take effect, by the statute (*h*).

It is also necessary that the use be one *in esse*, in 3rd Rule. possession, reversion, or remainder: thus, a man can- Use must be *in* not covenant to stand seised to the use of another, of *esse.* such land as he shall afterwards purchase (*i*). The use may, however, be either express or implied, for the But may be express or implied. statute speaks of a *trust or confidence* as well as of a press or implied. use; and the law will therefore imply a use, in many cases where equity would formerly have implied a trust. A simple instance of an implied use occurs if A has conveyed land to B, a stranger, without any consideration, and without any declaration of a use. In that case there will be implied a "resulting use" to A, and B will, in fact, take nothing. For although the conveyance to him will give him the legal estate momentarily, the resulting use will, by virtue of the statute, immediately take it back from him, and give it again to A.

Lastly, the statute provides that the estate of the 4th Rule. person seised of any use is to be deemed to be in him Use cannot be greater than that had the use, *after such quality* as the person seised the seisin. to his use previously had. It follows that the *cestui que use* cannot have an estate more extensive than that out of which the use is raised. Thus, if land be conveyed to A for life, to the use of B for life, in tail, or

---

(*g*) Bac. Uses, 54.
(*h*) *Samme's Case*, 13 Rep. 55; *Orme's Case*, L. R. 8 C. P. 281.
(*i*) *Yelverton v. Yelverton*, Cro. Eliz. 401; 1 Sand. Uses, 94.

in fee simple, the estate of B cannot, in any case, endure after the death of A (*j*).

Re-establish-ment of trusts. So far then the object of the framers of the statute had been accomplished. Uses had been turned into possession, and brought within the jurisdiction of the common law; and it seemed as if there were no room left for trusts. But the Court of Chancery soon contrived to re-establish trusts, and to bring them once more under its exclusive power. For the common law courts still adhered to their system of recognising the legal owner of an estate, but refusing to look beyond him. Thus, if land were now conveyed to A, to the use of B, to the use of C, the common law courts fixed upon B as the legal owner, and ignored the existence of C. For, they said, there cannot be a use (that is, a legal possession) upon (or after) a use (*k*)—a construction which seems opposed to the words, as well as to the spirit, of the statute. Not so, however, the Court of Chancery. This court declared the second use to be valid in equity, and compelled B to act as trustee for C, whom they now called the *cestui que trust*, in order to distinguish him from the *cestui que use*. Consequently, the only difference made in equitable estates was that trusts were substituted for uses, and the *cestui que trust* for the *cestui que use*. But as regards legal estates the statute effected far more important changes, since it led to the introduction of various new forms of limitations. These however we are to consider in subsequent chapters, and we will conclude the present with a few remarks on the subject of equitable estates.

Equitable estates. The rules relating to these do not materially differ from those which govern legal estates, for it is a

---

(*j*) 1 Sand. Uses, 107.
(*k*) *Tyrrell's Case*, Dyer, 155ᵃ.

maxim generally received, that equity adopts, with reference to equitable estates, the rules of law applicable to legal estates (*l*). Our task will, therefore, be limited to pointing out the principal instances in which this maxim does not hold good.

The first which we have to notice, applies to the creation and transfer of equitable estates. We have already seen that every legal estate of freehold, and most terms of years, must be created by deed. But this is not so with equitable estates, even of the highest nature. Suppose, for instance, that A, the owner both at law and in equity of an estate in fee simple, agrees to sell it to B, and afterwards refuses to perform his agreement. At law, A will be considered as having entered into a contract, for the breach of which the law will punish him, by making him pay a sum of money to B by way of damages. But the law does not consider that the estate has become the property of B by the contract, and will not therefore compel A to give him a deed formally evidencing that fact. Equity, however, considers that, from the moment when the agreement was made, the estate belonged to B, and the purchase-money to A. It will, therefore, (subject to the statutory provisions to be presently mentioned) if requested by B, and provided that he is prepared to pay the purchase-money, compel A to give him that legal title which is necessary to perfect his estate. A mere verbal agreement to buy and sell may therefore operate to create an equitable estate in fee simple. And similarly, if the owner of a fee simple were verbally to declare himself a trustee for A, or to convey his estate to another, with verbal directions to hold in trust for A, A would have an equitable estate in fee simple created by parol.

Their creation and transfer.

But the power of equity to act upon the assumption

(*l*) 1 Sand. Uses, 280.

Statute of Frauds.

that an equitable estate has been created, has been restricted by statute. For it has been enacted by the Statute of Frauds (*m*) that (*n*) no action (a term which includes a suit in equity) shall be brought to charge any person upon any contract or sale of lands, tenements, or hereditaments, or of any interest in or concerning them, unless the agreement upon which such action shall be brought, or some note or memorandum thereof, shall be in writing, and signed by the party to be charged therewith, or some other person thereunto by him lawfully authorized. And (*o*) that all declarations or creations of trusts or confidences of any lands, tenements, or hereditaments shall be manifested and proved by some writing, signed by the party who is by law enabled to declare such trust (that is, by the beneficial owner of the property (*p*)), or by his last will in writing, or else they shall be utterly void and of none effect.

Nor is there anything in the doctrines of equity which forbids the owner of an equitable estate from transferring it to another person by mere word of mouth. But here again, the Statute of Frauds (*q*) has interposed, by enacting (*r*) that no grants and assignments of any trust or confidence shall have any effect, unless in writing, signed by the party granting or assigning the same. Since however, in all these cases, the writing only serves to prove the existence of the equitable estate, not to create it, the Court of Chancery may act upon a writing, although it professes to prove the existence of an equitable estate created some time previous to the date of the writing (*s*).

(*m*) 29 Car. II. c. 3.
(*n*) S. 4.
(*o*) S. 7.
(*p*) *Tierney* v. *Wood*, 19 Beav. 330.
(*q*) 29 Car. II. c. 3.
(*r*) S. 9.
(*s*) *Gardner* v. *Rowe*, 2 S. & S. 346; 5 Russ. 258.

And, notwithstanding the words of the Statute of Frauds, the court will, in many cases, enforce contracts not evidenced by writing, where one of the parties has substantially performed his part of the contract (*t*).

It will be observed that a writing is all that is necessary, in any case, to create and transfer equitable estates, but it is the practice to employ the same species of instrument in the passing of legal as of equitable estates (*u*).

Equity also requires, in general, that the words used in creating or transferring an equitable estate should be the same as those necessary in the case of corresponding legal estates. But here again the rules of equity are more elastic than those of law. When there is a conveyance, or devise, of an estate to trustees upon trusts perfected and declared by the grantor or settlor, and said therefore to be "executed," the court will not interfere to give the grantee, or devisee, any other estate than that which the words of the instrument, read in their strict technical sense, purport to confer. If, however, the trust is "executory," that is, if the estate is given to a trustee with directions to limit it in a certain way, the court will pay regard to the plain meaning of the settlor or testator, although it may not have been expressed in the most appropriate words. Thus, in an early case (*v*), A devised land to trustees upon trust on the marriage of his grand-daughter to convey the estate to her for life, with remainder to the issue of her body. Here, according to the rule in *Shelley's Case* (*w*), to which we have before adverted, the grand-daughter, having an estate for life, followed by an estate to the heirs of her

Form of words.

(*t*) See *Lester* v. *Foxcroft*, and the notes to this case; 1 L. C. 768.
(*u*) Lewin on Trusts, 59.
(*v*) *Glenorchy* v. *Bosville*, Ca. t. Talb. 3, and, with notes, 1 L. C. 1.
(*w*) 1 Rep. 93.

body, would, if there had been a direct devise of the estate to her, have taken an estate tail, by barring which she might have deprived her issue of their chance of succession. But since the estate given to her by the will was only equitable, and the trust itself executory, the court decided to carry out the clear intention of the testator, and therefore only permitted the grand-daughter to take an estate for life, with remainder to her issue in tail.

Incidents of an equitable estate.

The incidents of an equitable estate are also, generally, the same as in a legal estate of a corresponding nature. For instance, there may be an estate by curtesy (*x*), and now, under the Dower Act (*y*), an estate in dower, in equitable estates of inheritance. An equitable estate tail may also be barred by the same means as a legal estate tail (*z*), But an equitable estate was never liable to escheat (*a*), a very considerable advantage in the turbulent days of our earlier history.

Alienation of equitable estates.

An equitable estate may, as we have seen, be alienated by writing during the owner's lifetime. It may also be disposed of by his will. And it is in the same position as a legal estate, as to liability to involuntary alienation under the statutes relating to judgments, bankruptcy, or the payment of the debts of a deceased person. Finally, it is to be mentioned that equitable estates are subject to the rules of descent which govern legal estates.

Descent of equitable estates.

(*x*) *Sweetapple* v. *Bindon*, 2 Ver. 536.
(*y*) 3 & 4 Wm. IV. c. ~~104~~. 105
(*z*) 3 & 4 Wm. IV. c. 74; 1 Hayes, Con. 155.
(*a*) *Burgess* v. *Wheate*, 1 Eden, 177.

CHAPTER IX.

OF A REVERSION AND OF A REMAINDER.

WE come now to the discussion of those estates which confer a present interest in land, but with a deferred possession. There are two ways in which an estate of this description may arise. For if A, the owner of an estate in fee simple, should part with a portion of it, as by giving out of it an estate to B for life; or if he should part with all of it, dividing it amongst different persons, as by giving C the rest of the estate, subject to B's life estate; then, in either case, A and C have no right to the possession of the land, so long as B's life estate continues to exist. But they have, each, an actual present estate, created at the same moment as that of B, and giving an immediate interest in the land, only with deferred possession. B has consequently a particular estate, whilst A and C have, respectively, an estate in reversion and in remainder, expectant on the determination of B's estate. A reversion has therefore been defined as the returning of land to the grantor or his heirs, after a grant of it is over (*a*); and a remainder as an estate limited to take effect, and be enjoyed, after another estate is determined (*b*). It is of reversions and remainders that we propose to treat in this chapter. Creation of a reversion and of a remainder.
Particular estate.
Reversion and Remainder.
Definition of a reversion.
And of a remainder.

The first point which we will notice, is one implied by the above definitions of these estates. It is, that a reversion always arises by operation of law, whilst a remainder cannot arise by operation of law, but must Reversion always created by operation of law. Re-

---

(*a*) Co. Litt. 142ª.
(*b*) 2 Bl. Com. 164.

mainder always by act of parties.

always be the result of some direct act of parties, which act may be repeated several times. Hence, there can be only one reversion, but almost any number of remainders, in the same estate. Thus, if land be granted to A for twenty-one years, and after the expiration of that time, or (as it is more shortly put) "with remainder" to B for life; with remainder to C in tail, B and C will each have an estate of freehold in remainder. And the same person may have both a remainder and a reversion in the same estate. If, for instance, a tenant in fee simple carves out of it a life estate for himself, and a remainder to his son in tail, he will still have a reversion in fee simple, which may take effect after the determination of the estate tail.

Remainder may be created by deed or will. But no remainder in a term of years.

A remainder may be created in freeholds or copyholds by either deed or will, but a remainder, properly so called, cannot be created in a term of years. For a term of years is personal property, and personal property is essentially the subject of an ownership which is absolute, and has no relation to property in others. If, therefore, the owner of a long term of years were to create out of it a series of terms, each to take effect after the determination of that preceding it, these would become independent interests, complete in themselves, and not related to one another. And if he were to attempt to assign the term to one person for life, and limit remainders after the life interest, the assignee for life would get the whole term, however long it might be, and the remainders over would be invalid. But, so far as regards limitations of terms of years by will, this doctrine has been modified in modern times; for a limitation in a term, although after a life interest in the same term can, at the present day, take effect if created by way of executory devise, the explanation of which will be attempted in the next chapter.

The few remaining remarks which we have to make on the subject of a reversion apply equally to a remainder, and, since we have already noticed the incidents of these estates, when considering the subject of estates in possession, it will be more convenient to pass on now to such points as are common to both of them, and then return to those which relate to remainders only.

A reversion, or remainder, may be alienated by the tenant of such an estate, if in other respects competent, by either deed or will. And if transferred to the tenant of the particular estate, it is said to be "released" to him. At one time, the transfer of a reversion or a remainder was not complete unless accompanied by the "attornment", or formal consent, of the tenant in possession of the land. Attornment had its origin in the feudal rule which prohibited the transfer of a fee without the consent of the tenant from whom military and other services were due to his feudal lord. This was afterwards extended to all cases where a tenant's rights might possibly be affected by a transfer of the fee, although in some, as for instance that of a tenant for life and remainder-man, there was never any feudal relation between the tenant of the estate to be transferred and the tenant whose consent was made requisite. It was subsequently enacted by the 4 & 5 Anne, c. 3 (c), that all grants or conveyances of any manors or rents, or of the reversion or remainder of any messuages or lands, should be as good and effectual, to all intents and purposes, without any attornment of the tenant of any such manors or of the land out of which such rents issued, or of the particular tenant upon whose particular estates any reversion or remainder might be expectant, as if their attornment had been had and made. Provided (d) that no such tenant should be prejudiced, or damaged, by payment of any rent to any

Alienation of a reversion or a remainder.

Attornment.

4 & 5 Anne, c. 3.

(c) S. 9.
(d) S. 10.

such grantor, or by breach of any condition for non-payment of rent, before notice should have been given to him of such grant by the grantee.

<small>11 Geo. II. c. 19.</small>

This statute was followed by the 11 Geo. II., c. 19, which (*e*), in order to put a stop to the practice of tenants fraudulently attorning to strangers who claimed a title to the estates of the tenants' landlords, enacted that all and every such attornment of any tenant of lands or hereditaments should be absolutely null and void, and that the possession of their landlords should not be deemed to be in any way affected thereby.

<small>Termination of a reversion or a remainder.</small>

A reversion or remainder may also cease to exist. For the particular estate on which it depends may be transferred, or "surrendered," to the reversioner or remainder-man, or it may come to an end. In such a case, the expectant estate will either become an estate in possession, and thus cease to be a reversion or a remainder; or if, in the case of a remainder, it is not capable of coming into possession, it will, for reasons to be presently explained, be destroyed altogether. And we have already seen how a reversion or a remainder, limited after an estate tail, may be destroyed by virtue of the Act for the Abolition of Fines and Recoveries (*f*).

<small>Remainders divided into Vested and Contingent. Example of a vested remainder.</small>

Returning to the consideration of remainders, as apart from reversions, we have to point out that they may be divided into the two principal classes of Vested Remainders and Contingent Remainders. Supposing that an estate is given to A for life, with remainder to B, a living person, in fee simple; then B's estate is always ready to become an estate in possession, whenever A's estate may come to an end. His estate

---

(*e*) S. 11.
(*f*) 3 & 4 Wm. IV. c. 74.

is therefore said to be a "vested" remainder, being fixed, as Blackstone puts it, to come to some determinate person after the particular estate is spent, and there being nothing which can defeat it, or set it aside (*g*). But if the remainder be given, not to B, but to B's eldest son, and B were at that time a bachelor, then the case is different. For it is necessary, as we have said, that every estate limited by way of remainder should be capable of becoming an estate in possession at the moment when the particular estate which precedes it comes to an end; otherwise it will fail of effect altogether. Now, in the case supposed, B may never have a son, or even if he has, that son may not be born until after the determination of A's life estate. It is evident, therefore, that until B's son is born, or until A dies (whichever event happens first), it is uncertain whether the estate in remainder will fail for want of compliance with the rule above stated. It is consequently said to be "contingent," as distinguished from that "vested" remainder which we have already defined. But if B's son is born in the lifetime of A, from that moment there is an ascertained owner of the remainder, which will thereupon cease to be contingent, and become vested.

Example of a contingent remainder.

A remainder may also be contingent, when the person to whom it is limited is in existence, but the estate is only to vest on the happening of some vague and uncertain event. As where land is given to A for life, and in case B survives him, then with remainder to B in fee: there B is a certain person, but the remainder to him is a contingent remainder, depending upon a dubious event, namely, the uncertainty of his surviving A. During the joint lives of A and B, it is contingent; and if B dies first, it never can vest, but if A dies first, the remainder to B becomes vested (*h*).

(*g*) 2 Bl. Com. 168.
(*h*) 2 Bl. Com. 170.

We see therefore that it is the *present* capacity of taking effect in possession, if the possession were to become vacant, which distinguishes a vested remainder from one which is contingent (*i*).

Rules for the creation of remainders.

We come next to the rules which relate to the creation of remainders, premising that remainders may be limited to take effect either with, or without, the instrumentality of a use (thus a remainder may be limited to A and his heirs, or to B and his heirs to the use of A and his heirs), but that the same rules apply in either case.

1st Rule. Remainder must await determination of particular estate, and cannot be limited after a fee simple.

The first which we will notice is, that every remainder must be so limited as to wait for the determination of the particular estate, before it is to take effect in possession; and not to take effect in prejudice or exclusion of the preceding estate (*j*). Also, that no remainder can be limited after an estate in fee simple. These propositions are derived from the definition of a remainder. For, as to the first, we saw that a remainder is an estate which is to be enjoyed after another estate is determined. We pointed out also, in our chapter on estates for years, that no one but a reversioner could, at common law, take advantage of a condition; a proviso, therefore, giving this advantage to a remainder-man would be void, as would also the estate dependent on the proviso. And as to the second, a fee simple is the greatest estate which can be enjoyed; the tenant of it has consequently the whole of the estate, and a remainder therefore, which is only a portion, or residuary part, of an estate, cannot be reserved after the whole is disposed of (*k*).

2nd Rule. Remainder must have precedent

With regard to the next rule, it has been already pointed out that a remainder will cease to exist, as

---

(*i*) Fearne, C. R. 216; *Borraston's Case*, 3 Rep. 20ᵃ.
(*j*) Fearne, C. R. 261.
(*k*) 2 Bl. Com. 164.

such, by becoming an estate in possession. That is particular to say, the existence of a particular estate is necessary estate. to the existence of a remainder, or, as the rule is usually stated, there must be some particular estate precedent to every estate in remainder (*l*).

If the remainder is vested, any estate greater than 3rd Rule. an estate at will is sufficient for this purpose; but the Freehold contingent remainder must proposition does not always hold good as regards contingent remainders. For the feudal law attached be supported by particular great importance to the seisin, or feudal ownership, estate of freehold. of land being a matter both of notoriety and of certainty. It, therefore, held that the seisin of land must never be in abeyance, and consequently forbad the transfer of any estate of freehold, unless accompanied by feoffment and livery of seisin, that is, by the open and immediate transfer of the estate to some ascertained person. It followed, that no estate of freehold could be granted unless it were to commence at the moment of the grant (since a man could not make present delivery of a future estate), but must take effect in possession, reversion, or remainder. This rule did not, however, apply to leases, which, being estates of an inferior nature, did not carry with them the seisin of the land, did not therefore require livery of seisin, and might consequently be granted to commence at some future time (*m*). Supposing then, that the owner of an estate in fee simple had (1) granted out of it an estate to A for life; or (2) granted an estate for years to B, with remainder to A for life; or (3) granted an estate to A for life, with remainder to B in fee simple. In the first case he would have had to make livery of seisin to A; in the second case he would have had to make it to B, as the bailiff or agent of A, and to take effect for the benefit of A's estate; and in the third case he would have had to

---

(*l*) 2 Bl. Com. 165.
(*m*) *Barwick's Case*, 5 Rep. 93ᵇ.

make it to A, and this would have taken effect for the benefit of B's estate as well as for that of A.

If the remainder-men in, the second and third of our cases, were ascertained, living, persons, or, in other words, if their remainders were vested, this would be simple enough. Nor would there be any difficulty in our third case, even if the remainder were contingent; since, as we said, livery of seisin could be made to A. But it would be otherwise if the remainder limited in our second supposed case were contingent. For B could not receive livery of seisin as the agent of a non-existent person; livery of seisin could not, therefore, be made to any one, and consequently the contingent remainder would be invalid, because the rule which required delivery of the seisin on the creation of every estate of freehold had not been complied with. And though estates of freehold may now be transferred without livery of seisin, this rule of law as to contingent remainders continues unaltered. Hence we arrive at another rule, namely: That every freehold contingent remainder must be supported by a freehold particular estate.

4th Rule. No remainder to issue of unborn person following estate for life to such person.

The next rule to be considered relates also exclusively to contingent remainders. These remainders were not, at one time, permitted at all; the law not allowing an estate in land to be given to a person who might possibly never exist. Afterwards however they were recognised, subject to the rules which we have stated. But a trace of the old prejudice against them was to be found in a rule which was in force in Coke's time (*n*), and which prohibited any remainder which depended upon the coming into existence of two unborn people, or, as it was said, endeavoured to limit a possibility after a possibility. This rule was not, it would seem, applied from any fear of such a

---

(*n*) See 2 Rep. 51ᵇ.

limitation acting as a restraint on alienation (*o*), and since the only cases to which it was likely to apply are those in which an endeavour is made to keep the same estate inalienable, in the same direct line of descent, it only survives (*p*) in a modified form derived from the general principle. The rule in its present shape may be stated as follows—If an estate is limited to an unborn person for life, with remainder to the children of such unborn person, this remainder is absolutely void (*q*). Hence, if an estate be given to A, a bachelor, for life, with remainder to his son for life, with remainder to that son's son, this last remainder cannot take effect. The operation of the above rule is however modified, in one particular case, by the application of what is known as the *Cy près* doctrine. For it sometimes happens that, in a will, an estate is given by words which, although when read in their strictly technical sense confer an estate for life only on an unborn person with remainder to his issue in tail, yet are considered by the courts to show that the testator's primary object was that the land should continue in the issue of the first taker, and that the mode in which the issue should take it was a secondary object (*r*). In such a case, the courts will give effect to his intention, as nearly as possible (*s*), by advancing the estate given by the will to the first taker, and holding that he has an estate tail, thus leaving his issue a chance of succeeding him as tenants in tail (*t*). But this indulgence is only shown where such limitations are endeavoured to be made by will (*u*), and is not extended to cases where the testator has shown an unmistakeable intention to infringe the rule of law, as where it is clearly intended that

Cy près doctrine.

(*o*) See judgment of Ld. Brougham in *Cole* v. *Sewell*, 2 H. L. C. 230.
(*p*) See *Cole* v. *Sewell*, 4 Dru. & War. 1, 32.
(*q*) Fearne, C. R. 502; *Spencer* v. *Marlborough*, 3 Bro. P. C. 232; *Brudenell* v. *Elwes*, 1 East, 442, 452 note (*e*), & 453.
(*r*) Fearne, C. R. 204ª.
(*s*) *Cy près*.
(*t*) See *Doe* v. *Aplin*, 4 T. R. 82; *Doe* v. *Halley*, 8 T. R. 5.
(*u*) See *Brudenell* v. *Elwes*, 7 Ves. 381, 389.

the first unborn person should take as tenant for life (*v*), or that the second should take as tenant in fee simple (*w*).

Rule as to vesting of contingent remainders.

Besides the above rules relating to the creation of remainders, there is another which applies to a contingent remainder after it has been created, and is a corollary to the rule that every remainder must have a particular estate to support it. Every vested remainder is, by its definition, ready to come into possession whenever the particular estate determines, and continues, therefore, to exist as an estate, though not as an estate in remainder, after the particular estate has come to an end. But it is otherwise, in such a case, with a contingent remainder, which being unable either to become an estate in possession, or (having lost its particular estate) to exist any longer as a remainder, is destroyed altogether. Hence we arrive at the rule that every contingent remainder must, in order to take effect in possession, be changed into a vested remainder either before, or at the moment when, the preceding particular estate comes to an end.

Child en ventre sa mère.

In the construction of this rule, it is now well settled that a child begotten, but not born, or as the legal phrase is *en ventre sa mère,* is to be considered as being already in existence. This was not the case formerly, and the way in which a change in the old law was brought about is somewhat curious. In a case (*x*) tried in the sixth year of William and Mary, a father had devised an estate to his son for life, with remainder to that son's sons in tail. The son died without having had a son born to him, but leaving his wife pregnant of a child, who was afterwards born and proved to be a son. The Courts of Common Pleas and

---

(*v*) *Seaward* v. *Willock,* 5 East, 108.
(*w*) *Hale* v. *Pew,* 25 Beav. 335.
(*x*) *Reeve* v. *Long,* Salk. 227.

of Queen's Bench were unanimous in holding that the grandson, not having been born at the expiration of the estate for life, could not take the estate tail. This decision was, however, afterwards reversed by the House of Lords, contrary to the opinion of all the judges. But the House of Commons, in reproof of what they considered an assumption of legislative authority by the Lords, brought in a bill which was passed as the 10 & 11 Wm. & Mary, c. 22, and which enacted that when any estate, by any marriage, or other, settlement, should be limited in remainder to the first or other son of the body, or to the daughter, or daughters, of any person, with any remainders over; any son or daughter of such person, born after the decease of his, or her, father, should take such estate so limited to the first or other sons, or to the daughter or daughters, in the same manner as if born in the lifetime of his, or her, father. And it is now laid down as a fixed principle, that when such consideration would be for his benefit every child *en ventre sa mère* is to be considered as absolutely born (y).

10 & 11 Wm. & M. c. 22. / 6

It may assist the reader if we pause here, in order to recapitulate the rules which we have deduced as governing the existence of remainders. They are:

1. That every remainder must await the determination of its particular estate, and that no remainder can be limited after an estate in fee simple.

2. That every remainder must have a particular estate to support it.

3. That if the remainder is contingent and also freehold, the particular estate must also be one of freehold.

4. That no remainder can be limited to an unborn person for life, followed by an estate to the issue of such unborn person. And,

---

(y) Watkins on Descents, 180; *Doe* v. *Clarke*, 2 H. Bl. 399; *Mogg* v. *Mogg*, 1 Mer. 654; *Trower* v. *Butts*, 1 S. & S. 181.

5. That every contingent remainder must vest before, or at the moment when, the precedent particular estate is determined.

It should be mentioned, at this stage of our subject, that the strict rules which applied to remainders, properly so called, were not, even in early times, enforced against limitations created by a will which sought to give estates by way of remainder. For wills have been always more leniently construed than deeds, and consequently from an early date it was allowable to make by will a limitation, distinguished as an "executory devise," which would have failed altogether if inserted in a deed. But executory devises having, since the passing of the Statute of Uses (z), been brought within the rules which govern limitations taking effect under that act, we will content ourselves for the present with noticing the fact of their existence, and reserve the consideration of them for the next chapter.

Alienation of possibility coupled with an interest.

We have already spoken generally of the alienation of remainders, but must add a few words on this point, with reference to contingent remainders. Such of these as are contingent on the birth of some unborn person are evidently inalienable. But one which depends upon the happening of a future event (as, to repeat a former example, an estate given to A for life, and if B survives him, then to B in fee), and which is sometimes spoken of as possibility coupled with an interest, is in a different position. In early times, indeed, it could not be disposed of either by deed or by will (a). Afterwards, however, it became disposable by will (b), and now it has been enacted by the Real Property Amendment Act (c) that a possi-

Real Property Amendment Act.

(z) 27 Hen. VIII. c. 10.
(a) *Bishop* v. *Fountaine*, 3 Lev. 427.
(b) *Roe* v. *Jones*, 1 H. Bl. 30.
(c) 8 & 9 Vict. c. 106, s. 6.

bility coupled with an interest, in any tenements or hereditaments, of any tenure, whether the limitation of such interest or possibility be or be not ascertained, may be disposed of by deed. And the Wills Act (d) provides that the power of disposition by will shall extend to all contingent interests in any real, or personal, estate, whether the testator may, or may not, be ascertained as the person, or one of the persons, in whom the same may become vested, and whether he may be entitled thereto under the instrument by which the same respectively were created, or under any dispositions thereof by deed or will.

<small>Wills Act.</small>

The fact that a contingent remainder is destroyed if not capable of vesting at the moment when the particular estate comes to an end, made it necessary formerly to take special precautions with reference to this point. For the particular estate might be destroyed by some act of the tenant; as if he did anything which caused it to be forfeited, or if he surrendered it to the owner of the reversion, or obtained a release of the reversion to himself, by both of which means the particular estate was merged in the reversion.

<small>Destruction of contingent remainders.</small>

In the case, then, of an estate being limited to A, a bachelor, for life, with remainder to his issue in tail, with remainder to B in fee simple; here A at any time before he had issue might, by any of the above-mentioned ways, put an end to his own estate, and, as a consequence, to that of his issue. It was necessary therefore to interpose another estate between those of A and of his issue, and this was done by giving to trustees, "upon trust to preserve contingent remainders," an estate which was to take effect if A's estate came to an end during his lifetime, and, in that case, to endure so long as A lived. By this means the con-

<small>Trustees to preserve contingent remainders.</small>

(d) 7 Wm. IV. & 1 Vict. c. 26, s. 3.

tingent remainder was protected against anything which A could do, and as to the trustees the Court of Chancery would interfere to prohibit them from doing anything which would amount to a breach of their trust (e).

Real Property Amendment Act.

But limitations to trustees, in order to preserve contingent remainders, have now been rendered unnecessary by the Real Property Amendment Act (f), which enacts (g) that a contingent remainder, existing at any time after the 31st of December 1834, shall be, and if created before the passing of the act shall be deemed to have been, capable of taking effect notwithstanding the determination by forfeiture, surrender, or merger, of any preceding estate of freehold, in the same manner in all respects as if such determination had not happened. It must be remembered, however, that a contingent remainder still remains liable to destruction if not ready to take effect when the particular estate comes to a natural determination.

(e) See *Moody* v. *Walters*, 16 Ves. 283 ; *Biscoe* v. *Perkins*, 1 Ves. & B. 485.
(f) 8 & 9 Vict. c. 106.
(g) S. 8.

CHAPTER X.

OF AN EXECUTORY INTEREST.

EXECUTORY interests, the explanation of which will be attempted in this chapter, came into existence as a consequence of the passing of the Statute of Uses (*a*). They may be created by deed or by will. If by deed they can only take effect by virtue of the statute, but if by will they may, or may not, be limited so to take effect by way of use (*b*). We will begin with the consideration of those executory interests which are created under the statute.

Executory interests a consequence of the Statute of Uses.
May take effect under the statute or by will.

It has been already shown how limitations of legal estates, by way of remainder, are subject to various restrictive rules, amongst which we may specially mention that which forbids the limitation of any estate after a fee simple, and that which compels every remainder to await the determination of its particular estate, before it can take effect. Prior to the passing of the Statute of Uses (*c*), uses, being subject to the rules of equity only, might be limited in ways not permissible in the case of legal estates. Thus, if land were given to A and his heirs, to hold to the use of B and his heirs until the happening of some future and uncertain event, and then to the use of C and his heirs; the Court of Chancery would compel A, on the happening of that event, to hold the land to the use of C and his heirs (*d*). But it is plain that this

Executory interests under the Statute of Uses.
Conditional limitations before the statute.

(*a*) 27 Hen. VIII. c. 10.
(*b*) Gilb. Uses, 356ª.
(*c*) 27 Hen. VIII. c. 10.
(*d*) Fearne, C. R. 384ª.

Limitations by way of use after the statute.

"conditional limitation" was one which, if made of a legal estate, would have been invalid as being obnoxious to the rules to which we have just referred.

After the Statute of Uses (e) was passed, uses conferred legal, as well as equitable, estates; limitations of them became, therefore, subject to the jurisdiction of law. But, nevertheless, they were still allowed to retain, in a great measure, the freedom which they had acquired when mere creatures of equity. For now, if land were limited by its owner to the use of himself and his heirs until the happening of some future event, and then to other uses, this would be perfectly good (f), although it would be a limitation of an estate after a fee simple. And an estate may also be well limited by means of uses, although it is to take effect by destroying a preceding estate, and is thus opposed to the rule governing remainders, which requires a subsequent estate to await the natural determination of that which precedes it. Thus, a limitation would be valid by which an estate was given to A, to hold to the use of B until C pays a sum of money (g), or until B acquires some other property (h); with a proviso that on the happening of either of these events the estate is to be held to the use of C. It may be noticed that it is the power of limiting an estate after a fee simple that enables a landowner, about to be married, to effect a settlement for the benefit of himself alone until marriage, and then for that of himself, his wife, and children.

Springing and Shifting Uses.

The uses, by means of which executory interests can be thus created, are divided into Springing Uses, and Shifting Uses. Springing uses are those which are limited, as in the first of the examples just given, to

---

(e) 27 Hen. VIII. c. 10.
(f) *Woodliff* v. *Drury*, Cro. Eliz. 439.
(g) *Lloyd* v. *Carew*, Prec. Ch. 72.
(h) *Nicolls* v. *Sheffield*, 2 Bro. C. C. 214; *Carr* v. *Erroll*, 6 East, 58.

arise on the happening of a future event, where no preceding use is limited; they do not, consequently, take effect in derogation of any interest other than that which results to the grantor, or remains in him in the mean time. Shifting uses are those which, as in our second example, do take effect in derogation of some other estate; they are either expressly limited by the deed, or are authorized to be created by some person named in the deed (*i*). In this latter case, the person so named acquires a Power of Appointment, a subject which it will be more convenient to discuss by itself later on.

An executory interest may also be created by a will, without calling in the aid of the Statute of Uses (*j*), and is, in that case, distinguished as an Executory Devise, the rules which govern it being nearly, if not entirely (*k*), the same as those to which such an interest is subject when created by way of use. *Executory Devise.*

We have seen that, before the passing of the statute, the use in land could be devised, whilst the legal estate in it, as a rule, could not; but that there were some exceptions to this rule, arising out of special local customs. It is probable that where land could be devised under a custom, limitations of it, similar to those permitted in a devise of uses, were sometimes attempted, and, from the liberality which our courts have always adopted in the construction of wills, were often allowed (*l*). When the Statute of Uses (*m*) was passed, both the legal and equitable estate in land ceased, for a time, to be devisable; but that statute was shortly afterwards followed by another (*n*), which permitted all land held in socage to be disposed of by *Origin of Executory Devises.*

(*i*) Gilb. Uses, 152ª.
(*j*) 27 Hen. VIII. c. 10.
(*k*) See Fearne, C. R. 40; Gilb. Uses, 35ª.
(*l*) Fearne, C. R. 384ª.
(*m*) 27 Hen. VIII. c. 10.
(*n*) 32 Hen. VIII. c. 1.

will; and when the greater part of the land in the kingdom became afterwards subject to this tenure (*o*), devises of land became general. Under these circumstances, the courts of law permitted direct limitations of it by will, similar to those already allowed in the creation of an executory interest, taking effect under the Statute of Uses (*p*). But it is to be remembered that every gift of real estate by will confers a use. For since every devise imports a consideration, there is also an implied use, by the common law, to the devisee, unless there is an express use to some other person, in which case the express use must prevail, and is executed by the statute (*q*).

Blackstone (*r*) defines an executory devise of lands as such a disposition of them, by will, that thereby no estate vests on the death of the testator, but only on some future contingency. It differs (he goes on to say) from a remainder in three very material points—1st, That it needs not any particular estate to support it. 2nd, That by it a fee simple, or other less estate, may be limited after a fee simple. 3rd, That by this means a remainder may be limited of a term of years, after a particular estate for life created in the same. The two first points apply, as we have seen, equally, to the case of an executory interest. As to the third, we have already said that such a limitation, if made by deed, would give the whole term to the person named as tenant for life. The same rule was formerly held to apply also if the limitation were made by will (*s*), and although, afterwards, the remainder-man was allowed to take the term, provided it had not been alienated by the first taker during his own lifetime, he had no remedy if it had been so disposed of (*t*). But

Executory devise of a term.

(*o*) 12 Car. II. c. 24.
(*p*) 27 Hen. VIII. c. 10.
(*q*) Gilb. Uses, 356, and note (2).
(*r*) 2 Bl. Com. 172.
(*s*) *Lore* v. *Windham*, 1 Sid. 450.
(*t*) *Anon.*, Dyer, 74[b].

later on, after the passing of the Statute of Uses (*u*), it was held that a limitation of the kind which we have been describing was to take effect as an executory devise, and not as a remainder, and could not be destroyed by any act of the first devisee (*v*). Such limitations were not, however, at first held to be good, unless all the persons named to take the term were in being and alive together (*w*); "so that," as it was said, "all the candles might be lighted and consumed together (*x*)." But this doctrine was subsequently overruled (*y*), and it is now settled that executory devises, of both real and leasehold estate, are subject, as to their creation, to the same rules. These, again, apply to the creation of all executory interests, whether under the Statute of Uses (*z*) or not, and we will next proceed to inquire what they are.

It is evident that limitations by way of executory interest allow much more freedom of action than is attainable in the creation of remainders. For an estate which is thus limited has no dependence upon any preceding particular estate, but, on the contrary, may take effect by destroying it, and cannot therefore be affected by any accident which may befall it. Being thus indestructible they might, if not restrained by the law, be so created as to render land inalienable for a very long period, and thus cause what is known as a perpetuity. To prevent this from being done, two principal rules have been framed. *Rules for the creation of executory interests.*

The first of these is that when an estate can take effect as a remainder, it shall never be construed to be an executory limitation (*a*). Thus in one case (*b*), by *1st Rule. No executory interest where limitation can*

(*u*) 27 Hen. VIII. c. 10.
(*v*) *Manning's Case*, 8 Rep. 94ᵇ; *Lampet's Case*, 10 Rep. 46ᵇ.
(*w*) *Goring* v. *Bickerstaffe*, 2 Free. 163.
(*x*) 2 Bl. Com. 175.
(*y*) *Howard* v. *Norfolk*, 2 Free. 72, 80; 2 Jur. Arg. 47.
(*z*) 27 Hen. VIII. c. 10.
(*a*) *Goodtitle* v. *Billington*, 2 Doug. 753ᵃ, 757.
(*b*) *Carwardine* v. *Carwardine*, Fearne, C. R. 388, & 1 Ed. n, 27.

take effect as remainder.

a settlement, made before marriage, land was conveyed to trustees to the use of A for life, with remainder to B, his intended wife, for life, with remainder to their issue in tail; but with a proviso that if A should die leaving such issue, and not having made provision for any of them during his lifetime, then the trustees should stand seised of one moiety of the settled estate upon trusts for the benefit of such issue. It was held that this proviso only created a contingent remainder, and not an indestructible executory interest, in favour of such of the issue as were left unprovided for. For, being preceded by, and bound to await the determination of, a particular estate, it was capable of being construed as a remainder, and came, therefore, within the rule. And the result is the same where a limitation which was originally an executory devise becomes capable, by some change of circumstances, of being construed as a remainder. For instance (c), land was devised to A for life, with remainder to B in fee simple; this being followed by a proviso that if B should happen to die before A, and A should have no child living at her death, she might devise the premises to whom she thought proper. B died in the lifetime of A. A had a child who survived her, but before her death she sold the property in question, having previously levied a fine with proclamations, a process which was at that time capable of destroying contingent remainders (d), but not executory interests. And it was held that, although at the death of the testator, and until the death of B, the power given to A to devise the land to such persons as she thought proper could only operate as an executory devise, yet upon the death of B the character of the limitation changed. For it had then a preceding particular estate whose determination it must await, and was consequently a contingent remainder, and well barred by the fine.

(c) *Doe* v. *Howell*, 10 B. & C. 191.
(d) *Archer's Case*, 1 Rep. 66ᵇ, 67ᵃ.

The other rule to which we have referred is that 2nd Rule.
generally known as the Rule against Perpetuities; Every executory limitation
the object of it is to prevent property becoming in- to take effect
alienable beyond a certain period, by fixing a time lives in being
within which every executory limitation must take and twenty one
effect. The necessity for such a rule became apparent wards.
as soon as executory limitations were permitted, but
no definite period appears, at first, to have been fixed
upon; the courts being content, for a while, with
defeating various attempts at creating perpetuities (e),
as where land was given in tail, with a proviso that
the estate should be forfeited if any attempt were
made to bar the entail (f); where it was given to a
succession of unborn children for life (g); or where it
was, indeed, given to an unborn person in tail, but
with a proviso that, on his being born, his estate tail
should be converted into one for life, with remainder
(subject to similar conditions) to his issue in tail (h).
But after a while a settled rule was laid down. This
is founded on an analogy to the rule of law relating to
remainders which forbids the gift of land to an unborn person for life, followed by any estate to the
issue of such unborn person. Under this rule, there
can be no greater restraint on alienation than that
which may be effected by means of a settlement
limiting one or more life estates to a person or persons
in being, followed by one or more estates tail expectant on the expiration of the preceding estate for
life (i). And since the estate tail can be barred by
the tenant in tail as soon as he has attained his
majority, the utmost restraint on alienation possible
by limitations of remainders, is for a life or lives in
being and twenty-one years afterwards. The full
extent of this period as that within which property

(e) See 2 Jur. Arg. 7.
(f) Corbet's Case, 1 Rep. 83ᵇ; Portington's Case, 10 Rep. 35ʰ.
(g) Humberston v. Humberston, 1 P. Wms. 333.
(h) Spencer v. Marlborough, 3 Bro. P. C. 232.
(i) Fearne, C. R. 562ª—9ª.

might be rendered incapable of alienation, was, in the case of executory limitations, at first allowed only where the limitation was to take effect in favour of an infant (*j*). But this was afterwards extended to all cases, and it is now clearly settled that every executory limitation is well created, which must either take effect, or fail to take effect, within the period of a life or lives in being, with an extension of a few months in favour of a limitation to a person who is *en ventre sa mère* at the expiration of the twenty-one years (*k*). It is to be remembered, however, that the event, or events, on which the limitation depends must be such as will necessarily take effect, or fail, within the period fixed by the rule. Thus, in one case (*l*), leasehold estate was given by will to trustees upon trust for A for life, and after his death upon trust, in effect, for the first heir male of A who should attain the age of twenty-one. At the death of A, his heir male by descent had already attained that age, but, nevertheless, the House of Lords held that the limitation to him was void. For it was said that the fact of his being both heir male and having attained his majority at the time of A's death was merely an accident, and that the events on which the limitation depended (namely, that A should have an heir male, and that such heir should attain the age of twenty-one) might not have happened in conjunction for many generations (*m*).

Accumulation of income.

It was at one time possible for a settlor to direct that the income derived from land should be accumulated for a period of time equal to that within which alienation of land itself might be restrained (*n*). But

---

(*j*) *Taylor* v. *Biddall*, 2 Mod. 289; *Stephens* v. *Stephens*, Ca. t. Talb. 228.
(*k*) *Beard* v. *Westcot*, 5 Taunt. 393; *Cadell* v. *Palmer*, 1 Cl. & F. 372, 421, and, with notes, Tu. R. P. 360.
(*l*) *Dungannon* v. *Smith*, 12 Cl. & F. 546, 622.
(*m*) And see *Gosling* v. *Gosling*, 1 N. R. 36; *Harrington* v. *Harrington*, L. R. 5 H. L. 87.
(*n*) *Thellusson* v. *Woodford*, 4 Ves. 227.

it is now enacted by the 39 & 40 Geo. III., c. 98, that (o) no person shall, after the passing of the act, settle, or dispose of, any real or personal property, so that the rents or produce thereof shall be wholly, or partially, accumulated for any longer term than the life of such settlor; or for the term of twenty-one years from the death of such settlor; or during the minority, or respective minorities, of any person or persons, who shall be living, or *en ventre sa mère*, at the death of such settlor; or during the minority, or respective minorities only, of any person or persons, who, under the uses or trusts of the instrument directing the accumulation, would, for the time being, if of full age, be entitled to the rents or produce so directed to be accumulated. And that in every case where such accumulations shall be directed otherwise than as aforesaid, such direction shall be null and void, and the rents of such property so directed to be accumulated shall, so long as the same shall be directed to be accumulated contrary to the provisions of the act, go to, and be received by, such person, or persons, as would have been entitled thereto had such accumulation not been directed. But (p) nothing in the act is to extend to any provision for the payment of the debts of the settlor (q); or to any provision for raising portions for any child or children of the settlor, or for any child or children of any person taking any interest under the instrument; or to any direction touching the produce of timber or woods upon any lands or tenements. An attempt at undue accumulation, unlike an excessive restraint on alienation, is not void altogether, but only so far as it exceeds the time allowed by the act. If, for instance, there is a direction to accumulate income during the life of some person other than the settlor, it is evident that this period of accumulation may happen to exceed

---

(o) S. 1.
(p) S. 2.
(q) See *Tewart v. Lawson*, W. N. (1874), 140.

the period of twenty-one years permitted by statute. But it is, nevertheless, good for twenty-one years, provided the person named lives so long; and will be only void for such further time as he may continue to live beyond the twenty-one years (*r*).

Alienation of executory interests.

The alienation of executory interests is governed by the same statutory enactments as those already mentioned in the case of contingent remainders. It will be enough, therefore, to refer the reader to what has been said on this point in the previous chapter; and we conclude the present with some remarks on the subject of powers of appointment.

Powers of appointment.

A springing or shifting use may be created, not only by the settlor or devisor of land, but also by any other person to whom he has given a power to create it. For such a person may have a power of appointing that land shall thenceforth be held, wholly or partially, to a use different from that to which it has been hitherto subject. As in the ordinary case of a power of sale, which is nothing more than a power to appoint the property which is sold to the use of the purchaser. Powers of this kind may be classified in two ways, according as it is wished to regard them with reference to their exercise, or to their destruction and alienation.

Powers may be Particular or General.

In the first case, they may be divided into Particular Powers and General Powers. A particular power is one which the donee of the power can only exercise in favour of particular objects; as, for instance, a power to appoint land amongst the children of A. A general power is one which may be exercised in favour of any person whom the donee may select, including himself.

Powers Colla-

The other division of powers is into Powers Col-

(*r*) *Griffiths* v. *Vere*, 9 Ves. 127, and, with notes, Tu..R. P. 430.

lateral, and Powers Not simply Collateral. Powers of the first kind are those given to a person who has no interest in the property settled, as where an estate is limited to the use of A, with power to B to revoke that use, and limit the property to the use of C. Powers not simply collateral are those which are given to some person who has an interest in the property subject to the power. These powers may be sub-divided into Powers Appendant and Powers in Gross. A power appendant is one which is strictly dependent upon the estate limited to the person to whom the power is given, and the exercise of which will affect his interest; as where a power is given to a tenant for life to make leases in possession (*s*). A power in gross is one which enables the donee to create such estates only as will <u>not</u> attach on the interest limited to him; as where a power is given to a tenant for life to create a term of years which is to commence after his death (*t*).

Powers may be created by any words which clearly indicate an intention to that effect. Trustees of settlements and mortgagees have also had various powers of sale and exchange conferred on them by statute (*u*), but to these we shall refer more fully in a later part of this work. We pass on therefore to consider, 1st, How powers may be exercised. 2nd, How they may be destroyed, or alienated.

It will be remembered that, for the purpose of the first question to be considered, powers are divided into those which are particular, and those which are general. The first point to be noticed as to their exercise, is that it must not tend to create a perpetuity. The application of this principle differs according to the class of the power. For as to par-

---

(*s*) Sug. Pow. 46.
(*t*) Sug. Pow. 47.
(*u*) 23 & 24 Vict. c. 145.

ticular powers, the rule is that, when the power is exercised, the limitation thus created is to be read as if it had been inserted in the instrument creating the power, at the time when that instrument came into operation (*v*); and then the validity of the execution of the power will turn upon the question whether the limitation, so read, sins against the rule against perpetuities (*w*). It will be seen from this statement that the power is not bad because the exercise of it might have tended to a perpetuity. It is the actual, and not the hypothetical, exercise of the power, which alone will be considered (*x*). As to general powers, the rule is simply that the exercise of the power must not create a limitation which, at the time of such exercise, is obnoxious to the rule against perpetuities. In this case the validity of the limitation is totally irrespective of the instrument creating the power. For the freedom of alienation is no more interfered with by the gift of a general power than if an absolute interest had been vested in the donee, and, consequently, there is no tendency towards a perpetuity (*y*).

Power need not be referred to.

The donee of a power may execute it without referring to it, provided the intention to execute appear (*z*) by his mentioning the property over which he has the power. Thus, it was held, in an early case (*a*), that if a man, having a general power to appoint land by will, devise the land itself, as owner of it, without reference to his authority, the land will pass by the will; for his intention is clear (*b*). But it is otherwise if the donee of a power refer neither

---

(*v*) See *Doe* v. *Cavendish*, 4 T. R. 741ª.
(*w*) *Spencer* v. *Marlborough*, 3 Bro. P. C. 232; *Jones* v. *Winwood*, 3 Mee & W. 653; *Massey* v. *Barton*, 7 Ir. Eq. Rep. 95.
(*x*) *Griffith* v. *Pownall*, 13 Sim. 393; *Attenborough* v. *Attenborough*, 1 K. & J. 296.
(*y*) Tu. R. P. 419.
(*z*) Sug. Pow. 289.
(*a*) *Clere's Case*, 6 Rep. 17ᵇ.
(*b*) And see *Hunloke* v. *Gell*, 1 Russ. & My. 515.

to it, nor to the property to which it is subject; and, as a general rule, it will be held, in such a case, that he did not intend to exercise his power (c). But an exception has been made in favour of a will made by a testator who has a general power of appointment over property. For it is enacted by the Wills Act (d) that a (e) general devise of the real estate of a testator, or of his real estate in any place, or in the occupation of any person mentioned in his will, or otherwise described in a general manner, or a bequest of the personal estate of a testator, or any bequest of personal property described in a general manner, shall be construed to include any real estate, or any real estate to which such description shall extend (as the case may be), or any personal estate, or any personal estate to which such description shall extend (as the case may be), which he may have power to appoint in any manner he may think proper; and shall operate as an execution of such power, unless a contrary intention shall appear by the will.

It is also necessary that the donee of a power should observe any conditions attached to its execution, as, for instance, that the consent of some particular person is to be first obtained. It was also necessary, formerly, scrupulously to observe, in the execution of a power, every formality which the caution or whim of the donor of the power had prescribed. But as to this it is now enacted by the Wills Act (f) that (g) no appointment made by will in exercise of any power shall be valid, unless the same shall be executed like a will (h); and that every will so executed shall, so far as respects the execution and attestation thereof, be a valid execution of a power

Observance of formalities.

(c) *Ex parte Caswall*, 1 Atk. 559; *Sloane v. Cadogan*, Sug. Pow. 915.
(d) 7 Wm. IV. & 1 Vict. c. 26.
(e) S. 27.
(f) 7 Wm. IV. & 1 Vict. c. 26.
(g) S. 10.
(h) As to which see s. 9 of the act.

of appointment by will, notwithstanding that it shall have been expressly required that a will made in exercise of such power should be executed with some additional or other form of execution or solemnity. And as to the execution of powers by other instruments, it is enacted by the 22 & 23 Vict., c. 35 (*i*) that a deed thereafter executed in the presence of, and attested by, two or more witnesses, in the manner in which deeds are ordinarily executed and attested, shall, so far as respects the execution and attestation thereof, be a valid execution of a power of appointment by deed, or by any instrument in writing not testamentary, notwithstanding it shall have been expressly required that a deed or instrument in writing, made in exercise of such power, should be executed or attested with some additional or other form of execution or attestation or solemnity.

Defective execution of powers aided. By Equity.
And on other points, besides those mentioned above, the Court of Chancery has been in the habit, in certain cases, of aiding the defective execution of a power, where it has been intended to execute it, and that intention has been sufficiently declared, but the act declaring the intention was not an execution of the power in the form prescribed. Where, for instance (*j*), a man, having power to make a provision for his wife out of certain land by deed, devised part of the land to her for life by a will made under seal, this was upheld in equity as a good execution of his power, although it was not strictly within the terms prescribed (*k*). Aid of this nature will be given to a wife or to children, although there has been no consideration given for the exercise of the power, and the rule is the same as to charities (*l*). But it will not be extended in other cases, to " volunteers "—persons, that

---

(*i*) S. 12.
(*j*) *Tollet* v. *Tollet*, 2 P. Wms. 489, and, with notes, 1 L. C. 227.
(*k*) And see *Bruce* v. *Bruce*, L. R. 11 Eq. 371.
(*l*) *Innes* v. *Sayer*, 3 M. & G. 606.

is, who have taken under a voluntary gift. The court will, however, aid the defective execution of a power in favour of other persons, provided that they have given consideration, such as purchasers (*m*) (including in this term mortgagees (*n*) and lessees (*o*)), and creditors (*p*); but it cannot aid the non-execution of a power, since this would be to go against the nature of a power, the exercise of which is left to the free will and election of the donee, and equity, therefore, will not say that he shall exercise it, or do that for him which he does not think fit to do for himself (*q*).

Equity will not aid the non-execution of a power.

Acting on this principle, the court formerly refused to give any aid in cases where trustees, having a power to sell an estate, had sold it without including that part of it which consisted of timber or minerals, or where, having sold an estate with timber or minerals, they had allowed the tenant for life, or some other party, to receive a part of the purchase-money on account of the timber or minerals. For the trustees had no power, at law, to sell the estate without these adjuncts, and consequently the case resolved itself into one of non-execution of a power to sell an estate in its entirety (*r*). We pointed out, however, in our chapter on estates for life, that a recent statute (*s*) has now provided a remedy in cases where there has been an inadvertent sale of an estate with the timber thereon, or any other articles attached thereto, and the trustees have allowed some other person to receive the purchase-money for such timber or articles. And to this we have to add that the 25 & 26 Vict., c. 108, has enacted (*t*) that no sale of land, made before the date

22 & 23 Vict. c. 35.

25 & 26 Vict. c. 108.

(*m*) *Affleck* v. *Affleck*, 3 Sm. & Giff. 394; *re Dykes*, L. R. 7 Eq. 337.
(*n*) *Taylor* v. *Wheeler*, 2 Ver. 564.
(*o*) *Shannon* v. *Bradstreet*, 1 Sch. & L. 52.
(*p*) *Wilkes* v. *Holmes*, 9 Mod. 485.
(*q*) Per Sir J. Jekyll, M. R. 2 P. Wms. 490.
(*r*) See *Cockerell* v. *Cholmeley*, 1 Russ. & My. 418, 421.
(*s*) 22 & 23 Vict. c. 35, s. 13.
(*t*) S. 1.

of the passing of the act (*u*), by any trustee or other person, expressed or intended to be made in exercise of any trust or power authorizing the sale of land and not forbidding the reservation of minerals, and which sale shall have been made with a reservation of minerals with or without rights or powers for working such minerals, shall be invalid on the ground only that the trust or power did not expressly authorize such exception or reservation: and that no sale, made before the date of the act, of any minerals separately from the residue of the land subject to the trust or power intended to have been exercised, and either with or without such rights or powers as aforesaid, shall be invalid on the ground only that the trust or power did not authorize such sale. And as to sales to be made after the act, it is enacted (*v*) that every trustee then or thereafter to become authorized to dispose of land by way of sale may, unless forbidden by the instrument creating the trust or power, so dispose of such land with an exception or reservation of any minerals, and with or without rights and powers of, or incidental to, the working, getting, or carrying away of such minerals, or may (unless forbidden as aforesaid) dispose of the minerals, by way of sale, with or without such rights or powers separately from the residue of the land; and, in either case, without prejudice to any future exercise of the authority with respect to the excepted minerals or (as the case may be) the undisposed of land (*w*).

Destruction and alienation of powers.

Coming now to the destruction and alienation of powers, we will first remind the reader that powers are for this purpose most conveniently divided into those which are, and those which are not, simply collateral.

(*u*) 7th August, 1862.
(*v*) S. 2.
(*w*) See *Buckley* v. *Howell*, 29 Beav. 546.

Powers simply collateral cannot be, in any way, destroyed or alienated (x). But it is otherwise with powers not simply collateral. For these may be, under certain circumstances, (1) suspended (or partially destroyed); (2) extinguished (or wholly destroyed); or (3) alienated. We will proceed to consider these points separately.

Powers simply collateral cannot be destroyed or alienated. But powers not simply collateral may be.

The suspension of powers can only occur in cases of powers appendant, and will happen where the exercise of the power would be in derogation of some previous estate or interest, created under the power. This is well illustrated by a leading case (y), in which the facts were as follows—Lord Bolingbroke was tenant for life of certain lands, with a power, if it should be desired to sell them, to revoke the uses to which they were held, and appoint new uses in favour of a purchaser. Lord Bolingbroke, in consideration of £3000, granted an annuity to last for his lifetime, and, in order to secure its payment, demised the lands to the annuitant for a term which was to expire on his (Lord Bolingbroke's) death. Afterwards, he purported to revoke the uses to which the lands were held, joined in a sale of them, and appointed them to new uses in favour of the purchaser. The latter claimed to hold them free from the lease to the annuitant, which he could, of course, do if Lord Bolingbroke's revocation of the use to himself for life was effectual. But the Court of Chancery held that the power of revocation was suspended, so far as regarded the estate of the tenant for life, since otherwise he would have been able, by the exercise of his power, to commit a gross fraud in taking away the security for the annuity (z).

Suspension of powers.

The extinguishment of powers not simply collateral *Extinguish-*

(x) *Digge's Case*, 1 Rep. 173ᵃ.
(y) *Goodright* v. *Cator*, 2 Doug. 477.
(z) And see *Bringloe* v. *Goodson*, 4 Bing. N. C. 726; *Hurst* v. *Hurst*, 16 Beav. 372.

ment of powers.

may occur in the case of either those which are appendant, or those which are in gross. It occurs with powers of the first kind where the donee of the power parts with all his interest in the property subject to his power. For the very definition of an appendant power points to this. Suppose, for instance, that a tenant for life has power to make leases to take effect in possession. If he assigns the whole of his interest to another person, it is clear that any subsequent lease of that property made by him could not take effect out of his interest in the property, since he no longer has any. His power of making leases is, therefore, extinguished. But the rule will not apply where he does not entirely part with his interest in the property; as if he conveys it to trustees, but on trust to hold it for himself, subject to payments, out of the profits of it, to other people (*a*).

Cases in which a power in gross is extinguished do not often happen. For since no estates created by the donee of such a power can affect his own interest, he cannot, by the exercise of the power, prejudice any person to whom he may have transferred his interest; such a transfer cannot, therefore, extinguish his power. But the power is extinguished where he has, subsequently to his acquisition of the power, done some act which would be defeated by any future exercise of the power. Thus, where a tenant for life who had a power of charging the land subject to the power with the payment of a sum of money to other persons, joined in revoking the settlement and making a new one, whereby he was made tenant for life of the property but without a power of charging it; it was held that this power had been extinguished by his joining in the new settlement (*b*).

(*a*) *Ren* v. *Bulkeley*, 1 Doug. 291; *Long* v. *Rankin*, Sug. Pow. 895.
(*b*) *Savile* v. *Blacket*, 1 P. Wms. 777.

OF AN EXECUTORY INTEREST.

Both powers appendant and those in gross may be alienated. Where the power is one which the donee may exercise for his own benefit he has, in fact, something reserved to him out of the property subject to his power, and this he may alienate at pleasure, by "releasing" his power. If, for example, having a power of charging land with the payment of a sum of money to himself, he joins in a conveyance of the land clear of the charge, this will operate as a release of his power (c). And a power in gross may also be released, although the exercise of such a power cannot confer any benefit on the donee of the power (d). But this is subject to the rule that the release must not be made with the object of obtaining for the donee of the power some benefit which he could not get otherwise. For, in such a case, equity will refuse to give present effect to the release, so far as it would operate in favour of the donee (e).

Alienation of powers.

By release.

Lastly, a power, the exercise of which can confer any benefit on the donee of the power, may be the subject of involuntary alienation; it being provided by the Bankruptcy Act 1869 (f), that (g) the property of any bankrupt divisible amongst his creditors shall include the capacity to exercise, and to take proceedings for exercising, all such powers in, or over, or in respect of property, as might have been exercised by the bankrupt for his own benefit at the commencement of the bankruptcy, or during its continuance, except the right of nomination to a vacant ecclesiastical benefice.

Involuntary alienation. Bankruptcy Act 1869.

(c) See *West* v. *Berney*, 1 Russ. & My. 431, 434.
(d) *Smith* v. *Death*, 5 Madd. 371; *Horner* v. *Swann*, Turn. & Russ. 430.
(e) *Cunynghame* v. *Thurlow*, 1 Russ. & My. 436ᵃ.
(f) 32 & 33 Vict. c. 71.
(g) S. 15.

CHAPTER XI.

OF ESTATES IN JOINT-TENANCY, TENANCY IN COMMON, AND CO-PARCENARY.

HITHERTO we have considered estates in land as belonging to one tenant only: we will, in this chapter, briefly consider some cases in which an estate may belong to more than one tenant.

Joint-tenancy. The first of these which we will notice is that of an estate being held in Joint-Tenancy, or by two or more Joint-Tenants.

A joint-tenancy may exist in any kind of estate in land. In order to constitute it, there must be, amongst the tenants, unity of interest, unity of title, unity of time, and unity of possession (a). In other words, the tenants must have the same quantity of interest (for instance, one cannot hold for life, and another in fee simple); their estates must be created by the same act, and must commence simultaneously, (except under circumstances to be presently noticed); and each must have entire possession of the land, concurrently with the others; thus constituting one owner and one estate. The exception above referred to occurs where joint-tenants take by way of use, or under a will. Thus, if there be a gift, made either by deed or by will, to the use of the children of A, or a gift by will to the children of A, those children of A who may be born after the deed or will has

---

(a) 2 Bl. Com. 180.

come into operation will take, each successively on birth, an estate in joint-tenancy with the others (b).

An estate may be granted to be held in joint-tenancy by any person capable of creating that estate. Joint-tenancy cannot arise by operation of law, but may be conferred by parol, when the estate in question can be created by parol; otherwise a deed or will is requisite. *Creation of a joint-tenancy.*

Such an estate occurs where lands are conveyed, or given, to two, or more, persons without any modifying words. Thus, a grant to A and B, or to A and B and their heirs, will confer upon A and B an estate in joint-tenancy, for life, or in fee simple, as the case may be. And if the gift is made by deed, it would seem to be doubtful whether the addition of the word "equally," or of the words "equally to be divided between them," or such like, would operate to prevent A and B from taking as joint-tenants (c). In a will, however, the apparent intention of the donor would, in such a case, be taken into consideration, and each donee would take a separate undivided share. *Form of words.*

The incidents of an estate by joint-tenancy will, to a great extent, depend upon the nature of the estate thus held. But since all the tenants constitute in law but a single owner, charges or grants made by any one of them on, or out of, the joint estate will cease with his death, and do not bind the others. For the same reason, one joint-tenant had not formerly any remedy against another who had received an undue proportion of the profits of the estate. But by the 4 & 5 Anne, c. 3, it was enacted (d) that an action of *Incidents of a joint-tenancy. Charges or grants. Receipt of profits. 4 & 5 Anne, c. 3.*

(b) *Shelley's Case,* note (Q), 1 Rep. 100ᵇ; *Kenworthy v. Ward,* 11 Ha. 196.
(c) Sug. Pow. 441, but see 1 Wat. Cop. 138, note (2); *Fisher v. Wigg,* 1 P. Wms. 14.
(d) S. 27.

account shall and may be brought and maintained by one joint-tenant against the other, for receiving more than comes to his just proportion, and against the executor or administrator of such joint-tenant. Joint-tenants may, if their estate permits, make leases either jointly or separately; but if they demise jointly, any one of them may separately put an end to his demise, whether his companions join him or not (*e*).

Leases.

Extinguishment of a joint-tenancy.

A joint-tenancy, as such, cannot be alienated either by deed or will; that is to say, if A and B are joint-tenants, A cannot transfer his estate to C to hold as joint-tenant with B. One joint-tenant may, however, "release" his interest to another, but this latter, if there are more than two joint-tenants, will not thereby obtain a larger proportion of the estate than the others, who will equally benefit by the release, although not professedly made to them. And a joint-tenant may sever his estate by conveying it, or even by entering into a binding agreement to convey it (*f*), to a third party; but the act of severance will, of itself, convert the estate of the transferee into a tenancy in common as between himself and the other joint-tenants, if more than one.

By release.

By severance.

Estate in joint-tenancy survives.

One advantage of the joint-tenant's having effected a severance of his estate during his lifetime is, that it will go to his representatives after his death; and partly on this account, partly because of the inconveniences to which a joint-tenancy gives rise, the Legislature has provided peculiar facilities for enabling joint-tenants to sever their estates. To these we will, however, refer a little later on, since they apply to other forms of ownership besides that of joint-tenancy.

(*e*) *Doe* v. *Chaplin*, 3 Taunt. 120.
(*f*) *Parteriche* v. *Powlet*, 2 Atk. 54; *Caldwell* v. *Fellowes*, L. R. 9 Eq. 410.

It will have been gathered, from the above remarks, that a joint-tenant cannot dispose of his estate by will. If he dies without having severed it during his lifetime, it will go to the surviving joint-tenants, or, as it is said, will "survive" to them, and the ultimate survivor will take the whole estate. This is so, notwithstanding that the estate may have been given to them "and their heirs." For the surviving joint-tenant, having continued for the longest time in possession of the estate, was presumed, in feudal days, to have done most service to the feud, and upon that account was allowed to transmit it to his heir (*g*), a privilege which still remains, although the reason for it has ceased to exist.

The next form of tenancy which we have to consider, is a Tenancy in Common. This occurs when two, or more, persons have each a distinct and separate, but undivided, share in an estate. Of the four requisites for constituting a joint-tenancy, only one is essential to a tenancy in common, namely, unity of possession; for tenants in common may have different quantities of interest, created by different acts, done at different times. All that is necessary is that they should hold the same land promiscuously. *Tenancy in common.*

A tenancy in common, like a joint-tenancy, cannot arise by operation of law, but may be conferred by any other means by which an estate in land can be created. As previously mentioned, it is necessary for that purpose to express in a deed, though not in a will, that the persons on whom the estate is conferred are to take as tenants in common. *Creation of a tenancy in common. Form of words.*

Each tenant in common is, in respect of his share, nearly in the same position as an independent tenant; but a tenant in common in fee simple *Incidents.*

(*g*) Bacon's Abridgement, Title Joint-Tenants, I. s. 1.

has been restrained from committing waste on what is, <u>until severance</u>, the joint property of himself and his co-tenants (*h*). The 4 & 5 Anne, c. 3, previously referred to, applies to the case of tenants in common, as well as to that of joint-tenants.

<small>Alienation.</small>

A tenancy in common may not only be alienated by the owner during his lifetime, but differs from a joint-tenancy in being <u>disposable</u> by will. If the tenant dies intestate, his estate will, if it is one which lasts beyond his lifetime, go to his heir, or administrator, according to its nature; and not survive to the other tenants in common.

<small>Estate in Coparcenary.</small>

The remaining form of tenancy which we have to notice, is that in Coparcenary. An estate in coparcenary arises either where the owner in fee simple of land has died intestate, and without male heirs; in which case all his female heiresses take jointly; or by some particular custom, as that of Gavelkind, where all a man's sons inherit his land equally, in the event of his dying without having disposed of it. Such an estate is neither a joint-tenancy nor a tenancy in common, <small>Always arises by operation of law.</small> and differs from both in that it always arises by operation of law, never by act of parties. On the other hand, it partakes in some degree of the nature of both. Thus, it resembles a joint-tenancy in re-<u>quiring</u> for its existence <u>unity</u> of interest, title, and possession, so that all the coparceners make but one heir between them. In other respects, it resembles a tenancy in common: thus, it does not require unity of time, for on the death of any of the coparceners, their estates will descend to their respective heirs, who will hold as coparceners with the others. <u>Nor</u> does such an estate <u>require unity</u>, although it does require entirety, <u>of interest</u>, since each coparcener is entitled to

---

(*h*) *Dougall* v. *Foster*, 4 Grant, 319.

a distinct share in the estate. It may be added here that a man can be coparcener with himself; as in the case where he holds one moiety of an estate as heir of his father, and the other moiety as heir of his mother.

A coparcener may alienate his estate by either deed or will, and his alienee will hold as tenant in common with the other coparceners. Alienation.

Coparceners could formerly, where they were all agreed, make a partition of their lands amongst themselves by parol. But the Statute of Frauds (*i*) first required all partitions to be evidenced by writing, and the Real Property Amendment Act (*j*) has now made a deed requisite for this purpose. The most convenient way, however, of making partition, either amongst coparceners, tenants in common, or joint-tenants, is that which we will now proceed to state.

The views of law and of equity were formerly different in regard to joint-tenancies and tenancies in common. The former were favoured by the law, because the divisible services issuing from land (as rent, &c.) are not divided, nor the entire services (as fealty) multiplied, by the existence of such a tenancy (*k*). But the latter were preferred by equity, which does not look favourably on the system of survivorship which obtains in a joint-tenancy (*l*). Statutes relating to partition.

Since law is older than equity, there was a time when joint-tenants, and tenants in common, had all to concur in order to divide the inheritance. This was first changed by the 31 Hen. VIII., c. 1, and the 32 31 Hen. VIII. c. 1.

(*i*) 29 Car. II. c. 3.
(*j*) 8 & 9 Vict. c. 106.
(*k*) 2 Bl. Com. 193.
(*l*) *Parteriche* v. *Powlet*, 2 Atk. 54, 55.

Hen. VIII., c. 32, which enabled any joint-tenant or tenant in common to compel the others to make partition. The writ by which this was effected under these statutes was abolished by the 3 & 4 Wm. IV., c. 27, but the Court of Chancery always exercised a power of compelling partition, in proper cases, between any of the tenants whose estates we have been considering in this chapter. And now, by the Partition Act 1868 (*m*), the court is empowered, in a suit for partition, where, if the act had not been passed, a decree for partition might have been made, to direct a sale of the property for the benefit of the parties interested; and (*n*) if a sale is requested by a party or parties interested, individually or collectively, to the extent of one moiety or upwards in the property to which the suit relates, such sale is to be directed, unless the court sees good reason to the contrary (*o*).

In cases where all the persons interested in the property agree to have a partition, recourse may be had to the Inclosure Commissioners, who, under the 11 & 12 Vict., c. 99, may (*p*), on the application in writing of the persons interested in the undivided parts or shares of any land, direct inquiries whether the proposed partition would be beneficial to the owners of such parts or shares. If the commissioners are of opinion that such partition would be beneficial, and that the terms of it are just and reasonable, they may cause to be framed, and confirm, an order of partition, showing the land allotted in severalty to each person so interested, in respect of the undivided part or share in which he shall be interested, and this order is of itself sufficient, without the necessity of any other deeds executed by the tenants themselves. And in order to facilitate the making of partitions, it is enacted

---

(*m*) 31 & 32 Vict. c. 40, s. 3.
(*n*) S. 4.
(*o*) See as to this *Pemberton* v. *Barnes*, L. R. 6 Ch. 685.
(*p*) S. 13.

by the 20 & 21 Vict., c. 31 (*q*), that when a partition is made, any disproportion in the value of the different allotments in severalty may be compensated by a rent charge.

20 & 21 Vict. c. 31.

(*q*) S. 7.

CHAPTER XII.

OF HUSBAND AND WIFE.

Term of Years.
IT is proposed to offer a few remarks, in this chapter, on the mutual rights of a husband and his wife, in respect of such property in land as previously to, or during the continuance of, the coverture belongs to the 'wife, or is acquired by her. And we will begin by stating the law on this subject when unaffected by any of the doctrines of equity. Commencing with a term of years belonging to the wife, we find that the husband has a right to receive the profits of it during their joint lives. He may also dispose of them at any time during the same period. Thus, in an old case before the House of Lords (*a*), a term had been assigned in trust for a married woman. Her husband died, whereby she became a single woman, or *feme sole* as it is called in legal phrase. She afterwards married again, and her husband sold the term and received the purchase-money. It was held that this was a valid disposition of it, and good as against the wife. It follows that the husband can make an under-lease of part of his wife's term. And if he survives her, he is entitled to the term, in virtue of his marital right, but subject to all charges and liabilities with which it was affected whilst in her possession (*b*).

But the husband cannot make any disposition of the term, by will, which will be binding upon the wife if she survives him. For, in that case, the term becomes her own property, and if he has made an under-lease

---

(*a*) *Turner's Case*, 1 Ver. 7.
(*b*) 1 Bright, H. & W. 96.

out of the term, any part of the under-lease which may exist at his death belongs to the wife (c).

If the wife's estate is one for life, the husband has a right to receive the profits of it during the joint lives of himself and his wife, the seisin of it being in them jointly; and he can impose charges on the estate, which charges will not, however, extend beyond their joint lives. Where the wife's estate is one of inheritance, she and her husband are jointly seised of it during their two lives, the husband being entitled to receive the profits of it during that time, and also for the rest of his life if he acquires an estate by curtesy, the requisites for which have been stated in our chapter on estates for life. And, in this case, any charges which he has created on the land will endure during his lifetime.

Estate for life, or in fee.

The husband cannot, however, by himself dispose of his wife's estate of freehold, by either deed or will, nor will he be entitled to her estate in fee simple if he survives her. For such an estate will, subject to his estate by curtesy (if any), belong to the heir of his wife. And if the wife survives the husband, her estate of freehold belongs to her absolutely. But the husband and wife may, during their joint lives, alienate the wife's estate of freehold, provided the alienation is made, if the land be of freehold tenure, by deed duly acknowledged by the wife (d); or, if the land be of copyhold tenure, by surrender preceded by the wife's separate examination by the steward of the manor.

The husband's interest in his wife's real or leasehold estate may, moreover, be entirely excluded. This will happen if the estate is conveyed, or given, to her by a

Doctrine of separate use.

(c) *Sym's Case*, Cro. Eliz. 33.
(d) 3 & 4 Wm. IV. c. 74, ss. 77, 79.

deed, or will, which states that it is to be held for her "separate use." In that case, if the property is vested in trustees for the wife, they will have the legal, and she the equitable, estate in it; whilst if there are no trustees appointed, the husband will take the legal estate, but the Court of Chancery will compel him to hold it as a trustee for his wife (*e*).

And although the gift of property to an unmarried woman for her separate use will have no effect so long as she remains unmarried, yet if she marries without having done anything to show that the property is not to be for her separate use, her husband's marital rights over it will be excluded (*f*). A woman may, moreover, in contemplation of marriage, with the consent of her intended husband, settle to her separate use any of her property which had not been expressed to be so held.

Form of words necessary to create separate use.

No particular form of words is necessary in order to vest property in a woman to her separate use, but the instrument conferring the property must be so worded as to show a manifest intention that the estate is to be at her absolute disposal (*g*), especially where it is given directly to her, without the intervention of any trustees (*h*). In all such cases the word "separate" is the proper one to use, having a fixed technical meaning appropriated to it (*i*).

Married Women's Property Act.

Moreover leasehold, or real, estate acquired by a married woman may, in certain cases, become her separate property, without any form of words. For it is enacted by the Married Women's Property Act

---

(*e*) *Bennet* v. *Davis*, 2 P. Wms. 316; *Newlands* v. *Paynter*, 10 Sim. 377.
(*f*) *Tullett* v. *Armstrong*, 1 Beav. 1, 4 My. & C. 377; *Hawkes* v. *Hubback*, L. R. 11 Eq. 5.
(*g*) *Stanton* v. *Hall*, 2 Russ. & My. 175; *Tyler* v. *Lake*, 2 Russ. & My. 183.
(*h*) *Gilbert* v. *Lewis*, 1 De G. J. & S. 38, 47, 48.
(*i*) *Massy* v. *Rowen*, L. R. 4 H. L. 288.

1870 (*j*) that where any woman, married after the passing of the act (*k*), 'shall, during her marriage, become entitled to any personal property as next of kin, or one of the next of kin, of an intestate, or to any sum of "money" (a word which may, in some cases, include leaseholds (*l*)) under any deed or will, such property shall, subject and without prejudice to the trusts of any settlement affecting the same, belong to the woman for her separate use. And that (*m*) where any freehold, copyhold, or customary property shall descend upon any woman, married after the passing of the act, as heiress or co-heiress of an intestate, the rents and profits of such property shall, subject and without prejudice to the trusts of any settlement affecting the same, belong to such woman for her separate use.

If a married woman has property belonging to her for her separate use, she has the same power of disposition over it as if she were a *feme sole*, unless the gift has been accompanied by a proviso restraining her from alienation by way of anticipation : in which case she cannot dispose of it, except by will, so long as she remains married.

Married woman's power of disposition over separate estate.

Her power of disposition over personal property settled to her separate use, without any restraint on alienation, was the first to be established (*n*). Subsequent decisions extended this privilege to her separate life interest in real estate (*o*). And now it has been finally decided that she has the same power over an estate in fee simple, provided that the whole estate is settled to her separate use (*p*). Her power of disposition extends to estates in reversion or remainder, as

---

(*j*) 33 & 34 Vict. c. 93, s. 7.
(*k*) 9th August, 1870.
(*l*) *Prichard* v. *Prichard*, L. R. 11 Eq. 232.
(*m*) S. 8.
(*n*) *Fettiplace* v. *Gorges*, 3 Bro. C. C. 7.
(*o*) *Stead* v. *Nelson*, 2 Beav. 245; *Major* v. *Lansley*, 2 Russ. & My. 355.
(*p*) <u>*Taylor* v. *Meads*</u>, 13 W. R. 394.

well as to those in possession (*q*), and may be exercised by either deed or will, without the consent of her husband, and without any acknowledgment by her of the disposing instrument (*r*). It follows that a married woman's separate estate is liable to the fulfilment of her contracts (*s*), and it would even seem that she may, if she has separate estate, be made a bankrupt if she fails to pay her debts (*t*). Moreover, a married woman who has separate estate is now bound to maintain her husband or children, if they become chargeable to the parish (*u*).

Case of property being given to a husband and wife.

Finally, we have to remark that if an estate is given to a man and a woman before marriage, and afterwards they marry, they will take as joint-tenants (*v*). But if an estate be given to a husband and wife, the case is different. For now the law considers them as but one person; they take, therefore, "by entireties," and neither can sever his, or her, share as joint-tenants can. Whatever the nature of the property may be, the husband is entitled to the rents and profits of it during his lifetime, and to the estate itself if he survives his wife. He can also, if the property is leasehold, make a valid assignment of it during his lifetime, which will be good against his wife if she survive him (*w*). But he cannot dispose of leaseholds by will; neither can he alienate freeholds or copyholds by any means, except with his wife's concurrence. Hence all estates in land given in the way we have supposed, and not disposed of by the husband and wife during their joint lives, will, subject to the husband's right to alienate such of it as is leasehold during his lifetime, belong ultimately to the husband or the wife, according as the one or the other may happen to be the survivor.

(*q*) *Sturgis* v. *Corp*, 13 Ves. 190.
(*r*) *Taylor* v. *Meads*, 13 W. R. 394.
(*s*) See notes to *Hulme* v. *Tenant*, 1 L. C. 481.
(*t*) *Ex parte Holland*, L. R. 9 Ch. 307.
(*u*) 33 & 34 Vict. c. 93, ss. 13, 14.
(*v*) Co. Litt. 187b.
(*w*) *Grute* v. *Locroft*, Cro. Eliz. 287.

CHAPTER XIII.

OF AN EQUITY OF REDEMPTION.

HITHERTO we have been occupied solely with the consideration of legal estates in land, and it is to them that our attention will be principally confined all through this work. But there is one variety of equitable estates, a notice of which comes fairly within the scope of our reading. This arises when land is pledged, or "mortgaged," to a lender or "mortgagee," as a security for money advanced by him. Here the borrower or "mortgagor" has still an estate or interest left in the land, and it is of this that we now propose to treat. *Equity of Redemption the result of a mortgage.*

The word "mortgage" (a dead pledge) is significant of a state of the law which has long passed away. A mortgage, in olden times, was effected by the use of two contemporaneous deeds, of which one set forth that the estate in question had been conveyed absolutely to the mortgagee, whilst the other, known as "the deed of defeasance," provided that it should be reconveyed to the mortgagor if he, on a specified day, repaid all sums for which the estate was a security. Failing this payment, on the precise day, the estate became the absolute property of the mortgagee. Thus, Littleton, writing in the reign of Edward the Fourth, says (*a*): If a feoffment be made upon such condition, that if the feoffor pay to the feoffee at a certain day £40 of money, then the feoffor may re-enter: if he doth not pay, then the land *Former law of redemption.*

(*a*) Litt. Ten. s. 332.

which is in pledge upon condition for the payment of the money is taken away from him for ever, and so dead to him upon condition.

Origin of an Equity of Redemption.

In time, however, the Court of Chancery began to consider this condition merely as a penalty imposed in order to secure punctual payment of the debt due from the mortgagor, and gave him, therefore, a right (subject to conditions to be presently noticed) to recover his estate, long after the time when a court of law looked upon it as the absolute property of the mortgagee. This right, from the fact of its being enforcible only in equity, came to be known as the mortgagor's Equity of Redemption, and is now inseparable from every mortgage. And it may be here mentioned that one result of this doctrine of equity is that (the former reasons for having two deeds no longer existing) the absolute conveyance of the estate to the mortgagee and a clause corresponding to the old deed of defeasance are now contained in the same instrument.

Creation of an Equity of Redemption.

It follows, from what has been said above, that an equity of redemption arises by operation of equity, without any act of parties. We will proceed to notice the principal points relating to it, premising that we shall treat only of that equity which arises in consequence of the pledge of one, or other, of those estates in land which have been considered in previous chapters of this work. At first, also, we will deal only with a mortgage of the legal interest in such property.

Equity of redemption is an estate in land.

An equity of redemption is more than a mere right. Lord Hale defined it as an estate in equity, recognised by the law as an equitable right inherent in the land, and of such consideration in the eye of the law, that the law takes notice of it, and makes it assignable and devisable (*b*). This statement has been confirmed

---

(*b*) *Pawlett* v. *Atty.-Genl.*, Hardres, 465, 469.

by other judges. Thus, in an early case (c), A, an unmarried woman, being seised in fee simple of a freehold estate, mortgaged it, and afterwards married B, by whom she had issue: A died, leaving the mortgage unredeemed, and the question arose whether B was entitled, subject to the mortgage, to an estate by curtesy in the land. On behalf of the heir of A, it was argued that the equity of redemption was not an actual estate or interest in A, but only a power to reduce the estate into possession again on paying off the mortgage, and that a man cannot have an estate by curtesy in a bare right. This view was acquiesced in by the Master of the Rolls (Sir J. Jekyll), but his decision was reversed, on appeal, by Lord Chancellor Hardwicke. The latter judge said that an equity of redemption had always been considered as an estate in land, and, therefore, the person entitled to the equity of redemption as the owner of the land, and a mortgage in fee as personal assets (d). He added that, with regard to that seisin in fact which is essential to entitle a husband to curtesy, there was, here, such a seisin in possession of the equitable estate of the wife as, in a court of equity, is considered equivalent to an actual seisin of a freehold estate at common law.

The result of the owner of the equity of redemption being considered as the owner of the land is that, subject to the rights of the mortgagee, he may deal with it as if it were a legal estate. Thus, an equity of redemption may, according to the quality of the legal estate, be devised, granted, mortgaged, or entailed: and an entail in it may be barred in the usual way. Moreover, an equity of redemption in an estate lasting beyond the lifetime of the tenant will go in the same way as its corresponding legal estate (e).

Incidents and alienation of equity of redemption similar to those of a legal estate.

(c) *Casborne* v. *Scarfe*, 1 Atk. 603, and, with notes, 2 L. C. 1035.
(d) See *Thornborough* v. *Baker*, 3 Swan. 628, and, with notes, 2 L. C. 1030.
(e) *Fawcet* v. *Lowther*, 2 Ves. 300, 303.

OF CORPOREAL HEREDITAMENTS.

Equity of redemption cannot be excluded. We have already referred to the fact that an equity of redemption is inseparable from every mortgage, and, besides this, any bargain entered into, at the time of executing the mortgage deed, with a view to making the subject of it irredeemable, will, generally speaking, be set aside in equity. This doctrine flows naturally from that which confers a right to redeem upon the mortgagor, and has been established from an early period. Thus, in a case (*f*) decided in the year 1683, a covenant in a mortgage deed, by which the right to redeem the mortgaged estate was confined to certain persons, *viz.*, the mortgagor and the heirs male of his body, was held to be void. On the same principle an attempt, in another case (*g*), to limit the time for redemption, by cutting it down to the joint lives of the mortgagor and the mortgagee, was not allowed to succeed (*h*). Any attempt, also, to prevent the equity of redemption from being exercised within a reasonable time will be set aside, and redemption allowed at an earlier period than that fixed by the mortgage deed (*i*).

Exception to the above rule. An exception to the rule that an equity of redemption cannot be restricted occurs, however, in cases where the mortgage is intended to be of the nature of a family settlement. Where, for instance, a mortgaged estate was made redeemable during the life of the mortgagor only, but it was proved that the mortgagee (who was a near relation of the mortgagor) had been intended by the latter to succeed to his estate if he died without issue, and that the clause of redemption was put in merely in order to provide for the case of the mortgagor's leaving issue: it was held that the clause could be sustained, and that the estate became,

---

(*f*) *Howard* v. *Harris*, 1 Ver. 190, and, with notes, 2 L. C. 1042.
(*g*) *Spurgeon* v. *Collier*, 1 Eden, 55.
(*h*) And see *Manlove* v. *Bale*, 2 Ver. 83.
(*i*) *Talbot* v. *Braddill*, 1 Ver. 183.

on the death of the mortgagor without issue, the absolute property of the mortgagee (*j*).

A distinction must also be made in this respect between a mortgage deed and a purchase deed conveying the property absolutely, but giving the vendor a right to re-purchase it : for, under such a deed, the vendor can only recover his property by complying precisely with the terms of the deed (*k*). Thus, in one case (*l*), A had conveyed a life estate to B in consideration of £4739, and, by a deed of even date, it was agreed between them that if A should, at any time, desire to re-purchase the life estate for £4739, B would convey it to him for that sum. B took possession of the estate and died, leaving a will in which he spoke of the life estate as "redeemable" on payment of £4739 and "interest," and referred to this interest as his "security." But it was held, on A's failing to prove any intention of the parties to make a mortgage, that the instruments in question did not amount to a mortgage deed. The Lord Chancellor (Lord Cranworth) in giving judgment remarked : " These deeds do not, on the face of them, constitute a mortgage. The rule of law is, that *primâ facie* an absolute conveyance, containing nothing to show that the relation of debtor and creditor is to exist between the parties, does not cease to become an absolute conveyance, and become a mortgage, merely because the vendor stipulates that he shall have the right to re-purchase. In every such case the question is what, upon a fair construction, is the meaning of the instruments (*m*) ? " The rule is the same with reference to dealings with an equity of redemption (*n*) ; and the leaning of the courts would

Distinction between a mortgage and a purchase with proviso for re-purchase.

(*j*) *Newcomb* v. *Bonham*, 1 Ver. 7, 214, 231.
(*k*) *Barrell* v. *Sabine*, 1 Ver. 268.
(*l*) *Alderson* v. *White*, 2 De G. & J. 97.
(*m*) And see *Perry* v. *Meddowcroft*, 4 Beav. 197 ; *Goodman* v. *Grierson*, 2 Ba. & B. 274 ; *Williams* v. *Owen*, 5 My. & C. 303.
(*n*) See *Ensworth* v. *Griffith*, 5 Bro. P. C. 184 ; *Davis* v. *Thomas*, 1 Russ. & My. 506 ; *Bulwer* v. *Astley*, 1 Ph. 422 ; *Gossip* v. *Wright*, 9 Jur. (N. S.) 592.

probably be to look upon such instruments as purchase deeds rather than as mortgage deeds, since mortgages with separate deeds of defeasance are not approved of in equity (*o*). Moreover, an agreement by the mortgagor, entered into after the time of making the mortgage, though restricting his ordinary right to redeem, would appear to be binding, if made for some consideration; for this is not the introduction of a stipulation by way of penalty or forfeiture, but the price to be paid in return for a privilege conferred (*p*).

Who is entitled to redeem. An ordinary mortgage deed contains a proviso for the redemption of the mortgaged premises, by "the mortgagor, his heirs, executors, administrators, or assigns;" but the estate may be redeemed, not only by the persons specified in this proviso, but also by all persons who have any interest in, or lien upon, it (*q*). Thus a surety who has paid off the mortgage debt (*r*), a joint-tenant (*s*), a tenant in common (*t*), in tail (*u*), or for life (*v*), or in dower, or by curtesy, of the equity of redemption, are each entitled to redeem on the same terms as the mortgagor himself might have done. Other assignees of a mortgagor, such as subsequent mortgagees, or judgment creditors, may also redeem, but in their case the right of redemption is only ancillary to their right to payment out of their debtor's land; they cannot, therefore, enforce it so long as a prior incumbrancer is in possession of the estate. And a judgment creditor cannot obtain the aid of equity for this purpose, unless he has previously complied with the provisions of the Judgment Acts, so far as circumstances will permit, and then applied to

---

(*o*) *Cotterell* v. *Purchase*, Ca. t. Talb. 61.
(*p*) See *Davis* v. *Thomas*, 1 Russ. & My. 506; *Ford* v. *Chesterfield*, 19 Beav. 428.
(*q*) *Pearce* v. *Morris*, L. R. 5 Ch. 227, 229.
(*r*) *Mayhew* v. *Crickitt*, 2 Swan. 185, 191; *Wade* v. *Coope*, 2 Sim. 155, 160.
(*s*) See *Waugh* v. *Land*, G. Coop. 129.
(*t*) See *Wynne* v. *Styan*, 2 Ph. 303, 306.
(*u*) *Playford* v. *Playford*, 4 Ha. 546.
(*v*) *Evans* v. *Jones*, Kay, 29.

the Court of Chancery to remove any further impediments to his obtaining delivery of the land (w). The general creditors of a mortgagor may also, under special circumstances, acquire a right to redeem his estate (x).

We come next to the consideration of the rights and liabilities of a mortgagor and of a mortgagee. These are, naturally, closely related to each other, but in dealing with them we will, as far as possible, treat of them separately, in the order in which they have been mentioned.

On the execution of a mortgage deed, the mortgagor becomes the equitable owner, and the mortgagee the legal owner, of the mortgaged estate. If there is, as sometimes happens, an express stipulation between them that the mortgagor shall remain in possession of the estate until a specified date, subject to his punctual payment of interest; that has the effect of a re-demise of the property by the mortgagee to the mortgagor, who becomes, therefore, a termor during the term so agreed upon, and cannot be dispossessed of the property during that time, provided that he observes his part of the agreement. If, however, as more frequently happens, the mortgagor remains in possession, without any agreement with his mortgagee, his exact position is not very clear. The mere receipt of interest by the mortgagee is not a recognition of the mortgagor as a tenant (y), and the mortgagor is consequently spoken of sometimes as a tenant at will, sometimes as a tenant by sufferance; but neither of these definitions is quite accurate. He is, perhaps, more correctly described as one who, having parted with his estate, remains in

<small>Rights and liabilities of a mortgagor.</small>

<small>Mortgagor may be a tenant for a term to the mortgagee.</small>

<small>But is not usually.</small>

<small>Position in such case.</small>

(w) *Re Cowbridge Ry. Co.*, L. R. 5 Eq. 413; *Mildred* v. *Austin*, L. R. 8 Eq. 220; *Hatton* v. *Heywood*, L. R. 9 Ch. 229; *Beckett* v. *Buckley*, L. R. 17 Eq. 435.
(x) Fisher on Mortgages, 316.
(y) *Doe* v. *Cadwallader*, 2 B. & Ad. 473.

246   OF CORPOREAL HEREDITAMENTS.

possession of it at the pleasure, and consistently with the rights, of the grantee; exercising the ordinary privileges of property, yet liable, at the option of the mortgagee, to be treated either as a tenant or as a trespasser, and to be ejected without notice or demand of possession, and without any claim, whether treated as tenant or as trespasser, to rents in arrear, or accruing, or to the growing crops (z). He is not bound to account for any rents or profits of the estate which he has received during his occupation (a), for he is not a receiver for the mortgagee (b); and he is entitled (whether in possession or not) to exercise rights incident to the estate which are not, presumably, a source of profit. Thus he may nominate to a vacant advowson, notwithstanding any previous agreement with his mortgagee to the contrary (c), or vote, in respect of the property, at an election for Parliament. He may, moreover, commit waste, except in cases where the security is thereby made insufficient (d), and is liable on account of the public burdens imposed on the property (e). But he cannot, on the other hand, deal with the legal estate in it, and cannot, therefore, make a good lease of the land without the consent of the mortgagee, for if he does, the mortgagee may eject his tenant, without any demand of possession or notice to quit (f).

Not bound to account for rents or profits.

May, in some cases, act as owner.

When mortgagor entitled to redeem.

But whether in possession, or not, of the mortgaged estate, the mortgagor still retains his equity of redemption unless, and until, it is lost to him by some of the means to be presently noticed. He is not en-

---

(z) Fisher on Mortgages, 464.
(a) *Colman* v. *St Albans*, 3 Ves. 25ᵃ.
(b) *Ex parte Wilson*, 2 Ves. & B. 252.
(c) *Mackensie* v. *Robinson*, 3 Atk. 558.
(d) *King* v. *Smith*, 4 Ha. 239; *Humphreys* v. *Harrison*, 1 Jac. & W. 581; *Ackroyd* v. *Mitchell*, 3 L. T. (N.S.) 236.
(e) *R.* v. *Baker*, L. R. 2 Q. B. 621.
(f) *Keech* v. *Hall*, 1 Doug. 21, and, with notes, 1 Smith, L. C. 523; *Doe* v. *Maisey*, 8 B. & C. 767.

titled, however, to redeem the mortgaged estate before the day named for that purpose in the mortgage deed; even though he tender to the mortgagee the principal sum due together with interest on it up to the day specified (*g*). On the named day he may redeem without having given any previous notice of his intention to do so; but after that day he is not entitled to redeem without giving six calendar months' previous notice, or paying interest up to the day when the time fixed by such a notice would have expired (*h*); because a mortgagee, as a rule, advances his money by way of investment, and is therefore entitled to time to look out for a new security.

If, from any reason, the mortgagor is unable to get the mortgagee to receive the mortgage money and reconvey the property (as, for instance, if the accounts are disputed, or it is doubtful who is the person entitled to a reconveyance) he must file a bill in equity for redemption, and, on proof that he is the person entitled to redeem, he will obtain a decree, ordering that an account shall be taken (by the proper officer of the court) of what is due to the mortgagee for principal, for interest calculated up to six calendar months from the date of the order, and (usually) for the costs of that suit; with a deduction, if necessary, of all the rents and profits which have been, or which ought to have been, received by the mortgagee; and that on payment being made by the mortgagor, on that day six months, of all sums thus found due to the mortgagee, the latter shall reconvey the property; but that in default of such payment the mortgagor's bill is to be dismissed with costs—a proceeding which has the effect of a decree that the equity of redemption shall be foreclosed (*i*). As has been mentioned, the

Bill for redemption.

(*g*) *Brown* v. *Cole*, 14 L. J. (Ch.) 167.
(*h*) *Sharpnell* v. *Blake*, 2 Eq. Ca. Ab. 603.
(*i*) *Cholmley* v. *Oxford*, 2 Atk. 267; *Winchester* v. *Paine*, 11 Ves. 194, 199; *Faulkner* v. *Bolton*, 7 Sim. 319.

costs of such a suit fall more usually upon the mortgagor (*j*), the exception occurring when the suit has been rendered necessary by the fault of the mortgagee, as where he has refused to accept a sum tendered to him which has been found ultimately, in working out the decree, to have been sufficient to pay everything due to him (*k*).

Rights and liabilities of a mortgagee.

Next, as to those points which relate more particularly to the mortgagee. Such a person has, as a consequence of his position, various rights which he may exercise in order to enforce his security. Thus, he may sue the mortgagor at law on the covenants for payment of the principal money lent and interest which are to be found in every properly drawn mortgage deed; he may enter into possession of the mortgaged property; and he may take proceedings for the foreclosure of the equity of redemption, or for the sale of the land. These rights, as well as any other

Mortgagee may exercise his rights concurrently.

remedies which he may happen to possess, he may exercise concurrently, without any interference by the courts (*l*). For instance, he may enter into possession of the property, and then sue at law on the mortgagor's covenant, bringing at the same time a bill for foreclosure (*m*); or he may sue on a bond, given as a collateral security, although he has already commenced a suit for foreclosure (*n*). Since, however, the exercise of any of these rights by the mortgagee involves corresponding liabilities on his part, we will proceed to consider each of them separately.

Action on the covenants for payment.

The mortgagee ought seldom to be obliged to have recourse to an action on the mortgagor's covenants in order to recover either his interest or his principal.

(*j*) See *Cotterell* v. *Stratton*, L. R. 8 Ch. 295.
(*k*) *Harmer* v. *Priestley*, 16 Beav. 569.
(*l*) See *Lockhart* v. *Hardy*, 9 Beav. 349; *Cockell* v. *Bacon*, 16 Beav. 158, 159.
(*m*) *Rees* v. *Parkinson*, 2 Anstr. 497.
(*n*) *Burnell* v. *Martin*, 2 Doug. 417.

This remedy may, however, be found useful where the interest has been allowed to get very much in arrear, or where the mortgaged estate proves to be an insufficient security for the amount due on it. For as to the first point, the mortgagee's power of recovering interest, in the absence of such a covenant, is restricted by the 3 & 4 Wm. IV., c. 27 (*o*), which enacts that no arrears of interest, in respect of any sum of money charged on land, shall be recovered by any action or suit but within six years after the same shall have become due, or after an acknowledgment of the same, in writing, shall have been given to the person entitled thereto, or his agent, signed by the person by whom the same was payable, or his agent; whereas under the 3 & 4 Wm. IV., c. 42 (*p*), an action of covenant, or of debt, upon any bond or other specialty may be brought within twenty years (*q*) (or longer in the case of persons under disability (*r*)) after the cause of such action or suit, or within twenty years after the time when the party liable by virtue of such specialty, or his agent, shall have given an acknowledgment of the debt either by writing, or by part payment, or part satisfaction of, or on account of, any principal, or interest, then due thereon. And since a mortgagee cannot recover, in a foreclosure suit, more than six years' arrears of interest (*s*), except when an express trust has been created in his favour (*t*) (an exception which will cease to exist when the Real Property Limitation Act 1874 (*u*) comes into operation (*v*)), the action on the covenant may be resorted to when his claim extends beyond that term.

To recover interest.

3 & 4 Wm. IV. c. 27.

3 & 4 Wm. IV. c. 42.

(*o*) S. 42.
(*p*) SS. 3, 5.
(*q*) *Paget* v. *Foley*, 2 Bing. N. C. 679.
(*r*) S. 4.
(*s*) *Round* v. *Bell*, 30 Beav. 121.
(*t*) 3 & 4 Wm. IV. c. 27, s. 25; *Cox* v. *Dolman*, 2 De G. M. & G. 592; *Shaw* v. *Johnson*, 1 D. & Sm. 412.
(*u*) 37 & 38 Vict. c. 57, s. 10.
(*v*) On the 1st of January, 1879.

To recover principal.

3 & 4 Wm. IV. c. 27.

The power of bringing an action on the mortgagor's covenant for payment of principal is also limited by the 3 & 4 Wm. IV., c. 27, which, by another section (*w*), enacts that no action shall be brought to recover any sum of money secured by any mortgage but within twenty years next after a present right to receive the same shall have accrued to some person capable of giving a discharge for, or release of, the same, unless in the mean time some part of the principal money, or some interest thereon, shall have been paid, or some acknowledgment of the right thereto shall have been given in writing, signed by the person by whom the same shall be payable, or his agent, to the person entitled thereto, or his agent; and in such case no such suit or action is to be brought but within twenty years after such payment or acknowledgment, or the last of such payments or acknowledgments, if more than one. And under the Real Property Limitation Act 1874 (*x*) (which will come into operation on the 1st of January 1879) the mortgagee will have to bring his action within twelve years (instead of twenty) from the time when his right first accrued, or from the time of his last receipt of some principal or interest, or of an acknowledgment of his right thereto. It has been held, in questions arising under the acts of William the Fourth, that no formal acknowledgment need be given by either the party liable or his agent (*y*), the statutes speaking only of some acknowledgment. It has also been decided (*z*) that if a part payment, or an acknowledgment, made by one of several parties interested in mortgaged property, has the effect of preserving any right of action, that right will be saved, not only against the

Acknowledgment need not be formal.

(*w*) S. 40.
(*x*) 37 & 38 Vict. c. 57, s. 8.
(*y*) *Blair* v. *Nugent*, 3 Jo. & L. 658, 677; *St John* v. *Boughton*, 9 Sim. 219.
(*z*) *Roddam* v. *Morley*, 1 De G. & J. 1; *Pears* v. *Laing*, L. R. 12 Eq. 41.

party making the payment, but against all other parties liable on the specialty (a).

The mortgagee's right to sue on the covenant may also be lost to him in consequence of certain acts of his own. For he will not be allowed to proceed on his collateral securities when he has put it out of his power to re-convey the mortgaged property. Thus (b), where a mortgagee, after foreclosure, sold the estate for less than was due to him, he was not allowed to sue on a bond given by way of collateral security, although the sale had been perfectly fair. And the same principle applies to a mortgagee suing on the covenant for the balance of the sum due to him (c). Hence we see that the mortgagee's better course, if he thinks the mortgaged estate an insufficient security, is first to sue on the covenant, and then to proceed against the estate for any money still owing to him. Of course if he has recovered in an action all that is due to him, on every account, he cannot take any further proceedings against the mortgagor, or against the estate, but must re-convey the mortgaged property. But, subject to this, the mere fact of his having sued on the covenant does not entail any responsibility upon him. *Mortgagee may lose his right of suing.*

The mortgagee may also enter into possession of the mortgaged property, and he has a right, in the absence of stipulation, to do this directly the mortgage deed is executed (d). Since the fact of such entry still leaves open the mortgagor's right to redeem, the mortgagee is bound to take due care of the property,—such care, that is, as a prudent man would take of his own.; subject however to his right to recover *Entering into possession. Is bound to take due care of the property.*

(a) But see *Coope* v. *Cresswell*, L. R. 2 Ch. 112, 125.
(b) *Lockhart* v. *Hardy*, 9 Beav. 349; and see *Walker* v. *Jones*, L. R. 1 P. C. 50.
(c) *Palmer* v. *Hendrie*, 27 Beav. 349.
(d) *Doe* v. *Lightfoot*, 8 Mee & W. 553.

his money. Hence, if the property is a sufficient security for the debt, the mortgagee will be liable for any unnecessary destruction of it (*e*), or for allowing any part of it to be abstracted by other persons, so as to make it impossible for the mortgagor to get back in specie what has been thus abstracted (*f*), and in such case he will be charged with his receipts from the property, but disallowed his expenses relating to it (*g*). And if he enters into possession of leasehold premises, he is bound to perform all the covenants in the lease, and is responsible to the mortgagor for a forfeiture occurring through his default in this respect (*h*). But, if the security is not sufficient, he may make the most of the mortgaged property for the purpose of realizing what is due to him. He may, therefore, on that ground, cut timber, or open a mine, but he does any speculative acts at his own peril, so that if he incurs a loss he cannot charge any of it against the mortgagor, whilst the whole of any profit which he may make must go in discharge of the mortgage debt (*i*). It is his duty to receive the rents, and he is bound to account, not only for the rents and profits which he has received, but also for those which he might have received but for his own wilful default (*j*), as, for instance, if he allows a tenant to remain for several years on the property, and does not receive or demand rent from him (*k*). On the other hand, he is entitled to charge the mortgagor with all sums fairly expended on the property, in keeping it in due repair, or even in respect of costs properly incurred in suits relating to it (*l*). He may do any

Rights if property is an insufficient security.

Must receive the rents and account for them.

May charge mortgagor with reasonable expenses.

(*e*) *Sandon* v. *Hooper*, 14 L. J. (Ch.) 120.
(*f*) *Hood* v. *Easton*, 2 Giff. 692; *Chisholm* v. *Sheldon*, 1 Grant, 318.
(*g*) *Thorneycroft* v. *Crockett*, 16 Sim. 445; 2 H. L. C. 239.
(*h*) *Perry* v. *Walker*, 1 Jur. (N. S.) 746.
(*i*) *Millett* v. *Davey*, 31 Beav. 470, 476.
(*j*) *Parkinson* v. *Hanbury*, L. R. 2 H. L. 1, 9.
(*k*) *Brandon* v. *Brandon*, 10 W. R. 287; and see *Hughes* v. *Williams*, 12 Ves. 493-4.
(*l*) *Parker* v. *Watkins*, John. 133; *Blackford* v. *Davis*, L. R. 4 Ch. 304.

acts, such as pulling down ruinous houses and building better, which may be necessary to prevent a forfeiture of the estate (m); and it would probably be his duty to do so, but he is not bound to do more than is required to keep the estate in necessary repair (n), or to speculate with the property on behalf of the mortgagor (o). Neither should he do anything which will unnecessarily increase the value of the estate, and thus make it more difficult for the mortgagor to redeem. He is not allowed to charge anything for his personal services in looking after the estate, or in collecting the rents (p), and any agreement to such an effect between him and the mortgagor will be set aside, and he will not be allowed to receive more than his principal, interest, and costs (q). But he was always entitled to appoint a receiver to collect the rent, and charge his expenses against the mortgagor (r); and this privilege is now expressly conferred on him by statute, where default has been made by the mortgagor (s). If he occupy any part of the property himself, he will be charged with a fair occupation rent for it (t). And he cannot, without the consent of the mortgagor, make any lease which will be binding upon the latter after he has redeemed, unless it has been necessary in order to avoid an apparent loss, in which case the lessee cannot be disturbed (u).

Must not unnecessarily increase the value of the estate.

Cannot charge for personal services.

But may appoint a receiver.

Occupation rent.

From the above remarks it will have been gathered that a mortgagee who has entered into possession is

Account.

(m) *Hardy* v. *Reeve*, 4 Ves. 466, 479ª.
(n) *Godfrey* v. *Watson*, 3 Atk. 517.
(o) *Rowe* v. *Wood*, 2 Jac. & W. 553, 555.
(p) *Bonithon* v. *Hockmore*, 1 Ver. 315; *Langstaffe* v. *Fenwick*, 10 Ves. 404.
(q) *French* v. *Baron*, 2 Atk. 120.
(r) *Bonithon* v. *Hockmore*, 1 Ver. 315; *Langstaffe* v. *Fenwick*, 10 Ves. 404; *Barrett* v. *Hartley*, 12 Jur. (N. S.) 426.
(s) 23 & 24 Vict. c. 145, ss. 11, 17—24.
(t) *Smart* v. *Hunt*, 1 Ver. 418ª.
(u) *Hungerford* v. *Clay*, 9 Mod. 1.

bound, when the mortgage is redeemed, to account for his receipts. If his annual receipts have exceeded the amount of interest annually due to him, he will have been gradually repaying himself the principal debt. But, if some interest was due to him when he entered into possession, he will, ordinarily, be allowed, in his accounts, to charge interest every year on the whole of the original principal (v); since he was not *Annual Rests.* bound to receive his money piecemeal. If, however, no interest was due to him at the time when he took possession, and there has been an excess of annual receipts over the annual interest due to him, the account will be taken against him with "annual rests." That is, the principal will be considered as having been, every year, diminished by the amount of such excess; and he will only be allowed to charge an annual interest on the principal thus actually due (w). And the same rule will apply to his possession during any part of a year. The account will be, also, taken with rests if he has entered into any agreement with the mortgagor by which the interest already due has been converted into principal (x).

An exception is, however, sometimes made to the general rule. For the mere fact of interest not being due to the mortgagee when he takes possession is not decisive upon the question of rests; every circumstance of the case will be regarded; and if the mortgagee has been driven to take possession, by the wrongful acts of parties interested in the estate, he will not be obliged to account with rests even though no interest was due to him at the time (y). This principle has also been applied to a case (z) where a mortgagee entered into possession in order to prevent a forfeiture for non-payment of rent and for non-

---

(v) *Scholefield* v. *Lockwood* (No. 3), 32 Beav. 439.
(w) *Shepherd* v. *Elliott*, 4 Madd. 254.
(x) *Wilson* v. *Cluer*, 3 Beav. 136.
(y) *Horlock* v. *Smith*, 1 Coll. 287, 297.
(z) *Patch* v. *Wild*, 30 Beav. 99.

assurance in accordance with a covenant (*a*). On the other hand, he may be held liable to account with rests although interest was due to him when he entered. Thus (*b*), where a mortgagee had sold part of the property, and there was a surplus out of the proceeds of the sale after payment of all interest then due and costs, it was held that this surplus must be deducted from the principal, and that from that time the account must be taken, on the diminished principal, with annual rests against the mortgagee (*c*).

The possession of the mortgagee may have the effect of destroying the mortgagor's equity of redemption. For, by an act already referred to (*d*), it is provided (*e*) that when a mortgagee shall have obtained possession or receipt of the profits of any land, or the receipt of any rent, comprised in his mortgage, the mortgagor, or any person claiming through him, shall not bring a suit to redeem the mortgage but within twenty years next after the time at which the mortgagee obtained such possession or receipt, unless in the mean time an acknowledgment of the title of the mortgagor, or of his right of redemption, shall have been given to the mortgagor, or to some person claiming his estate, or to the agent of such mortgagor or person, in writing signed by the mortgagee or some person claiming through him; and that in such case no such suit shall be brought but within twenty years next after the time at which such acknowledgment, or the last of such acknowledgments, if more than one, was given; and that when there shall be more than one mortgagor, or more than one person claiming through the mortgagor or mortgagors, such acknowledgment, if given to any of such mortgagors or persons, or his or their agent,

Mortgagee's possession may destroy the equity of redemption. 3 & 4 Wm. IV. c. 27.

(*a*) And see *Gordon* v. *Eakins*, 16 Grant, 363.
(*b*) *Thompson* v. *Hudson*, L. R. 10 Eq. 497.
(*c*) For the mode of taking such an account see *Binnington* v. *Harwood*, Turn. & Russ. 477, 481.
(*d*) 3 & 4 Wm. IV. c. 27.
(*e*) S. 28.

shall be as effectual as if the same had been given to all such mortgagors or persons; but that when there shall be more than one mortgagee, or more than one person claiming the estate or interest of the mortgagee or mortgagees, such acknowledgment, signed by one or more of such mortgagees or persons, shall be effectual only as against the party or parties signing as aforesaid, and the person or persons claiming through them, and shall not operate to give the mortgagor or mortgagors a right to redeem the mortgage, as against the person or persons entitled to any other undivided or divided part of the money, or land, or rent. And under the Real Property Limitation Act 1874 (*f*) the time of twelve years will, in all the above cases, be substituted for that of twenty years.

<small>Real Property Limitation Act 1874.</small>

Before the 3 & 4 Wm. IV., c. 27, was passed, the Court of Chancery had looked upon a twenty years' possession by the mortgagee, without any acknowledgment of the title of the mortgagor, as barring the latter's right to redeem, unless he had been under disability (acting on an analogy to the old Statute of Limitation (*g*)), or unless there had been some fraud, or unfair dealing, on the part of the mortgagee. But very slight acts of the mortgagee were held to be an acknowledgment by him of the mortgagor's right to redeem (*h*); such, for instance, as his having kept accounts of the sums due to him (*i*), or mentioning the estate in his will as "my mortgage" (*j*). This tendency of the court has been considerably restricted by the act, which requires, as we saw, an acknowledgment in writing; and this, it will be noticed, can only be given to the mortgagor or his agent, and not to any third person. But the acknowledg-

<small>Former rule as to acknowledgment.</small>

<small>Change made by the act.</small>

(*f*) 37 & 38 Vict. c. 57, s. 7.
(*g*) 21 Jac. I. c. 16; see *Anon.* 3 Atk. 313.
(*h*) See *Hodle* v. *Healey*, 6 Madd. 181.
(*i*) Per *Lord Loughborough*, 2 Ves. Junr. 83.
(*j*) *Ord* v. *Smith*, Eq. Ca. Ab. 600.

ment need not be formal. Thus (*k*), where a mortgagor's solicitor wrote, on the subject of the mortgage, to the mortgagee, who replied by letter "that he did not see the use of a meeting unless some one was ready to pay him off:" this was held a sufficient acknowledgment within the statute (*l*). Nor need the acknowledgment be given within twenty years from the time of taking possession, for in the case just referred to (*m*) it was not made until after twenty-five years' possession. And the mortgagee's posses- sion will not destroy the equity of redemption, unless he has held by a title adverse to the mortgagor; for otherwise there would not be (as the statute supposes) a person to whom the acknowledgment may be made, as well as a person to make it. Hence, where (*n*) a mortgagee, who had taken a mortgage of property from the tenant for life and the remainder-man of it, entered into possession, as mortgagee, and then purchased the equity of redemption of the tenant for life, it was held that the time during which he was in possession under the latter title did not run against the remainder-man. And the rule is the same, if the mortgagee acquires a non-adverse interest before he takes possession (*o*).

Mortgagee's possession must be adverse.

With reference to the acknowledgment being made by the "mortgagee," it has been held that where two or more mortgagees are trustees and joint-tenants, and the fact of their being so appears on the face of the mortgage deed, an acknowledgment made by one of them is not sufficient to let in the equity of redemption, since they, all together, only make up one mortgagee (*p*).

Acknowledgment by trustees.

(*k*) *Stansfield* v. *Hobson*, 3 De G. M. & G. 620.
(*l*) And see *France* v. *Sympson*, Kay, 678.
(*m*) *Stansfield* v. *Hobson*, 3 De G. M. & G. 620; and see *Pendleton* v. *Rooth*, 1 De G. F. & J. 81.
(*n*) *Hyde* v. *Dallaway*, 2 Ha. 528.
(*o*) *Raffety* v. *King*, 1 Keen, 601.
(*p*) *Richardson* v. *Younge*, L. R. 6 Ch. 478.

Bill for foreclosure.

Decree.

Final order.

Extension of time.

A mortgagee is not bound to trust only to his right of entering into possession, for the ultimate realization of his security. For when the Court of Chancery established the mortgagor's right to redeem, it also put a restriction on that right, by permitting the mortgagee to take proceedings to foreclose the equity of redemption. The consequence is that the mortgagee is entitled, so soon as the day fixed for payment by the mortgage deed is over, and provided his claim is not satisfied, to exercise his right of obtaining foreclosure. This he does by filing a bill in the Court of Chancery, and getting under it a decree that an account shall be taken of what is due to him for his principal, for interest on it, including six months' prospective interest, and for the costs of that suit: and that if the mortgagor shall, on that day six (calendar) months, pay all sums so found due, the mortgagee shall reconvey the mortgaged estate; but that, in default of such payment, the mortgagor shall, from thenceforth, stand absolutely debarred and foreclosed of and from all equity of redemption in and to the mortgaged premises (*q*). If default is not made, the mortgagee must, of course, re-convey the premises; but if default is made, he must next obtain a final order for absolute foreclosure in order to perfect his title (*r*).

Besides the indulgence thus shown to the mortgagor, in compelling the mortgagee to get a final order, the court is very lenient in extending the time within which the mortgagor may redeem. In the first place, if he comes before the time fixed for payment by the decree has arrived, he can generally, provided he can assign some reason for his request (*s*), get an order extending the time for another six months, on condition of his at once paying all interest then

---

(*q*) Seton, 364.
(*r*) See Seton, 393.
(*s*) *Holford* v. *Yate*, 1 K. & J. 677; *Nanny* v. *Edwards*, 4 Russ. 124.

due, and the costs of the suit. In one instance (*t*) as many as four such orders were made, but that was a very exceptional case, the mortgagor having already entered into an advantageous contract for the sale of the estate. And an order will not be readily made if the property is shown to be already an insufficient security (*u*). Not only can the mortgagor, generally speaking, get an extension before the time comes for payment, but he may even get one after the order for making the foreclosure absolute has been obtained and inrolled; this, however, has only been done under very peculiar circumstances, as, for instance, where it was clearly proved that the mortgagor's interest in the property was worth three or four times the amount of the debt (*v*).

Moreover, the court will often hold that the mortgagee has, after obtaining foreclosure, re-opened it by his dealings with the property before the foreclosure is made absolute. Thus, he opens the foreclosure if he receives any rents of the property between the time when a certificate has been made, showing the amount due to him, and the day fixed for payment by the mortgagor; even though default is afterwards made in such payment; since by receiving rents he has altered the amount found due to him (*w*). In that case a new day, not exceeding three months (*x*) from the time of his applying for an absolute order, must be fixed for payment (*y*). It was formerly thought that the foreclosure was not opened by the fact of the mortgagee receiving rents after the day fixed for payment, although he might not have obtained the final order (*z*); but it would seem from the decision in a recent case (*a*) that a receipt of rent

Foreclosure re-opened by acts of the mortgagee.

By receipt of rent.

(*t*) *Edwards* v. *Cunliffe*, 1 Madd. 287.
(*u*) *Eyre* v. *Hanson*, 2 Beav. 478.
(*v*) *Ford* v. *Wastell*, 2 Ph. 591; and see *Platt* v. *Ashbridge*, 12 Grant, 105.
(*w*) *Garlick* v. *Jackson*, 4 Beav. 154.
(*x*) *Buchanan* v. *Greenway*, 12 Beav. 355.
(*y*) *Alden* v. *Foster*, 5 Beav. 592; *Ellis* v. *Griffiths*, 7 Beav. 83.
(*z*) *Constable* v. *Howick*, 5 Jur. (N. S.) 331.
(*a*) *Prees* v. *Coke*, L. R. 6 Ch. 645.

at any time before obtaining the final order, re-opens the foreclosure.

By other acts. And although the court will not prevent a mortgagee who has foreclosed from pursuing his other remedies, if the value of the estate foreclosed proves to be less than the amount due to him, it will consider the foreclosure as thereby opened (b). We have also seen, previously, that parting with any of the property after foreclosure, stops the mortgagee from taking any further proceedings against the mortgagor.

Sale. The Court of Chancery would, under the old practice, sometimes direct a sale of the mortgaged property, instead of foreclosure of the equity of redemption, and now it is provided by the Chancery Improvement Act (c), that it shall be lawful for the court, in any suit for the foreclosure of the equity of redemption in any mortgaged property, upon the request of the mortgagee, or of any subsequent incumbrancer, or of the mortgagor, or of any person claiming under them respectively, to direct a sale of such property instead of a foreclosure of such equity of redemption, on such terms as the court may think fit to direct.

15 & 16 Vict. c. 86.

Sale may be immediate.

But time usually allowed to redeem.

The court may therefore direct a sale at once, even against the wish of the mortgagor (d), and it will incline to direct an immediate sale when the property is unproductive (e), or when such a sale is *primâ facie* for the benefit of all parties (f), but in other cases it will give a limited time, varying from six months (g) to one month (h), within which the mortgagor may re-

---

(b) *Dashwood* v. *Blythway*, 1 Eq. Ca. Ab. 317.
(c) 15 & 16 Vict. c. 86, s. 48.
(d) *Newman* v. *Selfe*, 33 Beav. 522.
(e) *Foster* v. *Harvey* (No. 2), 11 W. R. 899.
(f) *Hewitt* v. *Nanson*, 28 L. J. (Ch.) 49.
(g) *Bellamy* v. *Cockle*, 18 Jur. 465; Daniell, C. P. 1152.
(h) *Staines* v. *Rudlin*, 16 Jur. 965; *Smith* v. *Robinson*, 1 Sm. & Giff. 140.

deem. The proceeds of such a sale, after satisfying
the claims of the mortgagee, belong to the mortgagor.

It has already been pointed out how the mortgagee may, under the Statutes of Limitation, lose his right to bring a personal action against the mortgagor, and in like manner he may be prevented from proceeding directly against the mortgaged property. For it is enacted by the 3 & 4 Wm. IV., c. 27 (*i*), that no person is to make an entry, or bring an action to recover any land, but within twenty years next after the time at which the right to make such entry or to bring such action shall have first accrued to some person through whom he claims; or, if such right shall not have accrued to any person through whom he claims, within twenty years next after the time at which the right to make such entry or to bring such action shall have accrued to the person making or bringing the same. And the third section of the act explains that the right to make such entry or bring such action shall—if the grantee has been in possession—be deemed to have first accrued from the time when such possession was discontinued, or—if the grantee has not been in possession, and his claim is in respect of an estate or interest in land conveyed to him (by any instrument other than a will) by a person in possession of such estate or interest—from the time when he became entitled to take possession. But if such estate or interest was one in reversion or remainder, then the right is to be deemed to have accrued from the time when the estate or interest came into possession. A further proviso is made by another (the fourteenth) section, namely, that if any acknowledgment of the title of the person entitled to any land shall have been given to him, or his agent, in writing, signed by the person in possession, or in the receipt of the profits of such land, then the right to make such entry, or bring

Mortgagee may lose his security.

3 & 4 Wm. IV. c. 27.

(*i*) S. 2.

such action, shall be deemed to have accrued at the time when such acknowledgment, or the last of such acknowledgments, if more than one, was given.

A doubt was raised (*j*), on the wording of this section, whether payment of interest was equivalent to a written acknowledgment of the mortgagee's title, or whether a mortgagee's right to recover the land was gone if he, for twenty years, allowed the mortgagor to remain in possession, paying interest, but making no other acknowledgment of the mortgagee's title. In order to remove these doubts, it is enacted by the 7 Wm. IV. & 1 Vict., c. 28, that it shall and may be lawful for any person entitled to, or claiming under, any mortgage of land, to make an entry, or bring an action, or suit in equity, to recover such land, at any time within twenty years next after the last payment of any part of the principal money or interest secured by such mortgage, although more than twenty years have elapsed since the time at which the right to make such entry, or bring such action or suit shall have accrued. The Real Property Limitation Act 1874 (*k*), already referred to, substitutes (*l*) the term of twelve years for that of twenty years as the time within which the mortgagee is to bring his action under the circumstances mentioned in the 3 & 4 Wm. IV., c. 27, s. 2. It also (*m*) enacts that the provisions of the 7 Wm. IV. & 1 Vict., c. 28, are, after the 31st of December 1878 (*n*), to be construed as if the period of twelve years had been therein mentioned instead of the period of twenty years. It follows that the mortgagee's right to recover the land is, at present, lost if he permit the mortgagor to remain for twenty years in undisturbed possession without payment of interest, or written acknowledgment of title, and that after the

---

(*j*) *Doe* v. *Williams*, 5 A. & E. 291.
(*k*) 37 & 38 Vict. c. 57.
(*l*) S. 1.
(*m*) S. 9.
(*n*) S. 12.

31st of December 1878 such neglect on his part for a period of twelve years will bar his right to recover the mortgage security.

Reference has already been made to cases as to the acknowledgment required by other sections of the Statutes of Limitation, and those cases apply equally to acknowledgments under s. 14 of the 3 & 4 Wm. IV., c. 27. *Acknowledgment under these statutes.*

With regard to the possession necessary to bar the mortgagee's right to the land, it has been decided that if he is himself in possession of it, but under another title (as, for instance, where he is a tenant for life of the mortgaged estate), his possession in that capacity will not operate as a bar to his title as mortgagee (*o*).

It has also been held (*p*) that a mortgagee of land may, at any time within twenty years after his last receipt of interest or of acknowledgment of his title, recover the mortgaged land from a tenant of the mortgagor, even though, as between such tenant and the mortgagor, the latter's right to the land is barred, under the 3 & 4 Wm. IV., c. 27, in consequence of his not having received any rent, or any acknowledgment of his title, from the tenant for twenty years past. Moreover (*q*), a person who has purchased the mortgaged property from the mortgagee, and at the same time bought up the mortgagor's equity of redemption, (thus extinguishing the mortgage debt), still remains a person "claiming under," though not one "entitled to," a mortgage, within the meaning of the 7 Wm. IV. & 1 Vict., c. 28, and has, therefore, the same rights as against a tenant of the mortgagor, as the mortgagee himself would have had in the case last put. For

---

(*o*) *Wynne* v. *Styan*, 2 Ph. 303.
(*p*) *Doe* v. *Eyre*, 17 Q. B. 366.
(*q*) *Doe* v. *Massey*, 17 Q. B. 373.

otherwise the mortgagee, or persons claiming under him, might be prejudiced by the neglect of the mortgagor to receive rent, or an acknowledgment of title, from his own tenant—a contingency undesirable in the interest of the mortgagor himself, as tending to diminish the mortgagee's security, and thus make him less willing to allow the mortgagor time for repayment of the loan.

CHAPTER XIV.

OF AN EQUITY OF REDEMPTION (*continued*).

In addition to those privileges of a mortgagee which have been mentioned in the previous chapter, there are two others, of a somewhat different nature, which will require a brief notice.

The first of these arises from the fact of the mortgagee's being the legal owner of the mortgaged estate. This is his right to "Tack;" that is, to annex to his original security another which he holds for a subsequent debt due in respect of the same property. If, for instance, A has an estate conveyed to him by way of mortgage in the usual form, and subsequently, without notice of the existence of any other incumbrance on it, advances a further sum of money to the mortgagor on the security of the same estate, he will have a right to "tack" this last advance to his first, and claim payment of both before he re-conveys the property, even as against an incumbrancer who lent his money on the security of the equity of redemption, before A made his further advance.

Tacking.

It will be obvious that this right to tack is a great advantage where the mortgagor is insolvent, or, even if he is solvent, where the mortgaged estate is an insufficient security for all the money advanced on it by different persons. We will proceed, therefore, to consider the qualifications necessary to entitle a mortgagee to tack.

But, before doing so, we must point out that the

right does not obtain against any estate or interest which came into existence after the 7th of August 1874. For the Vendor and Purchaser Act 1874 (*a*) (which commenced on the date just mentioned) enacts (*b*) that after the commencement of the act no priority or protection shall be given or allowed to any estate, right, or interest in land, by reason of such estate right or interest being protected by or tacked to any legal or other estate or interest in such land. This, however, is followed by a proviso that the section containing this enactment shall not take away from any estate, right, title, or interest any priority or protection which but for the section would have been given or allowed thereto as against any estate or interest existing before the commencement of the act. It follows from the above that the right to tack may still be exercised, as against any equitable estate which was in existence before the commencement of the act, whether the protecting estate, or the estate sought to be tacked, was created before, or after, that date. And the reader will understand that the remarks about to be made on the subject of tacking apply to such cases only as are not affected by the act.

When a mortgagee may tack. Must have legal estate.

The first requisite for tacking is that the person claiming to exercise it must be in possession of, or have the power to obtain the possession of, the legal estate in the mortgaged property (*c*). For it is only in favour of a legal owner that an exception is made to the ordinary rule of equity, "that he who is first in point of time is to be considered as having the better right." The reason given for this exception is, that his right to be re-paid his further advance being equal (laying aside any question of priority) to the right of repayment of any other incumbrancer, equity will not prevent him from availing himself, in order

---
(*a*) 37 & 38 Vict. c. 78.
(*b*) S. 7.
(*c*) *Brace* v. *Marlborough*, 2 P. W. 490, 495.

to obtain payment, of any advantage which he has, in consequence of his possession of the legal estate in the mortgaged property. This reasoning cannot be called very satisfactory, and probably the best excuse that could be made for continuing the system of tacking is that given by a distinguished writer (*d*), namely, that it has been so long established as to have become a rule of real property. It does not, as a rule, prevail in our colonies, even where the system of law is the same as our own; and, in cases where it has been permitted, it would seem that the right to tack has been confined to the mortgagee himself (*e*), whereas our law (as we shall see presently) extends it to his assignee.

Next, the mortgagee must have made his advance on the credit of the mortgaged property. He will therefore, provided he possesses the other necessary qualifications, be, clearly, allowed to tack a subsequent advance if he has, at the time of making it, taken, by way of security, a second mortgage of, or further charge on, the same property. Before the passing of the present Judgment Acts (*f*) a mortgagee was allowed to tack, in like manner, a further advance secured by a statute or judgment given expressly for that purpose; for in such a case he was presumed, knowing that he had hold of the land by the mortgage, to have ventured his money upon a further security which, though it passed no present interest in the land, had the effect of a lien thereon (*g*). And his right to tack such an advance is still clearer if the judgment has been obtained since the passing of the Judgment Acts, and has been followed up by the measures required by those statutes, since such a judgment has the same effect as if the mortgagor had

Must have made his advance on the credit of the mortgaged property.

(*d*) Story, Eq. Jur. § 414.
(*e*) *Gordon* v. *Lothian*, 2 Grant, 293.
(*f*) 1 & 2 Vict. c. 110; 2 & 3 Vict. c. 11; 23 & 24 Vict. c. 38; 27 & 28 Vict. c. 112.
(*g*) *Brace* v. *Marlborough*, 2 P. W. 490, 493; *Shepherd* v. *Titley*, 2 Atk. 348, 351.

executed a written charge on the land (*h*). He may, if there are no other incumbrancers, tack advances secured only by bond, or by simple contract, against the mortgagor's heirs, or against his devisees beneficially interested (*i*), because these persons are liable for all the mortgagor's debts, to the extent of the value of his real estate. But bond, or simple contract, debts, since they give no peculiar remedy against the debtor's land, cannot be tacked against the mortgagor himself (*j*), and still less against subsequent incumbrancers (*k*).

<small>Must hold securities in the same right.</small> Again, the mortgagee can only tack those securities which he holds in the same right. Thus (*l*), where A had advanced money on a leasehold estate, and B subsequently made an advance on the equity of redemption of the same estate, and then died, leaving A his executor: it was held that A, although both the securities were thus vested in him, could not tack them against incumbrancers whose rights had accrued between the time when A and B respectively had made their advances. The mortgagee's right to tack will not, however, be affected by the fact that the deed securing his further advance provided for the payment of other incumbrancers besides himself (*m*).

<small>Must not have had notice of subsequent incumbrance.</small> Moreover, the mortgagee cannot tack if, at the time of his further advance, he had notice of the existence of any intervening incumbrance; for his equitable right to tack is expressly founded on the absence of such notice (*n*). And the right is lost, not only by actual notice (which must amount to more

---

(*h*) 1 & 2 Vict. c. 110, s. 13.
(*i*) *Coleman* v. *Winch*, 1 P. W. 775; *Rolfe* v. *Chester*, 20 Beav. 610; *Thomas* v. *Thomas*, 22 Beav. 341; *Carroll* v. *Robertson*, 15 Grant, 173.
(*j*) *Archer* v. *Snatt*, Str. 1106.
(*k*) *Jones* v. *Smith*, 2 Ves. Junr. 372, 376; and see *Lowthian* v. *Hasel*, 3 Bro. C. C. 161; *Irby* v. *Irby*, 22 Beav. 217.
(*l*) *Barnett* v. *Weston*, 12 Ves. 130.
(*m*) *Spencer* v. *Pearson*, 24 Beav. 266.
(*n*) *Bruce* v. *Marlborough*, 2 P. W. 490, 494.

than a vague rumour (*o*)) given to himself, or his agent, by some person interested in the property (*p*); but also by constructive notice, such, for instance, as the knowledge obtained by his agent, counsel, or solicitor (*q*), provided such knowledge was acquired with reference to the same transaction (*r*), and that it was such as the agent or professional man might be expected to have communicated to him (*s*); including in this category knowledge of acts arising out of the gross negligence (*t*) of those whom he employed, but not acts of fraud on their part (*u*). Notice may also, in certain cases, be given by entries in the public registers; and, however given, it is sufficient if it makes the mortgagee aware of the existence of incumbrances, although it may not be accurate as to the particulars or extent of such charges (*v*).

So strictly is the rule as to notice enforced in equity, that even though a mortgage be made expressly to secure, not only a sum of money then lent, but also further advances on the same property, yet the mortgagee cannot tack such further advances if, at the time of making them, he had become aware of the existence of an intermediate incumbrancer (*w*). For the deed does not bind him to make further advances, and if he chooses to make them under such circumstances, he must trust to the general solvency of his debtor. The result is the same, even where there is a mortgage deed to secure present and future advances, (the latter being limited to a certain amount) and

---

(*o*) *Wildgoose* v. *Wayland*, Gould. 147; *Jolland* v. *Stainbridge*, 3 Ves. 478, 485.
(*p*) *Barnhart* v. *Greenshields*, 9 Moo. P. C. 18, 86; and see *Natal Land, &c., Co.* v. *Good*, L. R. 2 P. C. 121, 129.
(*q*) *Le Neve* v. *Le Neve*, Amb. 436, 438; *Atterbury* v. *Wallis*, 8 De G. M. & G. 454.
(*r*) *Warrick* v. *Warrick*, 3 Atk. 290, 294; *Re Smallman*, Ir. R. 2 Eq. 34.
(*s*) *Wyllie* v. *Pollen*, 32 L. J. (Ch.) 782.
(*t*) *Rolland* v. *Hart*, L. R. 6 Ch. 678.
(*u*) *Kennedy* v. *Green*, 3 My. & K. 699.
(*v*) *Gibson* v. *Ingo*, 6 Ha. 112, 124; *Jones* v. *Williams*, 24 Beav. 47.
(*w*) *Shaw* v. *Neale*, 20 Beav. 157: *Hopkinson* v. *Rolt*, 9 H. L. C. 514.

another person, afterwards, but before any such future advances being made, lends money on the equity of redemption, "subject to the security already given (*x*)." But if the further advances are made without notice of an intervening charge, the mortgagee may tack although he may have, after its creation, substituted another form of security for that originally given (*y*).

Consolidating securities.

The last of the mortgagee's rights which we have to mention, is that of Consolidating his Securities. If, for instance, the owner of different estates mortgages them to one person separately for distinct debts, or successively to secure the same debt, or the same debt with further advances, the mortgagee may, provided the legal right of redemption be lost, insist that one security shall not be redeemed unless all the others are redeemed also (*z*); and it is immaterial, in such a case, that of the various securities to be consolidated some are legal and others merely equitable (*a*). This right, as exercised against the mortgagor, is founded on the maxim that he who seeks equity must do equity, and, consequently, a mortgagor, coming to a court of equity for help to redeem his mortgaged estate, forfeited at law, can get no assistance unless he is prepared to do equity by paying his creditor all that is due to him. It will be observed that this right differs from that of tacking, for that is the right to throw a series of debts on the same estate, this, the right to make separate estates liable for one consolidated debt; that is founded on legal possession, this, on a doctrine peculiar to equity; that is lost by notice, this (as we shall see presently) is entirely unaffected by notice (*b*). It may also be mentioned that the

Distinction between tacking and consolidating securities.

(*x*) *Menzies* v. *Lightfoot*, L. R. 11 Eq. 459.
(*y*) *Calisher* v. *Forbes*, L. R. 7 Ch. 109.
(*z*) Fisher on Mortgages, 679.
(*a*) *Watts* v. *Symes*, 1 De G. M. & G. 240; *Neve* v. *Pennell*, 2 H. & M. 170; *Tweedale* v. *Tweedale*, 23 Beav. 341.
(*b*) And see Fisher on Mortgages, 679.

Vendor and Purchaser Act 1874 does not appear to the author to have made any change in the law as to consolidating securities.

The rule as to consolidation extends to the case of a foreclosure suit, as well as to that of one for redemption, and a mortgagee could, therefore, in the cases put above, foreclose the equity of redemption of any one estate, unless paid the whole amount due on the security of all (c). Moreover, the benefit of the mortgagee's right to consolidate may remain, although one of his securities may have gone. If, for instance, two estates are mortgaged to the same person, and he cannot obtain, on selling one of them, the amount due on it, he may throw the balance owing to him on the property which remains in his hands (d).

Consolidation extends to foreclosure suit.

Nor does the right apply only to the simple case of an original mortgagor and mortgagee. Hence, if A mortgages two estates to B, and a third to C, and C afterwards takes an assignment of B's mortgage, he can consolidate his three securities and hold them all until he is paid in full (e). Neither is it necessary that any of the sums consolidated should have been advanced by the person claiming to exercise this right: it is sufficient that they are, at the time for redemption, vested in the same person. Where, for instance (f), the owner of two estates mortgaged them, one to A, the other to B, and afterwards mortgaged the equity of redemption of both estates to C, and subsequently A and B each transferred his mortgage to D: it was held that C could not redeem either estate without paying D all that was due to him on the security of both (g). It makes no

Assignee of a mortgagee may consolidate.

(c) *Watts* v. *Symes*, 1 De G. M. & G. 240; *Neve* v. *Pennell*, 2 H. & M. 170; *Tweedale* v. *Tweedale*, 23 Beav. 341.
(d) *Selby* v. *Pomfret*, 1 J. & H. 336.
(e) *Willie* v. *Lugg*, 2 Eden, 77.
(f) *Vint* v. *Padgett*, 2 De G. & J. 611.
(g) And see *Bovey* v. *Skipwith*, 1 Ca. Ch. 201; *Tweedale* v. *Tweedale*, 23 Beav. 341.

Right to consolidate not affected by notice.

difference (and this is perhaps the most important distinction between tacking and consolidating) that the party having one security and acquiring another, and claiming to consolidate them, had notice, when he acquired his second security, of the existence of other incumbrancers on either, or both, of the mortgaged estates, who would be prejudiced by his uniting his securities (*h*).

Securities may be consolidated as against mortgagor's assignee.

It will be seen from the above cases that the right to consolidate, thus given to a mortgagee or his assignee, can be exercised against an assignee of a mortgagor, as well as against a mortgagor himself; even though that assignee may have been himself a mortgagee or a purchaser for value. The justice of a rule which allows consolidating against such an assignee, by a person who has had previous notice of his rights, is not very apparent. The reason given for it is, that a mortgagee, or a purchaser, of an equity of redemption must be taken to have known of the rule which allows consolidation, and, consequently, of the risk which he was encountering (*i*); but this argument would seem to be valid only as furnishing a reason for continuing the existing rule, and not one for originating it. The practice, however, is now firmly established. Thus (*j*), where the purchaser of an equity of redemption filed a bill in Chancery against the mortgagee, for the purpose of redeeming the mortgage, and the defendant, by his answer, stated a subsequent mortgage made to him of the same premises, but for a distinct debt, it was decided that the purchaser had no right to redeem the first mortgage without redeeming the second also. Again, in a recent case (*k*) where the mortgages on seven different properties, originally made to different sets

---

(*h*) *Vint* v. *Padgett*, 2 De G. & J. 611.
(*i*) *Vint* v. *Padgett*, 2 De G. & J. 611, 613.
(*j*) *Ireson* v. *Denn*, 2 Cox, 425.
(*k*) *Beevor* v. *Luck*, L. R. 4 Eq. 537.

of mortgagees, had become vested in the same person; it was held that the purchaser of the equity of redemption of two of these estates could not redeem them without redeeming the other five also; and that it made no difference that some of the mortgages had been acquired by the then holder after the date of the purchase: also, that it was immaterial whether, or not, the purchaser had notice of the existence of the other mortgages, and that there is no difference in this respect between the position of a purchaser and that of a mortgagee of an equity of redemption. The rule, too, is the same where different mortgages are held by different trustees for the same person (*l*). All of which cases point emphatically to the danger of purchasing, or lending money on, a mere equity of redemption.

But the mortgagee's right to consolidate does not hold good against persons whose equities of redemption have been, all along, distinct from that of the mortgagor against whom he seeks to enforce it. Hence, where (*m*) A mortgaged his estate, and then B mortgaged his estate to the same person, and A at the same time gave a further charge on his estate in order to secure the loan to B; it was held that B was entitled to redeem his estate on payment of that sum only which had been advanced to him. On the same principle, if an estate, belonging partly to A and partly to B, be mortgaged to secure a joint advance to them; and then property belonging to A, and partly comprised in the first mortgage, be conveyed to the same person to secure a sum advanced to A alone; B can redeem on payment of the sum first advanced, without reference to the subsequent loan to A (*n*).

But no consolidation against distinct equities of redemption.

(*l*) *Tassell* v. *Smith*, 2 De G. & J. 713.
(*m*) *Aldworth* v. *Robinson*, 2 Beav. 287.
(*n*) *Higgins* v. *Frankis*, 15 L. J. (Chy.) 329; and see *Jones* v. *Griffiths*, 2 Coll. 207.

OF CORPOREAL HEREDITAMENTS.

Sub-mort-gagees.

Hitherto we have considered only the case of a mortgagee who has taken a conveyance of the legal estate in the property which forms his security, but a few remarks are now necessary respecting those mortgagees who advance their money on land which is already in pledge, and who may therefore be distinguished as submortgagees. Assuming that the mortgage of such an one is made by an ordinary mortgage deed, but subject to a pre-existing mortgage, we see at once that his rights are not identical with those of a legal mortgagee. He can sue the mortgagor on his covenants for payment, and the remarks previously made on this point apply to all mortgagees equally. But he cannot take possession of the property, for the right to take possession of land is founded on legal ownership of it. Again, if he wishes to realize his security by the aid of the Court of Chancery, his position is different from that of the legal mortgagee. For although, if he only wishes to foreclose the mortgagor or subsequent incumbrancers, he need not bring the first mortgagee before the court (*o*), yet, since this foreclosure will only extinguish the rights, in respect of the property, of the mortgagor and those claiming under him (including subsequent incumbrancers), he has still, if he wishes to satisfy his debt, to redeem the first mortgagee; his suit, therefore, more usually presents the two-fold aspect of seeking for redemption against the first mortgagee, and foreclosure against the mortgagor and all subsequent incumbrancers; in which case, or even where he only seeks to redeem the first mortgagee, all persons interested in the property must be made parties to the suit (*p*).

Rights not the same as a legal mortgagee's.
May sue on covenants for payment.
But cannot enter into possession.
Foreclosure suit.

Decree.

He can thus obtain a decree, which will begin with a direction for taking an account of what is due to the

---

(*o*) *Richards* v. *Cooper*, 3 Beav. 504; *Audsley* v. *Horn*, 26 Beav. 195.
(*p*) *Fell* v. *Brown*, 2 Bro. C. C. 275; *Farmer* v. *Curtis*, 2 Sim. 466.

first mortgagee, followed by an order that the plaintiff shall redeem him within six months, or have his bill dismissed with costs: but that, on his redeeming, an account shall be taken of what is due to him, with an option to be given to each incumbrancer in succession, and finally to the mortgagor, to redeem him, failing which their equities of redemption are to be foreclosed (*q*), and the plaintiff will then be in a position to acquire possession of the mortgaged property.

A sub-mortgagee's strict right is to a foreclosure only, and does not extend to a sale; but it will be remembered that the Court of Chancery has now (*r*) power to direct a sale instead of a foreclosure, and since the object of giving the court this power is to avoid the great delay and expense which is occasioned by foreclosure and redemption where an estate is subject to a number of successive mortgages (*s*), a sale will generally be ordered under such circumstances; the proceeds being, ordinarily, applied in paying off the several incumbrancers, according to their respective priorities, and the surplus, if any, belonging to the mortgagor. *Has not a right to a sale.* *But sale may be ordered by the court.*

We have already seen that a legal mortgagee has the right of tacking, subject to the provisions of the Vendor and Purchaser Act, and of consolidating his securities. This latter right, since it does not depend upon the possession of the legal estate, may be exercised by a sub-mortgagee against all mortgagees subsequent in date to himself, as well as against the mortgagor (*t*). But it is otherwise as regards consolidating against prior incumbrancers, and as regards tacking; for a sub-mortgagee cannot do either of these things, unless he can obtain priority in a way *Position of a sub-mortgagee as to tacking and consolidating.*

(*q*) Seton, 477.
(*r*) 15 & 16 Vict. c. 86, s. 48.
(*s*) *Hurst* v. *Hurst*, 16 Beav. 372, 374.
(*t*) *Watts* v. *Symes*, 16 Sim. 640; *Nevе* v. *Pennell*, 2 H. & M. 170, 183.

which we will presently endeavour to explain. It must also be remembered that his power of tacking, even when he obtains priority, only prevails against estates which were in existence before the 7th of August 1874, and that questions on this point can, therefore, only arise with reference to such estates.

Obtaining priority.

Supposing that there is a legal mortgage to A, followed by mortgages of the equity of redemption in the same property to B, C, and D, in succession. Then, so long as the legal estate remains in A, the right of B, C, and D to be paid ranks according to the priority, in date, of their mortgages. But if D has advanced his money in ignorance of the mortgages made to B and C respectively, he will be allowed, if he can get the legal estate in the property from A, and subject to the remarks just made as to the date of the other incumbrances, to stand as it were in A's place, as well as in his own. For he will then be entitled, not only to be paid the debt formerly due to A (supposing that he has bought it up) before any payment is made to B or to C, but also to tack his own advance to the sum due to him as claiming under A, and to be paid that also before B and C are paid at all. And even if nothing is due to him as claiming under A, he can still take advantage of his legal estate, and claim for his own mortgage priority over those of B and C (*u*). But since he cannot, under any circumstances, avail himself of the legal estate, so acquired, against a prior mortgagee of whose charge he was aware when he took his own, the questions, whenever a sub-mortgagee claims priority (which, as we have seen, involves a partial right to tack, and to consolidate), are whether he has really got the legal estate in the property (*v*); and

Must not have had notice.

(*u*) *Marsh* v. *Lee*, 2 Vent. 237, and, with notes, 1 L. C. 611; *Edmunds* v. *Povey*, 1 Ver. 187; *Brace* v. *Marlborough*, 2 P. W. 490, 491; and see *Rooper* v. *Harrison*, 2 K. & J. 86, 108.

(*v*) See *Brace* v. *Marlborough*, 2 P. W. 490, 495; *Thorpe* v. *Holdsworth*, L. R. 7 Eq. 139.

especially whether he had, at the time of making his advance, actual or constructive notice of those claims which he seeks to postpone to his own. The subject of the doctrines of equity with reference to notice, actual and constructive, is far too extensive for discussion here, but we may mention three points bearing on it, of which the two latter have given rise to some difference of opinion.

It has been, from an early period, clearly settled that a sub-mortgagee's right to acquire the legal estate is not prejudiced by mere notice given to him, after he has made his advance, of the existence of equitable incumbrances created before his own, for where the equities of several parties are equal, preference will be given to him who is clothed with the legal estate (*w*). But it would seem to have been at one time thought that a third mortgagee, although himself ignorant of the existence of a second, could not exclude him if the first mortgagee, when he conveyed the legal estate to the third and assigned his mortgage debt, knew of the second mortgagee (*x*). This opinion has, however, been overruled (*y*), and it may now be taken as beyond doubt that such knowledge on the part of the first mortgagee is immaterial, provided that he has still an unsatisfied claim against the property. But the case was more doubtful if the first mortgagee had been paid off, and had only a dry legal estate, for it was, until lately, doubted whether in such a case he was not in the position of an ordinary trustee, and unable, therefore, to part with his estate to the detriment of equitable claims on the property, of which he had notice (*z*). This somewhat fine distinction (*a*) has been swept away by a recent decision

Notice to a sub-mortgagee who has made his advance does not affect his right to tack.

Nor does notice to an unpaid first mortgagee.

And, *semble*, it makes no difference that the first mortgagee has been paid off.

(*w*) *Marsh* v. *Lee*, 2 Vent. 237, and, with notes, 1 L. C. 611; *Wortley* v. *Birkhead*, 2 Ves. 571, 574.
(*x*) See *Mackreth* v. *Symmons*, 15 Ves. 329, 335.
(*y*) *Peacock* v. *Burt*, 4 L. J. N. S. (Ch.) 33; *Bates* v. *Johnson*, John. 304.
(*z*) *Carter* v. *Carter*, 3 K. & J. 617; *Prosser* v. *Rice*, 28 Beav. 68, 74.
(*a*) See Dart, V. & P. 758-9.

of the Court of Appeal in Chancery (*b*), and it follows that the fact of the first mortgagee's having notice of the second does not, under any circumstances, prevent the third from obtaining priority by the means which we have been discussing.

<small>Sub-mortgagee may obtain priority over any equitable claimant.</small>

The mortgagee of an equitable interest may, as a rule, protect himself in like manner against the claims of any person interested in the property, whether as mortgagee or otherwise, by obtaining a conveyance of the legal estate in the property from any one in whom it is vested. But this rule is subject to the qualification that if the mortgagee gets the legal estate from one whom he knows at the time to be a trustee, in the ordinary sense of the word, then the legal estate will not protect him against the equities of those *cestuis que trust* of whose existence he had been along aware (*c*). There is also the limitation on his right, imposed by the Vendor and Purchaser Act, to which reference has been already frequently made. And, as might be expected, the mortgagor cannot prejudice sub-mortgagees or other incumbrancers by acquiring the legal estate of the first mortgagee: hence, where (*d*) a mortgaged estate, sold by a mortgagee under a power of sale, was purchased by the mortgagor for its full value, which was less than the amount due to the first mortgagee; it was held that the mortgagor could not thus obtain a title to the estate, free from the claims of subsequent incumbrancers.

<small>But not if he knows legal owner to be a trustee.</small>

<small>Mortgages by deposit of title-deeds.</small>

There remains one other class of mortgagees whom we must notice—those, namely, whose advances have been secured by a deposit of the title-deeds of land, with, or without, some written memorandum making

---

(*b*) *Pilcher* v. *Rawlins*, L. R. 7 Ch. 259, 273.
(*c*) *Saunders* v. *Dehew*, 2 Ver. 271; *Allen* v. *Knight*, 11 Jur. 527.
(*d*) *Otter* v. *Vaux*, 25 L. J. (Chy.) 734.

the loan a charge on the land. A mere deposit of title-deeds does not give the depositee any estate at law, nor did it, formerly, give him any in equity (e), being regarded as contrary to the provisions of the Statute of Frauds, which (f) forbids any action being brought upon any contract or sale of any interest in land, unless the agreement upon which such action is brought be in writing, and signed by the party to be charged therewith, or his agent. But since such a transaction is now considered as a contract— by the mortgagee that he will lend money, by the mortgagor that his interest in the property to which the title-deeds relate shall be liable for the debt so contracted, and that he will make such conveyance or assurance as may be necessary to vest his interest in the mortgagee (g)—the fact of the contract having been in part performed by the mortgagee, who has paid the money, is considered to take the case out of the Statute of Frauds (h); and since equity treats that as done which ought to be done, a deposit of title-deeds in return for a loan of money constitutes an equitable mortgage of the land comprised in the deeds. Such a mortgage may moreover be created even by an order, written by the mortgagor, but unsigned, directing a third person, in whose hands the title-deeds are, to deposit them with the mortgagee (i). And an equitable mortgagee is entitled to treat the mortgaged property as a security, not only for his original loan, but also for further advances, if they were agreed upon at the time when the deeds were deposited (j).

How viewed in equity.

Equitable mortgagee may secure future advances.

(e) *Ex parte Coming*, 9 Ves. 115, 117.
(f) 29 Car. II. c. 3, s. 4.
(g) *Price* v. *Bury*, 2 Drew. 41, 42.
(h) *Russel* v. *Russel*, 1 Bro. C. C. 269, and, with notes, 1 L. C. 674; *Ex parte Kensington*, 2 Ves. & B. 79, 83.
(i) *Daw* v. *Terrell*, 33 Beav. 218.
(j) *Ex parte Kensington*, 2 Ves. & B. 79; *Ex parte Whitbread*, 1 Ves. 209; *Ede* v. *Knowles*, 2 Yo. & C. 172; and see *National Bank of Australasia* v. *Cherry*, L. R. 3 P. C. 299.

Not necessary to deposit all the deeds.

It is not necessary that all the title-deeds relating to the mortgaged estate should have been deposited. For it has been held that the mere deposit of a copy of court roll (*k*), or of so many of the title-deeds of freeholds as form material evidence of title (*l*), makes a good equitable mortgage, even though the deeds do not show that the depositor has any interest in the property (*m*).

Equitable mortgagee entitled to legal mortgage.

An equitable mortgagee, being a person entitled, by virtue of his contract, to call for the legal estate in the mortgaged property, may compel the mortgagor to execute a formal mortgage of it to him, and it is immaterial for that purpose that the deposit was unaccompanied by any written memorandum. Should the mortgagee do this, he becomes an ordinary legal mortgagee, with all the rights and liabilities attendant on that position.

Equitable mortgagee may obtain a decree for foreclosure.

Or he may, without having obtained the legal estate in the mortgaged property, take proceedings in equity to realize his security. If the deposit was accompanied by a written agreement to execute a legal mortgage, there can be no doubt that the mortgagee's primary remedy, in default of payment by the mortgagor, is to obtain foreclosure of the latter's equity of redemption (*n*); since a right to a sale belongs, strictly, to those persons only who have a mere equitable charge on the property (*o*), unaccompanied by any estate in it, legal or equitable (*p*). And it is now settled (*q*), after some little fluctuation of opinion (*r*), that foreclosure is also the proper

---

(*k*) *Whitbread* v. *Jordan*, 1 Yo. & C. (Ex.) 303.
(*l*) *Lacon* v. *Allen*, 3 Drew. 579.
(*m*) *Roberts* v. *Croft*, 2 De G. & J. 1.
(*n*) *Perry* v. *Keane*, Coote on Mortgages, 582.
(*o*) *Tipping* v. *Power*, 1 Ha. 405, 410; *Footner* v. *Sturgis*, 5 De G. & Sm. 736.
(*p*) *Kennard* v. *Futvoye*, 2 Giff. 81, 89.
(*q*) *James* v. *James*, L. R. 16 Eq. 153.
(*r*) *Tuckley* v. *Thompson*, 1 J. & H. 126; and see *Matthews* v. *Goodday*, 10 W. R. 1060.

remedy, although there has been no agreement to execute a mortgage. The suit of an equitable mortgagee, and the proceedings under it, will therefore be the same as an ordinary foreclosure suit and its consequences (s); except that the decree will order the mortgagor, in default of payment, to execute a conveyance of the property (t) to the mortgagee, who can, if the mortgagor fails to comply with the decree, obtain the legal estate in the property under what is known as a vesting order (u). If no interest has been agreed upon between the parties, it will be allowed to the mortgagee at the rate of £4 per cent. (v).

Interest allowed at £4 per cent.

The position of an equitable mortgagee is not very secure, until he has obtained the legal estate in the property pledged to him; since, until then, he is liable to be postponed to a person who has *bonâ fide* taken a legal conveyance of the same estate for valuable consideration. But this must have been done without notice of the equitable mortgage, and, since the deeds of an estate should, as a rule, go with its legal possession, neglect on the part of a purchaser to inquire after the purchase deeds will cause him to be postponed to an equitable mortgagee, even though he had been unaware of the latter's existence (w). The result will be the same if he has inquired after the deeds, and been satisfied with an answer which ought to have put him on further inquiry (x). But the fact of his not having got in the title-deeds will not postpone him, if he has made proper inquiries for them, and a reasonable excuse has been given for their non-delivery (y).

Equitable mortgagee may be postponed.

(s) See as to time for redemption by the mortgagor, *Parker* v. *Housefield*, 2 My. & K. 419.
(t) Seton, 444.
(u) *Lechmere* v. *Clamp*, 30 Beav. 218.
(v) *Re Kerr's Policy*, L. R. 8 Eq. 331; and see *Carey* v. *Doyne*, 5 Ir. Ch. Rep. 104.
(w) *Worthington* v. *Morgan*, 16 Sim. 547; *Hunter* v. *Walters*, L. R. 7 Ch. 75.
(x) *Maxfield* v. *Burton*, L. R. 17 Eq. 15.

And on similar principles a mortgagee, whether legal (z) or equitable (a), who, without reasonable excuse, neglects to get in the title-deeds of the property comprised in his mortgage, or who, having got them, improperly parts with them (b), will be postponed to subsequent mortgagees who have bonâ fide advanced their money without notice of his mortgage. It may be added, in conclusion, that an equitable mortgagee will lose his rights against the mortgagor, if he voluntarily parts with the deposited title-deeds (c), although he will not be held liable for their accidental loss (d).

(y) *Hewitt* v. *Loosemore*, 9 Ha. 449, 458; *Dixon* v. *Muckleston*, L. R. 8 Ch. 155; and see *Colyer* v. *Finch*, 19 Beav. 500, 5 H. L. C. 901; *Evans* v. *Bicknell*, 6 Ves. 183; *Martinez* v. *Cooper*, 2 Russ. 198.
(z) *Hunter* v. *Walters*, L. R. 7 Ch. 75.
(a) *Waldron* v. *Sloper*, 1 Drew. 193.
(b) *Layard* v. *Maud*, L. R. 4 Eq. 397; *Briggs* v. *Jones*, L. R. 10 Eq. 92.
(c) *Re Driscoll*, Ir. R. 1 Eq. 285.
(d) *Baskett* v. *Skeel*, 11 W. R. 1019.

PART II.
OF CONVEYANCING.

CHAPTER I.

OF THE HISTORY OF CONVEYANCING.

THE first part of this work having been devoted to a consideration of the various estates in land, and of the manner in which they may be held, it is proposed in this, the second part, to try and explain the way in which the simplest forms of the principal conveyancing instruments are prepared. And in order to facilitate the comprehension of this part of our studies, it will be prefaced with a brief account of the history of conveyancing; so that the reader may understand the reasons for the changes which have been made, from time to time, in the various forms of assurance which we are about to consider.

We have seen how land may, with reference to its tenure, be regarded as being either freehold or copyhold. But it will be remembered that copyhold land is still transferred by the primitive method of surrendering it to the lord of the manor, who, in his turn, re-grants it to the tenant's nominee; and, since the various points relating to the subject of surrender have been discussed in our chapter on copyholds, land of this tenure will not, except incidentally, come under our present notice. *Assurances of copyholds not to be considered in this chapter.*

As to land of freehold tenure, we saw that the estates held in it may be either freehold or leasehold, *Estates in land of freehold tenure divisible into freeholds in possession; reversions and remainders; and terms of years.*

the former again being divisible into those in possession, and those in reversion or remainder, which may be placed, with reference to their mode of conveyance, in a class by themselves. We have, then, to consider the history of the assurances which relate to these divisions of freehold land. And since the principal changes introduced into conveyancing arose soon after, and in consequence of, the passing of the Statute of Uses (a), our three classes of property may, for this purpose, be conveniently treated of with reference to—1st, The manner of acquiring, and dealing with, them before the passing of the statute; 2nd, The changes and modifications in conveyancing introduced after that date; and 3rd, The further alterations in this respect made since the passing of the statute down to the present day.

Assurances before the Statute of Uses.

The right of alienating the various kinds of property which have been mentioned had been a thing of slow growth, and was subject to several restrictions, derived chiefly from the rules of feudal tenure. A consequence of this was, that the earlier forms of assurance were few in number, and comparatively simple in operation.

Feoffment with livery of seisin.

The earliest, and most important, form of conveyance was a Feoffment, accompanied by Livery of Seisin. This was employed for the creation of all estates of freehold in possession, and for the transfer of such of them as were alienable; namely, estates in fee simple, or for life. A Feoffment was a formal statement by the feoffor, or owner of the estate, that he gave it to the feoffee, and was completed by the feoffor's publicly putting the feoffee into possession of the land which he was to hold.

This public putting into possession, called Livery

(a) 27 Hen. VIII. c. 10.

(delivery) of the Seisin, or feudal possession of the land, was either "in deed" or "in law," according as it took place on, or in sight of, the land (b). It was essential that the feoffment and livery of seisin should be made simultaneously; and such a mode of assurance was, therefore, in general, applicable only to the creation of an estate which took effect in possession. It might, however, be employed for the creation of a remainder limited after a term of years, since the grant of a term did not transfer the feudal seisin to the termor. In such a case, livery could be made either to the lessee, to take effect for the benefit of the remainder-man (c); or to the latter himself, provided the lessee gave his consent (d). As early as the Conquest (e) it had become usual to embody the terms of a feoffment in a deed, or charter; but for a long time afterwards this was not essential, and a deed, if made, was only evidence of the transfer, and did not, of itself, pass any estate. It should here be mentioned that, after a time, the name "Feoffment" was applied only to an instrument conferring a fee simple, that which gave an estate tail, or one for life, being called either a Gift, or a Demise or Lease, as the case might be (f); but since the form of words used was, as nearly as possible, the same, and livery of seisin was requisite in every case, it will be sufficient if we associate the word "feoffment" with the grant of an estate of freehold in possession; remembering at the same time that an estate tail could only be created, and not transferred, by it.

Feoffment sometimes accompanied by a deed.

But this not essential.

Gift and Demise.

So great was the importance attached to a feoffment and livery of seisin, that it might have the effect of transferring an estate greater than that possessed by the transferor. Thus, if the tenant, in actual pos-

Tortious operation of a feoffment.

(b) Co. Litt. 48a.
(c) 2 Bl. Com. 166.
(d) Co. Litt. 48b, n. (8).
(e) Mad. Form. Ang. i., ii.
(f) 2 Bl. Com. 316.

session, of an estate less than a fee simple purported to convey a fee simple by feoffment and livery of seisin, his grantee did actually acquire the last-mentioned estate; subject, however, to the right of re-entry or action of the lawful tenant. Such a feoffment was said to have a "tortious" operation, because it conveyed an estate wrongfully; and if made by a tenant for life, or for years, caused a forfeiture of the estate of the wrong-doer.

Grant. — Reversions and remainders could not be the subject of livery of seisin except (as previously mentioned) in the case of a reversion or remainder expectant on the determination of a term of years. And even as to these estates it would seem that when the lessee had entered on the land, and was therefore in actual possession, the better way of passing the freehold was by the conveyance next to be considered (g).

Livery of seisin, then, being, in general, inapplicable to estates in reversion or remainder, other means were resorted to, in order to obtain as much notoriety as possible for their transfer. With this object, it was required that they should be conveyed by a Deed of Grant, followed by the delivery of the deed to the grantee. By this means the precise nature and amount of the property to be transferred was clearly ascertained, and since the execution and transfer of the deed operated as a transfer of the property comprised in it, reversions and remainders were said to "lie in grant" in distinction to estates in possession, which were said to "lie in livery." It was also necessary, as has been pointed out in a previous chapter, that the reversioner or remainder-man should obtain the attornment of those tenants whose estates preceded his own.

Lying in Grant and lying in Livery.

Lease. — We have next to mention a lease, which was the

(g) *Doe* v. *Cole*, 7 B. & C. 243, 248.

mode of granting a term of years. Terms of years, being of little value in early times, could be originated by mere word of mouth, without any ceremony or writing; their creation, therefore, calls for no remark, but it is to be remembered that a lease was never perfect until the lessee had actually taken possession of the land demised. For up to that time he had only an <u>*interesse termini* or right</u> of entry. But after entry he was capable of taking a conveyance of the reversion or remainder by deed alone, without any livery of seisin. A lease, moreover, might always be granted to commence at some future time, since the grant of a term of years does not, as we have seen, affect the feudal seisin of the land. *Entry by lessee was necessary.*

Closely connected with a lease is an Assignment, which is the transfer of the entirety of a term of years, and has the effect of putting the assignee in the place of the former lessee, and making him at once liable to all the obligations of the lease, although he may not have entered on the land. Like a lease, it required no ceremony, or writing, for its validity (h). *Assignment.*

The next modes of transfer to be stated are an Exchange and a Partition. An exchange was, as its name implies, the gift of one estate or interest, in consideration of receiving another. It might be made of estates in possession, or of those in reversion or remainder; but it was essential that the property exchanged should be of the same kind, although not necessarily of the same value (i) : thus a fee simple could only be exchanged for another fee simple, and not for an estate for life, or for years. *Exchange and Partition.*

No livery of seisin was necessary, even when the estates exchanged were freeholds in possession (j); for

---

(h) *Noke* v. *Awder*, Cro. Eliz. 373, 437.
(i) Co. Litt. 51ᵃ.
(j) 2 Bl. Com. 323.

since each owner simply changed places with the other, and each had, already, possession of his land, the transaction was made notorious without livery, especially as an exchange of estates in possession was not complete until perfected by the actual entry of both parties on their new lands. If the property exchanged consisted of estates not in possession, then a deed was necessary to make the transaction valid.

A Partition might be employed for the division between coparceners, joint-tenants, or tenants in common, of the estates previously held by them in severalty, but for the first two purposes (that is, partition between coparceners and joint-tenants) a release (to be presently noticed) was the more usual form of conveyance. Livery of seisin was necessary in every case of a partition, and if the partition was made between joint-tenants, or tenants in common, a deed was also necessary (*k*).

Release.

Another form of conveyance was a Release. This was used to convey a right in land to the owner of some existing estate in possession, whereby his estate became enlarged; as by adding a reversion or remainder to an estate for life, or for years; or by passing an undivided share in land to a joint-tenant. In both these cases it was necessary that there should be privity of estate between the relessor and the relessee. By "privity of estate," is meant that their estates must be so related to the other as to make but one and the same estate in law (*l*). The estate of the relessee being already in possession, no livery of seisin was necessary, but a deed was required in every case of an express release by act of parties. A release, preceded by a lease, was occasionally used to convey a fee simple, by first granting a lease for a short term

(*k*) 2 Bl. Com. 324.
(*l*) 2 Bl. Com. 325.

to an intending purchaser, and immediately afterwards
releasing the reversion to him. But since it was
necessary that the lessee should have actually entered
on the land to be conveyed, as much notoriety was
given to this mode of transfer as to a feoffment.

A Surrender was the converse of a release, being the yielding up of an estate in possession by its owner, with a view to its being merged in a greater (*m*). In this case, as in that of a release, it was essential that there should be privity of estate between the parties, but a surrender differed from a release in not requiring any deed or writing for its validity. Surrender.

Lastly we have to notice a Defeasance, which was a collateral deed made at the same time as a feoffment or other conveyance, and containing certain conditions, on the performance of which the estate then created might be defeated (*n*). It was in this manner that mortgages were usually made, but we may perhaps anticipate a little on this point by saying that after the passing of the Statute of Uses it became customary to insert the conveyance of an estate, and any conditions to which the conveyance was made subject, in the same deed; and thus separate deeds of defeasance have long fallen into disuse (*o*). Defeasance.

All the above-mentioned methods of dealing with land are called Common Law Conveyances, because they operate without reference to the Statute of Uses. They may also be divided into original or primary, and derivative or secondary, conveyances; the latter being those which presuppose some originating instrument, and only serve to transfer interests previously created. Thus, a feoffment, lease, exchange, and partition were original conveyances, an assign- Common Law Conveyances.
Are original or primary.
Or derivative or secondary.

(*m*) Co. Litt. 337ᵇ.
(*n*) 2 Bl. Com. 327.
(*o*) See *Cotterell* v. *Purchase*, Ca. t. Talb., 61, 64.

ment, a release, surrender, and defeasance were derivative; whilst a grant was either original or secondary, according to the nature of the property conveyed.

Extraordinary assurance. Besides the above, which, together with those subsequently introduced in consequence of the Statute of Uses, are called ordinary assurances, there was the method used for converting an estate tail into a fee simple, and thus rendering it alienable. This, Fine and Recovery. which was called an extraordinary assurance, was a Fine and Recovery, of which we need not say more than to remind the reader that it was a pre-arranged suit between the tenant in tail, as defendant, and a friendly plaintiff, in which the latter was declared owner in fee simple of the lands entailed; and was enabled, in consequence, to deal with them in any way which the tenant in tail might desire.

There were also two other forms of assurance which did not derive their force from the Common Law. We have already, in our chapter on the Statute of Uses, pointed out that before the passing of that act the Court of Chancery had recognised the custom of conveying land to some nominal owner, who was to hold it for the benefit of another person: and that the enforcement by equity of secret uses frustrated the policy of the law, by enabling land to be transferred without any notoriety. Such a transfer could be effected by the employment of one of two instruments, named respectively a Covenant to stand Seised Covenant to stand seised. and a Bargain and Sale; the former being a deed by which a man covenanted to stand seised of land to the Bargain and Sale. use of a wife, child, or kinsman; the other, a contract whereby the bargainor, for some pecuniary consideration, undertook to convey land to the bargainee. For since the Court of Chancery would enforce the use raised by these means, the covenantee or bargainee acquired the practical ownership of the land. These assurances were said to operate without transmutation of possession, as opposed to those which transferred a legal estate, and were therefore said to operate by transmutation of possession. The distinction still remains in name, although the Statute of Uses has, to use the words of Coke, " married uses to the law."

It was, as we know, in order to put a stop to these secret uses that the Statute of Uses (*p*) enacted that the *cestui que use* should be deemed to be in lawful seisin, estate, and possession of the estate held to his use. In this object it failed, owing to the peculiar view which the courts of law continued to take of trusts. But it made several important changes in the form of conveyancing instruments, and to these changes we will next turn our attention. The first and most general of them was the introduction into conveyances of an express declaration of the way in which the use was to be limited: thus, instead of making a feoffment simply "to" A and his heirs, it would now be made "unto and to the use of" A and his heirs, for by this means instruments were rendered effectual which might otherwise, from want of consideration, or from some omission or other imperfection, have failed to pass the legal estate in the land conveyed (*q*). [margin: Changes in consequence of the Statute of Uses.] [margin: Declaration of Use.]

But a still more important novelty was the invention of a new form of conveyance, which almost totally superseded that notorious and public mode of transferring property which the common law required, and the statute intended to restore (*r*). [margin: A new form of assurance.]

It will be recollected that, before the passing of the Statute of Uses, there were, besides the common law conveyances, two others, namely, the covenant to stand

---

(*p*) 27 Hen. VIII. c. 10.
(*q*) *Samme's Case*, 13 Rep. 54.
(*r*) Co. Litt. 271ᵇ, n. (1).

seised, and the bargain and sale, which served to raise a use although they did not, at that time, transmute the possession. But when the statute turned uses into possession, these assurances passed the legal, as well as the equitable, estate; and that without any necessity for livery of seisin or attornment. As regards the covenant to stand seised, this was not of much importance; for since no uses could be limited by it except to a child or near relation, the limitations to trustees, then necessary to support contingent remainders, could not be inserted in it, and consequently covenants to stand seised soon fell into disuse, and may be dismissed from our further notice.

Bargain and sale.

But a bargain and sale now obviously presented a ready means of making secret transfers of land from any one person to another. For a bargain and sale still raised a use in favour of the purchaser, and now, under the Statute of Uses, the fact of land being held to his use gave him the legal estate in possession in it also. In order, therefore, to restore notoriety in the transfer of land, it was enacted by the 27 Hen. VIII.,

Statute of Inrolments.

c. 16, called the Statute of Inrolments, that no hereditaments should pass from one to another, whereby any estate of inheritance or freehold should be made to take effect in any person, or any use thereof be made, by reason only of any bargain and sale thereof, except the same be made by writing, sealed, and inrolled within six months after execution. By this means, it was hoped, secret conveyances were made impossible; but the astuteness of the lawyers soon defeated the purpose of the law. For it was observed that the statute made mention only of estates of inheritance and of freeholds: a lease, therefore, for a term of years was exempt from its provisions. Now we have seen that if, before the statute, a lessee were in actual possession of the land demised, no livery of seisin was requisite to convey the remainder of the estate to him; and also, that if a man, in consideration of money paid to him, bargained that he would grant land to another, this raised a use in the bargainee. Then came the statute which turned uses into actual possession. If, therefore, a bargain were now made, for a pecuniary consideration, that a man should have land granted to him for one year, this was deemed to make him a lessee for a year in actual possession, and, as such, capable of taking a release of the remainder of the grantor's estate, without any livery of seisin, or other public ceremony.

From this sprung the conveyance known as a Lease and Release, which almost entirely superseded the ancient feoffment, and was, until lately, the ordinary way of conveying freehold estates of all kinds. The form of this assurance was, first, an instrument stating that the vendor, in consideration of some nominal sum, had bargained and sold the land to the purchaser for one year, to commence from the day previous to the date of the deed, to the intent that the purchaser might thereby, and by the statute for transmuting uses into possession, be in actual possession of the premises, and enabled to accept a grant of the reversion of the same. This was followed by a second deed releasing the reversion to him, and thus putting him into possession of the whole estate intended to be conveyed.

<small>Lease and Release.</small>

The Lease and Release, then, came to be the almost universal way of conveying freeholds, and was employed for the purpose of making an exchange or partition, as well as for conveyances between ordinary vendors and purchasers. Incorporeal hereditaments, proper, continued to be created and transferred by Deed of Grant, whilst of the other assurances previously enumerated the ordinary Release, the Surrender, Lease and Assignment, and Fine and Recovery remained unaffected by the Statute of Uses; and Covenants to stand Seised and Defeasances fell into general disuse.

Changes after the period of the Statute of Uses. It remains to notice the changes which have taken place, since the passing of the Statute of Uses, down to the present time.

Wills. The first of these, in point of date, had reference to Wills. It will be recollected that, before the date of the Statute of Uses, personal property was freely transmissible, but that real property could only be disposed of by will, by devising a use in it. When the statute turned uses into legal estates, even this mode of devise was no longer practicable; and so, for a short time, there existed no means by which real property could be disposed of by will.

Statute of Wills of Henry the Eighth. But some five years after the passing of the Statute of Uses, there came the first Statute of Wills, the 32 Hen. VIII., c. 1, which gave power to every person to devise, by his last will or testament in writing, all lands and hereditaments which he held in socage, and two-thirds of those which he held by knight service. *12 Car. II. c. 24.* This was followed up by the 12 Car. II., c. 24, which turned the tenure of all lands held by knight service into that of socage, and thus the fee simple of all hereditaments of freehold tenure became devisable. A will could moreover, since the Statute of Uses, operate as a settlement, as well as for the immediate passing of property. For it might contain, under the name of executory devises, those springing or shifting uses, and powers, which we have already considered. This Statute of Wills did not, however, apply to any hereditaments other than those belonging to the testator at the time of making his will; neither did it include copyholds (*s*). A will could, therefore, be only made to operate on copyholds, by first surrendering

---

(*s*) *Wainewright* v. *Elwell*, 1 Madd. 627.

them to the use of the testator's will, during his lifetime, and then devising the use.

The next statute which referred to wills was the Statute of Frauds (*t*), which, in addition to the writing required for a will of lands by the Statute of Wills of Henry the Eighth, prescribed its execution by the testator in the presence of three, or more, credible witnesses; who were also to append their signatures, by way of attestation. This statute also, practically, made it necessary for all wills of personal property to be in writing and signed by the testator. Next, after a long interval, came the 55 Geo. III., c. 192, which enacted that where, by the custom of a manor, a copyhold tenant might devise tenements previously surrendered to the use of his will, he might, thenceforth, devise them without any previous surrender. But this act did not enable a devisee (*u*), or purchaser of copyholds, to devise them (*v*) unless he had himself been previously admitted a tenant of the manor. Now, however, it is enacted by the present Wills Act, the 7 Wm. IV. & 1 Vict., c. 26 (*w*), that every person may devise all real and personal estate to which he is entitled, either at law or in equity; and this power is to extend to copyholds, notwithstanding that the testator, whether entitled as heir, devisee, or otherwise, has not been admitted thereto. The act also requires (*x*) that every will, whether of real or personal estate, shall be signed by the testator in the presence of, and be attested by, two witnesses.

Statute of Frauds.

55 Geo. III. c. 192.

Wills Act.

The Statute of Frauds made other desirable changes besides those relating to wills. Uses, as we know, had been upheld by the Court of Chancery even

Trusts.

(*t*) 29 Car. II. c. 3.
(*u*) *Doe* v. *Lawes*, 7 A. & E. 195.
(*v*) *Matthews* v. *Osborne*, 13 C. B. 919.
(*w*) S. 3.
(*x*) S. 9.

Statute of Frauds.

where there was no written evidence of their existence, and the same rule prevailed, at first, in regard to trusts. But the statute enacts (*y*) that all declarations of trust, except (*z*) in the case of a resulting trust, shall be manifested and proved by some writing, signed by the party enabled by the law to declare such trust. Upon these sections it has been held, that writing is necessary only as a proof of the existence of a trust, and not for its creation (*a*), and that the person "enabled by the law" to declare the trust is the settlor, and not the trustee (*b*).

Feoffments and Leases. Statute of Frauds.

The Statute of Frauds also made writing necessary in other cases where, as we have seen, it was not formerly required. For it enacted (*c*) that all leases, estates, interests of freehold or terms of years, or any uncertain interest of and in any hereditaments, created by livery of seisin only, or by parol, and not put in writing, and signed by the parties making or creating the same, or their agents thereunto lawfully authorized, should have the force and effect of leases or estates at will only. An exception was however (*d*) made in favour of leases not exceeding a term of three years, whereupon the rent reserved during the term amounts to two-thirds of the full and improved value of the thing demised. The statute also provided (*e*) that no leases, estates or interests of freehold, or terms of years, or any uncertain interests, not being copyhold or customary interests in, to, or out of any hereditaments, should be assigned, granted, or surrendered, unless it be by deed or note in writing, signed by the party assigning, granting, or surrendering the same,

---

(*y*) S. 7.
(*z*) S. 8.
(*a*) *Gardner* v. *Rowe*, 2 S. & S. 346, 5 Russ. 258.
(*b*) *Tierney* v. *Wood*, 19 Beav. 320.
(*c*) S. 1.
(*d*) S. 2.
(*e*) S. 3.

or by his agent thereunto lawfully authorized, or by act and operation of law.

These provisions of the Statute of Frauds were supplemented by the Real Property Amendment Act, the 8 & 9 Vict., c. 106, which (ƒ) makes void all feoffments, partitions, *exchanges* leases, assignments and surrenders unless made by deed, except feoffments made under a custom by an infant, partitions and exchanges of copyholds, and leases not required by law to be in writing—that is, those excepted by the Statute of Frauds. Real Property Amendment Act.

The next change effected in the transfer of land was by the 4 & 5 Anne, c. *3* This act (g) makes good all grants of any manors or rents, or of the reversion or remainder of any messuages or lands, without any attornment of the tenants of the manors or lands out of which such rent issues; or of the particular tenants upon whose particular estate any such reversions or remainders shall be expectant or depending. Attornment. 4 & 5 Anne, c. 3. /16

The next act to be mentioned is that for the Abolition of Fines and Recoveries (h), which substituted a deed, inrolled within six months after execution, for the ancient process of a fictitious suit. Fines and Recoveries Abolition Act.

Coming next to the reign of the present Queen, we find the 4 & 5 Vict., c. 21, which did away with the necessity for two deeds in a conveyance by Lease and Release; for it enacted that every deed of release of freehold estates, expressed to be made in pursuance of the act, should, thenceforth, be as effectual as if the releasor had also executed a deed or instrument of bargain and sale, or lease for a year, for giving effect to such release. Lease and Release made unnecessary. 4 & 5 Vict., c. 21.

(ƒ) S. 3.
(g) S. 9.
(h) 3 & 4 Wm. IV. c. 74.

Real Property Amendment Act.

Next to be noticed is the Real Property Amendment Act (*i*), already referred to, which, in addition to its other provisions, effected an important change in the mode of conveying freeholds. For it rendered unnecessary any conveyance of land by way of lease and release, by declaring (*j*) that from thenceforth all corporeal hereditaments should, as regards the immediate freehold thereof, lie in grant as well as in livery, thus enabling all hereditaments, whether corporeal or incorporeal, to be conveyed by a simple deed of grant. The act also (*k*) put an end to the tortious operation of feoffments, and thus caused a feoffment in fee simple by any tenant with a limited interest to operate as a conveyance of such interest only (*l*).

Tortious feoffments put an end to.

Inclosure Acts. 8 & 9 Vict., c. 118.

Lastly, we have to mention the Inclosure Acts (*m*), of which the 8 & 9 Vict., c. 118 (*n*), enabling exchanges to be made through the instrumentality of the Inclosure Commissioners (whose order permitting an exchange is good without any further conveyance or release), whilst the 11 & 12 Vict., c. 99 (*o*), extends the above provisions to cases of partition.

11 & 12 Vict., c. 99.

We have thus traced the history of conveyancing down to the date of the Statute of Uses; examined the great changes made by the statute, not only in the nature of legal estates, but in the modes also in which they could be settled and conveyed; and observed the origin and growth of the power of disposition by will; the safeguards against fraud provided by the Statute of Frauds and the Real Property Amendment Act; the abolition of the ceremony of attornment, and of the cumbrous process of fines and recoveries; the

---

(*i*) 8 & 9 Vict. c. 106.
(*j*) S. 2.
(*k*) S. 4.
(*l*) Shelf. R. P. Statutes, 637, note (k).
(*m*) 8 & 9 Vict. c. 118; 10 & 11 Vict. c. 111; 11 & 12 Vict. c. 99; 12 & 13 Vict. c. 83; 15 & 16 Vict. c. 79; 17 & 18 Vict. c. 97; 20 & 21 Vict. c. 31; 22 & 23 Vict. c. 43; 31 & 32 Vict. c. 89.
(*n*) S. 147.
(*o*) S. 13.

enactments by which the lease and release gave way, first to the release alone, and then to the simple grant; and finally the simplicity introduced by the Inclosure Acts into the exchange and partition of land. The result, from a conveyancing point of view, is that we have now the Grant and Assignment (comprehended under the general name of Purchase Deeds) for the sale of land; the Mortgage Deed for its pledge; the Lease to give its temporary possession; the Settlement whereby estates can, subject to due precautions, be preserved in families; and the Will, which can either operate as a settlement, or effect a direct transmission of property from one person to another.

The succeeding chapters will be devoted to the consideration of the assurances enumerated above, and we may take this opportunity of stating that our remarks will, as a rule, extend only to the simplest forms of those instruments which convey the legal estates in the various kinds of property which have been considered in the first part of this work.

CHAPTER II.

CONDITIONS OF SALE.

HAVING thus traced the history of conveyancing down to our own times, we have next to consider, in detail, the various instruments at present used for the transfer of real property. Now, each of these instruments marks the carrying out of some pre-existing purpose, which may have been that of one person, or of several. In the latter case, it will usually be found that the terms of the assurance have been the subject of previous negotiations, which have resulted in an agreement, or contract, and this contract forms an important part of the transaction, being the foundation of the edifice of which the assurance is the completion. This remark applies particularly to the ordinary case of vendors and purchasers of land. Hence, it is proposed, before considering purchase deeds of real and leasehold estates, to turn our attention to the contracts by which they are preceded.

Such a contract is, like all contracts, subject to various rules of law, non-compliance with which will render it invalid. There are also certain statutory requirements which are essential to the proof of its existence, though not to its creation. Under the former, a contract may be set aside on account of the incapacity of one, or more, of the parties to it; on account of there having been some fraud, or mistake, committed with reference to it; and on several other grounds which need not be further particularized. With these we shall not occupy ourselves, for our aim is simply to ascertain how a contract of sale of land ought to be drawn up, supposing it to have been properly entered into. This, however, involves the consideration of the statutory requisites for such a contract, and of the judicial decisions upon the wording of Acts of Parliament relating to these requisites.

And it may be as well here to remind the reader that an important change has been, very lately, made in our system of jurisprudence. For the Supreme Court of Judicature Act 1873 (a), which is to come into operation on the 1st of November 1875 (b), aims at doing away with the former distinction between law and equity. It therefore enacts (c), that except in matters therein particularly mentioned, (none of which relate to our subject) whenever there is any conflict or variance between the rules of equity and the rules of the common law with reference to the same matter, the rules of equity shall prevail. Consequently, although reference will occasionally be made in this and the following chapters to rules of law which differ from those of equity, it will only be in order to mark out equitable doctrines with more distinctness. The reader will also understand that such differences will shortly cease to have any existence.

Since, then, the preparation of a contract of sale of land is governed by the enactments and decisions to which reference has been made above, we will, in this chapter, discuss separately, 1st, The statutory requisites for such a contract; and 2nd, The proper form of the contract when embodied in an Agreement, or in Conditions of Sale. *Division of the subject.*

The principal statutory requisites for the contract are to be found in the fourth section of the Statute of Frauds (d). This section enacts that, from thence- *Statutory requisites for the contract. Statute of Frauds.*

(a) 36 & 37 Vict. c. 66.
(b) 37 & 38 Vict. c. 83.
(c) S. 25, sub s. 11.
(d) 29 Car. II. c. 3.

forth, no action shall be brought to charge any person upon any contract or sale of lands, tenements, or hereditaments, or any interest in or concerning them, unless the agreement upon which such action shall be brought, or some memorandum or note thereof, shall be in writing, and signed by the party to be charged therewith, or some other person thereunto by him lawfully authorized.

Statute applies to every interest in land. The first point to be noticed is, that these provisions of the statute apply to every agreement which is substantially one for the sale of an interest in land. Thus (e), where a lessee in possession had, verbally, agreed to give up his lease, in consideration that a third person (who had already obtained the promise of a lease from the lessor) should pay the lessee £150, and take certain fixtures at a valuation; this was held to be an agreement for the sale of an interest in land, and void for want of writing (f). We have next to consider what things are required by the statute.

What is required by the statute. These are, (1) a written agreement, and (2) signature by the party to be charged, or his agent lawfully authorized.

Written agreement. Since the agreement is to be in writing, it follows that the whole of it must be in writing, and the consequence is that an agreement is not binding upon either party unless it contains, in the body of it, or *What must be contained in the agreement.* by necessary implication, (1) the names of the contracting parties as such, (2) the consideration, and (3) the subject-matter or object of the contract (g). Hence, it has been decided that (h) a note of a sale of

---

(e) *Smith* v. *Tombs*, 3 Jur. 72.
(f) And see *Hodgson* v. *Johnson*, 5 Jur. N. S. 290; *Smart* v. *Harding*, 15 C. B. 652.
(g) Per C. J. *Tindal*, 2 Bing. N. C. 742.
(h) *Boyce* v. *Greene*, Batty, 608—a case under the Irish Statute of Frauds, 7 Wm. III. c. 12, containing the same provisions as the 29 Car. II. c. 3; and see *Williams* v. *Lake*, 29 L. J. (Q. B.) 1; *Williams* v. *Byrnes*, 2 N. R. 47.

mining shares, (which, under the circumstances, were held to be an interest in land) signed by the vendor, but consisting merely of a statement that he had "sold 100" shares, and not saying to whom, did not bind him; that (*i*) an agreement, signed by the purchaser, to purchase a horse over £10 in value (such an agreement being required by another section (*j*) of this statute to be in writing) was void, because it did not state the price; and (*k*) that a written agreement, signed by both parties to it, for the grant of a lease, was not binding on either of them, since it did not state for how long a term the lease was to be made (*l*). These cases, however, it must be remembered, only go to the length of deciding that the agreement must contain, within itself, the means of ascertaining the essential parts of the contract, but do not make it necessary that those parts should be precisely stated. It has, therefore, been held (*m*) that a contract signed by an agent "as agent for the vendors," but not naming them, was a sufficient description of the latter as contracting parties, when indorsed on a paper stating the vendors to be "the executors of Admiral F., deceased (*n*)." And (*o*) that a letter, signed by the vendor, stating that she had agreed to sell "this place," at a certain price, was a sufficient description of the subject-matter of the contract. It would also seem that the courts will enforce an agreement to purchase land "at a fair valuation (*p*)." For in this case the consideration can be collected or implied

---

(*i*) *Elmore* v. *Kingscote*, 5 B. & C. 583; and see *Blagden* v. *Bradbear*, 12 Ves. 466.
(*j*) S. 17.
(*k*) *Clinan* v. *Cooke*, 1 Sch. & L. 22; and see *Kenworthy* v. *Schofield*, 2 B. & C. 945.
(*l*) And see *Nesham* v. *Selby*, L. R. 7 Ch. 406.
(*m*) *Hood* v. *Barrington*, L. R. 6 Eq. 218.
(*n*) And see *Warner* v. *Willington*, 3 Drew. 523, 530; *Bourdillon* v. *Collins*, 24 L. T. (N. S.) 344.
(*o*) *Waldron* v. *Jacob*, Ir. R. 5 Eq. 131.
(*p*) 1 Dav. Con. 546, note (*f*).

from the instrument itself, not as a matter of conjecture, but with certainty (*q*).

Agreement need not be in one document.
But different parts must be related.

The written agreement need not, necessarily, be contained in one document, but, if it is not, all the separate documents from which it is sought to extract the agreement must have reference to each other, and must point to the same contract (*r*). And if one part of the agreement is contained in a letter, signed by one of the parties to be charged, it is not necessary that the letter should be addressed to the other party to the contract; since, as we said before, such a writing is only required to prove the terms of the contract, and does not constitute it (*s*). It has also been held, in a case (*t*) turning on another section of the Statute of Frauds, that a man was bound by a letter written by him, and setting out the terms of a parol contract; although the object of the letter was to state his reasons for declining to carry out the contract.

Parol evidence when admissible.
When terms of agreement are clear.

If the terms of the written agreement are clear, and complete without reference to anything else, then it is a general rule of the law of evidence, irrespective of the Statute of Frauds, that no parol evidence is admissible to contradict or vary the written agreement (*u*), and the same rule prevails in equity, so far as regards the tendering of parol evidence by a plaintiff. But an exception is made in the case of a defendant against whom specific performance of a contract is sought. For he may adduce parol evidence to show

---

(*q*) See as to this, *James* v. *Williams*, 5 B. & Ad. 1109; *Raikes* v. *Todd*, 8 A. & E. 846; *Dinham* v. *Bradford*, L. R. 5 Ch. 519.
(*r*) *Clinan* v. *Cooke*, 1 Sch. & L. 22; *Bayley* v. *Fitzmaurice*, 8 E. & B. 664; *Boydell* v. *Drummond*, 11 East, 142.
(*s*) *Gibson* v. *Holland*, L. R. 1 C. P. 1; *Baumann* v. *James*, L. R. 3 Ch. 508.
(*t*) *Buxton* v. *Rust*, L. R. 7 Ex. 1 & 279.
(*u*) *Goss* v. *Nugent*, 5 B. & Ad. 58, 64.

that the written agreement does not represent the real intention of the parties to it (v).

If the instrument contains a patent ambiguity, one, that is, apparent upon the face of the instrument itself, the latter is entirely void (w). But if there be a latent ambiguity, that is, one of such a nature that its existence is first shown by extrinsic evidence, whether written or verbal, it may be explained by extrinsic evidence which may be either written or verbal (x). If a man, for instance, agrees in writing to sell "his manor of A:" this appears, on the face of the document, to be straightforward enough. But if it can be shown that the vendor has two manors, one called North A, and the other South A; then, since the agreement does not specify which of them he has contracted to sell, parol evidence is admissible to explain this latent ambiguity raised by extrinsic evidence (y). Where there has been a verbal contract, followed by a partial performance of it by one party, equity will, as a rule, compel the other party to the contract to perform his part, notwithstanding the absence of any written agreement. For in all questions on the Statute of Frauds, the end and purport of making it has been considered, namely, to prevent frauds and perjuries; so that any agreement in which there is no chance of either, the court has considered as out of the statute (z). On this ground also, it seems that the statute never extended to sales under the order of the Court of Chancery; nor to purchases under the order of the court, if the purchaser made no opposition to the confirmation of the report approving of the purchase (a).

When agreement is ambiguous.

Part performance.

(v) *Woollam* v. *Hearn*, 7 Ves. 211ᵇ, and, with notes, 2 L. C. 484.
(w) *Hitchin* v. *Groom*, 5 C. B. 515.
(x) 5 B. & C. 520ᵃ; and see *Shore* v. *Wilson*, 9 Cl. & F. 355, 555, & 565.
(y) See *Jones* v. *Newman*, 1 W. Bl. 60.
(z) *Per Hardwicke* C. *Atty.-Genl.* v. *Day*, 1 Ves. 218, 220. See also *Lester* v. *Foxcroft*, 1 Colles. P. C. 108, and, with notes, 1 L. C. 768; and note to *Pym* v. *Blackburn*, 3 Ves. p. 38.
(a) Dart. V. & P. 183.

C.   U

Signature.

Next, as to the signature. It is clearly settled that the signature of the party to be charged is sufficient to bind him at law, and also to induce equity to decree specific performance of his contract by him, although there may not have been any signing by the other party to the contract (*b*). It has also been held, in a modern case, that a proposal in writing, if accepted by parol, becomes thereupon a binding agreement upon the person making it (*c*). And it seems that putting a man's initials to a document (*d*), or his printed signature, if ordinarily used (*e*), satisfies the requirements of the statute. Nor does it matter in what part of the agreement the signature is to be found; unless the document is evidently incomplete (*f*). Thus, a paper beginning "I, James Crockford, agree to sell," and written by James Crockford, was held to contain a sufficient signature (*g*).

What is a sufficient signature.

A corporation aggregate which has a common seal must use that seal as its ordinary signature. It cannot, therefore, at common law, either enforce (*h*) or be bound by ordinary contracts not under its seal (*i*); but it will, in equity, be bound by contracts within its province, although not under seal, where there has been part performance by the other contracting party (*j*).

Signature by agent.

Auctioneer.

The statute also makes a signature by a lawfully authorized agent binding on his principal. On this point it may be mentioned that the auctioneer at a

---

(*b*) See *Williams* v. *Lake*, 29 L. J. (Q. B.) 1, 3; *Western* v. *Russell*, 3 Ves. & B. 187, 192. Fry on Specific Performance, 136-7.
(*c*) *Reuss* v. *Picksley*, L. R. 1 Ex. 342; a case of a contract not to be performed within a year.
(*d*) *Phillimore* v. *Barry*, 1 Camp. 513.
(*e*) *Saunderson* v. *Jackson*, 2 Bos. & P. 238.
(*f*) *Hubert* v. *Treherne*, 3 Man. & Gr. 743.
(*g*) *Knight* v. *Crockford*, 1 Esp. 190.
(*h*) *Mayor of Kidderminster* v. *Hardwick*, L. R. 9 Ex. 13.
(*i*) Grant, Corp. 65. *East London Water-works Co.* v. *Bailey*, 4 Bing. 283.
(*j*) *Crook* v. *Corporation of Seaford*, L. R. 6 Ch. 551.

sale is the agent of both parties (*k*), and that his signature is binding upon either the vendor or the purchaser. The signature of his clerk is also sufficient to bind a party who has authorized the clerk to sign for him (*l*). But in the absence of such authority the clerk's signature has no binding effect (*m*). If the auctioneer be himself the vendor, his signature will not bind the purchaser, since the signature as agent must be made by some third person (*n*). It has also been held that an acceptance of an offer, first signed on the ordinary telegraph form, and then correctly transmitted by telegraph, is binding on the sender, who has thus constituted the telegraph company his agent for the purpose of forwarding an exact copy of the written acceptance (*o*). It follows that the sender is not bound by an inaccurate copy (*p*).

Auctioneer's Clerk.

Telegraph Company.

We have now arrived at the consideration of the manner in which a contract for the sale of land should be prepared. If the sale is to be by private contract, the particulars of the property to be sold and the terms mutually assented to by the parties are, in general, contained in numbered clauses of the same document, which is known as the Agreement. If it is to be by public auction, the particulars of the property are kept apart from those clauses in which the vendor states the terms on which he is prepared to sell, and which are consequently known as the Conditions of Sale. It is proposed first to offer a very few remarks on the preparation of the particulars, and then to go through the clauses of an ordinary precedent of conditions of sale of freeholds, or copyholds, in lots; calling attention to the leading principles on which

The written contract.

(*k*) *Kemeys* v. *Proctor*, 3 Ves. & B. 57; *Simon* v. *Motivos*, Burr. 1922; *Coles* v. *Trecothick*, 9 Ves. 234.
(*l*) *Emmerson* v. *Heelis*, 2 Taunt. 38; *Bird* v. *Boulter*, 1 Nev. & M. 313.
(*m*) *Pierce* v. *Corf*, L. R. 9 Q. B. 210.
(*n*) *Wright* v. *Dannah*, 2 Camp. 203; *Farebrother* v. *Simmons*, 5 B. & Ald. 333; *Sharman* v. *Brandt*, L. R. 6 Q. B. 720.
(*o*) *Godwin* v. *Francis*, L. R. 5 C. P. 295, 301, 302.
(*p*) *Henkel* v. *Pape*, L. R. 6 Ex. 7.

they are prepared, and adverting when necessary to such modifications as would be needed in order to adapt them to a sale by private contract, or to the sale of leaseholds (*q*).

The Particulars.

In the preparation of the particulars, two points must be specially attended to. The first is, that they must comply with the rules before mentioned as founded on the Statute of Frauds, by stating, distinctly or by necessary implication, that which is the subject matter of the contract (*r*). The second is, that they must not be so worded as to mislead a purchaser by any statement which describes the property inaccurately with regard to its advantages or value. Thus, in a well-known case (*s*), the particulars of an estate described it as being "about one mile from Horsham;" it being, in fact, between three and four miles from that place. Lord Ellenborough left it to the jury to say whether this misdescription was wilfully introduced in order to make the estate appear more valuable; and the jury finding in the affirmative, the contract was set aside (*t*). The same principle was acted upon in another case (*u*). There, a large farm, on an estate to be sold, was described as "late in the occupation of A at the rent of £290." In fact, A had occupied the farm for a year at the rent of £290, but for the previous quarter of a year he had only paid a rent of £1; and thus had paid only £291 for a tenancy of a year and a quarter. At the end of that time he had quitted the farm, and another person who had, subsequently, agreed to give £225 a year for it, had paid £20 to be off his bargain. The statement in the particulars was consequently held to be one calculated

---

(*q*) The student is recommended, in reading this and similar chapters, to have by him a simple precedent of the instrument under discussion.
(*r*) See *Hooke* v. *McQueen*, 2 Grant, 450.
(*s*) *Norfolk* v. *Worthy*, 1 Camp. 337.
(*t*) And see *Stanton* v. *Tattersall*, 1 Sm. & Giff. 529.
(*u*) *Dimmock* v. *Hallett*, L. R. 2 Ch. 21.

to mislead the purchaser of the estate, who was therefore allowed to rescind his contract. And a misstatement as to the nature of the property, such as describing leaseholds, for however long a term, as freeholds, has had the same result (v). It may be added that maps, or plans, of the property, forming as they do a part of the particulars, are subject to the same rules (w).

Next, as to the preparation of the conditions of sale. This is always a matter which requires care, for, as has been said, it is "an undertaking to defend the title to the property against the whole world (x)." And since these conditions are inserted in order to restrict the ordinary rights of a purchaser, who has not had any voice in their preparation, it is essential that they should be clear and intelligible in stating to a man of ordinary understanding what he is not to require; and that they should not be of such a nature as to mislead or deceive him (y). Care should also be taken that they are not too stringent. Where the vendor is selling his own property he need, of course, only be guided by the consideration of the probability of depreciating the value of the property, added to the certainty of preventing a purchase of it by trustees; but where the vendor is himself a trustee, he must remember that the sale may be set aside by a *cestui que trust* if the conditions are unnecessarily depreciatory (z), and that he may become personally liable for any consequent loss.

Conditions of Sale.

General rules for their preparation.

We will now, as previously arranged, consider *seriatim* those ordinary conditions of sale to which we have referred. But first it may be as well to mention

---

(v) *Fordyce* v. *Ford*, 4 Bro. C. C. 494; *Drewe* v. *Corp*, 9 Ves. 368.
(w) *Dykes* v. *Blake*, 4 Bing. N. C. 463; *Denny* v. *Hancock*, L. R. 6 Ch. 1.
(x) 1 Dav. Con. 439.
(y) 1 Dav. Con. 442.
(z) See *Dance* v. *Goldingham*, L. R. 8 Ch. 902.

that the "abstract" consists of connected summaries of the deeds which show the vendor's title to the property to be sold. This is delivered to the purchaser, who founds on it such "requisitions" (by way of further inquiry or objection) on the vendor's title as he thinks proper; and also verifies it, by comparing it with the original deeds from which it is taken.

1st Condition.
Conduct of the sale.

The 1st condition usually relates to the manner of conducting the sale. It fixes a sum as the *minimum* advance which may be made at each bidding, this being regulated generally by the value of the property. It also provides that the highest bidder shall be the purchaser; that if any dispute arises respecting a bidding to any lot, the same shall be put up again and resold; and that no bidding shall be retracted. It is not clear that this last stipulation can be enforced (a); but it is clear that, in the absence of it, any bidding may be audibly retracted before the fall of the auctioneer's hammer (b). If the property is leasehold, it should also be stipulated that the production of a receipt for the last payment of rent accrued previously to the completion of the purchase shall be conclusive evidence that all the covenants and conditions of the lease have been observed up to the date of completion. The lease, or a copy of it, should be produced at the sale, and the condition should provide that each purchaser is to be deemed to have notice of the contents of the lease.

Sale subject to a reserve price should be so stated.
Sales of land by Auction Act.

If it is intended that the sale should be subject to a reserve price, this fact should be stated in the conditions. For it is now enacted, by the Sales of Land by Auction Act (c) (passed to put an end to the previously conflicting rules of law and equity on this point (d)), that the particulars or conditions of sale by

---

(a) 1 Dav. Con. 449; Sug. V. & P. 14; Dart. V. & P. 113.
(b) *Payne* v. *Cave*, 3 T. R. 148.
(c) 30 & 31 Vict. c. 48, s. 5.
(d) S. 4, and see *Mortimer* v. *Bell*, L. R. 1 Ch. 10.

auction, of any land, shall state whether such land will be sold without reserve, or subject to a reserved price, or whether the right to bid is reserved; and that, if it is stated that the sale is to be without reserve, it shall not be lawful for the seller to employ any person to bid at such sale, or for the auctioneer, knowingly, to take any bidding from such person. But (e) that when it is declared that the sale is subject to a right for the seller to bid, it shall be lawful for the seller, or any one person on his behalf, to bid at such auction, in such manner as he may think proper. It will be noticed that a right to bid is only given when the sale is declared to be subject to such a right. Hence, it has been held (f) that where the conditions merely state that the sale is subject to a reserved bidding, it is illegal to employ an agent to bid on behalf of the vendor, even in order to bring the biddings up to the reserve price.

The corresponding clause in an agreement for sale by private contract has, of course, no reference to the manner of conducting the sale, but it serves to set out the names of the vendor and purchaser respectively, the consideration, and the particulars of the property to be sold; all of which come under separate headings when the sale is to be by public auction. *Clause where sale is by private contract.*

The 2nd condition provides for the payment, by each purchaser, of a deposit; which is usually fixed at from £10 to £20 *per cent.* of the purchase-money. This condition is commonly dispensed with in sales by private contract, where the purchaser is already known to the vendor. The payment of a deposit is a part payment of the purchase-money (g); and will, of course, be allowed for on completing the purchase, but the object of the condition is chiefly (as we shall see hereafter) to provide for the imposition of a penalty on *2nd Condition. Deposit.*

(e) S. 6.
(f) *Gilliatt* v. *Gilliatt*, L. R. 9 Eq. 60.
(g) 1 Dav. Con. 419.

the purchaser if he fail to complete the purchase, and to give the vendor a security in respect of any damage which he may sustain by such failure. It is also stipulated, by this condition, that the purchaser shall sign a memorandum annexed to the conditions, acknowledging that he has purchased the property at the price named, and subject to the conditions. A written memorandum is necessary because sales by auction are within the Statute of Frauds (*h*), but it will be remembered that the auctioneer is the agent of the purchaser, and he can therefore bind the latter by, himself, signing the memorandum of sale, should the purchaser improperly refuse to do so.

3rd Condition. Valuation of fixtures and timber.

The 3rd condition provides for the fixtures, timber, and other trees, and underwood, being taken by the purchaser at a valuation, to be made by two valuers, or their umpire, appointed in the usual way. And in order to prevent any question arising from its being impracticable to carry out this stipulation (*i*), it is generally added that, if the valuation is not so made, the fixtures, &c., shall be paid for by the purchaser at their fair value.

4th Condition. Title to be shown. Present length of title which may be required.

The 4th condition has for its object the restriction of the purchaser's ordinary rights in respect of the vendor's title to the property. In the absence of any condition, the purchaser of freehold or copyhold land has, at present, a right to require a title commencing at least sixty years before the date of his conveyance; the Statute of Limitation (*j*) not having made any difference in this respect (*k*). But it has recently been enacted by the Vendor and Purchaser Act 1874 (*l*), that in the completion of any

Vendor and Purchaser Act 1874.

(*h*) *Buckmaster* v. *Harrop,* 7 Ves. 340.
(*i*) See as to this *Potts* v. *Thames Haven &c. Co.,* 15 Jur. 1004; *Morgan* v. *Milman,* 3 De G. M. & G. 24.
(*j*) 3 & 4 Wm. IV. c. 27.
(*k*) *Cooper* v. *Emery,* 1 Ph. 388.
(*l*) 37 & 38 Vict. c. 78, s. 1.

contract of sale of land made after the 31st of December 1874, and subject to any stipulation to the contrary in the contract, forty years shall be substituted as the period of commencement of title which a purchaser may require, in place of sixty years, the present period of such commencement.

There are very few freehold or copyhold titles to which a clear sixty years' title can be shown. It has become, therefore, almost a matter of course to insert a stipulation that the title shall commence with a specified deed or document which is less than sixty years old. And it is probable that, even under the new act, a similar condition will often be necessary, with a view to guarding the vendor against having to show a forty years' title. To select the best instrument to form a "root of title," as it is called, is often somewhat difficult. Without attempting to lay down any definite rule on this point, we may mention that the further back the title goes the more attractive it is likely to prove to an intending purchaser (although not to so great an extent as might be supposed), and that, on the other hand, it is essential to have a clear root of title, standing of itself independently of any other instrument, and with which the subsequent dealings with the property are connected by a well-defined and natural growth. In endeavouring to combine these advantages of a long and of a clear title, it may be remembered that, other things being equal, a conveyance to a purchaser for value is the best root of title: or, failing that, a marriage settlement made by a person acting as the owner of a fee simple. In the absence of any condition on the subject, a vendor of leaseholds (excepting when the lease has been granted by a corporation under a disabling statute (*m*)) cannot, at present, enforce the contract unless he can show that the original lessor had a right to demise

Selection of a root of title.

Vendor of leaseholds must show lessor's title.

(*m*) *Fane* v. *Spencer*, 2 Madd. 438; 1 Dav. Con. 478.

the property in question (n). He must also, if the lease is less than sixty years old, show the lessor's title for such a period as is necessary, when added to the time for which the property has been held under the lease, to make up a sixty years' title to the property. It appears, however, to be doubtful whether a purchaser insisting on these points could compel the vendor to complete the purchase (o).

But a vendor of leasehold property can scarcely ever produce his lessor's title, nor is it desirable that he should do so, even if he can. A stipulation has, therefore, always been inserted in every properly framed contract of sale of leaseholds, with a view to guard the vendor against liability in this respect. The condition should also, if necessary, limit the length of leasehold title which is to be shown, since, in the absence of agreement, the vendor of leasehold property must produce the lease under which he claims, however old it may be (p). If the property is held by a sub-lease the purchaser should also be precluded from inquiring into the title of the sub-lessor.

<small>Vendor and Purchaser Act 1874.</small> The Vendor and Purchaser Act 1874 (q) has provided that in the completion of contracts entered into after the 31st of December, 1874, and subject to any stipulation to the contrary in the contract, the intended assignee of a term of years shall not be entitled to call for the title to the freehold. The condition under discussion will, consequently, be unnecessary when the act comes into operation, so far as regards production of the freeholder's title by a vendor of leaseholds. But the act does not apply

---

(n) *Purvis* v. *Rayer*, 9 Pri. 488; *Souter* v. *Drake*, 5 B. & Ad. 992; *Hall* v. *Betty*, 4 Man. & Gr. 410.
(o) 1 Platt on Leases, 618.
(p) *Frend* v. *Buckley*, L. R. 5 Q. B. 213.
(q) 37 & 38 Vict. c. 78, s. 2.

to an assignment of a sub-lease. In that case, therefore, a stipulation against calling for the title of the sub-lessor will still be necessary; as may be also one limiting the length of leasehold title to be shown.

Besides fixing a date from which the title is to commence, and prohibiting a demand for any earlier title, the condition should also provide against the purchaser's making any investigation at all as to any prior title, or founding any objection on such prior title, as appearing by recitals contained in any of the title-deeds or otherwise. For a more condition as to the commencement of the title, or one prohibiting the purchaser from making any inquiry as to any earlier title, will be held to mean nothing more than that there shall be no obligation upon the vendor to produce any earlier title, and not to preclude the purchaser from making investigations on his own account (r). And this part of the condition will, it is apprehended, continue to be necessary in every case, even in that of a sale of leaseholds. For the Vendor and Purchaser Act only takes away the right of a purchaser of a term of years to "call for" the title to the freehold. It would appear, therefore, that he still remains entitled to make inquiries for himself, and to avail himself of any objections to completing the purchase which he may thus be enabled to raise.

<small>Condition should prohibit investigation by the purchaser.</small>

The 5th condition provides against inquiries about dower, which it may be difficult or impossible to answer, and which since the Dower Act (s) can seldom be of any value, by providing that it shall be assumed that every former owner of any part of the property, whose widow (if any) would have been entitled to dower, and is not mentioned in the abstract, did not

<small>5th Condition. Dower.</small>

(r) *Shepherd* v. *Keatley*, 1 Cr. Mee & R. 117, 127; *Waddell* v. *Wolffe*, W. N. (1874), 122.
(s) 3 & 4 Wm. IV. c. 105.

leave a widow. If any of the property is copyhold the condition should extend to freebench.

6th Condition. Recitals. A purchaser is entitled, in the absence of stipulation, to have at the vendor's expense strict proof of every statement of fact appearing on the abstract; and also the verification of the abstract itself, by a comparison of it with the originals of all the deeds or documents abstracted or recited which are in the vendor's possession, and even of those which are not, unless they are more than sixty years old (*t*). It often happens that strict proof cannot, except at great expense, be given of matters as to which there can be little real doubt, as, for instance, the death of a former trustee, or the solemnization of a marriage. In order, therefore, to relieve a vendor from the heavy burden which might, otherwise, be imposed upon him by a captious or over-cautious purchaser, it is conditioned that every deed and (in the case of copyholds) entry on, or copy of, court roll, and also every document which is more than a specified number of years old (generally twenty), shall be considered conclusive evidence of everything recited, noticed, assumed, or implied therein.

The Vendor and Purchaser Act 1874 (*u*) enacts (*v*) that in the completion of any contract of sale of land made after the 31st of December 1874, and subject to any stipulation to the contrary in the contract, recitals, statements, and descriptions of facts, matters, and parties contained in deeds, instruments, Acts of Parliament, or statutory declarations, twenty years old at the date of the contract, shall, unless and except so far as they shall be proved to be inaccurate, be taken to be sufficient evidence of the truth of such facts, matters, and descriptions. This condition will,

---

(*t*) *Prosser* v. *Watts*, 6 Madd. 59.
(*u*) 37 & 38 Vict. s. 78.
(*v*) S. 2.

therefore, be unnecessary after the act takes effect, except in cases where it is desired to render unimpeachable recitals, &c., less than twenty years old.

This condition is followed up by the 7th, which throws upon the purchaser all expenses attendant upon the production of any muniment of title not in the vendor's possession; and of producing and obtaining evidence, such as copies of registers, wills, and so on, required by the purchaser for the verification of the title. There can be little doubt that these stringent conditions do often prevent a willing purchaser from insisting upon being supplied with information which is really necessary to make a satisfactory title; but they seem to have very little effect in deterring purchasers, who probably calculate on putting the same obstacle in the way of inquiries by subsequent purchasers. *7th Condition. Expenses of Searches, &c.*

The 8th condition is necessary when, from the removal of landmarks such as hedges or walls, it is impossible accurately to identify the component parts, or "parcels," of the property sold with those mentioned in older deeds (*w*). It provides that the purchaser shall be satisfied, on this point, by a comparison of the description of the property in the particulars with that in the title-deeds, fortified, if necessary, by declarations of the ~~purchaser~~ or of other persons, evidencing long and undisputed possession of the property under those title-deeds. *8th Condition. Identity of Property.*

[margin: Vendor]

The 9th condition provides against the sale being annulled on account of there being any error, mistake, or omission, in the particulars of the property sold. It is either to the effect that in such case compensation shall be given or taken, as the case may be, or else stipulates against any compensation *9th Condition. Compensation.*

(*w*) See as to this *Flower* v. *Hartopp*, 6 Beav. 476.

being received, whether by the vendor or by the purchaser. The doctrine of the common law is, that misdescription of the property debars the vendor from obtaining any damages against a purchaser who refuses to complete the contract. But, on the other hand, the purchaser, if he wishes to fulfil the contract, cannot, at law, get any compensation in respect of that part of the property agreed to be sold which he could not obtain. Equity, however, holds that, under such circumstances, the contract ought not, in general, to be altogether set aside, but enforced so far as practicable; compensation being given, or taken, for that part of it which cannot be performed. This doctrine was carried to a great length in some of the older cases (*x*); but it is now settled that the court will not compel a purchaser specifically to perform his agreement, with an abatement in the price, unless he gets substantially what he bargained for. A purchaser, for instance, has been held (*y*) not to be bound to carry out a contract to buy a wharf and jetty, when it turned out that the jetty was removable at the pleasure of a third person; nor (*z*) one for the purchase of land described as containing 349 acres or thereabouts, the real number being about 100 acres less; and that, notwithstanding a condition that the property should be taken at the quantity stated, whether more or less (*a*).

But where the purchaser can get that which it was his real object to obtain, he must carry out his contract, and take compensation for the deficiency in value (*b*). The compensation will be fixed according

---

(*x*) *Howland* v. *Norris*, 1 Cox, 59; *Poole* v. *Shergold*, 2 Bro. C. C. 117, and the case cited, *ib.* 118ª.
(*y*) *Peers* v. *Lambert*, 7 Beav. 546.
(*z*) *Portman* v. *Mill*, 2 Russ. 570.
(*a*) And see *Perkins* v. *Ede*, 16 Beav. 193; and as to the purchase of more than one lot, *Cassamajor* v. *Strode*, 2 My. & K. 706, 725.
(*b*) *Dyer* v. *Hargrave*, 10 Ves. 505, 507; and see *Drewe* v. *Hanson*, 6 Ves. 675, 678; *Halsey* v. *Grant*, 13 Ves. 73, 78.

to the actual loss sustained by him, not rateably according to the quantity of the property sold (c). A purchaser therefore has been compelled to perform his contract, with an abatement in the price, where a good title could be shown to the whole of a large estate except six acres (d); and where a lot sold contained ten acres less than stated (e). And the same principle has been applied in a case where the property was not in as good a state of cultivation as represented (f). Conversely, a vendor has been compelled to carry out a contract, making compensation, where he contracted to sell a fee simple in possession, and it turned out to be a fee simple in remainder (g); where the estate was said to contain 217 acres, and wanted 26 acres out of that number (h); and where it contained 573 square yards instead of 753 as stated (i), although in this last case there was a special condition against the vendor's being bound to give compensation (j).

It will be gathered from some of these cases that the insertion of the condition under consideration, whichever way it may be framed, is not allowed to override the rule of equity that a purchaser is only bound to carry out his contract, with an abatement in the price, if he can get substantially that which he bargained for. Still less will the condition be permitted to cover wilful omissions or mis-statements. Thus, it has been held that a condition providing for compensation was of no force where (k) property was

---

(c) *Hill* v. *Buckley*, 17 Ves. 394.
(d) *McQueen* v. *Farquhar*, 11 Ves. 467.
(e) *Leslie* v. *Thompson*, 9 Ha. 268.
(f) *Dyer* v. *Hargrave*, 10 Ves. 505; *Canada Permanent Building Society* v. *Young*, 18 Grant, 566.
(g) *Nelthorpe* v. *Holgate*, 1 Coll. 203; and see *Hoy* v. *Smithies*, 22 Beav. 510.
(h) *Hill* v. *Buckley*, 17 Ves. 394.
(i) *Whittemore* v. *Whittemore*, L. R. 8 Eq. 603.
(j) And see *Dyas* v. *Currie*, 2 Jo. & L. 460.
(k) *Phillips* v. *Caldeleugh*, L. R. 4 Q. B. 159.

sold as "freehold," without mentioning that it was subject to restrictive covenants; where (*l*) it turned out that the mines and minerals under the property were reserved to a third person; and, in a case (*m*) of the sale of leasehold property, where the conditions stated that no "offensive trade" could be carried on upon the premises, which were situate in Covent Garden, but concealed the fact that the business of a fruiterer was amongst the prohibited trades (*n*). It has also been held (*o*) that a clause providing against any compensation being claimed by either party only covers small errors, and that a purchaser may, notwithstanding, claim compensation for a serious deficiency. But if the deficiency is great, and there is, besides the condition against compensation, another, entitling the vendor to rescind the contract, the purchaser cannot enforce specific performance of the contract unless he waives his claim to compensation (*p*). Since it is the vendor's duty to ascertain the nature and particulars of the property which he offers for sale, a condition against compensation would probably be construed more strictly against him, if the property should turn out to be larger or more valuable than stated (*q*).

10th Condition. Payment of the purchase-money.

The 10th condition provides for the payment of the remainder of the purchase-money on a specified day (which should be such as will allow of a fair interval for investigating the title, and preparing the conveyance (*r*)), and the execution by the vendor, on payment

---

(*l*) *Upperton* v. *Nickolson*, L. R. 6 Ch. 436.
(*m*) *Flight* v. *Booth*, 1 Bing. N. C. 370.
(*n*) And see *Price* v. *North*, 2 Yo. & C. (Ex.) 620; *Robinson* v. *Musgrove*, 2 Moo. & R. 92.
(*o*) *Whittemore* v. *Whittemore*, L. R. 8 Eq. 603.
(*p*) *Cordingley* v. *Cheeseborough*, 31 L. J. (Ch.) 617; *Durham* v. *Legard*, 11 Jur. (N. S.) 706; *Mawson* v. *Fletcher*, L. R. 6 Ch. 91.
(*q*) *Martin* v. *Cotter*, 3 Jo. & L. 496, 512; and see a case of *Walker* v. *Barnett*, Dart, V. & P. 594.
(*r*) 1 Dav. Con. 559, note (*c*).

of the purchase-money, of a proper assurance of the property. It is the duty of the purchaser, in any case, and at his own expense, to prepare the conveyance, and tender it to the vendor for execution. The condition, however, goes beyond that, for besides stipulating that the conveyance shall be left, at a fixed time beforehand (usually ten days or so), for perusal by the vendor's solicitors, it proceeds to throw upon the purchaser many expenses which would not, otherwise, fall upon him. Such are those attending the getting in of any outstanding estate or interest, or procuring the execution of the conveyance by any parties other than the vendor. It will be observed that the vendor is not relieved by this condition from his ordinary duty of getting in such estates or procuring such execution (*s*). For it only provides for the expenses attendant on his so doing. This condition also, when necessary, restricts the purchaser's rights to the usual covenants for title, but since we propose to go into this question when treating of purchase deeds, we will not, at present, do more than refer to it.

The 11th condition provides that the rents and possession shall be received and retained, and the outgoings paid, by the vendor up to the day fixed for completing the purchase, after which date both the benefit and the liabilities of the property are to devolve upon the purchaser; the rents and outgoings being, if necessary, apportioned between the parties. If leasehold property is sold in lots, considerable difficulty is often felt as to the apportionment of the liability to pay the rent, and observe the covenants, of the original lease; since the lessor is entitled to distrain upon any part of the property for the whole rent due from it. The best plan seems to be (*t*) to

11th Condition.
Rents and outgoings.

(*s*) 1 Dav. Con. 500.
(*t*) 1 Dav. Con. 476; Dart. V. & P. 120.

c.   x

insert a condition providing for the assignment of the lease to the purchaser of the largest lot; the other purchasers taking underleases from him of the term, wanting one day; and, each of them, covenanting to indemnify the holder of the original lease against the acts of all the other sub-lessees.

The effect of the 11th condition, coupled with the previous one, is to raise implied covenants, by the vendor and purchaser respectively, that, on a specified day, the purchase shall be completed, by execution of the conveyance on the one side, and payment of the purchase-money on the other (*u*). But since the covenants are mutual, it follows that a purchaser cannot claim possession of the property unless he is ready to pay the purchase-money, nor can the vendor claim payment unless he has shown a good title to the property. At law, the party not ready, on the specified day, to perform his part of the contract loses all his rights under the contract. But, if he be subsequently ready to carry it out, equity will enforce specific performance of it, at his suit (*v*); unless there has been an express condition as to time (*w*); or unless the nature of the property (*x*), or the known object of one of the contracting parties for entering into the contract (*y*), made time "of the essence of the contract." Under the Judicature Act 1873 (*z*) the rules of the Courts of Equity as to time being of the essence of the contract are to obtain in all the courts.

The condition goes on to provide that if "from any cause whatever" any purchase shall not be completed

---

(*u*) *Neath New Gas Co.* v. *Gwyn*, W. N. (1873), 200.
(*v*) *Seton* v. *Slade*, 7 Ves. 265, and, with notes, 2 L. C. 513; *Boehm* v. *Wood*, 1 Jac. & W. 419; *Roberts* v. *Berry*, 3 De G. M. & G. 284.
(*w*) *Hudson* v. *Temple*, 30 L. J. (Ch.) 251.
(*x*) *Hudson* v. *Temple*, 30 L. J. (Ch.) 251; *Coslake* v. *Till*, 1 Russ. 376.
(*y*) *Tilley* v. *Thomas*, L. R. 3 Ch. 61.
(*z*) 36 & 37 Vict. c. 66, s. 25, sub s. 7.

on the specified day, the purchaser shall pay a fixed rate of interest on all money due from him, until completion; and shall not be entitled to any compensation for the vendor's delay, or otherwise. In the absence of such a condition, a purchaser is liable to pay interest on his purchase-money from the time only when he has taken, or might safely have taken, possession of the property (a). And if there is a delay in completion, arising from the vendor's fault, the purchaser may elect whether he will pay interest on his purchase-money from the day fixed, charging the vendor with the rents and profits of the estate, or whether he will waive his right to the rents and profits and pay no interest. In cases where the above condition is inserted, some little hesitation appears to have been felt at one time by the Court of Chancery as to enforcing it, where the delay did not arise from any fault of the purchaser. In one case it was suggested that a purchaser paying interest under such circumstances was entitled, notwithstanding the condition, to receive from the vendor compensation for non-performance of the latter's part of the contract (b). But it is now settled that the mere existence of difficulties in the title, although justifying the purchaser in refusing to complete until they are ~~renewed~~ removed, does not exempt him from the condition respecting payment of interest (c). And he will only be entitled to the clear rents and profits actually received, without any claim for compensation. But he may charge the vendor with an occupation rent, if the latter remains in actual occupation of the property (d).

The condition, however, will not be enforced by the Court where there has been gross misconduct, or

---

(a) *Binks* v. *Rokeby*, 2 Swan. 222; *Jones* v. *Mudd*, 4 Russ. 118.
(b) *De Visme* v. *De Visme*, 1 M. & G. 336, 347.
(c) *Palmerston* v. *Turner*, 33 Beav. 524; *Williams* v. *Glenton*, L. R. 1 Ch. 200.
(d) See as to this, *Sherwin* v. *Shakspear*, 5 De G. M. & G. 517.

wilful delay on the part of the vendor (*e*). The purchaser's best plan, in such a case, appears to be to lodge the purchase-money at a bank, to a separate account, giving notice of his having done so to the vendor, and stating at the same time that he will not be bound by the condition (*f*). It may be added that if the vendor remains in possession he is bound to keep the property in repair (of course at the purchaser's expense), and that the purchaser may set off against the interest payable by him the amount of any extra deterioration arising from the vendor's neglect in this respect (*g*).

12th Condition.
Title-deeds.

The 12th condition provides for the retention, by the vendor, of such of the title-deeds as relate to property other than that sold; he entering into a covenant to produce them when required by any purchaser, at the expense of the latter. It also stipulates that such of the title-deeds as do not relate to any other property than that sold, but which embrace more than one lot, shall be handed over to the purchaser of the largest part, in value, of property held by the same title, who is, in like manner, to covenant to produce them, when required, to the purchasers of the other lots or purchasers from them. But the greater part of this condition will be rendered unnecessary by the Vendor and Purchaser Act 1874 (*h*), which enacts (*i*), with reference to contracts entered into after the 31st December 1874, that, subject to any stipulation to the contrary, when a vendor retains any part of an estate to which documents of title relate, he shall be entitled to retain all such documents.

13th Condition.

The 13th condition is one which occasionally gives

(*e*) See *Esdaile* v. *Stephenson*, 1 S. & S. 122.
(*f*) See *Winter* v. *Blades*, 2 S. & S. 393.
(*g*) *Philipps* v. *Silvester*, L. R. 8 Ch. 173.
(*h*) 37 & 38 Vict. c. 78.
(*i*) S. 2.

rise to disputes between vendors and purchasers, but its proper construction is now tolerably well settled. It provides that each purchaser shall send in his objections and requisitions, in respect of the title and of all matters appearing on the abstract, particulars, or conditions of sale, within a limited time from the date of the delivery of his abstract; that, in this respect, time shall be of the essence of the contract; and that in default of such requisitions or objections the purchaser shall be deemed to have accepted the title. The condition is sometimes so worded as to fix times for the various matters consequent on sending in requisitions, such as that for making further requisitions, and so on; but this mathematical accuracy can seldom be attained in practice, and an attempt at it is very likely to lead to difficulties.

Objections and Requisitions.

The abstract delivered must be a "perfect" abstract; that is, an abstract as perfect as the vendor can make it at the time; and if this is done, time will begin to run against the purchaser from the delivery of the abstract, although it shows a defective title (*j*). For the condition only precludes the purchaser from making, after the expiration of the time fixed, any requisitions which he might have made before that date, and does not prevent him from making further inquiries arising out of the answers given to his first set of requisitions (*k*). He is not bound by the condition if the abstract shows that the vendor has in fact no title; as where (*l*) trustees profess to sell under a power of sale which the abstract shows not to have arisen; for, in such a case, the abstract of itself points out that the purchaser is entitled to rescind the contract. Neither is the condition as to time being of the essence of the contract binding on a purchaser,

---

(*j*) Dart. V. & P. 115.
(*k*) *Ward* v. *Ghrimes*, 9 Jur. N. S. 1097.
(*l*) *Want* v. *Stallibrass*, L. R. 8 Ex. 175.

if a day is fixed for delivering the abstract, and it is not delivered on that day. It has been laid down that in such a case the time for taking the objections, and the mode in which they are to be considered as waived, should depend upon the general principles of equity (*m*). No precise rule appears to exist as to what would be considered a proper time, but it is clear that an unreasonable length of time in delivering the abstract may entitle the purchaser to rescind the contract altogether (*n*).

The condition goes on to provide that if the purchaser shall insist on any objection or requisition, as to the title, particulars, or conditions, which the vendor is unable, or unwilling, to remove, or comply with, the vendor may, by notice in writing, rescind the contract, notwithstanding any negotiation or litigation in respect of the requisitions; and shall thereupon return the purchaser his deposit, but without any interest, costs of investigating the title, or other compensation or payment whatever. It will be remembered that the vendor has, by a previous condition, guarded himself against the contract being annulled on the ground of mistake or misstatement, and the present condition will not, therefore, be allowed to operate in cases which come clearly within the former. The power of rescinding the contract, when allowed, extends to requisitions or objections made in respect of matters arising subsequently to the delivery of the abstract, and not appearing on the original abstract (*o*). But it would seem that the "unwillingness" of the vendor to comply with requisitions must in any case be reasonable (*p*).

If the purchaser has insisted on requisitions which

(*m*) *Upperton* v. *Nickolson*, L. R. 6 Ch. 436, 443.
(*n*) *Venn* v. *Cattell*, W. N. (1872), 183.
(*o*) *Gray* v. *Fowler*, L. R. 8 Ex. 249.
(*p*) *Mawson* v. *Fletcher*, L. R. 6 Ch. 91, 94; *Gray* v. *Fowler*, L. R. 8 Ex. 249, 265, but see *S. C.* p. 273.

he knows the vendor cannot comply with, the latter may at once rescind the contract, without giving him further time in which to waive his requisitions (*q*). But the very wording of the condition shows that the mere fact of a requisition being made does not allow the vendor immediately to rescind the contract. Nor can he, under colour of such a condition, evade compliance with reasonable requisitions, nor rescind against a purchaser who is willing to waive his objections to the title and take the property without an abatement in price. The value of the condition consists in enabling a vendor who has, in fact, a good title, to rescind upon a requisition being insisted on, which is either frivolous or untenable, or with which, on the ground of expense, or other sufficient cause, he cannot reasonably be expected to comply (*r*).

The 14th and last condition provides that if any purchaser fail to comply with the conditions, his deposit shall be, thereupon, forfeited, and that the vendor may proceed to resell the property; the purchaser being liable for all expenses attending the resale, as well as for any deficiency in the price so obtained. It seems to be doubtful how far this condition would be allowed to be enforced. Probably not at all, where the purchaser is able and willing to put the vendor in the situation in which he would have been had the contract been carried out (*s*). The purchaser would, in any case, be held liable for the expenses of a re-sale, and the deficiency, if any, in price at such a sale, but the condition should always be inserted, as it enables the vendor to make a re-sale without having recourse to the courts, and prevents any question being raised as to his right of forfeiting the deposit—at least to the extent necessary to pay all such expenses and deficiency.

14th Condition. Forfeiture of Deposit.

(*q*) *Duddell* v. *Simpson*, L. R. 2 Ch. 102.
(*r*) Dart. V. & P. 146; and see *Mawson* v. *Fletcher*, L. R. 6 Ch. 91.
(*s*) 1 Dav. Con. 453.

Memorandum of sale.

Attached to the conditions of sale is the memorandum referred to in the first condition. The form of this often provides for the auctioneer signing as agent for "the vendor" without naming him, but having regard to the somewhat conflicting decisions as to whether this is a sufficient compliance with the Statute of Frauds (*t*), it is at any rate safer for the name of the vendor to appear on the memorandum of sale (*u*).

Besides these ordinary conditions of sale, there will have to be inserted, in almost every case, special conditions rendered necessary by the nature of the title, or of the property to be sold. Into these we do not propose to enter. Their number is, practically, infinite; and little advice can be given beforehand as to their preparation, since this varies with each case. But a careful study of the conditions ordinarily employed, and of the principles on which they are construed by the courts, will form a solid foundation on which to construct these more complicated forms of drafting.

(*t*) 29 Car. II. c. 3.
(*u*) See *Williams* v. *Byrnes*, 2 N. R. 47; 2 Dav. Con. 2; Dart. V. & P. 202; *Hood* v. *Barrington*, L. R. 6 Eq. 218; *Bourdillon* v. *Collins*, 24 L. T. (N. S.) 344; *Sale* v. *Lambert*, L. R. 18 Eq. 1; *Potter* v. *Duffield*, L. R. 18 Eq. 4.

CHAPTER III.

OF PURCHASE DEEDS.

WE now come to the consideration of those Purchase Deeds which form the final step in carrying out contracts for the sale of land, and cause them to lose their character of executory, and to assume that of executed, contracts. And in doing this, we propose to notice, in turn, the various clauses of which such a deed is composed, pointing out, when necessary, the different ways in which they are framed, according as the estate dealt with is freehold, copyhold, or leasehold.

An ordinary purchase deed may be conveniently divided into the following parts:—1st, the Premises, which include all that part of the deed which comes before the habendum; 2nd, the Habendum, which defines the estates to be held in the property dealt with; 3rd, the Covenants; and 4th, the Testatum, or witnessing part. If the deed is more complex, it may contain, in addition to the above, Declarations of any trusts which may be fastened on the legal estate, followed by such Provisos or explanatory statements, as may be necessary. These parts, if inserted, come immediately after the habendum (*a*). *Division of a Purchase Deed.*

The Premises are again subdivided into various clauses. Of these the first is the Introductory Part, which consists merely of the words "This Indenture made on" such and such a date. It does not call therefore for further remark. *The Premises. Introductory Part.*

(*a*) 1 Dav. Con. 33.

Parties.

Next come the Parties to the deed. These should, in general, comprise, besides the vendor and purchaser, every person from whom any legal or equitable estate or interest is transferred to the purchaser (*b*); and also all persons who enter into any of the covenants contained in the deed. The most convenient order of their arrangement is to place first the party or parties from whom the legal estate in the property is transferred; next, any persons whose concurrence is requisite, or who enter into any covenants; and last, the party or parties to whom the legal estate is to be given by the deed. The names and descriptions of all the parties should be set out in full, so as to prevent any difficulty in their subsequent identification, but a deed is not invalidated by a defect in this respect, so long as the name or description given to any party is that by which he, or she, is generally known (*c*).

Recitals.

After the parties come such Recitals as may be considered necessary. Recitals are of two kinds, namely, narrative recitals, which set out the facts and instruments necessary to show the title and the relation of the parties to the subject-matter of the deed (*d*); and introductory recitals, which explain the motives for the preparation and execution of the deed.

Narrative recitals.

Narrative recitals, when used, should go back far enough to show a clear root of title (*e*), which can only be done by showing the creation of the estates and interests of the conveying parties; but they should not go beyond this, neither should they, as a rule, contain anything which is not logically connected with the particular matter in hand. It has, however, been pointed out by an eminent writer (*f*) that, in

---

(*b*) See Dart. V. & P. 469, as to an exception to this rule.
(*c*) *Williams* v. *Bryant*, 5 Mee. & W. 447.
(*d*) 1 Dav. Con 43.
(*e*) Dart. V. & P. 476.
(*f*) Ibid.

view of the common condition of sale as to recitals being evidence, they may sometimes be used 'as a statement of facts tending to validate the title, even where they do not strictly comply with the above rule ; and the effect of the Vendor and Purchaser Act 1874 (*g*) (which makes all recitals twenty years old at the date of the contract, unless proved to be inaccurate, sufficient evidence of the statements contained in them) will probably be to increase the practice of introducing them.

Introductory recitals, when used, should come immediately after the narrative recitals, which they connect with the rest of the deed by showing why, and how, the state of things previously existing is about to be altered by the deed. It follows that introductory recitals are unnecessary when the deed contains no narrative recitals, nor is their employment essential in every case where narrative recitals have been introduced. But whenever there have been narrative recitals, an introductory recital, stating an agreement for the sale or purchase of the property at the price fixed, makes the deed more complete and scarcely adds to its length. This recital should not refer to the formal written agreement, or to the conditions of sale (whichever may have been used), except in cases when it is necessary to do so, as in that of a sale under an order of court.

Introductory recitals.

In the simplest form of purchase deeds no recitals of any kind need be introduced (*h*) ; and opinions would appear to be somewhat divided as to the extent to which they should be used, even in preparing more complicated deeds. There can, however, be no doubt that the tendency of modern conveyancing is to do away with the amount of unnecessary recitals,

When recitals are to be used.

(*g*) 37 & 38 Vict. c. 78.
(*h*) See 1 Dav. Con. 43, and 2 Dav. Con. 206, note (*a*).

as well as to omit the verbiage, with which deeds of all kinds were formerly overloaded. The better rule appears to be, that recitals are necessary whenever the deed itself does not clearly imply for what purpose any person joining in it is made a party (*i*); or whenever the covenants into which he enters show that he has only a qualified interest in the property sold. From this it would follow that recitals are requisite in all cases where the property is vested in different persons, each having partial estates; or in trustees, or others, selling under a power of sale; and also, whenever the estate is subject to incumbrances which are noticed in the deed.

Recitals should, as a rule, be in general terms. On the assignment of leaseholds it is customary to describe them fully in the recitals, by setting out the parcels as worded in the original lease; and then in the operative part (or that in which the property is transferred to the purchaser) to describe them merely by reference to that lease. In other cases, as we shall see presently, the parcels are described fully in the operative part. Subject to the exception just noticed in the case of leaseholds, care should be taken that the recitals are expressed in general terms; since otherwise they may conflict with the operative part (*j*). When they do so their tendency is to override the latter. Thus (*k*), when the owner of land situate in Middlesex and comprising a certain manor, mortgaged to A some of his property in Middlesex, but not the manor, and afterwards, by a deed reciting that he was seised of the property intended to be granted " subject to the mortgage " to A, conveyed to B all the lands comprised in the mortgage to A, and " all other lands, if any, belonging to him situate in the county of Middlesex : " it was held that these

---

(*i*) 1 Prid. Con. 180.
(*j*) See *Jenner* v. *Jenner*, L. R. 1 Eq. 361.
(*k*) *Rooke* v. *Kensington*, 2 K. & J. 753.

sweeping words were restricted by the previous recital, and that the manor, consequently, did not pass by the grant to B. It may be added that recitals in a deed estop all persons on whose behalf they are made from disputing their accuracy (*l*), but that they cannot bind any other parties to the deed (*m*). *When they estop.*

The next division of the premises consists of the operative part. This commences with a witnessing clause which refers to the introductory recital of the agreement (where this recital has been used) and also to the consideration which is to be paid. The receipt of the purchase-money is acknowledged here parenthetically, and a formal receipt for it is also indorsed on the back of the deed. The acknowledgment on the back of the deed does not estop the vendor, or those claiming under him, from showing that the consideration was never paid (*n*); but it has the advantage of relieving a subsequent purchaser from the necessity of ascertaining that the consideration was, in fact, paid (*o*); and it is so universally employed that its absence would, probably, bind him to make further inquiries on the subject. The acknowledgment of the receipt in the body of the deed is of little practical value. It does not, it would seem, even at law, estop a vendor from disputing the fact of the receipt (*p*) unless it is followed by a formal release from all claims on account of the purchase-money (*q*); and it cannot, in any case, prevent him from disproving the receipt in equity (*r*). *Operative Part.* *Receipt clause and endorsement.*

(*l*) *Lainson* v. *Tremere*, 1 A. & E. 792; *Bowman* v. *Taylor*, 2 Ad. & E. 278, 290.
(*m*) *Hills* v. *Laming*, 9 Exch. 256, Sug. V. & P. 559.
(*n*) *Lampon* v. *Corke*, 5 B. & Ald. 606, 611.
(*o*) 1 Dav. Con. 65.
(*p*) *Skaife* v. *Jackson*, 3 B. & C. 421; *Lee* v. *Lancashire Ry. Co.* L. R. 6 Ch. 527, 534.
(*q*) *Baker* v. *Dewey*, 1 B. & C. 704.
(*r*) *Winter* v. *Anson*, 3 Russ. 488; *Hawkins* v. *Gardiner*, 2 Sm. & Giff. 441.

Words of Conveyance. The operative part includes also the words of conveyance which transfer the property: these varying according to the nature of the estate. It will be remembered that all hereditaments now lie in grant. Hence the word "grant," alone, is that proper to be used in an ordinary conveyance of freehold land to a person who has had no previous interest in it. Where the grantee has already some estate in the land, the words "release" or "surrender," as the case may be, are more appropriate. If the vendor is acting under a power the word "appoint" is best, and if he has a mere power of sale (as in the case of an executor selling copyholds under a power in a will), the words "bargain and sell" are commonly employed (*s*). A party joining to transfer a beneficial interest should "confirm" the assurance of the property. But it will be understood that the various expressions given above are merely those which are considered most appropriate; and that a deed will not, necessarily, fail of effect from the mere use of an inappropriate word, provided that the intention of the conveying parties appears clearly. If the property is copyhold, it can only be legally transferred by a surrender and admittance recorded on the court rolls. The purchase deed, consequently, in this case, takes the form of a covenant by the vendor that he will make the necessary surrender, in order to enable the purchaser to obtain admittance. If the property is leasehold, the vendor "assigns" it to the purchaser. Care must, of course, be taken to define the purchaser's estate accurately. A conveyance in fee simple of freeholds or copyholds limits it to him, "his heirs, and assigns," whilst leaseholds, being personal property, are limited to him, "his executors, administrators, and assigns."

The Parcels. The operative part is followed by the description of the property. This is technically known as the

---

(*s*) 1 Dav. Con. 70.

Parcels, and should, when practicable, be the same as in former title-deeds, so as to prevent any question as to the identity of the property conveyed with that comprised in such deeds. When this is not possible, there should be a reference connecting the parcels with former descriptions, but without specifying the deeds in which they are so described. Except in small purchases, it is preferable that the parcels should refer to, and be accompanied by, a map or plan of the property, drawn on the deed; but care must, in that case, be taken to have in the body of the deed, such a description of the property as will be sufficient to prevent any difficulties arising should the plan prove to be inaccurate. For an inaccurate plan, if not corrected by the wording of the deed, may override the real intention of the parties. Thus, in a modern case (*t*), the parcels described the property as "bounded by a line drawn from J. V.'s house to a certain bound stone," and stated that the premises were "particularly described by the map drawn on the back" of the deed. It was proved that the position of J. V.'s house was wrongly marked on the map; but it was held that, since the map formed part of the deed, and was not contradicted by any other part of it, the boundary line must be accepted as drawn on the map (*u*). The above remarks apply also to a description of property by reference to its present or former occupants (*v*). When the parcels are numerous, they may be conveniently set out in a schedule to the deed, the schedule and map being referred to in the words of conveyance.

Description by reference to a plan.

Schedule.

After the parcels come what are known as the General Words; those, namely, which purport to con-

General Words.

(*t*) *Lyle* v. *Richards,* L. R. 1 H. L. 222.
(*u*) And see *Llewylln* v. *Jersey,* 11 Mee. & W. 183; *Davis* v. *Shepherd,* L. R. 1 Ch. 410.
(*v*) *Dyne* v. *Nutley,* 14 C. B. 122; *Fox* v. *Clarke,* L. R. 7 Q. B. 748, W. N. (1874), 141.

vey to the purchaser all rights and easements (*w*) appurtenant to the property, or at any time enjoyed with it, or reputed to form part of it. These are often contained in a long string of words, but the whole clause is of little use. For easements or appurtenances legally belonging to land pass with it, without any express words of grant (*x*); and a vendor of land cannot, evidently, put his purchaser in a position better than that in which he himself is, so as to confer upon the property sold, as against a third person, any easements which do not already legally belong to it. The latter part of the clause, therefore (that which refers to reputed easements), has, alone, any value; and this is limited to preserving, as against the vendor of part of an estate, easements which, though not existing legally, have been exercised for its benefit over the part retained by him. And even in this case, the value of the clause has been considerably lessened by recent decisions. For, in the first place, all continuous and apparent easements, such as rights of drainage, which have been, and are at the time of the grant, used by the owner of the entirety for the benefit of the parcel granted, will pass, although not legally existing, by a conveyance of that parcel (*y*). In the next place, a discontinuous easement, such as a right of way, if it has only been created whilst the entirety of a property has been held by the same owner, will not pass by a conveyance in the ordinary general form of words relating to easements now or heretofore enjoyed (*z*). The only advantage, therefore, of the clause is that it may serve to revive and transfer a previously exist-

---

(*w*) An easement is a privilege which the owner of one neighbouring tenement has of another, existing in respect of their several tenements, by which that other is obliged to suffer, or not to do, something on his own land for the advantage of the possessor of the easement.—Gale on Easements, 1.
(*x*) *Colegrave* v. *Dias Santos*, 3 Dow. & R. 255.
(*y*) *Suffield* v. *Brown*, 3 N. R. 340, 343.
(*z*) *Thomson* v. *Waterlow*, L. R. 6 Eq. 36; *Langley* v. *Hammond*, L. R. 3 Ex. 161.

ing easement which has become suspended or extinguished by the fact of two properties having been united in the possession of one owner (a), and which would not otherwise pass by the deed (b). It would seem to be safer to word the clause generally, without specifying any particular rights or easements, since otherwise the accidental omission of any of them might prevent its passing by the conveyance (c).

The parcels and general words are followed by what is known as the "Estate" Clause, which finishes this part of the deed by a general transfer of all the vendor's estate and interest in the property. This clause is, as has been generally pointed out, simply useless (d); and its retention only shows the difficulty of altering any long-established custom. Indeed, so firmly is its use established, that it is inserted even in one of the latest forms of statutory conveyances (e), which certainly does not, otherwise, sin in unnecessary length. It is, however, omitted in assurances made in pursuance of powers of appointment. Estate Clause.

This finishes the premises, and we come next to the Habendum, which, commencing with the words "To have and to hold," is intended to define the estate of the purchaser: it also refers generally to the premises which have been granted by the operative part. The proper office of the habendum is to limit, explain, and qualify, the words in the premises, provided it be not contradictory or repugnant to them. It cannot therefore give a man more than he would take under the words of conveyance, for that would be to contradict them; but it may restrict those words, by the explanation which it affords of the intention of the Habendum.

(a) Lanes v. Plant, 4 Ad. & E. 749.
(b) *Barlow* v. *Rhodes*, 1 Cr. & Mee. 439, 448.
(c) See *Holliday* v. *Denison*, 4 Jur. N. S. 1002.
(d) 1 Dav. Con. 88.
(e) See 36 & 37 Vict. c. 50.

parties. These two rules are well illustrated by a decision of the Court of Queen's Bench. In that case (*f*) there was a demise " to H, her heirs and assigns, to have and to hold to the said H and her assigns during the life of G." The habendum, which showed a clear intention that H should take an estate *pur autre vie* only, was allowed to restrict the words of conveyance which, taken alone, would have conferred on her an estate in fee simple; whilst, on the other hand, it was not allowed to contradict them by limiting the estate to the assigns of H only, so as to prevent the heirs of H from taking, on her decease, as special occupants.

Covenants for title

Next come the Covenants, which, in the simplest form of conveyance, consist only of covenants for title entered into by the vendor. To these must be added, on a sale of leaseholds, some other covenants which will be particularized later on.

The covenants for title are substantially the same in a sale of freeholds, copyholds, or leaseholds. The

For right to convey.

first is that the vendor has a right to convey the property according to the terms of the deed. If the vendor has acquired the property by any means other than by descent, the covenant is to the effect that no acts of his have affected his right to convey; but if he has taken the property by descent, he should also co-

For quiet enjoyment.

venant against any acts of his ancestors. Then come covenants that the purchaser shall, from thenceforth, peaceably enjoy the premises without any molestation by the vendor or any person lawfully or equitably

Free from incumbrances.

claiming under him, and that the property is free from any incumbrances, created by the vendor or any person claiming through, or in trust, for him: to which again must be added, if the vendor has acquired the property by descent, incumbrances created by his an-

---

(*f*) *Doe* v. *Steele*, 3 Ga. & D. 622.

cestors. And these covenants conclude by an undertaking on the part of the vendor, that he and all persons claiming through him, or (under the circumstances before mentioned) through his ancestors, will, at the purchaser's expense, do anything which may be reasonably required to perfect the assurance of the property to the purchaser. *For further assurance.*

The covenant for quiet enjoyment is merely intended to secure the purchaser's title and possession, and only guarantees to him that he may use it in any way in which his vendor might have used it. Therefore, when (g) land had been conveyed in fee simple to B, who had covenanted with his vendor that he would not carry on, upon the premises, the trade of a seller of beer; and B afterwards demised the land by a lease which contained no prohibition against carrying on such a trade: it was held that his lessee had no right of action against him on account of loss which the lessee had incurred from being restrained, at the suit of B's vendor, from fitting up the premises as a beer-shop (h). It will be noticed that the covenant against incumbrances does not say that the estate is free from incumbrances, but merely that there shall not be any disturbance by incumbrancers; in which case the vendor would be bound to discharge their claims, or indemnify the purchaser against them. *Effect of the covenant for quiet enjoyment.* *Wording of the covenant against incumbrances.*

These covenants for title are entered into by the vendor for himself, his heirs, executors, and administrators, with the purchaser, his heirs and assigns. The benefit of them runs with the land whether freehold, copyhold, or leasehold (i). Their object is to give the purchaser, or those claiming under him, a remedy, if necessary, against the vendor and his re- *By whom, and with whom, covenants for title are entered into.*

(g) *Dennett* v. *Atherton,* L. R. 7 Q. B. 316.
(h) See also, as to the effect of this covenant, *Leech* v. *Schweder,* L. R. 9 Ch. 463.
(i) *Riddell* v. *Riddell,* 7 Sim. 529; *Campbell* v. *Lewis,* 3 B. & Ald. 392.

presentatives, by means of an action on the express covenants which the latter has entered into, without being limited to such covenants as are implied on the

Absolute owner.

sale of an estate. Every vendor who is the absolute owner of the property which he sells, is bound to enter into them (*j*), as is also a husband on the sale by him and his wife of the latter's real estate not held to her separate use.

Trustee.

If the vendor is only a trustee, or a mortgagee selling under a power of sale, he is not compellable to enter into any covenant except that he himself has not incumbered the property. And the rule is the same on a sale by executors in pursuance of a contract entered into by their testator during his lifetime (*k*). Where there is a sale by a trustee, it is the settled practice of conveyancers, in the absence of any special condition, to make all the beneficiaries who take a substantial interest in the proceeds of the sale enter into covenants for title to the extent of that interest (*l*). It is, however, doubtful how far this practice can be enforced; and it has been decided that it cannot, where the trustee is selling under the order of the Court of Chancery (*m*). On the other hand, it has been held that where a sale is made by a trustee under a power which only authorizes the sale at the direction of a tenant for life, the latter must enter into the usual covenants for title (*n*). It would seem, however, that any limited owner who sells under a statutory power need not enter into covenants for title extending beyond his own interest (*o*), and that owners of land whose estates are altogether taken compulsorily, as, for instance, by a railway company,

Cestui que trust.

(*j*) *Church* v. *Brown*, 15 Ves. 258, 263, & 263ª.
(*k*) *Worley* v. *Frampton*, 5 Ha. 560.
(*l*) Dart. V. & P. 500.
(*m*) *Cottrell* v. *Cottrell*, L. R. 2 Eq. 330.
(*n*) *Poulett* v. *Hood*, L. R. 5 Eq. 115.
(*o*) Dart. V. & P. 503.

need not enter into any covenants at all (*p*). It may be added that the Crown, if selling land, never enters into covenants for title.

The Crown.

The time for bringing an action on covenants for title is limited by the 3 & 4 Wm. IV., c. 42, to twenty years from the date when the cause of such action arose. The time for bringing actions on the covenant that a vendor has a good right to convey, and also on that against incumbrances, when entered into by trustees, begins to run from the date of the conveyance; but that for bringing actions on any of the other covenants for title, entered into by an ordinary vendor, does not begin to run until some actual breach of the covenant in question.

Limitation of time for suing on these covenants.

3 & 4 Wm. IV., c. 42.

It was mentioned previously that there are additional covenants to be inserted on a sale of leaseholds. These are, covenants by the vendor that the lease which he assigns is valid and subsisting, and that the rents and covenants of the lease have been, respectively, paid and observed, so far as he is concerned, up to the date of the conveyance. There is, also, a covenant by the purchaser that he will, from thenceforth, pay that rent and observe those covenants, and indemnify the vendor against any further liability in this respect. The covenant by the vendor that the lease is valid is implied by the covenants for title, and may, therefore, be safely omitted. The covenant by the purchaser that he will indemnify the vendor against any further liability in respect of the rent and covenants of the lease is one which he cannot refuse to give (*q*). On this point it may be remarked that when a vendor is himself an assignee of a lease, a purchaser from him is liable to indemnify the original lessee against breaches of covenant in the lease, com-

Covenants on a sale of leaseholds.

(*p*) Dart. V. & P. 502.
(*q*) *Staines* v. *Morris*, 1 Ves. & B. 9.

mitted during his own tenancy, without reference to the covenants which such a purchaser may have entered into with his vendor (*r*).

Testatum.   Having thus gone through the essential parts of a purchase deed, it only remains to mention that the whole is concluded by a Testatum, which sets forth that the several parties to the deed have duly affixed thereto their respective hands and seals; and to point out that the fact of their having done so should be attested by at least one witness, whose attestation is usually to be found indorsed on the deed along with the receipt clause.

(*r*) *Moule* v. *Garrett*, L. R. 7 Ex. 101.

CHAPTER IV.

OF LEASES.

HAVING thus considered the instruments which relate to the sale of land, we come next to those which are employed when it is to be let. These, as we know, are called leases, and will form the subject of discussion in this chapter. The simplest form perhaps of a lease is that of a dwelling-house and grounds for a short term of years which is to commence on, or very shortly after, the execution of the instrument of demise. And since our object is to deal only with the more ordinary and simple forms of conveyancing, we will confine our remarks to leases of this description. And, in so doing, we will follow the plan adopted in the case of purchase deeds, and divide our present subject into, 1st, Agreements for Leases, and 2nd, Leases.

Agreements for leases, again, may be classified under two headings; namely, those instruments which have been expressly entered into by the parties as agreements for leases, and those instruments which operate as agreements by construction of law, although not expressly entered into as such. Before, however, considering agreements for leases with reference to this classification, we have to say a few words on the statutory requisites relating to all such agreements generally. *Agreements for Leases.*

Prior to the passing of the Statute of Frauds (a),

(a) 29 Car. II. c. 3.

Statute of Frauds.

any lease, and also any agreement for a lease, of land, might be made by parol. But by this statute it is enacted (*b*) that no action shall be brought whereby to charge any person upon any contract or sale of lands, tenements, or hereditaments, or any interest in, or concerning, them, unless the agreement upon which such action shall be brought, or some memorandum or note thereof, shall be in writing, and signed by the party to be charged therewith, or some other person thereunto by him lawfully authorized.

Part Performance.

It follows, therefore, that no person is liable on a mere contract to grant, or take, a lease, unless he has signed some written document which, either in itself, or in conjunction with other writings, contains the substantial parts of the contract. But if something more has been done than simply entering into a non-binding agreement, the contract may come within the class of cases which are considered as taken out of the Statute of Frauds by part-performance. Thus, it has been held that possession taken by a lessee, and payment of rent by him, when these acts are distinctly referable to a parol or unsigned agreement, were sufficient to induce a court of equity to decree specific performance of the agreement, against either the lessor (*c*) or the lessee (*d*). And this rule extends also to the representatives of a lessor or of a lessee. Thus, where there had been a verbal agreement for a lease, and the lessee had entered into possession of the property, paid rent, and made improvements on the property, and afterwards died : it was held that his representatives were entitled to have, from the representative of the lessor, a formal lease, in terms corresponding to those of a draft lease found amongst the papers of the lessor, who was also dead (*e*).

(*b*) S. 4.
(*c*) *Pain* v. *Coombs*, 1 De G. & J. 34.
(*d*) *Kine* v. *Balfe*, 2 Ba. & B. 343.
(*e*) *McFarlane* v. *Dickson*, 13 Grant, 263.

We now come to agreements for leases, expressly *Express agreements for leases.* entered into as such. We shall not, however, dwell long on this point, since, as a rule, preliminary agree- *Not in general desirable.* ments are neither usual, nor desirable, in the case of those ordinary leases with which alone we are concerned. Where the lease is to take effect at once, and is not to contain any but the ordinary covenants, there can be no object in having a formal preliminary agreement (which can only be safely prepared by inserting in it all the covenants and clauses literally as they are to stand in the lease (*f*)), this agreement being immediately followed by a formal lease. Still less is it desirable to have, as is sometimes done, a formal agreement not followed by a lease. For in this case, besides the risk of raising questions, where the term is less than three years, as to whether the instrument is an agreement or an actual lease (a point to which we shall advert presently), both parties are, under an agreement, in a much less favourable position than under a lease. For the lessee, having no legal interest, is *primâ facie* liable to ejectment at the will of the lessor, and can only remedy this injury by establishing an equitable defence; whilst the lessor, until some rent has been paid, cannot distrain for unpaid rent,.but is driven to bring an action for use and occupation of the premises (*g*).

We will, therefore, with regard to formal agreements *Stipulations which should be inserted when agreements are prepared.* for leases, only call attention to two stipulations, both of which should, at present, be inserted when these instruments are prepared by the conveyancer, but which would be out of place in the lease itself: premising, that the fact of their being necessary, if there is an agreement, does not conflict with the statement that an agreement is not usually desirable. The first of these stipulations is, that the lessee is not to require

---

(*f*) See 5 Dav. Con. 46ª.
(*g*) 5 Dav. Con. 17.

proof of, or investigate, his lessor's title. It is now settled (h), notwithstanding former doubts to the contrary (i), that a lessor is bound, in the absence of any stipulation to the contrary, to make out his title to the property which he purports to demise; and although a court of equity will not compel one party specifically to perform his contract to grant a lease, unless the right to see his title is waived, neither will it compel the other to carry out his contract to take a lease, unless the title is produced (j). The necessity for one part of this stipulation will, however, shortly come to an end. For the Vendor and Purchaser Act 1874 (k) enacts (l) that in the completion of any contract entered into after the 31st of December, 1874, and subject to any stipulation to the contrary contained in the contract, an intended lessee shall not be entitled to call for the title to the freehold. But the remarks made in a former chapter as to the necessity of precluding a purchaser from investigating, as well as from inquiring for, his vendor's title, will still apply equally to the case of lessor and lessee, and a stipulation to that effect will, therefore, continue to be necessary. The agreement should also, whatever may be the length of the term to be granted, contain a statement that the instrument is intended only as an agreement, and does not pass any legal interest to the lessee. We will enter into the reasons for this when speaking of the second of the headings under which agreements have been classified. It may be added that, unless otherwise provided, all the expenses attending the preparation of the agreement, and of the lease, fall upon the lessee (m), whilst the expense of preparing the copy of the lease retained by the lessor, and known as the "counter-

(h) *Stranks* v. *St John*, L. R. 2 C. P. 376.
(i) *Fildes* v. *Hooker*, 2 Mer. 424, 427.
(j) *Fildes* v. *Hooker*, 2 Mer. 424; 1 Platt on Leases, 618.
(k) 37 & 38 Vict. c. 78.
(l) S. 2.
(m) *Grissell* v. *Robinson*, 3 Bing. N. C. 10.

part," must be borne by him (*n*). Hence if some different plan is contemplated it should be so stated in the agreement.

It was remarked just now that no agreement for a lease could be drawn safely unless it set out, literally, the covenants to be contained in the lease. But it may not be out of place to point out here how agreements will be construed which are either silent on the question of covenants or (which comes to the same thing) merely provide that the lease to be prepared shall contain the "usual" or "proper" covenants. Whenever an open agreement of this kind is executed, the law will imply a further agreement by both parties to enter into certain covenants which are applicable to all leases, and no covenants can, generally speaking, be inserted in a lease made in pursuance of an open agreement other than those which are implied by the law as being strictly incidental to the subject-matter of the contract. It seems to be pretty well settled that these are—covenants by the lessee (1) to pay rent, (2) to pay taxes, except such as are expressly payable by the lessor, (3) to keep and deliver up the premises in repair, and (4) to allow the lessor to enter and view the state of repair; and a covenant by the lessor that the lessee shall quietly enjoy the premises (*o*). It follows that, in the absence of precise stipulation, a lessee is not bound to enter into a covenant not to assign the lease without licence from the lessor (*p*); or not to carry on trade on the premises (*q*), even where there is a covenant not to keep a school (*r*); or into a covenant to pay such taxes as land tax or tithe rent charge. But where there is some special local or trade custom, under which certain covenants

Usual and proper covenants.

(*n*) *Jennings* v. *Major*, 8 C. & P. 61.
(*o*) 5 Dav. Con. 49ⁿ.
(*p*) *Church* v. *Brown*, 15 Ves. 259.
(*q*) *Propert* v. *Parker*, 3 My. & K. 280.
(*r*) *Van* v. *Corpe*, 3 My. & K. 269.

are always contained in leases, these will be held, with reference to the particular case, to be "usual" covenants, and therefore implied by law. Thus, a covenant not to assign without licence appears to be "usual" in London (*s*); as may be also covenants in restriction of trade in particular cases (*t*), so that there is still plenty of room for litigation under an open or informal agreement.

Other questions sometimes arise on such agreements, as to the construction to be put upon concise statements of the covenants which are to be inserted in the lease. As to these, we may mention that it has been decided that a covenant to pay a "net rent" binds a lessee to pay every kind of tax (*u*), as does also a covenant to pay rent "free from all outgoings (*v*)."

Agreements for leases by operation of law.

We have next to consider those instruments which amount to agreements for leases by operation of law, and in order to explain this point we must go back to the law as it stood after the passing of the Statute of Frauds (*w*), but before the year 1845.

Statute of Frauds.

The Statute of Frauds enacted (*x*) that all leases, except those not exceeding the term of three years whereupon the rent reserved during the term amounted to two-thirds at least of the full value of the thing demised, should have the force and effect of leases at will only, unless they were put in writing, and signed by the parties making or creating the same, or their agents thereunto lawfully authorized in writing. And it will be remembered that, by another section (*y*) of

---

(*s*) *Strangways* v. *Bishop*, 29 L. T. 120.
(*t*) See *Bennett* v. *Womack*, 7 B. & C. 627.
(*u*) Ibid.
(*v*) *Parish* v. *Sleeman*, 1 De G. F. & J. 326; *Amfield* v. *White*, Ry. & Moo. 246.
(*w*) 29 Car. II. c. 3.
(*x*) SS. 1, 2.
(*y*) S. 4.

this act, all agreements for leases must also be in writing. Supposing then that a man were found in possession of land under a written instrument, it might be a question, upon the wording of the instrument, whether he held under a lease, or only under an agreement for a lease, or, in other words, whether he had, or had not, a legal interest in the land. In deciding these questions, the courts inclined to holding such instruments to be leases. For the general rule was, that where there was an instrument by which it appeared that one party was to give possession and the other to take it, that was a lease, unless it could be collected, from the instrument itself, that it was only an agreement for a lease to be afterwards made (z). And on this principle, instruments not containing words of express present demise might be, and often were, held to be leases; provided they contained with sufficient certainty all the terms of the lease (a); still more if they were followed by some act, such as possession of the premises by the lessee, which showed an intention to pass an immediate interest (b).

It being, evidently, undesirable that doubts should be possible as to whether a written document passed a legal interest or not, two acts were passed in the present reign, each of which sought to put such questions beyond doubt. Of these the 7 & 8 Vict., c. 76, enacted (c) that no lease in writing should be valid, as a lease, unless made by deed, but that every agreement in writing to let land should take effect as an agreement to execute a lease. This act took no notice of the exception in favour of short leases made by the Statute of Frauds (d), and was repealed in the next year by the Real Property Amendment Act (e), 7 & 8 Vict. c. 76.

Real Property Amendment Act.

(z) *Morgan* v. *Bissell*, 3 Taunt. 65, 72.
(a) *Dunk* v. *Hunter*, 5 B. & Ald. 322; *Clayton* v. *Burtenshaw*, 7 Dow. & Ry. 800.
(b) *Doe* v. *Ries*, 8 Bing. 178.
(c) S. 4.
(d) 29 Car. II. c. 3.
(e) 8 & 9 Vict. c. 106.

which enacts (*f*) that a lease required by law to be in writing, made after the 1st day of October 1845, shall be void at law unless made by deed. This act, it will be observed, does not touch leases exempted from the operation of the Statute of Frauds. Hence, since the 1st of October 1845, there can be no doubt, when the term does not come within the exception of the Statute of Frauds, that an instrument which is in writing only, and not by deed, cannot operate as a lease. But although it cannot be a lease, it may be held to be an agreement for a lease, and probably will, reversing the former rule of construction, be so held in all cases where its wording makes it possible for the court to do so. Thus, in a case in equity (*g*), there was an instrument relating to a term of more than three years, made after the 1st of October 1845, and not under seal, which, although it would formerly have been construed as a lease, was so worded as to admit of its being considered an agreement. The lessee entered into possession under it, but disputes arising between him and the lessor, the latter brought an action of ejectment against him, and he thereupon filed a bill in Chancery to restrain the action, and to compel the grant of a proper lease. It was argued on behalf of the lessor (*h*) that the instrument, being void as a lease, was void altogether, but the court held that it was admissible as an agreement for a lease: pointing out that the statute only made it "void at law as a lease," and not "void to all intents and purposes." This decision was soon followed by one at law (*i*), in which it was held that an action for breach of contract to take a lease might be founded on such an instrument, for it was said that the words of the statute meant no more than that the instrument, not

New rule of construction.

(*f*) S. 3.
(*g*) *Parker* v. *Taswell*, 2 De G. & J. 559, 570.
(*h*) Relying on *Stratton* v. *Pettit*, 16 C. B. 420, now overruled.
(*i*) *Bond* v. *Rosling*, 1 B. & S. 371, 374.

being under seal, should pass no legal interest (*j*). From these cases it will be seen that the courts incline, now, to consider as agreements for leases writings which, from their ambiguous wording, would formerly have been treated as leases; and the fact that the parties have executed an instrument which, as they may be presumed to know, cannot take effect as a lease, will be looked upon as an additional reason for holding it to be an agreement only. It is in order to assist the courts in arriving at such a conclusion that it is still desirable to state in an agreement for a lease that it is not intended to pass any legal interest. Moreover, the 8 & 9 Vict., c. 106, still leaves open questions upon instruments dealing with terms which need not be granted by writing, and upon those under seal; consequently, the precaution above mentioned should be specially observed when these instruments are intended to be agreements only.

Not only may an instrument, void as a lease for a term over three years, be treated as an agreement for a lease, but it may, in some cases, operate to create a tenancy from year to year. For the effect of the statutes which we have been considering is to give to such a lease the effect of a lease at will; and since, ordinarily speaking, payment of rent converts a tenancy at will into a tenancy from year to year, such a lease may, if rent is paid under it, operate to create a tenancy from year to year (*k*), in which case all the covenants and conditions of the lease will apply to the yearly tenancy (*l*).

Intended lease for a term may operate to create a yearly tenancy.

In treating of the second part of our subject, namely, Leases, we will first remind the reader that, under the

Leases.

(*j*) And see *Tidey* v. *Mollett*, 33 L. J. (C. P.) 235; *Martin* v. *Smith*, L. R. 9 Ex. 50.
(*k*) *Doe* v. *Bell*, 5 T. R. 471, and, with notes, 2 Smith, L. C. 98; *Clayton* v. *Blakey*, 8 T. R. 3, and, with notes, 2 Smith, L. C. 103.
(*l*) *Richardson* v. *Gifford*, 1 A. & E. 52; *Beale* v. *Sanders*, 3 Bing. N. C. 850.

Statute of Frauds (*m*), a lease (unlike an agreement for a lease) cannot be made by an agent unless the latter be authorized in writing, and that wherever the lease is made by deed the agent must be authorized by deed (*n*). We will next, following our former system in the case of purchase deeds, go through the clauses of a simple lease in its ordinary form.

Ordinary form of a lease. The component parts of such an instrument are—1st, The Premises; 2nd, The Habendum; 3rd, The Reddendum; 4th, The Covenants; and 5th, The Testatum.

The Premises. The Premises begin with the Introductory part which is in the usual form, and this is followed by the names Parties. of the Parties, who should be fully described, as in purchase deeds. It was formerly a matter of great importance that every person intended to take an immediate estate or benefit in a lease should be made a party to it, since otherwise he could not sue on the covenants contained in the lease. This, however, is Real Property Amendment Act. now remedied by the Real Property Amendment Act (*o*), which enacts (*p*) that under an indenture executed after the 1st of October 1845, an immediate estate or interest in any tenement or hereditament, and the benefit of a condition, or covenant, respecting any tenement or hereditament, may be taken, although the taker thereof be not named a party to the said indenture. Ordinary convenience, however, still makes desirable the insertion of the names of all such persons as parties to the lease.

Recitals are, generally, unnecessary. A simple form of lease does not require any Recitals. Sometimes when the lease is made under a power the power is recited, but this does not appear to be usual(*q*),

---

(*m*) 29 Car. II. c. 3, s. 1.
(*n*) *Berkeley* v. *Hardy*, 5 B. & C. 355.
(*o*) 8 & 9 Vict. c. 106.
(*p*) S. 5.
(*q*) 5 Dav. Con. 113ª.

although recommended by some conveyancers (r). If the power is recited, care should be taken to set it out literally, and whether it is recited or not, the operative part must correspond with the wording of the power.

If there are no recitals, the parties are immediately followed by the Operative Part, which begins by setting out the consideration for the lease. The consideration consists usually in the rent to be paid, and the covenants to be observed, by the lessee. But it may be raised by any benefit conferred on the lessor by the lessee, or by any one on his behalf; and it often consists, besides the rent and covenants, in the payment of a premium, or the execution of repairs or improvements on the property demised. Next come the words of demise by which the term is created. The word "demise" is the best for expressing the fact that the lessor leases the property, and is the only word which need be employed for that purpose. But any words showing a clear intention to lease will have the same effect. The demise is to the lessee, his executors, administrators, and assigns; for, as we know, a term of years is personal, and not real, property. Words of demise.

Next come the Parcels. The general rules to be observed in framing parcels were referred to in our last chapter, and need not therefore be repeated, further than to remind the student of the importance of this clause being accurate, and not containing more, either expressly or by implication, than is intended to pass, whether as part of the property itself or as subsidiary to its enjoyment. These precautions will be especially necessary in drawing leases of property which has never been demised before. Parcels.

Thus, in a recent case (s), the demised property was

(r) 2 Platt on Leases, 17.
(s) *Espley* v. *Wilkes*, L. R. 7 Ex. 298.

described as "bounded on the east and north by newly-made streets." The piece of ground by which it was bounded on the east was, at the time of the demise, and remained for some years afterwards, a piece of rough waste ground, but it was held that its description in the lease, and on a plan attached, as a "street," gave the lessee a right of way over it to the demised premises, and so debarred the lessor from letting it to a third person as building ground (*t*). Moreover, since leases sometimes contain penalties for altering the nature of the property demised, care should be taken that no mistake is made in this respect, since the description given in the lease is presumed to be correct unless proved to be otherwise (*u*).

General Words.

After the parcels come the General Words, which are followed by any exception or reservation which may be agreed upon. These vary with the circumstances of each particular case, but it may be pointed out that the two words have entirely distinct meanings, although they are sometimes used indiscriminately. For the word "exception" is properly applied to some already existing part of the property which, by force of the exception, does not pass by the demise, and the absolute ownership in which remains, therefore, with the lessor; whilst the word "reservation" should be used to express some new right or easement over the property, created by the reservation, but taking effect by way of re-grant by the lessee to the lessor, who can therefore only use it for the express purpose for which it was reserved (*v*).

The Habendum.

The Estate clause is not inserted in leases: so we are now at the end of the premises, and come next to the Habendum. The Habendum states the term during

---

(*t*) And see *Roberts* v. *Karr*, 1 Taunt. 495.
(*u*) *Birch* v. *Stephenson*, 3 Taunt. 469.
(*v*) See *Hamilton* v. *Graham*, L. R. 2 H. L. (Sc.) 166, 168; *Wickham* v. *Hawker*, 7 Mee. & W. 63; *Proud* v. *Bates*, 34 L. J. (Ch.) 406.

which the lessee, his executors, administrators, and assigns are to hold the property, and the day on which the term is to begin. This day should be named precisely, not, for instance, as the 1st day of March "next," or as "Lady Day" in such a year. For this wording may give rise to difficulties if there is any mistake in the date of the lease, or delay in its execution, or if any question can arise as to whether old or new style was referred to.

Then follows the Reddendum, which takes up the story at the point where it was left by the habendum; and states the rent which the lessee is (to use the common form) to "yield and pay," and the days on which it is to be paid. Quarterly payments are the most usual, and the reddendum should fix them with reference to precisely named days of certain months; the day on which the first payment is to be made being also expressly stated. If the property is let at a yearly rent, without specifying any particular mode of payment, the lessor is only entitled to rent at the end of each year (*w*). It is a good plan to make the last payment payable in advance, before the expiration of the term, so as to give the lessor the opportunity of exercising his power of distress, in case this payment should not be made. The reddendum should not state to whom the rent is to be paid, for if rent is reserved generally the law will always carry it to the owner of the reversion, whoever he may be, after the lessor's death (*x*); whilst an incomplete or mistaken reservation may give rise to difficulties; although it will as a rule be regarded as a mere slip of the pen by the courts, who will, notwithstanding such a reservation, hold the rent to be incident to the reversion (*y*). The lease should contain also a stipulation, in the event of the term being put an end to by the lessor's

The Reddendum.

(*w*) *Coomber* v. *Howard*, 1 C. B. 440.
(*x*) 2 Platt on Leases, 18.
(*y*) *Sachererel* v. *Frogat*, 2 Lev. 13.

re-entry, for payment by the lessee of a proportionate part of the rent for the fraction of the current quarter up to the day of such re-entry. Without this stipulation the lessor, if he re-enters for a breach of covenant before the next day of payment, loses the current instalment of rent, whilst, on the other hand, he cannot enter after a receipt of rent, for the receipt will have been a waiver of his right of re-entry (*z*). With reference to the first point, it has been decided that the Apportionment Act, 4 & 5 Wm. IV., c. 22, does not confer any right to an apportionment of rent upon a lessor who puts an end to a lease by his own act: the statute only applying to cases of apportionment between the individual who was entitled to it when it began to accrue, and another who has come in as a remainder-man or reversioner, or otherwise (*a*). And the Apportionment Act, 33 & 34 Vict., c. 35, does not seem to have made any change in this respect.

The Covenants. We next come to the Covenants, beginning with those entered into by the lessee for himself, his heirs, executors, administrators, and assigns, with the lessor, his heirs and assigns; or, in the case of a sub-lease, with the lessor, his executors, administrators, and assigns.

Lessee's covenants. These covenants are (1) to pay rent; (2) to pay taxes; (3) to repair; (4) to permit the lessor to enter and inspect the state of repair; (5) to repair upon notice being given of want of repair; (6) to insure; (7) not to use the premises otherwise than as a private dwelling-house, without licence; (8) not to assign the premises, without licence; and (9) to deliver up the premises in good repair at the end of the term.

Covenant to pay rent. A covenant to pay a fair rent is implied on every

---

(*z*) 5 Dav. Con. 100, note (c).
(*a*) *Oldershaw* v. *Holt*, 12 A. & E. 590, 596.

demise, and the reservation of rent in the reddendum raises an implied covenant to pay the particular rent reserved, but an additional express covenant to pay the rent, on the days and in the manner previously mentioned in the lease, is always inserted in order to enable the lessor to maintain an action of covenant for non-payment. The rent is sometimes covenanted to be paid without any deduction except income tax, but these last words are entirely superfluous, as the legislature has already made absolutely void any contract for payment of rent without such deduction (*b*).

The object of the covenant for payment of taxes is to throw upon the lessee certain burdens which would, in the absence of agreement, have to be borne by the lessor. These are the payment of land tax, sewers' rates, and tithe rent charge, and also of all assessments made in respect of permanent improvements done by order of a local authority, and which assessments are primarily payable, under the various acts authorizing the improvements, by the owners of the adjoining premises. The ordinary wording of this covenant is, that the lessee shall pay all future as well as existing taxes, rates, assessments, and outgoings, payable either by landlord or tenant in respect of the premises. The proper wording of the covenant is a matter of importance, since it will be construed strictly against the lessor. It should include future taxes, &c., because although a general covenant to pay taxes will probably include all future taxes of the same kind as covenanted to be paid, it will not embrace any of a different nature. It is also necessary to specify "assessments and outgoings," for although a covenant to pay taxes generally will include all parliamentary taxes (*c*), it will not embrace any other

Covenant to pay taxes.

(*b*) 5 & 6 Vict. c. 35, s. 73.
(*c*) *Brewster* v. *Kidgill*, 12 Mod. 167; *Amfield* v. *Moore*, Ry. & Moo. 246.

impositions, although they may be ordinarily spoken of as taxes, such for instance as a sewer's rate (*d*); and for these the word "assessments" is required. The covenant must also extend to "outgoings," for it has been held (*e*) that a covenant to pay "all taxes and assessments whatsoever," does not include tithe rent charge. The form above mentioned will probably include every kind of tax or charge imposed on the lessor or lessee in respect of the premises, although made on account of a permanent improvement, such as paving a street on which the premises abut, by order of a local authority (*f*). But it will not preclude the lessee from recovering from the lessor money paid by the lessee to a local authority, when an act of parliament has imposed a duty in respect of the premises on the lessor personally, with power to the local authority, if the lessor neglect his duty, to perform it for him, and, "by way of additional remedy," to recover the sums thus expended from the lessee (*g*). But it would seem that this difficulty can be got over by including in the covenant "burdens, duties, and services," as well as taxes, rates, assessments, and outgoings (*h*).

Covenant to repair.

The next covenant is, that the lessee will, during the term, and without being required to do so, repair, maintain, and keep, the premises in good and substantial repair; and this is followed up by specifying such particular kinds of repair as are applicable to the property demised.

Effect of the covenant.

A covenant to repair does not mean that an old building is to be restored in a renewed form at the end of the term, thus making it of greater value than

---

(*d*) *Palmer* v. *Earith*, 14 Mee. & W. 428.
(*e*) *Jeffrey* v. *Neale*, L. R. 6 C. P. 240.
(*f*) *Thompson* v. *Lapworth*, L. R. 3 C. P. 149; *Crosse* v. *Raw*, L. R. 9 Ex. 209.
(*g*) *Tidswell* v. *Whitworth*, L. R. 2 C. P. 326.
(*h*) See *Payne* v. *Burridge*, 12 Mee. & W. 727; *Sweet* v. *Seager*, 2 C. B. (N. S.) 119.

at the commencement of the term. It only binds the lessee to take care, by keeping the premises as nearly as possible in the same condition as when they were demised, that they do not suffer more than the operation of time and nature would effect (*i*). But a covenant to keep the premises in repair, binds the lessee, if they are out of repair, to put them in repair, and he cannot therefore leave them in bad repair because they were in that state when he took them (*j*). This covenant moreover binds the lessee to rebuild the premises if they are burnt down (*k*), nor is this liability affected by the fact of the lessor's having insured them, and having received the insurance money (*l*).

The general covenant to repair without notice is followed by another, by which the lessee undertakes to permit the lessor, at all reasonable times, to enter upon the premises, in order to view their condition; a thing which the lessor could not do without a stipulation to that effect (*m*). It is also provided that the lessor may give notice in writing of all defects and wants of repair on the premises, and the lessee covenants that he will, within a specified time (generally three months), make good all defects of which notice has been given. The object of this covenant is to prevent any question arising under the general covenant to repair, as to what repairs are necessary, or whether the lessee is using due expedition in repairing, by enabling the lessor to specify the repairs which he requires to be done, and by fixing a time within which they are to be finished. Care should be taken that the covenant to repair after

<!-- sidenotes: Covenant to permit the lessor to enter and view the state of repair. Covenant to repair on notice. -->

(*i*) *Gutteridge* v. *Munyard*, 7 C. & P. 129; *Stanley* v. *Towgood*, 3 Scott, 313.
(*j*) *Payne* v. *Hayne*, 16 Mee. & W. 541; *Easton* v. *Pratt*, 33 L. J. (Ex.) 233, 235.
(*k*) *Bullock* v. *Dommit*, 6 T. R. 650; *Digby* v. *Atkinson*, 4 Camp. 275.
(*l*) *Leeds* v. *Cheetham*, 1 Sim. 146.
(*m*) *Barker* v. *Barker*, 3 C. & P. 557.

notice does not restrict the general covenant to repair without notice, and it should therefore be contained in a separate sentence, since those covenants only are held to be distinct which severally make a distinct sentence. Thus (n), where there was a covenant that the lessee should repair at all times when, where, and as often as, occasion should require, and at furthest within three months after notice of want of repair: it was held that this sentence comprised but one covenant, and that the lessee was not liable for a breach of it, unless he had received notice of want of repair. The form given above obviates any risk of that kind (o).

Covenant to insure.

This covenant is followed by one to the effect that the lessee will insure the premises in the joint names of the lessor and of the lessee; that he will, if required, produce the insurance policy and the various receipts for premiums, and will, in case of fire, lay out the insurance moneys in rebuilding the premises. By this means the lessor obtains a security that the premises will be rebuilt which is additional to, and, presumably, more effectual than, that which he has under the lessee's covenant to repair; and its insertion is therefore a matter of common form.

Covenant not to use the premises for the purpose of any trade.

Where the premises, or part of them, consist of a dwelling-house, it is usual to insert a covenant that the lessee will not use the house for purposes of trade or business, or otherwise than as a private dwelling-house, without the licence of the lessor, his heirs, or assigns; and also that he will not, without such licence, assign, or underlet, the whole or any part of the premises. The general restriction against carrying on trade appears to be preferable to a form saying that particular kinds of business are not to be carried

And not to assign or underlet.

(n) *Horsefall* v. *Testar*, 7 Taunt. 385.
(o) See *Doe* v. *Meux*, 4 B. & C. 606; *Baylis* v. *Le Gros*, 4 C. B. (N. S.) 537.

on without licence, or one restraining "offensive" trades only. For such clauses often give rise to disputes (p), whereas the general prohibition allows the lessor to exercise his judgment upon each application made to him, and in that case his rights under the covenant will not be limited by any consideration as to the nature of the trade or business proposed to be carried on (q). It may be added that the word "business" includes keeping a school (r).

The covenant against assignment should, if intended to prohibit under-letting, be expressly worded to that effect, for a covenant merely not to assign or put away the lease or the premises, does not prevent the lessee from making an underlease of part of the term (s); although an underlease of the whole term amounts to an assignment (t). A covenant not to assign is not broken by the deposit of a lease by way of security for money lent, since this is not a parting with the legal interest (u), nor by giving a warrant of attorney to confess judgment in an action, although the result may be that the lease is taken in execution and sold (v), for the covenant does not apply to an involuntary alienation by operation of law (w). But it. is broken by an assignment by one joint-tenant to another, since although it relates to the estate of all the joint-tenants, it necessarily involves the interest of each (x).

As to under-letting.

The lessee's covenants terminate by a general under-

Covenant to

(p) See as to this *Doe* v. *Bird*, 2 A. & E. 161; *Jones* v. *Thorne*, 1 B. & C. 715; *Gutteridge* v. *Munyard*, 7 C. & P. 129; *Harrison* v. *Good*, L. R. 11 Eq. 338.
(q) *Macher* v. *Foundling Hospital*, 1 Ves. & B. 186.
(r) *Doe* v. *Keeling*, 1 Mau. & Sel. 95, 100.
(s) *Crusoe* v. *Bugby*, 3 Wil. 234; *Kinnersley* v. *Orpe*, 1 Doug. 56.
(t) *Beardman* v. *Wilson*, L. R. 4 C. P. 57.
(u) *Doe* v. *Hogg*, 4 Dow. & Ry. 226; *Ex parte Cocks*, 2 Deac. 14.
(v) *Doe* v. *Carter*, 8 T. R. 57.
(w) *Croft* v. *Lumley*, 6 H. L. C. 672.
(x) *Varley* v. *Coppard*, L. R. 7 C. P. 505, 507.

deliver up in good repair.
taking on his part that he will, at the end of the term, deliver up the premises in good repair, and in such a condition as shall be consistent with the due performance of his covenants.

Proviso for Re-entry.
These covenants are followed by a very important clause, which is known as the Proviso for Re-entry. This is to the effect that whenever any part of the rent shall have been in arrear for (generally) three weeks, 21a whether the same shall have been legally demanded or not, or whenever the lessee shall commit a breach of any of his covenants, the lessor may re-enter upon the premises, and that thereupon the term granted shall absolutely determine.

The proviso should particularly state that the re-entry may be made whether the rent has been legally demanded or not, for this wording enables the lessor to re-enter for non-payment of rent without any demand for rent (*y*), and it also avoids the common law niceties which were formerly requisite in making a re-entry for non-payment, and which still apply (*z*), in the absence of such a stipulation, unless there is a half-year's rent due, and no sufficient distress can be found upon the premises (*a*).

The grounds on which a lessor will be held to have lost his right to enforce a forfeiture have been already discussed in our chapter on estates for years. We will, therefore, only add here, with reference to another clause in the lease, that a notice requiring a lessee to repair within a certain (named) time, prevents the lessor from re-entering until after the expiration of

---

(*y*) *Doe* v. *Masters*, 2 B. & C. 490.
(*z*) 2 Platt on Leases, 341.
(*a*) See 4 Geo. II. c. 28, s. 2; 15 & 16 Vict. c. 76, s. 210; and *Doe* v. *Alexander*, 2 Mau. & Sel. 525; *Doe* v. *Wilson*, 5 B. & Ald. 363; *Philipps* v. *Bridge*, L. R. 9 C. P. 48, 49 note (2).

that time (b); although the case is otherwise when the notice requires him to repair "forthwith" (c).

The proviso for re-entry is followed by a covenant on the part of the lessor, that the lessee and his representatives shall, provided that they pay the rent and observe the covenants mentioned in the lease, peaceably enjoy the premises without any interruption by the lessor, his heirs, or assigns, or any person lawfully claiming through him or them. It will be noticed that this is not an absolute covenant for quiet enjoyment, and it should always be inserted in the lessor's interest; for, in the absence of any covenant, the lessor will be presumed to have given an absolute covenant for quiet enjoyment (d), and will thus be liable for the acts of persons claiming adversely to him (e), whereas the qualified covenant saves him from any risk of this kind (f). It is to be observed that the covenant for quiet enjoyment, whether in a purchase deed or in a lease, does not enlarge or increase the rights granted by the previous part of the deed. Its only effect is that an additional remedy, namely, an action for damages, is given if the lessee cannot get, or is deprived of, anything which has been previously professed to be granted or demised (g).

Lessor's covenant for quiet enjoyment.

The deed concludes with the ordinary Testatum, which should, if there is no counterpart, be signed by both the lessor and the lessee, but it is more usual to have a counterpart, in which case the lease is signed by the lessor, and the counterpart by the lessee. Both instruments should be properly attested, and the lease,

The Testatum

(b) *Doe* v. *Meux*, 4 B. & C. 606.
(c) *Roe* v. *Paine*, 2 Camp. 520.
(d) *Nokes' Case*, 4 Rep. 80ᵇ.
(e) *Bandy* v. *Cartwright*, 22 L. J. (Ex.) 285; *Hall* v. *City of London Brewery Co.* 31 L. J. (Q. B.) 257.
(f) *Line* v. *Stephenson*, 4 Bing. N. C. 678; *Stanley* v. *Hayes*, 3 Q. B. 105.
(g) *Leech* v. *Schweder*, L. R. 9 Ch. 463, 474.

if made of land belonging to a married woman, but not settled to her separate use, must be duly acknowledged by her.

Statutory provisions as to leases.

8 & 9 Vict., c. 124.

We may conclude these remarks by calling attention to an Act of Parliament, passed with the object of shortening the ordinary form of leases, but remarkable chiefly on account of its utter failure to carry out that object. This act is the 8 & 9 Vict., c. 124, entitled " An Act to Facilitate the Granting of Certain Leases." It contains in the schedule two parallel columns, in one of which are the ordinary clauses of a lease as drawn by conveyancers, whilst in the other are as many marginal notes, each relating to a separate clause. The act gives to each marginal note the effect of its corresponding clause, but these notes are too concise to give sufficient information to an ordinary person looking at a lease so drawn, in order to ascertain his rights or obligations under it (*h*), and the act appears to be very seldom made use of.

(*h*) See also Dart. V. & P. 463.

CHAPTER V.

OF MORTGAGE DEEDS.

WE come next to the consideration of the ordinary form of a mortgage deed of land. This, as we have noticed already, consists essentially of a conveyance of the mortgaged property to the mortgagee, with a proviso for its reconveyance when the debt secured by it is paid off. It contains, in addition, various other clauses which are necessary to give completeness to the transaction. Where the subject of the mortgage is a freehold estate in land, the conveyance, ordinarily, takes the form of an absolute grant of it, subject to the proviso for redemption. On a mortgage of leaseholds, it is open to the mortgagee to take either an assignment of the whole term for which the property is held by the mortgagor or else a lease for a period a few days short of the whole term. A question as to which plan is the better can only be answered by reference to the circumstances of each case. Generally speaking, if the covenants of the lease are not onerous, the mortgagee had better take an assignment of the whole term, as he thus obviates any risk of the lease being forfeited by the mortgagor's dealings with the reversion, and has also the certainty of any fixtures which may be on the property forming a part of his security: a point which will be presently referred to. On the other hand, the mortgagee, if he takes the whole term, and even though he never enters into possession of the property, becomes liable to all the rents and covenants of the lease; since he who takes an estate must, without reference to his object in taking it, bear all burdens

<sub>Form of mortgage.
Freeholds.</sub>

_{Leaseholds.}

incident thereto (a). And since the mortgagee escapes this liability by taking a sub-lease only (b), this latter plan is preferable where the rent of the mortgaged premises is more than nominal, or where the covenants are stringent or burdensome. It may also be remarked that, in the case of mortgages of leaseholds made after the 28th August 1860, the mortgagee can, if he sells the property under a power of sale, convey to a purchaser the reversion which had been left in the mortgagor (c), and is, therefore, in that respect, in as good a position as if he had taken the whole of the term.

Copyholds. Since copyholds do not pass by deed, a mortgage of them takes, in the first place, the form of a covenant by the mortgagor that he will, immediately after the execution of the mortgage deed, surrender them to the lord of the manor to the use of the mortgagee. This is followed by the formal surrender, which is duly entered on the manor rolls, but expressed to be subject to a condition that on payment by the mortgagor, on a specified date, of all sums secured by his covenants in the mortgage deed (and to which we will refer presently) the surrender shall be void and of no effect (d): The mortgagee has not a legal title to the copyholds unless they are thus surrendered to him; and cannot, therefore, safely part with his money until the surrender is made, since, up to that time, he is liable to be postponed to any subsequent purchaser for value who has obtained a surrender without notice of the earlier mortgage (e). This conditional surrender, as it is called, leaves the mortgagor tenant of the manor (f), but prevents him from dealing with the property to the prejudice of the mortgagee, whilst

---

(a) *Williams* v. *Bosanquet*, 1 Brod. & B. 238; overruling *Eaton* v. *Jaques*, 2 Doug. 455.
(b) *Halford* v. *Hatch*, 1 Doug. 183.
(c) 23 & 24 Vict. c. 145, s. 15; *Hiatt* v. *Hillman*, 19 W. R. 694.
(d) Scriv. Cop. 839.
(e) *Oxwith* v. *Plummer*, 2 Ver. 636.
(f) *Doe* v. *Wroot*, 5 East, 132.

it has, at the same time, the advantage of freeing the mortgagee from any liability to the lord of the manor, who, having the tenancy "full" already, has no further claims in respect of it. The mortgagee must, however, be admitted a tenant of the manor if he wishes to realize his security by a sale of the property (*g*). We may add here that if the mortgage is paid off, an entry of its satisfaction, made on the manor rolls, is sufficient to restore the mortgagor to his original position (*h*).

Having premised thus much, we will, pursuing our system in other cases, go through the various clauses of an ordinary mortgage deed of freeholds in fee simple, adverting, when necessary, to the differences between such clauses and those of a mortgage deed which deals with leaseholds, or with copyholds.

The mortgage deed.

The introductory part of such a deed conforms to the rules which govern the corresponding portion of a purchase deed, as do also the recitals (*i*), except that the last introductory recital, when inserted, consists of a statement of the agreement for a loan, subject to its repayment being secured in the manner to be described in the deed.

Introductory Part.

Recitals.

Next comes the first Witnessing Part. This consists more generally, though by no means universally, of a covenant by the mortgagor which, referring to, and acknowledging the receipt of, the sum lent, promises that in consideration thereof the mortgagor or his representatives will, on a specified day (usually six calendar months from the date of the deed), pay to the mortgagee, his executors, administrators, or assigns, the same sum, with interest in the mean

First Witnessing Part.

(*g*) See *Flack* v. *Downing College*, 13 C. B. 945 ; 2 Dav. Con. 667.
(*h*) Scriv. Cop. 842.
(*i*) As to the construction put on recitals in a mortgage deed, see *Francis* v. *Minton*, L. R. 2 C. P. 543.

time at a given rate *per cent.* We have, in our chapter on an equity of redemption, seen the advantages gained by inserting this covenant, which makes the mortgagee a specialty creditor of the mortgagor; a position which he would not hold otherwise, since the implied contract for repayment arising out of the loan raises a simple contract debt only (*j*).

Second Witnessing Part.

Then follows the second Witnessing Part. This corresponds to the operative part of a purchase deed, and contains the words which convey the mortgaged property, by grant or by demise or assignment, according as it is freehold or leasehold, to the mortgagee, his heirs and assigns, or to him, his executors, administrators, and assigns. If the property is copyhold, the words of conveyance find a substitute in the covenant for surrender previously mentioned. The conveyance however, whatever its form may be, is made subject, in the case of freeholds or leaseholds, to a proviso for redemption on repayment of the sum advanced; and in the case of copyholds, to a condition for making void the surrender, corresponding with the proviso for redemption.

Parcels. General Words and Estate Clause.

After the operative part come the Parcels, which are described in the usual way. These are followed by the General Words, and the Estate Clause, if the property is freehold; by the General Words only if the property is leasehold; and after these comes the

Habendum.

Habendum, which limits the mortgagee's estate, according to the nature of the mortgaged premises, and subject to the proviso for redemption which immediately follows.

Effect of a mortgage deed in transferring fixtures.

Before noticing this proviso, however, we will call attention to one way in which the operative part of a

---

(*j*) *Yates* v. *Aston,* 4 Q. B. 182; *Isaacson* v. *Harwood,* L. R. 3 Ch. 225.

mortgage deed has a different effect, according as the deed is made by an absolute, or by a limited, owner of land. Fixtures, as we know, are personal chattels, which, having been annexed to land, become part of it, subject to a right to remove them, vested in the party who has annexed them or his representatives, as against the owner of the freehold : this right, however, being lost if not exercised either during the term or, in the case of a tenant for life, during or immediately after the term. Now, since a man cannot have a right as against himself, it follows that an absolute owner of land has no right in respect of fixtures as distinct from any other part of the freehold, and therefore fixtures having, in such a case, no separate existence will pass on a sale or mortgage of an estate in fee simple without being specifically mentioned (*k*). Mortgage by an absolute owner passes fixtures though not named.

But in the case of a limited owner of land there are two distinct interests possessed by him—a limited interest in the land, an absolute interest in the fixtures. These last have, therefore, in such a case, a separate existence apart from the freehold, and although they will pass without being specifically mentioned on an assignment of the whole of a limited interest (*l*), because the person who has annexed them has, by the assignment, parted with his right of removal, which will therefore be assumed to have been passed to the transferee; the case is different where the limited interest is not entirely parted with, as, for instance, where there is a mortgage by sub-lease : for here the fixtures do not pass unless specifically mentioned (*m*), and the right to remove them will remain, therefore, in the mortgagor. We see then that, as against the mortgagor, the mortgagee acquires a right to the fixtures, although not named, if the mortgage is by So on the assignment of the whole of a limited interest.
But it is otherwise where the limited interest is not entirely parted with.

(*k*) *Ex parte Reynal*, 2 M. D. & De G. 443.
(*l*) *Longstaff* v. *Meagoe*, 2 A. & E. 167.
(*m*) *Hawtrey* v. *Butlin*, L. R. 8 Q. B. 290, 293.

Further step required on mortgage of a limited interest.

way of grant of a fee simple or assignment of the whole of a limited interest, but that they must be definitely mentioned in order to pass, on a mortgage by demise. But, except in the case of a grant in fee simple, something more than the operative part, however framed, is necessary to give the mortgagee a perfectly good title to the fixtures.

Bills of Sale Registration Act.

For by the Bills of Sale Act, 1854 (*n*), it is enacted (*o*) that every bill of sale of personal chattels, made after the passing of the act, shall be registered, in manner provided by the act, within twenty-one days after the making or giving thereof: otherwise such bill of sale is, as against the trustee in bankruptcy, or the execution creditors of the giver of it, to be null and void to all intents and purposes whatever, so far as regards the property in, or right to the possession of, any personal chattels comprised in such bill of sale, which at or after the time of the giver's bankruptcy, or of his goods being taken in execution, and after the expiration of the said period of twenty-one days, shall be in his possession, or apparent possession. And under another section of this act (*p*), the term "bill of sale" is to include every assurance of personal chattels, and this latter term again, is to include fixtures. It is evident, therefore, that a mortgage of fixtures, unaccompanied by any mortgage of the land to which they are attached, requires, in every case, registration under the act, in order to be good against the mortgagor's trustee in bankruptcy, or his execution creditor (*q*). If the mortgage comprises both the fixtures and the land, the rule is somewhat different. For if the mortgaged estate is a fee simple, registration is unnecessary because, in fact, no fixtures as such have

---

(*n*) 17 & 18 Vict. 36.
(*o*) S. 1.
(*p*) S. 7.
(*q*) *Waterfall* v. *Penistone*, 6 E. & B. 876.

passed (r), and a mortgage of land does not require registration under this act.

But where there is a mortgage of a limited interest, there are really two separate interests parted with, and one of these being the absolute ownership of the fixtures, as distinct and apart from the ownership of the land, the mortgage deed requires registration under the Bills of Sale Act, in order to give the mortgagee a perfect title to the fixtures, just as much as if they had been assigned by a separate deed altogether (s). The importance of attending to this point will probably be fully appreciated when it is considered that on a mortgage of (say) manufacturing premises, the machinery on them, which comes within the definition of fixtures (t), forms by far the most important part of the mortgagee's security.

We now arrive at the Proviso for Redemption which, in modern practice, takes the form of an agreement that if the mortgagor or those claiming under him shall, on the day already fixed by his covenant for payment of the principal and current interest, pay those sums to the mortgagee, his executors, administrators, or assigns, then the mortgagee will re-convey the property to the mortgagor, his heirs, or assigns. This covenant, it will be noticed, provides for repayment of the mortgage money to the mortgagee or his personal representatives, whilst the mortgaged estate is, when re-conveyed, to go to those persons to whom

Proviso for Redemption.

(r) *Cullwick* v. *Swindell*, L. R. 3 Eq. 249; *Climie* v. *Wood*, L. R. 3 Ex. 257; *Holland* v. *Hodgson*, L. R. 7 C. P. 328.
(s) *Beglie* v. *Fenwick*, 24 L. T. (N. S.) 58; *Hawtrey* v. *Butlin*, L. R. 8 Q. B. 290; *Ex parte Daglish*, L. R. 8 Ch. 1072; *Meux* v. *Allen*, W. N. (1874) 16, overruling *Boyd* v. *Shorrock*, L. R. 5 Eq. 72.
(t) *Longbotham* v. *Berry*, L. R. 5 Q. B. 123; *Holland* v. *Hodgson*, L. R. 7 C. P. 328.

it would have belonged had there been no mortgage, that is, to the mortgagor and his heirs.

Mortgage money made payable to personal representatives of the mortgagee.

The personal representatives of the mortgagee should be designated as those who are to receive the mortgage money, since a mortgage even in fee is always considered personal assets, and it is therefore inconsistent to introduce any words which seem to give the mortgagee's real representatives any right to the mortgage money. But it does not appear that any mistake of this kind would be of essential importance. For it has been decided (*u*)—where the mortgagee has died before the day fixed for payment—that if no person ·besides himself has been named as the recipient of the mortgage money, his personal representatives alone are entitled to take it; and that if the proviso is for re-payment to the mortgagee's heirs *or* his personal representatives, the mortgagor, if he redeems after the day fixed for that purpose, can pay his money to the personal representatives only; although if he comes on the precise day he may pay it either to them or to the heir, who will, however, in that case, be considered a trustee for them (*v*) ; as he will be, also, if the mortgagee and· his heirs have alone been named as the persons to whom payment is to be made.

Re-conveyance of the mortgaged estate:

A question of more importance may arise if the proviso for re-conveyance of the mortgaged premises would, if literally carried out, alter the devolution of the equity of redemption.

If it is intended to transfer the beneficial ownership of the equity of redemption from the person entitled to the beneficial ownership of the estate at the time of the mortgage, or· to vary his rights in any

---
(*u*) *Thornborough* v. *Baker,* 3 Swan. 628, and, with notes, 2 L. C. 1030.
(*v*) *Kendall* v. *Micfield,* Barnard. 46, 50.

way, a full recital of this intention should be inserted in the deed (*w*), for a mere change in the ordinary wording will not be sufficient for this purpose (*x*). But of course, if no change in this respect is intended, care should be taken to avoid, as far as possible, any language which may seem to indicate an intention of change. And this precaution is the more necessary since it is now settled (*y*), contrary to the opinion formerly prevalent, that the absence of a recital is not, of itself, sufficient to preclude the person in whose favour such a change would appear to have been made from relying on the wording of the deed, in support of his claim (*z*).

The proviso for redemption is followed by a covenant by the mortgagor that if the principal sum lent, or any part of it, shall remain unpaid after the day fixed for payment he will, so long as it remains unpaid, pay interest on it at a specified rate. The covenant should also name the days on which such interest is to be paid; these being usually arranged so as to secure half-yearly payments. Here, too, should be inserted any proviso which may have been agreed upon for reduction of the rate of interest, on punctual payment of the sums secured by the last-mentioned covenant. The covenant for payment of interest at a higher rate, followed by a proviso for reducing that rate, is a circuitous method of imposing a penalty on the mortgagor if he does not pay his interest regularly. This object cannot be effected directly, owing to the somewhat unsatisfactory doctrine of equity which treats a proviso that the rate of interest shall be increased

Covenant for payment of interest.

(*w*) Co. Litt. 208*, note (1).
(*x*) *Stansfield* v. *Hallam*, 29 L. J. (Ch.) 173; *Hastings* v. *Astley*, 30 Beav. 260.
(*y*) *Jackson* v. *Innes*, 1 Bli. 104.
(*z*) See *Eldleston* v. *Collins*, 3 De G. M. & G. 1; *Atkinson* v. *Smith*, 3 De G. & J. 186.

in default of punctual payment as a penalty to be relieved against. Thus, in an early case (*a*), a proviso raising the rate of interest from £5 *per cent.* to £5 10s. *per cent.* per annum, if the interest were not paid within two months from the time fixed for payment, was set aside, although the interest was greatly in arrear. And the court decreed payment at the lower rate without allowing the mortgagee anything on account of the delay in payment, notwithstanding that the decision was founded upon the principle that such a proviso was a penalty to be relieved against, and that such relief is, ordinarily, given only to a person making full recompense in respect of the act, or neglect, for which the penalty was imposed. But both in that and in other cases (*b*) the court has approved of covenants for payment of interest at a certain rate which is to be reduced if the interest be paid punctually, although, as observed by the editor of Vernon's Reports (*c*), the agreement of the parties seems to be the same in either case, and whether interest is to be reduced on compliance with the times of payment, or advanced in default thereof, seems to be only a difference in expressing one and the same thing.

In one case (*d*) it was attempted to enforce regular payment of interest by inserting a proviso that all interest not paid within six months from the time when it was due should be accounted principal and carry interest. This, however, was set aside, the Lord Chancellor (Lord Cowper) remarking that no agreement entered into at the time of the mortgage could turn future interest into principal, but that to make interest into principal it is necessary that interest be first due, and then an agreement concerning

---

(*a*) *Strode* v. *Parker*, 2 Ver. 316; and see *Holles* v. *Wise*, 2 Ver. 289; *Nicholls* v. *Maynard*, 3 Atk. 519.
(*b*) *Stanhope* v. *Manners*, 2 Eden. 196; *Wayne* v. *Lewis*, 25 L. T. 264; and see *Herbert* v. *Salisbury Ry. Co.*, L. R. 2 Eq. 221, 224.
(*c*) 2 Ver. 317.
(*d*) *Ossulton* v. *Yarmouth*, Salk. 448.

it may turn it into principal. But in a case decided in Upper Canada (where the law relating to mortgages is much the same as in this country), a stipulation in a mortgage deed that the interest should be at the rate of £8 *per cent.* per annum, up to a certain day ; and that if the principal was not paid on that day the rate of interest should be raised to £12 *per cent.* per annum, was held to be not a penalty but a valid agreement (*e*). By the custom of bankers, compound interest is charged on overdrawn accounts, and this custom holds good although a banker may have taken a mortgage of land as a collateral security for the balance of an account, for in that case the mutual relation of the parties is still that of banker and customer (*f*). Where, however, a mortgage is given by a customer to his banker for a fixed sum, and not by way of collateral security for the running balance of his account, the banker cannot include that sum in the banking account, and charge compound interest upon it (*g*), for, as regards it, the parties occupy the position of mortgagor and mortgagee respectively.

Where the mortgage money is advanced by trustees, it is necessary to insert at this point a declaration that it belongs to them on a joint account in equity as well as at law: and that, consequently, the survivor shall remain entitled in equity, as well as at law, to the sums secured by the mortgage deed. It is necessary to mention expressly that the money belongs to the trustees jointly, in equity as well as at law ; for in the case of two people lending money jointly, equity, differing therein from law, says, in the absence of a distinct statement to the contrary, that it could not have been their intention that the right to it should belong exclusively to the survivor, but that, although

Declaration on loan by trustees.

(*e*) *Waddell* v. *McColl*, 14 Grant, 211.
(*f*) *Rufford* v. *Bishop*, 5 Russ. 346.
(*g*) *Mosse* v. *Salt*, 32 Beav. 269.

they took a joint security, each means to lend his own money, and to take back his own (*h*).

It is not desirable to state in the mortgage deed that the money lent is trust money, for that would have the disadvantage of affecting every person dealing with the property with notice of the trust, whilst the advantage arising from the rule that an acknowledgment of title by one of several mortgagees who appear on the face of the mortgage deed to be both joint-tenants and trustees, does not keep alive the mortgagor's right of redemption (*i*), is too remote to be of much value.

Covenants by the mortgagor.
If the property consists of buildings, the mortgagor should next enter into covenants to repair, and to allow the mortgagee to enter and view the state of repair, similar to those contained in leases. He should also covenant to insure all buildings and fixtures on the property; to keep them, so long as the mortgage lasts, insured for an amount equal at least to that of the sum lent; and to apply all moneys which may be received under such insurance in repairing any part of the premises, or fixtures, which may be destroyed by fire. The mortgagee has, even without this proviso, a right to insist upon money received under the insurance being laid out in repairing the mortgaged houses or buildings damaged or destroyed by fire (*j*), but he cannot, in the absence of agreement, compel the application of such money to the repair of fixtures removable by a tenant (*k*), except, perhaps, where the mortgagor has received money under an insurance which existed before the mortgage, and which he has kept up in pursuance of a covenant to that effect (*l*).

(*h*) Per Sir R. *Arden*, M. R. 3 Ves. 631.
(*i*) *Richardson* v. *Younge*, L. R. 6 Ch. 478.
(*j*) 14 Geo. II. c. 78, s. 83 ; *Ex parte Goreley*, 13 W. R. 60.
(*k*) *Ex parte Goreley*, 13 W. R. 60 ; *Lees* v. *Whiteley*, L. R. 2 Eq. 143.
(*l*) *Garden* v. *Ingram*, 23 L. J. (Ch.) 478.

The mortgagor's covenant to insure should, in any case, be followed by a proviso that, in default of his keeping the premises insured, the mortgagee may do so, and add all money thus expended to the principal sum lent.

If any part of the mortgaged property consists of leaseholds which the mortgagor has a right to have renewed, he should next covenant that he will exercise this right, if necessary; for otherwise the mortgagee cannot compel him to renew, but must himself pay the expenses of any renewal, and may then reimburse himself by adding the sums thus expended to his principal (in which case they will carry interest), and may also hold the renewed lease as a security both for the sum originally advanced by him and for that expended in obtaining the renewal (*m*).

We have already seen that foreclosure, which is the primary right of a mortgagee, is a slow and expensive process, especially where there are several incumbrances on the mortgaged estate. Hence, it has been, for some time, the almost universal custom to insert in mortgage deeds a power for the mortgagee, his executors, administrators, or assigns, at any time after the day fixed for payment of the principal sum due, and without any further consent on the part of the mortgagor, to sell the mortgaged property in such manner as they think fit, and to do all things necessary for effectuating and completing such sale. If there are two or more mortgagees, the power should be extended to them, or the survivors or survivor of them, or the executors or administrators of such survivor, or their or his assigns. Provision should also be made for the concurrence, if necessary, of any

Power of Sale

(*m*) *Lacon* v. *Mertins*, 3 Atk. 1, 4.

other person in whom the legal estate in the property may have become vested.

It will be observed that the power of sale is limited to the mortgagee and his personal representatives, or his or their assigns: since, as will be remembered, a mortgage debt is personal assets, and it is desirable that the sale, if it takes place, should be made by the persons entitled to receive the purchase-money under it. Care should be taken to include the mortgagee's assigns amongst the persons who may exercise the power, for it has been held (*n*), that a power of sale vested in A "and his heirs" cannot be exercised by an "assign" of A, even though the deed empowers the "assigns" of A (amongst others) to give a receipt for the purchase-moneys obtained by such a sale; and since the same reasoning would apply to a power given to A "his executors and administrators" only, the word "assigns" is necessary to allow of the power of sale being exercised by any person who has taken a transfer of the mortgage.

A purchaser is not entitled, in the event of a sale, to require the concurrence of the mortgagor, even if the mortgage deed contains a covenant that, on a sale being made, the mortgagor shall concur therein (*o*); for such a covenant is a mere contract between the mortgagor and the mortgagee, to the benefit of which a purchaser is not entitled.

Events on which exercise of power depends.

This absolute power to sell is followed by provisoes which restrict its operation, by declaring that the power is not to be exercised unless the mortgagor has made default in payment, at the specified time, of the principal and interest secured by the deed, and

---

(*n*) *Bradford* v. *Belfield*, 2 Sim. 264; and see *Townsend* v. *Wilson*, 1 B. & Ald. 608.
(*o*) *Clay* v. *Sharpe*, 18 Ves. 346ⁿ; *Corder* v. *Morgan*, 18 Ves. 344.

has also failed for a period of (generally) six months to comply with a notice requiring him to pay off all sums then due from him; or unless some payment of interest has been in arrear for (generally) three months, in which latter case no notice is requisite. It is provided that the notice referred to may be given to the mortgagor, his heirs, executors, administrators, or assigns, or left at his or their usual or last known residence, or on some part of the mortgaged premises, and shall be sufficient notwithstanding any clerical error therein, and notwithstanding the disability of any person to whom it is addressed.

In order to prevent any question being raised, on a sale, of the sufficiency or otherwise of any notice, it is further provided that no purchaser shall be bound to see whether there has been any default in payment of either principal or interest; or whether any notice, proper or otherwise, has been given of the mortgagee's intention to sell; or whether there has been any impropriety, or irregularity, in the sale; and that the mortgagor's only remedy in these events shall be in damages against the mortgagee. But if the purchaser knows that the sale is irregular, it cannot be maintained, even though the deed contains a proviso that notwithstanding any irregularity or impropriety in the sale, the same shall be deemed, as regards a purchaser, to be within the power of sale, and be valid accordingly (p).

But purchaser not to be bound to inquire whether any of them have happened.

The purchaser is further secured by a declaration that a receipt for the purchase-money, given by the persons who are to exercise the power of sale, shall be a sufficient discharge to him, and that he shall not be bound to see to its application, or be answerable for its misapplication. It has been decided with

Mortgagee's receipt to be a sufficient discharge.

(p) *Jenkins* v. *Jones*, 2 Giff. 99; and see *Parkinson* v. *Hanbury*, 2 De G. J. & S. 450, 452.

reference to this clause that the power to give a receipt for the purchase-money does not oblige the mortgagee actually to receive the purchase-money, provided he accounts for it to the mortgagor; and that, consequently, his having allowed part of it to remain on a new mortgage of the property is a good exercise of his power, and does not keep alive the first mortgagor's equity of redemption (*q*).

<small>Application of proceeds of sale.</small>   Next comes a clause to the effect that the mortgagee shall, out of the money obtained by any sale, first, reimburse himself all the expenses of the sale; next, repay himself all sums secured by the mortgage deed; and, finally, hand over the surplus, if any, to the mortgagor. The result is that the mortgagee is in the position of a fiduciary vendor (*r*), and he cannot, therefore, purchase the property which he is selling under his power. But this rule does not extend to a second mortgagee with the ordinary power of sale, for he may purchase from the first mortgagee, and on doing so stands in the position of any other purchaser, thus putting an end to the mortgagor's equity of redemption (*s*). Whether he can purchase, if his own mortgage has taken the form of a trust for sale, does not seem to be quite clear (*t*). It follows from the fact of a mortgagee selling under his power being looked upon as a fiduciary vendor, that he is bound to take every reasonable precaution to prevent the property being sacrificed at the sale (*u*).

The surplus moneys arising from the sale should be made payable to the mortgagor, his heirs, and

---

(*q*) *Davey* v. *Durrant*, 1 De G. & J. 535; *Thurlow* v. *Mackeson*, L. R. 4 Q. B. 97.
(*r*) *Jenkins* v. *Jones*, 2 Giff. 99, 108; *Davey* v. *Durrant*, 1 De G. & J. 535.
(*s*) *Shaw* v. *Bunny*, 11 Jur. (N. S.) 99; *Kirkwood* v. *Thompson*, 2 De G. J. & S. 613, 618; *Watkins* v. *McKeller*, 7 Grant, 584.
(*t*) See *Parkinson* v. *Hanbury*, 2 De G. J. & S. 450, 455; and *contrd Kirkwood* v. *Thompson*, 2 De G. J. & S. 613.
(*u*) *Richmond* v. *Evans*, 8 Grant, 508; *Latch* v. *Furlong*, 12 Grant, 303.

assigns, only: for it is no part of the office of a mortgagor to alter the character of the surplus, as between the heir and the personal representatives of a mortgagor (v). It has been decided that where a mortgage deed contains a power of sale, and provides for the surplus moneys arising thereby being paid to the mortgagor, his executors, administrators, and assigns, such surplus, if the sale is made after the mortgagor's death, belongs, notwithstanding the wording of the deed, to the mortgagor's heir or devisee, according as the equity of redemption has descended or been devised (w).

The clauses relating to the power of sale are completed by a declaration that the power may be exercised by any person entitled to give a receipt for the mortgage money, and that the mortgagee, or those representing him, shall not be answerable for any involuntary losses which may happen in the exercise of the power.

If the mortgagor is in actual occupation of the mortgaged property, the power of sale is sometimes followed by a third Witnessing Part, in which the mortgagor declares himself to be tenant to the mortgagee in respect of all the mortgaged premises, and agrees to pay a yearly rent accordingly. This rent, both in its amount and time of payment, corresponds, usually, with the interest payable by the mortgagor, for which it is, in the absence of agreement, an equivalent, so far as the two amounts are equal (x); any excess of rent over interest going in reduction of the principal sum lent. The attornment gives the mortgagee a power to distrain for any rent which may be in arrear, and thus affords him a ready means of

Attornment by mortgagor to mortgagee.

(v) 5 Dav. Con. 629.
(w) *Wright* v. *Rose*, 2 S. & S. 323; *Re Clarke*, 22 L. J. (Ch.) 230; *Hardey* v. *Felton*, 14 L. T. 346.
(x) *Hampton* v. *Fellows*, L. R. 6 Eq. 575.

enforcing payment of the interest, or instalments, due from the mortgagor.

The reservation of rent would, if standing alone, create a yearly tenancy between the mortgagor and the mortgagee, which could not be put an end to without six months' notice. In order to obviate this, the attornment clause should be followed by a proviso enabling the mortgagee to enter upon the premises at any time, without notice, and thus to determine the tenancy created by the attornment. The efficiency of such a clause as enabling the mortgagee, whatever may be the meaning of the clause of attornment, to enter at any time without notice has been decisively established (*y*). And it would seem that the same result may be obtained even without it, by expressly stating the tenancy to be one at will; and that distraining for rent in such a case is not a recognition of a yearly tenancy (*z*).

Mortgagor's covenant for title.

Then come the mortgagor's covenants for title. These are—that he has good right to convey; that if the principal sum lent and interest are not paid on the day fixed for that purpose, the mortgagee may enter upon, and peaceably enjoy, the mortgaged property, without disturbance from any person, and that free from all incumbrances; and for further assurance, which is to be made, until foreclosure or sale, at the cost of the mortgagor, and after that time, at the cost of any person requiring the same. These covenants closely resemble the covenants for title in ordinary purchase deeds, but differ from them in being absolute instead of qualified. They are not of much use to the mortgagee, as such, since by bringing an action upon them he could only recover his mortgage money

---

(*y*) *Doe* v. *Olley*, 12 A. & E. 481; *Doe* v. *Tom*, 4 Q. B. 615; *Morton* v. *Woods*, L. R. 3 Q. B. 658.
(*z*) *Doe* v. *Cox*, 11 Q. B. 122.

OF MORTGAGE DEEDS.

which he could more easily obtain by suing on the covenant for its payment (a). If, however, he forecloses or sells the property, he, or a purchaser from him, has the advantage of absolute, instead of qualified, covenants for title; and it has, therefore, been pointed out (b), that there is no good reason why such covenants should not be as restricted in mortgage, as in purchase, deeds; but the general custom to the contrary would seem to be too firmly established to be easily altered.

The deed is concluded by the ordinary Testatum, and should have the mortgagor's receipt for the money paid to him indorsed on the back. It may be mentioned that the mortgagee appears to be bound at all times to produce this deed to the mortgagor (c), although he cannot be compelled to show any other of the title-deeds of the mortgaged property which have been handed over to him to any person whatever (d), unless he is first paid his principal, interest, and costs.

Testatum.

A few words are necessary, in concluding this subject, as to the statutory provisions relating to mortgage deeds. These are to be found in what is generally known as Lord Cranworth's Act, the 23 & 24 Vict., c. 145, ss. 11—23, both inclusive, and have reference to selling, insuring, and appointing a receiver over, mortgaged property. The act, which, it is to be remembered, applies only to mortgage deeds executed after the date of its commencement (e), recites in the preamble that it is expedient that certain powers and provisions, which it is now usual to insert in mort-

Statutory provisions as to mortgage deeds. Lord Cranworth's Act.

(a) 2 Dav. Con. 659.
(b) 1 Dav. Con. 115.
(c) *Patch* v. *Ward*, L. R. 1 Eq. 436; but see *Dell* v. *Chamberlain*, 3 Cham. Rep. 429.
(d) *Chichester* v. *Donegall*, L. R. 5 Ch. 497.
(e) 28th August, 1860.

gages should be made incident to the estates of the persons interested, so as to dispense with the necessity of inserting the same in terms in every instrument. It then says, in effect, that every mortgage deed of any hereditaments of any tenure, or of any interest therein, shall be deemed to contain certain powers, subject to anything in it which may contradict, vary, or limit them (*f*). These are powers (*g*) for the mortgagee, his executors, administrators, or assigns, at any time after the expiration of one year from the time when the principal money lent shall have become payable according to the terms of the deed, or after any interest on such principal money shall have been in arrear for six months, or after any omission to pay any premium on any insurance which by the terms of the deed ought to be paid by the person entitled to the property subject to the mortgage; (1) to sell the property as he, or they, may think fit, and give receipts for the purchase-money (*h*); (2) to insure the property, and add the money so paid for premiums to the principal debt; and (3) to appoint a receiver who is to collect the rents and profits of the property, and whose powers and duties are defined by the act (*i*). The power of sale is not to be exercised unless six months' previous notice has been given to the person, or one of the persons, entitled to the property subject to the charge, or left upon some conspicuous part of the property (*j*): but protection is given to a *bonâ fide* purchaser both as to the notice required by the act (*k*), and as to the application of the purchase-money (*l*). The vendor has to apply the purchase-money in the usual way (*m*), and is empowered to vest in the purchaser the property sold

(*f*) S. 32.
(*g*) S. 11.
(*h*) S. 12.
(*i*) SS. 18—23.
(*j*) S. 13.
(*k*) Ibid.
(*l*) S. 12.
(*m*) S. 14.

for all the estate and interest of the mortgagor therein (*n*), and to demand the assignment of any outstanding legal estate which may be held in trust for the mortgagor (*o*).

So far as regards the appointment of a receiver, this act has answered its purpose, since its provisions on this subject are much the same as those formerly inserted by conveyancers. But, unfortunately, the powers and provisions relating to insurance and to sale contained in the act are not "those which it is usual to insert in mortgages," and not being so complete or so advantageous to the mortgagee as those which they seek to supplant, are not generally adopted. The clauses relating to insurance are merely incomplete, since they do not oblige the mortgagor to insure, and therefore only supply the place of the ordinary proviso which enables the mortgagee to insure on the mortgagor's failing to do so. But those conferring a power of sale are open to more serious objection. For the power of sale given by the act can only be exercised after twelve months from the time fixed for payment of the principal, or when the interest is six months in arrear, and requires six months' notice to be given in every case; whereas, as we saw, the power of sale ordinarily inserted in mortgage deeds can be exercised, if necessary, after six months from the time fixed for payment of the principal, or when the interest is three months in arrear, and requires no notice to be given in the latter case. The requirements, too, in the act, as to notice, oblige the mortgagee, if he cannot leave the notice upon some conspicuous part of the premises (a process, of course, impossible where they consist of incorporeal hereditaments), first to ascertain the precise person entitled to the equity of redemption,

Objections to relying entirely on this Act.

(*n*) S. 15.
(*o*) S. 16.

and then to serve him with the notice, although he may be at the other end of the world; thus encountering an amount of risk and difficulty sufficient to deter most people from lending money on mortgage at all. From these considerations it would seem that the better plan is to insert, as heretofore, in a mortgage deed, the ordinary clauses relating to the insurance and sale of the mortgaged property, and at the same time to obtain all the benefits derivable from the act, by abstaining from any express declaration that it is not to apply to the deed in question.

CHAPTER VI.

OF SETTLEMENTS.

HITHERTO we have dealt only with instruments having for their object the alienation of land, either absolutely or temporarily: we turn now to those which seek to prevent its alienation, so far as the law will allow. This object may be attained either by wills operating as settlements, or by settlements proper. These latter again are divided into family settlements, whereby provision is often made for several branches of one family, and marriage settlements, the benefits of which are primarily conferred only on two persons about to marry, and their issue. Settlements made by wills, or by means of family settlements, may, evidently, take almost innumerable forms, varying with the wishes of each individual settlor, and cannot be properly dealt with in an elementary work like the present. We will, therefore, confine our attention to the less complex subject of marriage settlements of land, selecting as a specimen the most ordinary form, that, namely, which is usually known as a "strict" settlement.

The object of such an instrument is to give the settled property to the eldest son of the marriage in tail male, subject to its providing a life income for the husband and wife and portions for the younger children: the deed containing, in addition to the clauses apt for these purposes, some which provide for various contingencies, and others whereby the wishes of the settlors can be more effectually carried out. A "strict" settlement.

The settlement, after the usual formal introduction, Parties.

states the parties to the deed. These consist of the intended husband and wife respectively, and of four different sets of trustees, whose functions we shall presently consider. Supposing that, as is more ordinarily the case, the estate to be settled belongs to the future husband, the first thing to be done is to keep it in his absolute possession until the marriage is solemnized. This can be accomplished by means of a shifting use, the application of which to this purpose is one of the many advantages derived from the passing of the Statute of Uses (a). With this object the deed proceeds to witness that, in consideration of the intended marriage, and in pursuance of a previous agreement, the husband, with the consent of the wife, conveys the property in fee simple to the first set of trustees, whom we may distinguish as the "general trustees." This he does by assuring it to them by means of the same words of conveyance and clauses as fare usually contained in purchase deeds; the habendum being to the use of himself (the husband) in fee simple until the solemnization of the marriage; thus effecting no change in his ownership until that event takes place.

Term to secure wife's income during the coverture. The settlement then goes on to declare the uses which are to take effect after the marriage. Of these, the first is limited for a term of ninety-nine years, without impeachment of waste, to the second set of trustees. The declaration of the trusts of the term are, however, postponed, for the sake of convenience, to a subsequent part of the settlement, and we will, therefore, only mention now, that its object is to give a separate income to the wife during the coverture.

Husband's life estate. Subject to this term, the next use is to the husband for life, without impeachment of waste: thus giving him the legal estate in the property during his life-

---

(a) 27 Hen. VIII. c. 10.

time, with as much power over it as is consistent with its due preservation for the remainder-men. He is, therefore, in a position to deal with the estate much as a prudent man would deal with one of which he was absolute owner; being allowed to open mines and quarries, pull down buildings when necessary, and cut ordinary timber for his own benefit (b); whilst, on the other hand, he cannot commit that which is known as "equitable waste," such as pulling down the mansion-house of the estate (c), or cutting ornamental timber (d).

Provisions having been thus made for the wife during the coverture, and for the husband during his life, the next thing is to give an income to the wife in case she survives her husband. With this object the next limitation is to the use that if the wife survive the husband she may receive during her lifetime, in lieu of all dower and freebench, a specified yearly sum for her jointure, such sum being charged upon the property, and payable quarterly: the first payment being made at the expiration of three calendar months from the death of her husband. *Wife's jointure.*

The word "jointure" is synonymous with "provision" (e); the old way of securing a jointure was to set aside, for that purpose, the rents and profits of some particular estate belonging to the husband; and in most great families the same estate was commonly so settled from generation to generation. Hence the frequent occurrence, on large estates, of a house distinguished as "the jointure house." *Meaning of jointure.*

A jointure made in conformity with the require-

(b) *Bowles' Case*, 11 Rep. 79ᵇ; and Tu. L. C. 27.
(c) *Vane* v. *Barnard*, 2 Ver. 738.
(d) *Downshire* v. *Sandys*, 6 Ves. 107; see also the notes to *Garth* v. *Cotton*, 1 L. C. 697.
(e) See *Hervey* v. *Hervey*, 1 Atk. 560, 562.

ments of the Statute of Uses (*f*) will bar the widow's right to dower; but it is better to state in the deed that the provision thus made for her is to be in lieu of all dower and freebench, because the intention to bar dower must, in order to operate under the statute, be either expressed (*g*) or clearly implied (*h*); and because, although jointure may act as a bar to freebench in equity (*i*), the statute itself does not extend to copyholds.

The form of limitation mentioned above gives the widow a legal rent charge, in the same way as if it had been granted to her directly. For the Statute of Uses (*j*) enacts that where any person shall be seised of any lands, to the use and intent that some other person shall have any annual rent thereout, the person that has such use shall be deemed to be in possession and seisin of the same rent, of and in such like estate as they had in the use of it; and as if a sufficient grant of such rent had been made to them by the persons seised of the use. The grant of a rent charge did not formerly give a power to distrain for rent due, unless this power were expressly conferred on the grantee; but this has been altered by an act (*k*), which gives the legal owner of a rent charge the same power of distress as is possessed by a lessor (*l*). Nevertheless, it is still customary to insert in the settlement an express power for the wife to distrain upon the premises, in case any part of the rent charge is in arrear for twenty-one days after the time of payment thereof, and to apply the distress in payment of such arrears and of the costs thus incurred by her.

Power of distress.

4 Geo. II., c. 28.

(*f*) 27 Hen. VIII. c. 10, s. 6.
(*g*) Co. Litt. 36^b.
(*h*) Co. Litt. 36^b, note B.; *Vizard* v. *Longdale*, cited 3 Atk. 8; *Garthshore* v. *Chalie*, 10 Ves. 1; *Hamilton* v. *Jackson*, 2 Jo. & L. 295.
(*i*) *Walker* v. *Walker*, 1 Ves. 54.
(*j*) 27 Hen. VIII. c. 10, ss. 4, 5.
(*k*) 4 Geo. II. c. 28, s. 5.
(*l*) *Dodds* v. *Thompson*, L. R. 1 C. P. 133.

In addition to this power of distress, the wife has Power of entry.
given to her a power, if any part of the rent is in
arrear for forty days from the time of payment, and
whether the rent has been legally demanded or not (*m*),
to enter upon the land, and hold it without impeachment of waste, and take the rents and profits of it,
until she has been, by this means, paid all sums due
on account of the rent charge, including those which
have become due during the time of her possession.
This power does not go with the grant of a rent
charge, unless expressly conferred, nor will its deficiency be supplied by the courts, even though the
power of distress be an insufficient remedy, except in
cases where some fraud is being practised (*n*). It
should, therefore, always be inserted, and will, coupled
with the power of distress, give the widow an efficient
means of enforcing payment of her jointure, if it
should be necessary for her so to do. An additional Term for secur-
security is, moreover, provided for her, by limiting a ing jointure.
further term to the third set of trustees: the statement of the trusts of the term being put off to
another part of the deed.

The husband and wife being thus provided for, the Term for secur-
claims of the younger children have next to be at- ing portions.
tended to; for this purpose a third long term is
limited to the fourth set of trustees, the trusts of this
term also being set out later.

Then comes the limitation which gives the property,
subject to the various estates and charges which we
have enumerated, to the first and other sons successively of the marriage in tail male, with a final limitation in default of such issue, to the husband, his heirs
and assigns, for ever.

The settlement next proceeds to declare the trusts Trusts of the

---

(*m*) See L. R. 9 C. P. 49 note (2).
(*n*) *Champernoon* v. *Gubbs*, 2 Ver. 382.

of the several terms previously created. The first is that which secures the wife's income during the coverture. The trustees of it are empowered, during the joint lives of the husband and wife, out of the rents and profits of the property, or by the sale of timber or minerals, or by mortgage of the property for the whole or part of the term, to raise an annual sum, of a specified amount, and to pay the income so obtained, quarterly, to the wife for her separate use, by way of pin money, but without her having any power to deprive herself of it by way of anticipation, and, subject thereto and to the payment of their expenses, to allow the rents to be received by the husband or his assigns. Pin money is, as its name applies, money applicable to the personal expenses of the wife, for her dress and for her pocket-money (*o*). It is not like other money given to her for her separate use, for she cannot claim more than one year's arrears of it (*p*); nor can she even claim this if her husband, instead of paying her pin money, has furnished her, at his own expense, with clothes and other necessaries (*q*). Neither have her personal representatives any claim for arrears of it, under any circumstances, after her death (*r*); it being given in order that she may be enabled to dress so as to keep up the dignity of her husband, and she being under an implied obligation to spend it for that purpose, and not accumulate it (*s*).

Next in order comes the declaration of the trusts of the second term which further secures the wife's jointure. These are, that, if any part of her jointure shall remain unpaid for sixty days after any of the

---

(*o*) See on this subject Sug. Law of Property, 165ª.
(*p*) *Townshend* v. *Windham*, 2 Ves. 1, 6.
(*q*) *Thomas* v. *Bennet*, 2 P. W. 339; *Fowler* v. *Fowler*, 3 P. W. 353, 354.
(*r*) *Howard* v. *Digby*, 2 Cl. & F. 634.
(*s*) *Jodrell* v. *Jodrell*, 9 Beav. 45.

days appointed for payment of it, the trustees shall, out of the rents and profits of the estate, or by the sale of its timber or minerals, or by mortgage or demise of it, during the whole, or part, of the term, raise a sufficient sum to pay the wife all that is then due to her on account of jointure, and pay also all expenses attending the execution of their trust. The powers already given to the wife for the same purpose are so extensive that this term may be safely omitted, especially as her right to enter and take the "rents and profits" will include a power of charging the corpus of the estate with all arrears of jointure, if an intention that it shall have that effect can be collected from the various parts of the instrument (*t*).

Trusts of the third term. To secure portions.

The third term is created in order to secure the portions for the younger children. With this object, it is limited to the fourth set of trustees upon trust, after the death of the husband, by mortgage of the whole or any part of the premises, or by the sale of the minerals or timber thereof, or out of the rents and profits of the estate, to raise a sum of money for the portions of such of the children (other than the first or only son, or than any son who before attaining the age of twenty-one shall become entitled to the property as first tenant in tail male) who, being a son, shall attain the age of twenty-one years, or who, being a daughter, shall attain that age or marry under that age. The sum thus raiseable generally varies in amount, being gradually increased according to the number of such children, but with a fixed *maximum* which is not to be exceeded in any case. The result of this form of trust is, that no child can acquire a vested interest in a portion except on attaining majority, or (in the case of a daughter) on attaining majority or being married: and this plan seems pre-

---

(*t*) *Re Tyndall,* 7 Ir. Ch. Rep. 181.

ferable to making the number of portions raiseable depend merely on the number of children born, for under such an arrangement a younger child who happens to be the only survivor amongst several others may get a portion very much larger than that raiseable under the settlement in the event of there being only one younger child born (*u*). It will be observed that the firstborn son of the marriage is entirely precluded from having any share of the portions fund, but that a younger son who happens to succeed to the estate will not necessarily lose his portion, except when he has become tenant in tail before attaining his majority. But if it is intended that he should be so favoured, there must be an express statement to that effect in the settlement, for the general rule is, that, unless there is a strong presumption to the contrary, as where the words used are the same as, or similar (*v*) to, those employed here, a son who at any time before his father's death becomes entitled to the estate (*w*) shall not have any share in the portions fund, even though an appointment of part of it has been already made in his favour (*x*).

Who may take a portion.

The clause next goes on to point out when, and how, children enabled to take a portion shall be entitled to payment of it. It says, therefore, that if there is only one such child, and he, or she, shall not attain twenty-one, or (if a daughter) attain that age, or marry, until after the death of the husband, such child's portion is to be paid at once, at majority or marriage as the case may be. If, however, the husband is alive at that time, then the payment of the portion is to be postponed until after his death. When there are two or more younger children in a position to take por-

Time for payment of portions.

(*u*) See *Hemming* v. *Griffith*, 2 Giff. 403; *Knapp* v. *Knapp*, L. R. 12 Eq. 238.
(*v*) *Windham* v. *Graham*, 1 Russ. 331, 344.
(*w*) *Ellison* v. *Thomas*, 1 De G. J. & S. 18, 27; *Collingwood* v. *Stanhope*, L. R. 4 H. L. 43.
(*x*) *Chadwick* v. *Doleman*, 2 Ver. 527; *Teynham* v. *Webb*, 2 Ves. 197.

tions, the portions fund is either to be divided amongst such of them, and in such shares, and at such age or time (not earlier than their majority, if sons, or majority or marriage, if daughters), and in such manner, as their father shall appoint; or, in default of his making any appointment, each such child is to receive an equal portion, which is to be paid under conditions similar to those already stated in the event of there being one such younger child only. It follows that, subject to any appointment by the husband, the time for payment of the portions does not arise until after his death, although the time when they become vested may be earlier in date. It is necessary to state in the settlement that the payment of the portions is not to take place during the husband's lifetime, for the general rule is that if there is nothing more than a limitation to the parent for life, with a term to raise portions at the age of twenty-one or at marriage, the portions must be raised as soon as they are vested, by mortgaging the term created for raising them, although the term itself has not yet come into existence (y). In order to prevent any one child from getting an undue share of the portions fund, there comes next a "hotch-pot" clause, providing that no child in whose favour any appointment has been made shall have any share in the unappointed part of the fund, unless he throws into it the share which he has received already, and thus, as it is technically expressed, brings the latter into hotch-pot.

Hotchpot Clause.

Of the other trusts of this term, the first provides for the case of the husband's dying before all the younger children have become entitled to their respective portions. It is to the effect that the trustees shall, after the death of the husband, raise a sum out of the rents and profits of the estate, and apply it for

Trust for maintenance.

(y) *Greaves* v. *Mattison*, T. Jones, 201; *Codrington* v. *Foley*, 6 Ves. 364, 379; *Smyth* v. *Foley*, 3 Yo. & C. (Ex.) 142; *Massy* v. *Lloyd*, 10 H. L. C. 248.

the maintenance of such children. The amount of this sum is not to exceed, in the case of any child, what the interest of his or her expectant portion would come to at £4 *per cent.* per annum, and, subject to this condition, is to be fixed in accordance with the husband's appointment, if he has made any; if he has made none, its amount is left to the discretion of the trustees. This is followed by a clause which empowers the trustees, after the death of the husband, or on his written request during his lifetime, to raise a sum not exceeding one-half of the then-expectant or presumptive portion of any son, (daughters not being usually included) and apply the same for the advancement of the son, as the husband, during his lifetime, or the trustees, after his death, shall think fit. The advancement clause ends with a proviso that no advancement shall be deemed to be part of the amount raiseable for portions, unless the child in whose favour it is made becomes afterwards competent to take a portion; or unless the sums advanced would, together with those still to be raised, exceed the *maximum* amount allowed by the settlement for portions, in which latter case the sums still raiseable are to be reduced by the amount of such excess. The object of this proviso is to throw any advance made to a son who afterwards dies before attaining twenty-one upon the estate, and not upon the portions fund, so long as the limit fixed for portions is not in any case exceeded: thus enlarging, to a certain extent, the scope of the clause which charges the estate only in favour of children who may attain their majority, or marry, as the case may be.

Advancement Clause.

A further proviso permits the husband to require the trustees to raise, in his lifetime, the whole or part of the portion in which any child has acquired a vested interest: but the trustees may in such a case, at their option, instead of actually raising any portion, mortgage a sufficient part of the property to the child by way of security for it, and pay him, or her, interest on

Proviso for raising portions during the husband's lifetime.

such mortgage, so as to provide an income in lieu of that which would otherwise be derived from the severed portion. They may also, if they think fit, include in such mortgage the husband's life interest in the estate, in which case he will be bound to keep down the interest on the sum so raised; receiving the surplus income only, after providing for all the expenses incurred by the trustees in the execution of their trust.

The next clause provides for the death of the husband during the minority of any tenant in tail. Should this happen, the general trustees are empowered to enter upon the property, with ample powers of management, to receive the rents and profits of it, and, after paying all expenses, keeping down any interest chargeable on the estate, and providing a suitable sum for the maintenance or benefit of the minor, to invest the surplus, and accumulate all sums invested until the minor either dies under age or attains his majority. On the happening of the first-named event they are to invest the fund thus formed in the purchase of new land to be settled to the same uses, whilst if the child lives they are to hand over the fund to him on his attaining his full age. *Powers of the general trustees.*

After these clauses come others, whereby the husband is enabled to appoint, in favour of any future wife, a rent charge of a specified amount by way of jointure, with or without its being in bar of dower, and to confer upon her the usual powers of distress and entry in order to enforce its payment. He is also empowered, in the event of his marrying again, to charge the estate with portions for the children of any such marriage, under conditions similar to those already stated in the case of his having younger children by his first marriage; and with the usual maintenance and advancement clauses. *Power to husband to jointure future wife.* *And to charge portions for children of future marriage.*

Powers of Leasing.

These are followed by powers given to the husband during his life, and, after his death, to the general trustees during the minority of any tenant in tail of the settled estate, to appoint the property, by way of occupation or agricultural leases, for terms not exceeding twenty-one years, each lease to take effect in possession, or within six months after the date of the appointment, and to reserve the best rent obtainable. The husband, or the trustees, may also make building leases for ninety-nine years, under conditions similar to the above, but with a proviso enabling a nominal rent to be accepted for the first five years of every such term. They are also empowered to make mining leases for sixty years; if any part of the property consists of copyholds, to grant licences to the tenants to build on, or let, any part of their lands; and to enfranchise copyholds. These powers should, generally speaking, be inserted in every strict settlement of real estate, being far larger, and more easily carried out, than those given by the Settled Estates Act (z), or by the Settled Estates Amendment Act (a). But the particular nature of each estate will, of course, be taken into consideration before inserting any, or either, of them.

Powers of sale and exchange.

The powers of leasing are sometimes supplemented by others, given to the same persons, and authorizing them to sell, or exchange, any part of the settled estate, with or without the minerals belonging to it, and to settle the lands bought or taken in exchange to such uses as are already subsisting by virtue of the settlement. They have also power to renew leases, and to raise, by mortgage of the property, any money which may be required for any of the above purposes. They may, moreover, if they think fit, apply the money produced by any sale, exchange, or enfranchise-

---

(z) 19 & 20 Vict. c. 120.
(a) 21 & 22 Vict. c. 77.

ment of copyholds, in paying off incumbrances on the estate, instead of in the purchase of land; investing surplus moneys in the public funds until an opportunity arises for their use. But this series of clauses is, in most cases, rendered unnecessary by the provisions relating to settlements which are contained in Lord Cranworth's Act (b), and may ordinarily be safely dispensed with if the deed contains a declaration that the general trustees shall have a power of sale and exchange over all the settled estate, exercisable during the life of the husband, with his consent in writing, and after his death, and during the minority of any tenant in tail, at their own discretion.

Finally, the deed concludes with covenants for title, entered into by the husband with the general trustees. These are the same as in ordinary purchase deeds made by way of appointment, and are for the benefit, not only of the trustees and others claiming under the settlement, but also for that of any person purchasing any part of the estate under the powers of sale contained in the settlement.

<small>Covenants for title.</small>

(b) 23 & 24 Vict. c. 145, ss. 1—10, both inclusive.

CHAPTER VII.

OF WILLS.

THE subject for our consideration in this, our final chapter, is a Will of Land. In the previous chapters of this part of our work we have gone through the clauses of a simple form of the particular instrument under discussion, in order to show how the practical work of conveyancing is made to comply with the rules of law. But when we come to the subject of wills it is not possible for us to adopt our usual plan. All the other instruments to which our attention has hitherto been directed, however much they may vary in detail, have some parts common to the class to which they belong. The covenants for title in a purchase deed, the lessee's covenants in a lease, the limitations in a strict settlement, vary only within moderate limits; and the observation, therefore, of any one set of them serves as a guide in framing all other assurances of a like nature. But with wills the case is different. There may be, and often is, a similarity between one will and another. The conveyancer may be able to lay his finger upon this and that form, and say that they ought, respectively, to be made use of in certain cases, but he cannot say of any of the important parts of any one will that they are matters of common form.

We will, therefore, after a few words on the qualifications necessary to enable a person to make a will, arrange our subject under three headings, namely:—

Proposed division of the subject. 1st, the execution and attestation of wills; 2nd, the estates and interests in land which can be disposed of by will; and, 3rd, the revocation of wills; the first and third of these divisions applying to all wills equally.

The principal rules which govern the making of wills at the present day are to be found in the 7 Wm. IV., and 1 Vict., c. 26 (generally known as the Wills Act), which applies to all wills made in England and Wales, or Ireland, since the 31st of December 1837. The act first says that it shall be lawful for every person (*a*) to make a will, and subsequently excepts two classes from this general rule. These are, persons under the age of twenty-one years (*b*), and married women, except in so far as they might have made a will before the passing of the act (*c*). To the incapacity of an infant to make a will of real property (an exception to his general incapacity being made, by another section (*d*) of the act, with regard to a will of personalty by a soldier or sailor who is an infant (*e*)) we may add that of persons who cannot make a will on account of natural or temporal incapacity, such as idiots, lunatics, those who from old age or other causes have outlived their understanding, or who are subject to undue influence, and of persons who are disabled by statute (*f*) on account of their being sentenced to death, or undergoing penal servitude, for any crime. *[margin: The Wills Act. Who may make a will. Infants may not make a will of real property. Exception as to personal property.]*

Married women, it will be noticed, are under the same disability as before the act (*g*). By an old statute relating to wills (*h*), repealed by the present Wills Act (*i*), it was enacted (*j*) that no will made of *[margin: Wills of married women.]*

(*a*) S. 3.
(*b*) S. 7.
(*c*) S. 8.
(*d*) S. 11.
(*e*) *Re McMurdo*, L. R. 1 P. & M. 540.
(*f*) 33 & 34 Vict. c. 23.
(*g*) See *Thomas* v. *Jones*, 2 J. & H. 475, 483.
(*h*) 34 & 35 Hen. VIII. c. 5.
(*i*) 1 Vict. 26, s. 2.
(*j*) S. 14.

any lands, manors, or other hereditaments, by any married woman, should be effectual. A married woman is, therefore, unable to make a will of freeholds or copyholds, not settled to her separate use, except in execution of a power of appointment; which must, moreover, in the case of copyholds, have been created by a surrender in her favour (*k*). But if the power exists, it is no objection to her exercise of it that she has thereby a dominion over land, and is not merely an agent carrying out the wishes of the person who created the power (*l*). She may dispose by will of her equitable estate or interest in any land which has been settled to her separate use (*m*), or to which she has become entitled for her separate use under the provisions of the Divorce Acts (*n*), or of the Married Women's Property Act (*o*); since in respect of these she is considered a *feme sole*, the statute of Henry the Eighth being held not to apply to land settled to a married woman's separate use, inasmuch as this form of property did not exist at the time when the statute was passed. She may also dispose by will of leaseholds, although not held to her separate use, provided her husband gives his consent to her doing so by some specified will (*p*), does not die during the coverture, (for this operates as a revocation of his assent (*q*)) and, if he survives her, either expressly repeats his assent (*r*), or does not revoke it before her will is proved (*s*).

Execution and attestation of wills.

We next come to the execution and attestation of wills. Before the passing of the Wills Act, a will of

---

(*k*) *Doe* v. *Bartle*, 5 B. & Ald. 492, Sug. Wills, 9.
(*l*) Sug. Pow. 153.
(*m*) *Taylor* v. *Meads*, 13 W. R. 394.
(*n*) 20 & 21 Vict. c. 85, ss. 21, 25; 21 & 22 Vict. c. 108; *re Elliott*, L. R. 2 P. & M. 274.
(*o*) 33 & 34 Vict. c. 93.
(*p*) *R.* v. *Bettesworth*, Str. 891.
(*q*) *Noble* v. *Willock*, L. R. 8 Ch. 778.
(*r*) *Maas* v. *Sheffield*, 1 Rob. 364.
(*s*) 1 Wms. Exors, 54.

personal estate might, under certain circumstances, be made by parol, and if in writing did not require any attestation. A will of real estate, on the other hand, was invalid unless attested by three witnesses. The present act has established a uniform rule for the execution of every kind of will. It enacts that no will (a term which includes a codicil to a will) shall be valid unless it shall be in writing and executed in the manner thereinafter mentioned; (that is to say) it shall be signed at the foot or end thereof, by the testator, or by some other person in his presence and by his direction; and such signature shall be made or acknowledged by the testator in the presence of two, or more, witnesses, present at the same time; and such witnesses shall attest and shall subscribe the will in the presence of the testator, but no form of attestation shall be necessary. It is further enacted (t) that no appointment made by will, in exercise of any power, shall be valid, unless the same be executed in the manner required by the act for the execution of wills: and that every will so executed shall, so far as regards the execution and attestation thereof, be a valid execution of a power of appointment by will, notwithstanding it shall have been expressly required that a will made in exercise of such power should be executed with some additional or other form of execution or solemnity.

The writing of a will need not, necessarily, be in ink: pencil writing will be sufficient, although objectionable both on account of its liability to obliteration, and because where a will is partly in ink and partly in pencil the words in pencil may be rejected if the will is sensible without them (u). The will may consist also, in part, of a printed form filled up in writing, or may even be in numbers and letters (v)

<small>Will need not, necessarily, be in ink.</small>

(t) S. 10.
(u) Re Adams, L. R. 2 P. & M. 367.
(v) East v. Twyford, 4 H. L. C. 517.

explained by a key, but the first-mentioned form of will may give rise to difficulties in probate (*w*), whilst the disadvantages of the second are obvious.

If the will is in writing nothing inserted in it by the testator before its execution can be altered after his death. In a recent case (*x*), the residuary clause of a will was in the following terms :—" the trustees to stand possessed of all the residue of my real estate in trust, &c." It was proved, conclusively, that the testator had intended to include his personal estate in this clause, and the Court of Probate was asked to carry out his wishes by striking out the word " real," but the judge (Sir J. Hannen) refused to do so, holding that, in the absence of fraud or mistake made without the knowledge of the testator, the court has no jurisdiction to correct any error which may have crept into a will. With respect to changes made in a will after its execution the case is different, for the act, says (*y*) that no obliteration, interlineation, or other alteration, made in any will after the execution thereof shall be valid or have any effect, except so far as the words or effect of the will before such alteration shall not be apparent, unless such alteration shall be executed and attested in the same manner as a will. But it is provided that such alteration shall be duly executed if the signature of the testator and the subscription of the witnesses be made in the margin of the will near such alteration, or near a memorandum referring to such alteration, and written in some part of the will. If, therefore, there is an unattested alteration in a will, and the will is intelligible without such alteration, the latter will be struck out of the will unless it can be proved to have been made before the will was executed. It has been said that there is no presumption of law that an alteration

---

(*w*) See 2 Rob. 115ª; *Re Dilkes*, W. N. (1874) 76.
(*x*) *Harter* v. *Harter*, L. R. 3 P. & M. 11.
(*y*) S. 21.

was made at any particular time, but that the *onus* of proving that it was made before execution lies, generally speaking, upon the person who would derive advantage from it (z). In a more recent case (a), however, a distinction was made between interlineations and any other alterations; it being held that the court is not precluded, by the absence of direct evidence, from considering the nature of an interlineation and the internal evidence, if any, furnished by the document itself; but may admit the interlineation to probate, although there is no evidence that it was made before the will (b). However, it is always better to attest every alteration in a will, although it may have been made before the will was executed; since, unless the signature (c), or the initials (d), of the testator, and of the witnesses, are placed in the margin near the alteration, or unless there is some attested memorandum referring to the alteration, the Court of Probate will require evidence that it was made before the execution of the will.

The next point to be noticed is, that the will must be signed at the foot or end thereof. Non-compliance with this apparently simple direction formerly made many wills invalid (e), and consequently there was passed the Wills Act Amendment Act (f), which applies to every will which had not, prior to the 17th of June, 1852, been pronounced to be defectively executed. This act provides (g) that a will shall be valid if the testator's signature shall be so placed at, or after, or following, or under, or beside, or opposite to, the end of the will, that it shall be apparent on

Signature.
Position of the signatures.
Wills Act Amendment Act.

(z) Per V.-C. *Wood*, *Williams* v. *Ashton*, 1 J. & H. 115, 118.
(a) *Re Cadge*, L. R. 1 P. & M. 543.
(b) And see *Re Hindmarch*, L. R. 1 P. & M. 307.
(c) *Re Wingrove*, 15 Jur. 91.
(d) *Re Hinds*, 16 Jur. 1161.
(e) See the cases collected in Deane on Wills, pp. 75, *et seq.*
(f) 15 & 16 Vict. c. 24.
(g) S. 1.

the face of the will that the testator intended to give effect by such his signature to the writing signed as his will: and that no such will shall be affected by the circumstance that a blank space shall intervene between the concluding word of the will and the signature; or by the circumstance that the signature shall be placed amongst the words of the testimonium clause, or of the clause of attestation; or shall follow, or be after, or under, or beside, the names, or one of the names, of the subscribing witnesses; or by the circumstance that the signature shall be on a side, or page, or other portion of the paper or papers containing the will, whereon no clause, or paragraph, or disposing part, of the will shall be written above the signature; or by the circumstance that there shall appear to be sufficient space on, or at, the bottom of, the preceding side, or page, or other portion of the same paper on which the will is written, to contain the signature. Under this act, a will has been held to be well executed where the testator's signature and the attestation of the witnesses were alone written across a side of a sheet of paper of which two other sheets were filled up by the words of the will (*h*); and where they were written alone on one of several sheets of paper, although there was room for them at the end of the previous sheet (*i*).

Signature by the testator.

The will may be signed either by the testator or by some other person in his presence and by his direction; but such signature must be made or acknowledged by him in the presence of two or more witnesses, present at the same time. If the testator cannot write, or is too ill to write, he may either make his mark (*j*), or direct his signature to be made for

Signature on behalf of the testator.

(*h*) *Re Wright*, 4 Sw. & Tr. 35; *Re Coombs*, L. R. 1 P. & M. 302; *Re Jones*, 13 W. R. 414; *Re Archer*, L. R. 2 P. & M. 252.
(*i*) *Re Williams*, L. R. 1 P. & M. 4; *Hunt* v. *Hunt*, L. R. 1 P. & M. 209; see also *Re Ainsworth*, L. R. 2 P. & M. 151; *Re Arthur*, L. R. 2 P. & M. 273; *Re Wotton*, L. R. 3 P. & M. 159.
(*j*) See 1 Jar. Wills, 104.

him. This may be done by one of the attesting witnesses (k); and it will be a good execution if the witness signs his own name, stating in the will that he does so on behalf of the testator, in his presence, and by his direction (l). But it is essential that the testator should know, and approve of, the contents of the will at the time of its execution (m).

Both the witnesses must be present when the will is signed or when it is acknowledged (n); but no particular form of acknowledgment is necessary, nor need the testator say in so many words that the signature to the will is his (o); and very slight acts on his part will be held to amount to an acknowledgment of his signature (p). Although the act requires the signature to be made in the presence of two witnesses, it does not make it requisite that they should actually see the testator write. It is sufficient if they see him in the act of writing what is presumably his signature (q); or even if they are in such a position that they may, if they please, see him in the act of writing (r). But it is essential that there should be a possibility of the witnesses seeing the testator write (s), and that his signature should be made or acknowledged before those of the witnesses are affixed to the will (t). Similar rules apply to the signature of the witnesses, for a witness may sign by means of a mark, which will be a good signature although a wrong surname is written opposite to it, if it is clear that the will was

Acknowledgment by the testator.

Presence of the witnesses.

Signature by witnesses.

(k) Re Bailey, 1 Curt. 914; Smith v. Harris, 1 Rob. 262.
(l) Re Clark, 2 Curt. 329.
(m) Hastilow v. Stobie, L. R. 1 P. & M. 64; see Cleare v. Cleare, L. R. 1 P. & M. 655; Atter v. Atkinson, L. R. 1 P. & M. 665.
(n) Re Ayling, 1 Curt. 913; Re Mansfield, 1 No. Cas. 362.
(o) Keigwin v. Keigwin, 3 Curt. 607, 611.
(p) See Re Warden, 2 Curt. 334; Gaze v. Gaze, 3 Curt. 451; Beckett v. Howe, L. R. 2 P. & M. 1; Morritt v. Douglas, L. R. 3 P. & M. 1.
(q) Smith v. Smith, L. R. 1 P. & M. 143.
(r) Newton v. Clarke, 2 Curt. 320; and see Casson v. Dade, 1 Bro. C. C. 98.
(s) Re Colman, 3 Curt. 118.
(t) Re Olding, 2 Curt. 865; Re Byrd, 3 Curt. 117.

otherwise properly attested (*u*); and a witness may make a mark even though he can write (*v*). His signature, also, must be made so that the testator can see him write (*w*), but it is not necessary that one witness should sign in the presence of the other.

<small>Attestation of the will.</small>
The witnesses must not only subscribe the will: they must also attest it. Now to "attest" a will means to put one's name to it as bearing witness to the fact of its having been signed by the testator. A signature, therefore, appended without the intention of attesting the will does not constitute the person signing a witness. Where, for instance (*x*), a will was signed at the end of the first page by the testator and by one other person as a witness, and at the top of the next page there was a memorandum referring to the testator's property, followed by the signatures of three other persons, it was held that these last had not signed as witnesses, and that the will was, therefore, invalid. But the fact of a witness signing also in another capacity, as where a man witnessed a will, and wrote opposite his name "executor," instead of "witness," will make no difference (*y*).

<small>Form of attestation.</small>
The act says that no form of attestation shall be necessary; and it has been decided that this obviates the necessity of any form at all, not merely of any particular form (*z*). But it is always desirable to add an attestation clause to a will, since, without it, probate will not be granted unless evidence is given, if

---

(*u*) *Re Ashmore*, 3 Curt. 756.
(*v*) *Re Amiss*, 2 Rob. 116.
(*w*) *Newton* v. *Clarke*, 2 Curt. 320; *Norton* v. *Bazett*, 3 Jur. (N. S.) 1084.
(*x*) *Re Wilson*, L. R. 1 P. & M. 269.
(*y*) *Griffiths* v. *Griffiths*, L. R. 2 P. & M. 300.
(*z*) *Re Thomas*, 7 W. R. 270; *Bryan* v. *White*, 2 Rob. 315.

obtainable, that all the formalities required by the Act have been complied with (a).

In selecting witnesses for a will, care should be taken not to include any persons on whom any benefit is conferred by the will. For the Wills Act enacts (b) that if any person shall attest the execution of any will to whom, or to whose wife or husband, any beneficial devise, estate, interest, or appointment, of, or affecting, any real or personal estate (other than charges and directions for the payment of debts) shall be thereby given, such devise, estate, interest, or appointment, shall, so far as regards such person, or the wife or husband of such person, be utterly null and void: but such person may still be admitted as a witness to prove the execution of the will. It is also provided that a creditor who attests a will providing for payment of debts (c), or a person attesting a will of which he is appointed executor (d), shall be competent to prove its due execution. The fact of a witness being a trustee does not invalidate a gift made to him on trust, even when the particular way in which the gift is to be applied for the benefit of the object designated is left to his discretion (e). If a will has been inadvertently attested by two persons, one of whom takes some benefit under it, it is not necessary to make a new will: for a codicil witnessed by two indifferent persons, and confirming the will, makes the gift valid (f). When a will has been signed by the testator and attested by two witnesses, and afterwards a third person adds his name, the Court of Probate will not, without cogent evidence, come to the conclusion that that third person signed as a witness, and will there-

Selection of witnesses.

(a) *Re Diaper*, 3 N. R. 215.
(b) S. 15.
(c) S. 16.
(d) S. 17.
(e) *Cresswell* v. *Cresswell*, L. R. 6 Eq. 69.
(f) *Anderson* v. *Anderson*, L. R. 13 Eq. 381.

fore incline to strike out his name (*g*). But if he has signed as a witness, although after the other two, and the will has been admitted to probate with the names of the three as witnesses, he cannot take any benefit under the will (*h*). It would seem to be clear that the subsequent marriage of a witness to a person entitled to the benefit of a devise or bequest would not invalidate that devise or bequest (*i*).

By what law a will is governed.

It may be mentioned here that a will of land is governed by the law of the country in which the land is, not by that of the country where the testator is domiciled. Hence, a will devising real estate situate in England must, in order to be effectual, be made in compliance with the law of this country; if written in a foreign language must contain expressions which would, if translated into English, comprise and destine the land in question (*j*); and must not contain any provisions contrary to the law of this country respecting real estate. And although a will of personal property is, generally speaking, governed by the law of the testator's domicile, an exception obtains to this rule in the case of leaseholds; since leasehold property is part of the territory of the country in which it is situate, and a will disposing of leasehold estate in England must, therefore, conform to the requirements of the English law (*k*).

What property may be disposed of by will.

The Wills Act also defines the estates and interests in land which may be disposed of by will. These include (*l*) all real, and all personal, estate to which a testator is entitled, either at law or in equity, at the time of his death; and which, if not so devised,

---

(*g*) *Re Sharman*, L. R. 1 P. & M. 661, 663; *Re Pursglove*, 26 L. T. (N. S.) 405.
(*h*) *Cozens* v. *Crout*, W. N. (1873) 144.
(*i*) Hay. & Jar. Wills, 29a.
(*j*) 1 Jar. Wills, 1.
(*k*) *Freke* v. *Carbery*, L. R. 16 Eq. 461.
(*l*) S. 3.

bequeathed, or disposed of, would descend upon the heir at law or customary heir of him, or, if he became entitled by descent, of his ancestor, or upon his executor or administrator. It is also provided that the power of disposition by will shall extend to copyholds, notwithstanding that the testator may not have surrendered the same to the use of his will, or notwithstanding that, being entitled as heir, devisee, or otherwise, to be admitted thereto, he shall not have been admitted thereto, or that the same, but for the act, could not have been disposed of by will. The power of disposition extends, moreover, to estates *pur autre vie ;* to all contingent, and future, interests in real or personal estate; and to rights of entry, including also such of the above-mentioned estates and interests as the testator may be entitled to at the time of his death, notwithstanding that he may have become entitled to the same subsequently to the execution of his will.

The act, therefore, enables a testator to devise and bequeath all estates in land except those held in joint-tenancy, or for an estate tail, or an estate in *quasi* tail (that is, an estate *pur autre vie* given to a man and the heirs of his body), all of which do not descend to a man's heir, executor, or administrator, and consequently do not come within the act. This statute enlarges the former rule of law, by enabling a man to devise all freeholds to which he is entitled at the time of his death, although he may have acquired them subsequently to the date of his will; whereas, previously to the act, a devise of freeholds could only include those belonging to the testator at the time when he made his will; even though the will purported to devise all lands which he should have at the time of his decease (*m*). The act also increases the power of devising copyholds, for a former act (*n*) Change made by the act. Freeholds.

Copyholds.

(*m*) *Bunter* v. *Coke,* Salk. 237.
(*n*) 55 Geo. III. c. 192.

which partially did away with the necessity of a surrender of such estates before they could be disposed of by will, did not extend to the case of a devise by a devisee (*o*), or by a purchaser (*p*), who had not himself been admitted. But, notwithstanding the expression, "which if not so devised would devolve upon his customary heir," the act has not done away with the old rule that a devise of copyholds conveys no title to the property until the devisee has been admitted: and the legal estate therefore, in such a case, still remains in the heir of the copyholder until the admittance of the devisee (*q*).

Wills to be construed as speaking immediately before the death of the testator.

In order still more effectually to guard against a testator's dying intestate as to any part of his property, the act provides that, unless a contrary intention shall appear by the will, every will shall be construed, with reference to the real and personal estate comprised in it, to speak and take effect as if it had been executed immediately before the death of the testator (*r*);

Residuary devise to include lapsed and void devises.

that a residuary devise shall include estates comprised in lapsed and void devises (*s*); that

General devise to include copyholds and leaseholds.

a general devise of the land of the testator, or of his land in any place, or in the occupation of any person, or otherwise described in a general manner, shall include copyhold and leasehold as well as freehold land (*t*);

General power of appointment executed by general devise.

that a general devise or bequest of the real or personal estate of a testator shall include any real or personal estate which he may have power to appoint in any manner he may think proper (*u*); and

Devise without words of limitation to pass fee simple.

that a devise of real estate without any words of limitation shall pass the whole of the estate or interest

---

(*o*) *Doe* v. *Laws*, 7 A. & E. 195.
(*p*) *Matthew* v. *Osborne*, 13 C. B. 919.
(*q*) *Glass* v. *Richardson*, 2 De G. M. & G. 658; *Garland* v. *Mead*, L. R. 6 Q. B. 441, 449.
(*r*) S. 24.
(*s*) S. 25.
(*t*) S. 26.
(*u*) S. 27.

therein which the testator had power to dispose of by will (v).

In considering whether property passes under any of these sections, the test is whether the will shows a contrary intention when read as if it had been executed immediately before the death of the testator. If it does, of course, the sections do not apply. Thus, in a case (w) where a testator devised "all the real estate of which I am now seised," bequeathed his personal estate without any such form of expression, and, in other parts of his will, when using the word "now," clearly alluded to the time when he was making his will: it was held that this devise did not pass real estate which he had acquired after the date of his will. Again, where (x) a testator devised "all my freehold estate which I purchased from B," it was held that this particular description of the property as "freehold" prevented the will from passing a piece of leasehold land, mixed up with the freehold, which the testator had purchased from B, and the freehold reversion in which he had acquired after the date of his will. But the mere use of words which might refer to the date of the will does not prevent after acquired property from passing, when such words are only used in order to describe property included in the will. Hence, a devise of "the house in which A now resides" has been held to pass a garden purchased by the testator after the date of his will, and attached to the house (y). On the same principle, a devise of "real estate of which I am seised," has been held to include after acquired property (z): and a gift of "my mansion called C. Court," to comprehend lands afterwards

How contrary intention is shown.

(v) S. 28.
(w) *Cole* v. *Scott*, 1 M. & G. 518.
(x) *Emuss* v. *Smith*, 2 De G. & Sm. 722.
(y) *Re Midland Ry. Co.* 34 Beav. 525.
(z) *Lilford* v. *Ponyskeck*, 30 Beav. 300; *Langdale* v. *Briggs*, 8 De G. M. & G. 391; and see *Goodlad* v. *Burnett*, 1 K. & J. 341, 348; *O'Toole* v. *Browne*, 3 E. & B. 572.

purchased, and thrown into the grounds attached to the mansion (a). As regards a contrary intention appearing in the will by a reference to the tenure of property, it was decided, in one case, that the mere description of land as "leasehold" did not prevent the whole of the testator's estate in it from passing by the will, although he had, after the date of his will, purchased the fee simple reversion in the land and thus put an end to its character of leasehold (b).

Change made by the act in case of leaseholds.

In making a general devise of the testator's land include leaseholds, unless the will shows a contrary intention, the act has made another change in the law of wills. Formerly a devise of "lands," or of "lands and tenements," did not include leaseholds unless, at the time of the devise, the testator had no freehold lands which could pass by his will (c). Since the passing of the act, the presumption is that such words do include leaseholds (d). And not only the word "lands", standing alone, but even additional expressions, which would seem to apply particularly to freeholds, may now, when used in a general devise, pass the testator's leaseholds. Thus, in one case (e), leaseholds were held to be included in a devise of "all my lands and all other my real estate;" and the same effect was given to a devise of "all my freehold land," when the leasehold property, sought to be included in this devise, was one of which the testator had the reversion in fee simple at the expiration of three years from the end of his term (f).

As to land of

A general devise of real and leasehold estate would,

(a) *Castle* v. *Fox*, L. R. 11 Eq. 542.
(b) *Cox* v. *Bennett*, L. R. 6 Eq. 422; and see *Miles* v. *Miles*, L. R. 1 Eq. 462.
(c) *Rose* v. *Bartlett*, Cro. Car. 292; *Thompson* v. *Lawley*, 2 Bos. & Pul. 303.
(d) See *Prescott* v. *Barker*, L. R. 9 Ch. 174, 186.
(e) *Wilson* v. *Eden*, 21 L. J. (Q. B.) 385.
(f) *Matthews* v. *Matthews*, L. R. 4 Eq. 278; and see *Gully* v. *Davis*, L. R. 10 Eq. 562.

before the Wills Act, have passed all land of which *which testator* the testator was, at the time of making his will, seised *is trustee or mortgagee.* or possessed as a trustee, or as a mortgagee (*g*), unless there was something in the will inconsistent with such a construction (*h*). The rule still holds good, and is extended by the operation of the statute to all estates or interests so vested in the testator at the time of his death. And a general devise of land, with a direction to pay the testator's just debts out of his residuary estate (*i*), or even a general devise of real estate to a married woman for her separate use (*j*), will not prevent mortgage or trust property from being included in the devise. But a mortgaged estate has been held not to pass by a general devise of property of which one moiety was given to A and B as tenants in common, and the other moiety to C to hold upon trusts declared by the will (*k*).

The old rule as to the exercise of a power of appointment by will was that a general devise did not operate as an execution of a power, unless the testator showed by his will an intention that it should have that effect; the presumption, therefore, being against the power having been so exercised (*l*). Now, under the act, the rule is the other way, and the presumption is that the testator did intend to exercise his power; and any one maintaining the negative must establish his case by showing that a contrary intention appears by the will. In a case (*m*) where there were two settled estates, A and B, the testator, who had no power of appointment over estate A, but a general power of

As to powers of appointment.

(*g*) *Wall* v. *Bright*, 1 J. & W. 494; *Braybroke* v. *Inskip*, 8 Ves. 417, and, with notes, Tu. L. C. 876.
(*h*) *Ex parte Marshall*, 9 Sim. 555; *Rackham* v. *Siddall*, 16 Sim. 297.
(*i*) *Re Stevens*, L. R. 6 Eq. 597.
(*j*) *Lewis* v. *Matthews*, L. R. 2 Eq. 177.
(*k*) *Martin* v. *Laverton*, L. R. 9 Eq. 663.
(*l*) *Clere's Case*, 6 Rep. 17^b; *Andrews* v. *Emmott*, 2 Bro. C. C. 297, 300.
(*m*) *Lake* v. *Currie*, 2 De G. M. & G. 636, 650.

appointment over estate B, with a remainder, in default of his appointment, in favour of other persons, in his will referred to, and confirmed, the deeds by which both estates had been settled, and then made a general devise of his real estate; it was held that the reference to the settlement applied only to estate A, and that the general devise operated as an execution of his power to appoint estate B, especially as he had no real estate besides A and B (*n*). It is to be noticed that the act only speaks of a power to appoint in any manner the testator may think proper. A general devise cannot, therefore, operate under the act as the execution of a power to appoint in such manner as the testator may think fit, but amongst specified objects only (*o*).

As to devise without words of limitation. Before the passing of the Wills Act, a devise, by an owner in fee simple, of "lands," or even of "lands, tenements, and hereditaments" (*p*), conferred on the devisee an estate for life only, unless the devise contained words of limitation. Now, as we have seen, such a devise will, in the absence of apparent intention to the contrary, give an estate in fee simple. It has been decided (*q*) that a general devise to A, followed by an expression of intention that B should enjoy all the testator's estate, which was to be absolutely at his free will and disposal, gave A an estate for life only; the fact that the gift to B could have no effect if A took an estate in fee simple, being considered a sufficient indication of an intention that the latter should not take more than a limited estate. But a gift to a person of "the house she now lives in," although without words of limitation, was held not to show any intention to give her a life estate only; she therefore took the whole of the testator's estate in the property

---

(*n*) And see *Hutchins* v. *Osborne*, 3 De G. & J. 142.
(*o*) *Clove* v. *Awdry*, 12 Beav. 604.
(*p*) *Hopewell* v. *Ackland*, Salk. 238.
(*q*) *Gravenor* v. *Watkins*, L. R. 6 C. P. 500.

in question (r). And an intention to confer a limited estate will not be implied from the fact that proper words of inheritance have been employed in conferring estates in fee in other parts of the will (s).

The next branch of our subject is the Revocation of Wills. Before the passing of the Wills Act, a man's will was presumed to be revoked by the fact of his subsequently marrying and having a child born to him. But this presumption might be rebutted by the surrounding circumstances, as when the testator had, by such a will, provided for a future wife or for future children (t); or where the children of the marriage could obtain no benefit by the revocation of the will (u). A woman's will was absolutely revoked by her marriage alone, although she might happen to survive her husband. The law relating to the will of a woman remains almost unaltered, but a change is made by the present act with regard to the will of a man. For it is enacted (v) that every will made by a man, or woman, shall be revoked by his, or her, marriage, except a will made in exercise of a power of appointment, when the real or personal estate thereby appointed would not, in default of such appointment, pass to his, or her, heir, customary heir, executor, or administrator, or the person entitled as his, or her, next of kin under the Statute of Distributions (w). A will is revoked under this section if made on the same day as, but previously to, the testator's marriage; even though it appears from the terms of the will that he did not intend it to take effect until after the marriage (x). Nothing, therefore, can keep alive any will made before marriage, except the fact that its revocation cannot give

Revocation of a Will. By marriage.

(r) *Reay* v. *Rawlinson*, 29 Beav. 88.
(s) *Wisden* v. *Wisden*, 2 Sm. & Giff. 396, 405.
(t) Sug. Wills, 58.
(u) See *Sheath* v. *York*, 1 Ves. & B. 390.
(v) S. 18.
(w) See Sug. Wills, 55—60.
(x) *Ottway* v. *Sadleir*, 33 L. T. 46.

the property in question to any of the persons mentioned in the act. And the rule is not affected by the circumstance that the revocation of the will cannot possibly benefit any future husband, wife, or children. Thus (*y*), a woman who had a general power of appointment over freeholds, with remainder, in default of such appointment, to her heirs and assigns, exercised the power in favour of her two children by a first marriage, and then married again: it was held that her will was revoked, although the only result of this was to give the whole property to one of those two children, as her heir-at-law, without conferring any benefit on the children of the second marriage. But a will made in exercise of a power of appointment is not revoked when its revocation could only give the appointed property to the same persons as would take under the settlement in default of appointment, although they would take in that case as next of kin of the deceased (*z*).

By presumption of intention.

The act goes on to say that no will shall be revoked by any presumption of an intention to that effect, founded on an alteration in the circumstances of the testator (*a*); and that no conveyance, or other act, made or done subsequently to the execution of a will of, or relating to, any real or personal estate therein comprised (except any act declared by the statute to amount to a revocation), shall prevent the operation of the will with respect to such estate or interest in such real or personal estate as the testator shall have power to dispose of by will at the time of his death (*b*). This enactment puts an end to the former unsatisfactory rule that a devise should not take effect unless the estate to which the testator was entitled when he made his will remained unaltered until the time of his

---

(*y*) *Vaughan* v. *Vanderstegen*, 2 Drew. 165, 168.
(*z*) *Re Fenwick*, L. R. 1 P. & M. 319; *Re McVicar*, L. R. 1 P. & M. 671; *Re Worthington*, 20 W. R. 260.
(*a*) S. 19.
(*b*) S. 23.

death. The result of this rule was that a fine or recovery, made expressly in order to give effect to a will, operated, instead, as a revocation of it; and, in like manner, that a devise of an estate was revoked if the testator mortgaged it after making his will, even though it was re-conveyed to him during his lifetime. The act does not, however, apply to cases where the thing meant to be given is altogether gone. If, for instance, a man by his will gives an estate in land, and afterwards sells that estate, the devisee has no claim to the purchase-money, even though the purchase is not completed until after the testator's death (c). But if the contract is not carried out, the devisee is, of course, unaffected by it, and it would seem that a devise of an estate stated in the will to be already contracted to be sold would give the devisee the purchase-money of the estate (d).

With regard to revocation by other means, the act provides (e) that no will or codicil, or any part thereof, shall be revoked otherwise than as aforesaid; or by another will or codicil executed in the manner required by the act; or by some writing declaring an intention to revoke the same, and executed in the manner in which a will is required by the act to be executed; or by the burning, tearing, or otherwise destroying the same by the testator, or by some person in his presence and by his direction, with the intention of revoking the same. It will be noticed that a subsequent will, or codicil, need not be expressly stated to be a revocation of a former will. If, therefore, there are two properly executed wills, making different dispositions of the same property, the former of them will be revoked, so far as concerns that property, by the mere making of the latter (f). But if the first of two such

<small>Other modes of revocation.</small>

<small>By will or codicil.</small>

(c) *Farrar* v. *Winterton*, 5 Beav. 1; and see *Moor* v. *Raisbeck*, 12 Sim. 123.
(d) Sug V. & P. 191.
(e) S. 20.
(f) *Henfrey* v. *Henfrey*, 2 Curt. 468.

wills disposes of property which does not pass under the second, then the first is not revoked, so far as that disposition is concerned, by the fact that the second will begins with the words "this is my will" (g), or even with the words "this is my last will" (h). Similarly, a codicil to a will confirms such parts of it as it does not revoke (i). • If, however, the second will, or the codicil, expressly revokes all former wills, no previous will can, in general, be admitted to probate, even though it may be referred to by the subsequent revoking will (j), or though such revoking will cannot be found (k). But if the clause of revocation in the second will can be clearly proved to have been introduced by mistake, without the knowledge of the testator, probate will be granted of the will without the clause (l).

By writing executed like a will.

A will may also be revoked by a writing not in any way dealing with the testator's property, provided it be executed like a will and declare an intention to make a revocation. Consequently in a recent case, where a testator in a letter, signed by him in the presence of two witnesses, directed his brother to obtain his will from a third person and burn it without reading it; this was held to be a writing declaring an intention to revoke the will, which was consequently pronounced invalid (m).

By destruction of the will.

The other ways in which a will can be revoked are the burning, tearing, or otherwise destroying it, by the testator, or by some person in his presence and by his direction, with the intention of revoking the

---

(g) *Stoddart* v. *Grant*, 19 L. T. 305.
(h) *Freeman* v. *Freeman*, 5 De G. M. & G. 704; *Lemage* v. *Goodban*, L. R. 1 P. & M. 57; *Re Petchell*, L. R. 3 P. & M. 153.
(i) *Re Howard*, L. R. 1 P. & M. 636.
(j) *Re Sinclair*, 3 Curt. 746.
(k) *Wood* v. *Wood*, L. R. 1 P. & M. 309.
(l) *Re Oswald*, W. N. (1874) 52.
(m) *Re Durance*, L. R. 2 P. & M. 406.

same. Before the Wills Act any part of a will cancelled by a testator became thereby revoked, but cancellation does not now revoke a will unless it is afterwards re-executed (*n*); for the words "otherwise destroying" only include acts of a nature similar to those just before enumerated. This rule must often have disappointed the intention of testators who had imagined that they had sufficiently revoked the whole, or part, of their wills. For instance, a will was held valid in one case (*o*), notwithstanding that the whole body of the will was struck through with a pen, the name of the testator crossed out, and the attestation clause and the names of the witnesses likewise run through with a pen; and in another case (*p*), notwithstanding that the testator had written the word "cancelled" across his signature, and added a written declaration that the will in question was revoked, and that he intended to make another will. But, of course, a complete obliteration of any part of an executed will revokes that part; such a case coming within those provisions of the act (*q*) which give effect to alterations so made that words contained in the will before such alteration are no longer apparent (*r*).

Cancellation not a revocation.

As to the various modes of destroying a will which are mentioned in the act, it is to be observed that there are two things requisite to make them effectual revocations. The first is that the destruction, if not the act of the testator himself, must be in his presence as well as by his direction. Thus, where a person who had made a will afterwards expressed a wish, in the presence of two witnesses, to revoke it, and desired them to take it into another room and burn it, which was done, it was held that this did not amount to a revocation, and probate was accordingly granted of a

How destruction must be accomplished.

(*n*) Sug. Wills, 47.
(*o*) *Stephens* v. *Taprell*, 2 Curt. 458.
(*p*) *Re Brewster*, 6 Jur. N. S. 56.
(*q*) S. 21.
(*r*) *Townley* v. *Watson*, 3 Curt. 761.

draft copy of the will (s). And, of course, the destruction of a will after the testator's death, although done in pursuance of his written request to that effect, is inoperative as a revocation of the will (t). The other point is, that the destruction of a will must, in order to be effectual, be accompanied by an intention on the part of the testator to revoke it. Hence, where a testator tore up his will under a mistaken impression that it was invalid, and then on second thoughts collected and preserved the pieces, it was held that there had been no revocation of the will (u). And a similar decision was given in a case (v) where a testator, having torn up his will when suffering from delirium tremens, on his recovery expressed his regret for what he had done, and preserved the pieces, which had been collected at the time (w). It must also be clearly proved that the intention to revoke existed at the time of the will being destroyed; subsequent declarations by a testatrix that she had destroyed her will with the intention of revoking it having been held insufficient (x). The Court of Probate will, however, presume that a will which has remained in the custody of a deceased person until the time of his death, and the non-existence of which at his death is clearly proved (y), has been revoked by him during his lifetime (z).

It may be added here that whereas, formerly, a codicil was revoked whenever the will to which it belonged was revoked, a codicil now takes effect, independently of a will, unless revoked by one of the modes indicated by the Wills Act. Thus, in one case, a

(s) *Re Dadds*, 29 L. T. 99; and see *Rooke* v. *Langdon*, 2 L. T. 495.
(t) *Stockwell* v. *Ritherdon*, 1 Rob. 661, 667.
(u) *Giles* v. *Warren*, L. R. 2 P. & M. 401.
(v) *Brunt* v. *Brunt*, L. R. 3 P. & M. 37.
(w) And see *Powell* v. *Powell*, L. R. 1 P. & M. 209, 212.
(x) *Re Weston*, L. R. 1 P. & M. 633.
(y) *Finch* v. *Finch*, L. R. 1 P. & M. 371.
(z) *Eckersley* v. *Platt*, L. R. 1 P. & M. 281, 284.

testator had executed a will and a codicil to that will, and after his death, his will, not being forthcoming, was presumed to have been revoked: it was held, nevertheless, that the codicil, having been duly executed, must be admitted to probate as a will (a). Neither does a codicil revoking a will necessarily revoke a prior codicil to that will. Where a testator had made a will and two codicils, and afterwards by a third codicil revoked the will except as to a bequest stated to have been made by it, the two codicils remained valid notwithstanding the revocation of the will (b).

The sections of the Act which have been referred to on the subject of revocation are completed by another (c), which provides that no will or codicil, or any part thereof, which shall be in any manner revoked, shall be revived otherwise than by the re-execution thereof; or by a codicil executed in the manner required by the Act, and showing an intention to revive the same; and that when any will or codicil which shall be partly revoked and afterwards wholly revoked shall be revived, such revival shall not extend to so much thereof as shall have been revoked before the revocation of the whole thereof, unless an intention to the contrary shall be shown. Under the old law, if a man made a will, and then a second will revoking the first, and afterwards revoked the second, it would be presumed, if the first remained in existence, that the testator had intended to give it the same effect as if it had never been revoked (d). The Wills Act requires either that the will should be re-executed, which is tantamount to making a new will in the same terms, or, where the will is revived by a codicil,

Revival of a will.

Former rule as to revival.

Change made by the act.

(a) *Black* v. *Jobling*, L. R. 1 P. & M. 685; and see *Re Savage*, L. R. 2 P. & M. 78; *Re Turner*, L. R. 2 P. & M. 403.
(b) *Furrer* v. *St Catharine's College Cambridge*, L. R. 16 Eq. 19.
(c) S. 22.
(d) *Goodwright* v. *Glazier*, Burr. 2512.

that the intention of which it speaks should appear on the face of the codicil, either by express words referring to the will as revoked and importing an intention to revive it, or by a disposition of the testator's property inconsistent with any other intention, or by some other expressions conveying with reasonable certainty the existence of the intention in question. In other words, it was designed by the statute to do away with the revival of wills by mere implication (*e*). Therefore the fact that a codicil refers to a previous revoked will is not a sufficient indication of an intention to revive that will, when it appears from the codicil itself that the reference to the will was made by mistake (*f*). Neither can a codicil revive a will which has been destroyed with the intention of revoking it, for in that case the will has ceased to exist both in law and in fact, and a will or codicil cannot incorporate, or revive, a document which has no existence at the time when the will or codicil is executed (*g*).

Lastly, it may be mentioned that, just as a codicil is not necessarily revoked by the revocation of the will to which it belongs, so, on the other hand, it is not, after having been revoked, revived by another codicil reviving the will, unless the subsequent codicil shows an intention to revive the revoked codicil as well as the will (*h*).

(*e*) *Re Steele*, L. R. 1 P. & M. 575, 578.
(*f*) *Re Wilson*, L. R. 1 P. & M. 582.
(*g*) *Hale* v. *Tokelove*, 2 Rob. 318; *Newton* v. *Newton*, 5 L. T. (N. S.) 218; *Rogers* v. *Goodenough*, 2 Sw. & Tr. 342, 350.
(*h*) *Re Reynolds*, L. R. 3 P. & M. 35.

INDEX.

ABSTRACT—
Definition of an, 310.
Condition of sale as to sending in requisitions after delivery of the, 325.
Vendor must deliver a perfect, ib.

ACCOUNT—
Between mortgagor and mortgagee, when taken with rests, 254.
Doctrine of equity as to money lent on a joint, 375.

ACCUMULATION—
Of income, restrictions on, 214.

ACKNOWLEDGMENT—
By married woman, to bar an estate tail, 121.
Written, extends time for recovery of land, 142.
Of mortgagee's rights to principal and interest, 249, 250.
Required by Statutes of Limitation, need not be formal, 250.
Of mortgagor's title, by a mortgagee, 255.
Of mortgagor's title, by a trustee who is one of several mortgagees, 257.
Of mortgagee's title, by mortgagor, 261, 263.
Of a will, by the testator, witnesses must be present at the, 407.

ADMINISTRATOR—
Of a lessee, how protected, 65.
Of a tenant for life, must remove fixtures within a reasonable time, 105.
Of a tenant for life, is entitled to emblements, 109.
Of a tenant in tail, right of to remove fixtures, 113.
Of a tenant in tail, is entitled to emblements, 124.

ADMITTANCE—
New tenant of a manor requires, 158.
Surrender and, theory of, ib.
Enactments relating to surrender and, 158—161.
Of tenant of manor, may take place within or without the manor, and without holding any court, 160.
Of new tenant, to be immediately inrolled, ib.
When made, dates back to surrender, 161.
Lord cannot compel, of a purchaser of copyholds, 162.
Of heir of copyholder, may be compulsory, 164.
Fine payable on, to several copyhold tenements, ib.

ADMITTANCE—(*continued.*)
Fine payable on, of more than one tenant, to copyholds, 164.
Fine payable on, of tenant for life and remainder-man to copyholds, *ib.*
Fine payable on, of joint tenants to copyholds, 165.
Fine payable on, of heir or devisee of an unadmitted copyholder, *ib.*

ADVANCEMENT—
Power of, in a marriage settlement, 396.

AGREEMENT—
For sale of any interest in land, must be in writing, 302.
For sale of land, what must be contained in an, *ib.*
For sale, need not be contained in one document, 304.
For sale, parol evidence when admissible to prove terms of an, *ib.*
For sale, when enforced on the ground of part performance, 305.
For sale, signature to an, 306.
Difference between an, and Conditions of Sale, 307.
For a lease, two kinds of, 343.
For a lease, must, as a rule, be in writing, 344.
For a lease, may be enforced on the ground of part performance, *ib.*
Express, for leases not usually desirable, 345.
Stipulations to be inserted in, for leases, *ib.*
For a lease, should be stated to be such, 346.
For a lease, should contain all the covenants to be inserted in the lease, 347.
For a lease, may arise by operation of law, 348.

AIDS—
Definition of, 15.
At first voluntary but afterwards regular incidents of tenure, *ib.*
Abolished, 21.

ALIEN—
May now acquire and hold land like a natural-born British subject, 129.

ALIENATION—
Of land, restrictions formerly imposed on, 23.
Of land, permitted by statute of *Quia Emptores*, 24.
Of land, by will formerly unknown, 27.
Of a term of years, 63—66.
Of an estate for life, 105, 106.
Of an estate in fee simple, 131—138.
Of copyholds, 173—175.
Of equitable estates, 192.
Of a reversion or a remainder, 195.
Of a possibility coupled with an interest, 204.
Of powers, 222.
Of a tenancy in common, 230.

ANCIENT DEMESNE—
What are lands of, 14.
Villein Socage called also tenure by, *ib.*
Probable origin of, *ib.*

APPORTIONMENT—
No, formerly, on death of tenant for life, 107.
Statutes relating to, 107, 108, 109.
Act 1870, applies to all instruments whether coming into operation before, or not until after, its passing, 109.
Of rent on lease made by a tenant in tail, 123.
Of rent reserved by tenant in fee simple, 144.

ASSETS—
Estate pur autre vie in hands of heir chargeable as, by descent, 91.

ASSIGNEE—
Of a reversion, was unable to take advantage of covenants or conditions in a lease on which the reversion was expectant, 60.
Of part of a reversion on a lease, now entitled to the benefit of all conditions contained in the lease, 61.
Of a term, is liable on the covenants of the lease, 63.
Of a term must indemnify his assignor, 64.
Mesne, of a term must indemnify original lessee, *ib.*
Of a term, protected against previous breach of covenant to insure, *ib.*
Of a mortgagee, may consolidate securities, 271.

ASSIGNMENT—
Of a term of years, 63.
Of a lease, must be by deed, 65.
Restriction against, not effectual as against a lessee's trustee in bankruptcy, *ib.*
Of an estate for life, must be by deed, 105.

ASSIGNOR—
Of a lease, must take back lease if disclaimed by lessee's trustee in bankruptcy, 66.

ATTENDANT TERM—
How term became an, 76.
Satisfied term formerly presumed to be an, *ib.*
Satisfied term is not now an, 79.
When term considered an, 80.

ATTESTATION—
A will requires, 408.
Of a will, need not be formal, *ib.*
Of a will, advantages of a formal, *ib.*

ATTORNMENT—
Definition of, 195.
Formerly necessary on transfer of a fee, *ib.*
Transfer of a fee now complete without, *ib.*
By mortgagor, to mortgagee, 381.

AUCTION—
Sale by, conduct of, 310.
Sale by, subject to reserved price must be so stated, *ib.*
Sale by, is within the Statute of Frauds, 312.

BANKRUPT—
  Trustee of, may lease land belonging to, 41.
  Trustee of, may disclaim lease, 66.
BANKRUPTCY—
  Effect of, when bankrupt has an estate in land, 137.
  Effect of, on powers, 225.
BARGAIN AND SALE—
  Conveyance by, before the Statute of Uses, 290.
  Conveyance by, after the Statute of Uses, 292.
BLACKSTONE—
  His canons of descent, 145—153.
BOROUGH ENGLISH—
  Custom of, 14.
BURGAGE TENURE—
  Definition of, 14.

CESSER—
  Proviso for, 76.
CESTUI QUE TRUST—
  Who is a, 33.
  In actual occupation is tenant at will, *ib.*
  Substituted for *cestui que use*, 188.
  Covenants for title to be entered into by a, 343.
CESTUI QUE USE—
  Meaning of term, 188.
CESTUI QUE VIE—
  Definition of, 90.
  Production of, may be ordered, 92.
CHARGE—
  Tenant for life in possession is bound to keep down the interest on, affecting the estate, 97.
  Tenant for life paying off, may keep it alive for his own benefit, 98.
  Tenant in tail is not bound to keep down the interest on, 113.
  Tenant in tail paying off, is presumed to have done so for the benefit of the inheritance, *ib.*
CHATTELS—
  What, are exempted from distress, 51.
  Of a lodger, protected from distress, *ib.*
CHILD—
  En ventre sa mère, considered in existence, 202.
  What, entitled to a portion, under a marriage settlement, 394.
  Time for payment of portion given to a, *ib.*
  Trust in a marriage settlement for maintenance of children, 395.
  Trust in a marriage settlement for advancement of children, 396.
  Proviso in a marriage settlement for raising the expectant portion of a, *ib.*

CITY OF LONDON—
Custom of the, 14.

CODICIL—
Must be executed and attested like a will, 403.
Revocation of a will by a, 419.
Revival of a will by a, 423.
Revival of a, by another codicil, 424.

COMMON—
Different kinds of, 170.
Copyholder's right to, is founded on prescription, ib.
Copyholder's prescription to rights of, must be reasonable, 171.

COMPENSATION—
Conditions of sale as to, 317—320.
Doctrine of the common law as to, on sales, 318.
Doctrine of equity as to, on sales, ib.
Purchaser when bound to fulfil contract and take, ib.
Condition of sale as to, cannot cover wilful mis-statements, 319.
Condition of sale as to, only applies to small errors, 320.

CONDITION—
Stranger to a, could not formerly take advantage of it, 59.
Was held to be indivisible, 60.
Present law as to conditions in leases, 61.

CONDITIONAL—
Fee, meaning of, 26.
Estate tail in a manor is a conditional fee, except under a custom, 156.
Limitations, before the Statute of Uses, 207.

CONDITIONS OF SALE—
Difference between, and an agreement, 307.
General rules for preparation of, 309.
As to conduct of sale by auction, 310.
As to payment of a deposit, 311.
As to valuation of fixtures and timber, 312.
As to title to be shown by a vendor, ib.
As to dower, 315.
As to recitals, 316.
As to expenses of searches, 317.
As to identity of property, ib.
As to compensation, ib.
As to payment of purchase-money, 320.
As to rents and out goings, and payment of interest by the purchaser, 321.
As to title-deeds, 324.
As to objections and requisitions, and rescision of the contract of sale, 325.
As to forfeiture of the purchaser's deposit, 327.

CONSOLIDATING SECURITIES—
Definition of, 270.
Distinction between, and tacking, ib.

CONSOLIDATING SECURITIES—(continued.)
Right of, extends to foreclosure suit, 271.
Assignee of a mortgagee has right of, ib.
Right of, not affected by notice, 272.
Right of, may be exercised against mortgagor's assignee, ib.
No right of, against distinct equities of redemption, 273.
When sub-mortgagee may have right of, 275—278.

CONVICT—
Administrator of, may lease land belonging to, 41.

CO-PARCENARY—
Estate in, 230.
Always arises by operation of law, ib.
Alienation of an estate in, 231.
Partition of estates in, 231—234.

COPYHOLD—
Tenure, origin of, 21.
Tenure, still considered base, ib.
Tenure, cannot be created at the present day, 153.
Estates, incidents of, 161—173.
Land, may be extended under the Judgment Acts, 173.
Land, may be forfeited to the lord, ib.
Land, may be devised without previous surrender, 174.
Land, devise of, on trust for sale, ib.
Land, descent of, 175.
Land, enfranchisement of, ib.
Land, statutes relating to enfranchisement of, 175—182.
Land, form of mortgage of, 366.
Devise of a, does not pass the legal estate to the devisee until admittance, 411.
A general devise, includes devise of a, 412.

COPYHOLDER—
Derivation of the word, 21.
Fine is due to lord, on death of a, 162.
May be liable to a fine on change of lord, and for licence to demise, 165.
Cannot cut timber or dig for minerals, except by custom, 169.
Right of, to common is founded on prescription, 170.
Prescription of, for rights of common must be reasonable, 171.
Alienation of estate of a, 173—175.
Estate of a, may be seized under a judgment, 173.
Estate of a, may be subject to forfeiture, ib.

CORPORATION—
Ecclesiastical, leases by, 42.
Municipal, leases by, 43.
Religious and charitable, restrictions on acquiring land, ib.
Power of a, to hold land, 127.
Charitable, Mortmain Act relating to, ib.
Not charitable, has a limited power of holding land, 129.

CORPOREAL HEREDITAMENTS—
Definition of, 2.

COUNTERPART—
Of a lease, what is the, 346.
Of a lease, expense of preparing, must be borne by the lessor, 347.

COURT BARON—
Incident to every manor, 12.
Object of holding, ib.
Fell into disuse, ib.

COVENANT—
Contained in a lease, formerly put an end to by merger or surrender of the reversion, 49.
Now preserved, notwithstanding merger or surrender of the reversion, ib.
As to fixtures, effect of, 58.
Stranger to a, could not formerly take advantage of it, 59.
Statute of Henry the Eighth relating to covenants in leases, ib.
In a lease, when runs with the land, 62.
In a lease, running with the land, run with the reversion, 63.
To insure, in a lease, relief against forfeiture for breach of, 70.
To stand seised, 290.
In a purchase deed, for right to convey, 338.
In a purchase deed, for quiet enjoyment, 338, 339.
In a purchase deed, for freedom from incumbrances, ib.
In a purchase deed, for further assurance, 339.
Covenants for title, who must enter into, ib.
Covenants on a sale of leaseholds, 341.
What are usual and proper covenants in leases, 347.
In a lease, to pay rent, 356.
In a lease, to pay taxes, 357.
In a lease, to repair, 358, 359.
In a lease, to permit lessor to enter and view the state of repair, 359.
In a lease, to insure, 360.
In a lease, not to use premises for purposes of trade, 360, 361.
In a lease, not to assign or underlet, ib.
In a lease, to deliver up the premises in good repair, 362.
In a lease, lessor's, for quiet enjoyment, 363.
In a mortgage deed, for repayment of sum lent, 368.
In a mortgage deed, for payment of interest, 373.
Mortgagor's covenants, in a mortgage deed, 376.
Covenants for title, in a marriage settlement, 399.

CROWN—
May make ordinary leases for thirty-one years or three lives, 41.
May make repairing leases for fifty years, ib.
Commissioners of Woods and Forests may grant leases of lands belonging to the, ib.
Debts due to the, when a charge on land, 137.
Never enters into covenants for title, 341.

CROWN DEBTS—
Estate tail is liable for, 123.
Present law relating to, 137.

CURTESY—
Estate by, is a legal estate for life, 82.
When husband entitled to estate by, 87.
Cannot be out of an estate for lives, *ib*.
May be barred by instrument conferring the wife's estate, *ib*.
Takes effect out of both legal and equitable estates, *ib*.
None in a manor except by custom, 171.
In manors, birth of issue not always necessary for, 172.
In manors, may be in equitable estates, *ib*.

CUSTOM—
All dealings in manors are regulated by, 155.
Grants in manors must conform to the, 157.
Amount of fine on admittance to a manor depends upon the, 162.
As to amount of fine on admittance must be reasonable, *ib*.
May be a special, compelling admittance of a copyholder's heir, 164.
Amount of steward's fees in a manor regulated by the, 166.
Heriot, origin of, 167.
No curtesy in manors except by, 171.
No freebench in manors except by, 172.

CUSTOMARY COURT—
Establishment of, 20.
All customary tenants bound to attend, *ib*.
Lord's steward judge of, *ib*.
Proceedings at, *ib*.
Lord or steward of a manor may hold, although no tenant be present, 155.

CY PRES—
Doctrine of, 201.
Application of doctrine of, in limitations by will, *ib*.

DE DONIS, STATUTE OF—
Reason for passing, 26.
Enactments of, *ib*.
Remained in force until the year 1473, 114.

DEBTS—
Crown, when a charge on land, 137.
Payment of, out of real estate, 138, 139.

DEED—
Usually accompanied livery of seisin, 11.
What leases must be made by, 46.
Assignment of a term of years must be made by, 65.
Surrender of a term of years when to be made by, 73.
Creation of an estate for life by, 88.
Assignment of an estate for life must be by, 105.
Surrender of an estate for life must be by, *ib*.
Barring an estate must be inrolled, 121.
Containing protector's consent to barring an estate tail must be inrolled, 122.

DEED—(continued.)
　Barring a *quasi* estate tail need not be inrolled, 122.
　Giving land in mortmain requires inrolment, 127.
　Barring an estate tail in copyholds requires inrolment, 157.

DEFEASANCE—
　Deed of, 280.
　Deeds of, have long fallen into disuse, *ib.*

DEMISE—
　Grant of a term of years is called a, 36.
　Words of, in a lease, 353.

DEPOSIT—
　Condition of sale as to payment of a, 311.
　Payment of a, is part payment of the purchase-money, *ib.*
　Condition of sale as to forfeiture of purchaser's, 327.

DESCENT—
　Of a fee simple, 145—152.
　Of copyholds, 175.
　Of equitable estates, 192.

DETERMINATION—
　Of an estate for life by death of the tenant, 106.

DEVISE—
　Of leaseholds must be made in accordance with the law of England, 410.
　Of copyholds does not pass the legal estate to the devisee until admittance, 412.
　Residuary, includes lapsed and void devises, *ib.*
　General, includes copyholds and leaseholds, *ib.*
　Power of appointment may be exercised by a general, *ib.*
　Without words of limitation may pass a fee simple, *ib.*
　General, may include land of which the testator is trustee or mortgagee, 415.

DISTRESS—
　For rent at common law, on what dependent, 50.
　Definition of, *ib.*
　For rent, in pursuance of common law right, waives lessor's right to a forfeiture, 67.
　By lessor under statutory power, 73.
　Power of, to secure a wife's jointure, 390.

DOUBLE VALUE—
　Tenant holding over liable to pay, 72.

DOWER—
　Estate in, is a legal estate for life, 82.
　Definition of estate in, *ib.*
　Former law of, 83.
　Inconvenience of former law of, 84.
　What arrears of, may be claimed, *ib.*
　Act relating to, 85.
　Widow may now have, in equitable as well as in legal estates of a deceased husband, *ib.*

DOWER—*(continued.)*
  Widow's chance of, dependent upon her husband's pleasure, 85.
  Covenant not to bar will be enforced, 86.
  Condition of sale as to, 315.
  Is barred by jointure, 390.

EASEMENT—
  Definition of an, 336, note (*w*).
  Legally belonging to land passes without express words of grant, *ib.*
  Continuous, passes by grant of the parcel to which it belongs, *ib.*
  Discontinuous, does not pass by the ordinary form of General Words, *ib.*

ELEGIT—
  Effect of writ of, under the Statute of Westminster, 132.
  Sheriff may now take all debtor's land under a writ of, 133.

EMBLEMENTS—
  Definition of, 33.
  Tenant at will when entitled to, *ib.*
  Statute relating to, *ib.*
  Executors or administrators of a tenant for life are entitled to, 109.
  Executors or administrators of a tenant in tail are entitled to, 124.

ENFRANCHISEMENT—
  Of copyholds, 175.
  Of copyholds, statutes relating to, 175—183.

EQUITABLE ESTATES—
  Rules relating to, similar to those governing legal estates, 188.
  Creation and transfer of, 189.
  Creation and transfer of, how to be proved, 190.
  Form of words for creating or transferring, 191.
  Incidents of, 192.
  Alienation of, *ib.*
  Descent of, *ib.*

EQUITY OF REDEMPTION—
  Is the result of a mortgage, 239.
  Did not, at one time, exist, *ib.*
  Origin of an, 240.
  Creation of an, *ib.*
  Is an estate in land, *ib.*
  Incidents of an, similar to those of a legal estate, 241.
  Cannot, in general, be excluded, 242.
  Who may have an, 244.
  May be destroyed by mortgagee's possession, 255.
  Mortgagee's possession, to bar, must be adverse, 257.

ESCHEAT—
  Derivation of word, 16, note (*u*).
  When occurred, *ib.*
  Became an incident of villein tenure, 19.

INDEX. 435

ESCUAGE—
   Meaning of term, 18.
   Became universal in time of Henry III., *ib.*
   Tenure by knight-service sometimes called tenure by, *ib.*
   Tenant in socage liable to payment of, *ib.*
   Tenure by, abolished, 21.

ESTATE—
   In land, definition of, 2.
   Reason for use of the term, 12.
   In land is either freehold or less than freehold, 31.
   In a manor, how to be granted, 156.

ESTATE AT WILL—
   Definition of an, 32.
   Must be at the will of both lessor and lessee, *ib.*
   Usually arises by implication of law, *ib.*
   May exist by express agreement, 33.
   Incidents of an, *ib.*
   How put an end to, 34.
   Not favoured by the law, 35.

ESTATE BY SUFFERANCE—
   Definition of an, 32.
   Can only arise by implication of law, *ib.*
   Any recognition of an, converts it into an estate at will, *ib.*

ESTATE FOR LIFE—
   Is an estate of freehold, 81.
   Two kinds of, *ib.*
   Who may create a conventional, *ib.*
   Tenant for years cannot create an, *ib.*
   Mode of creating an, 82.
   Legal estates for life, *ib.*
   Conventional, may be created by deed, 88.
   May be created by will, 89.
   Form of words for creating an, *ib.*
   Incidents of an, 93.
   Assignment of an, must be by deed, 105.
   Surrender of an, must be by deed, 106.
   Will not now be forfeited by tenants' making a feoffment, 106.
   Given to a husband by a marriage-settlement, 388.

ESTATE FOR YEARS—
   Origin of, 28.
   Is less than freehold, 29.
   Is a "term," 35.
   Definition of an, *ib.*
   May be for shorter period than a year, *ib.*
   May arise by implication of law, 45.
   For more than three years cannot be created by parol or by writing, 46.
   Where rent reserved is less than two-thirds of the full improved value of the land, cannot be created by parol or by writing, *ib.*
   Formal words not necessary to create an, *ib.*

ESTATE FOR YEARS—(continued.)
Incidents of an, 48.
Determined by forfeiture, 66.
Determined by effluxion of time, 70.

ESTATE IN FEE SIMPLE—
Is absolute or qualified, 125.
By whom created, *ib*.
Restrictions on holding an, 126.
How may be created, 129.
Incidents of an, 130.
Alienation of an, 131.
May be taken in execution under the Judgment Acts, *ib*.
Descent of an, 145—153.
Act relating to inheritance of an, 145—153.
May be devised without words of limitation, 412.

ESTATE PUR AUTRE VIE—
Meaning of term, 25.
Limitation of an, 90.
Not devisable before the passing of the Statute of Frauds, *ib*.
General occupant of an, *ib*.
Special occupant of an, 91.
General occupancy in an, now abolished, *ib*.
Is chargeable in hands of the heir, as assets by descent, *ib*.
If no special occupant of an, it goes to executor or administrator, *ib*.
In hands of executor or administrator to be applied as personal estate, 92.

ESTATE TAIL
Different kinds of, 110.
Quasi, 111.
Who can create an, *ib*.
May be created by deed or by will, *ib*.
Form of words for creating an, *ib*.
Rule in *Shelley's Case* applicable to an, 112.
Incidents of an, *ib*.
Former ways of barring an, 114.
Right of suffering a recovery was inseparable from an, 116.
How barred, under the Fines and Recoveries Abolition Act, 118—122.
How barred, when tenant is a married woman, 121.
Assurance barring an, must be inrolled, *ib*.
Quasi, how barred, 122.
Alienation of an, *ib*.
May be taken in execution under the Judgment Acts, 123.
Is liable for debts due to the Crown, *ib*.
Determination of an, *ib*.
None, in a manor, except by custom, 156.
In manors how barred, *ib*.

ESTOPPEL—
Lease by, 44.

ESTOVERS—
Definition of, 54.
Tenant for years is entitled to, *ib*.
Tenant for life is entitled to, 93.

EXCHANGE—
: Definition of, 287.
: Of what property could formerly be made, ib.
: Livery of seisin was not necessary for, ib.
: May be made under the Inclosure Acts, 298.
: Powers of, in a marriage-settlement, 398.

EXECUTOR—
: Of a lessee, how protected, 65.
: Of a tenant for life must remove fixtures within a reasonable time, 105.
: Of a tenant for life is entitled to emblements, 109.
: Of a tenant in tail, right of, to remove fixtures, 113.
: Of a tenant in tail is entitled to emblements, 124.
: Of a tenant in fee simple, right of, to remove fixtures, 130.
: Covenant for title to be entered into by an, 340.

EXECUTORY DEVISE—
: Origin of, 209.
: Blackstone's definition of an, 210.
: Of a term, ib.

EXECUTORY INTEREST—
: A consequence of the Statute of Uses, 207.
: Rules for the creation of an, 211—214.
: None, where limitation can take effect as a remainder, 211.
: Time within which an, must take effect, 213.
: Alienation of an, 216.

EXTINGUISHMENT—
: Of powers, 223.

FEALTY—
: Meaning of, 8.
: A principal incident of tenure by Knight Service, ib.
: Mode of taking oath of, ib.
: Was an incident of socage tenure, 10.

FEE—
: Steward of a manor when entitled to a, from tenant, 166.
: Occasions on which steward of a manor is entitled to a, regulated by custom, ib.
: Amount of steward's, in a manor must be reasonable, ib.

FEE TAIL—
: Origin of, 25.
: Originally known as conditional fee, 26.
: Reason of name, 27.
: For long time inalienable, ib.

FEOFFEE—
: Meaning of word, 22.

FEOFFMENT—
: Was accompanied by livery of seisin, 284.
: Was sometimes accompanied by a deed, 285.
: Former tortious operation of a, ib.
: Changes in the law relating to feoffments, 296.
: Has not now a tortious operation, 298.

FEUD OR FEE—
Meaning of, 6.
Ultimate ownership of a, remained with the lord, *ib.*
All fees granted at the Conquest held by Knight Service, 8.
Originally descended only to the tenant's issue, 22.
If tenant had no issue, escheated to the lord, *ib.*
Base, meaning of term, 117.

FEUDAL SYSTEM—
Description of, 6.

FINE—
When payable, 15.
Amount of a, at first arbitrary, 17.
Amount of a, is now regulated by the value of the land, *ib.*
Became an incident of villein tenure, 19.
Levying a, to bar an estate tail, 116.
Less efficacious than a recovery, *ib.*
Levying a, recognized by statute, 117.
And recovery, abolished, 118.
Lord of a' manor is entitled to a, on the admittance of every new tenant, 161.
On admittance, is not due until after admittance, 161.
Amount of, on admittance to copyholds depends upon custom, 162.
Rule as to amount of, on admission of one tenant to a single tenement, 162.
Amount of, on admission to several copyhold tenements, 164.
Amount of, on admittance of more than one tenant to copyholds, *ib.*
Amount of, on admittance of tenant for life and remainder-man to copyholds, *ib.*
Amount of, on admittance of joint tenants to copyholds, 165.
Amount of, on admittance of heir or devisee of an unadmitted copyholder, *ib.*
Copyholder may be liable to pay, on change of lord and for licence to demise, *ib.*

FIXTURES—
Definition of, 55.
Right to remove, gradually established, 56.
Trade, when removable by lessee, *ib.*
Domestic, lessee's right to remove, *ib.*
Agricultural, not formerly removable, 57.
Present law as to removal of agricultural, *ib.*
Right to remove, by lessee should be exercised during his term, 58.
Effect of covenant as to, *ib.*
Rules as to, between tenant for life and remainder-man, 104.
Executors of tenant for life may remove, within a reasonable time, 105.
Tenant in tail may remove any, 113.
Right of executor or administrator of a tenant in tail to remove, *ib.*
Tenant in fee simple may remove any, 130.
Right of executor or administrator of a tenant in fee simple to remove, *ib.*
Condition of sale as to valuation of, 312.
When passed by operative part of a mortgage-deed, 369.
Mortgage of, when requires registration, 370.

FORECLOSURE—
　　Bill by mortgagee for, 258.
　　Bill for, decree under, ib.
　　Final order for, necessary, ib.
　　Extension of time under decree for, ib.
　　Re-opened by mortgagee's receipt of rent, 259.
　　Re-opened by mortgagee's parting with the mortgaged property, and by other acts, 260.
　　Sale instead of, when ordered by the Court of Chancery, ib.
　　Bill for, by sub-mortgagee, 274.
　　Sale instead of, may be ordered at the suit of a sub-mortgagee, 275.
　　Equitable mortgagee may obtain, 280.

FORFEITURE—
　　Meaning of term, 16.
　　When took place, ib.
　　Of a lease, 67.
　　Lessor's right to a, when presumed to have been waived, ib.
　　Lessee may obtain relief against, for non-payment of rent, 68.
　　For breach of covenant to insure when relieved against, 70.
　　Copyholder's land may be subject to, 173.
　　Of a purchaser's deposit, condition of sale as to, 327.

FRANKALMOIGN—
　　Tenure in, 14.
　　Fealty not due from tenant by, 15.
　　Exists at the present day, ib.

FREEBENCH—
　　Definition of, 172.
　　None, except by custom, ib.
　　Husband may defeat, ib.
　　Dower Act does not apply to, ib.

FREEHOLD—
　　What are estates of, 31.
　　Land, form of mortgage of, 365.

FREEHOLDER—
　　Who is a, 29.

GAVELKIND—
　　Custom of, 14.
　　Still prevails in Kent, ib.
　　Characteristics of, ib.

GENERAL WORDS—
　　In a purchase-deed, object of, 335.
　　Clause containing, is of little value, 336.
　　Ordinary form of, does not pass discontinuous easements, ib.
　　Advantage of clause containing, 337.
　　Clause containing, should be worded generally, ib.
　　In a lease, 354.
　　In a mortgage deed, 368.

GRAND SERJEANTY—
    Tenure by, 21.
GRANT—
    Of estates in copyholds must conform to the custom of the manor, 157.
    Fitness of lord or steward to make, in copyholds is immaterial, *ib.*
    What property formerly passed by, 286.
    Lying in, and lying in livery, *ib.*
GUARDIAN—
    Lord was, of infant tenant by Knight Service, 16.
    Lord not, of infant tenant by socage, 19.
    Of infant tenant by socage was his nearest relation not capable of succeeding him by descent, *ib.*
    Of infant tenant by socage was bound to account on the infant's attaining majority, *ib.*
    Of infant tenant by socage could gain no benefit by his marriage, *ib.*
    Of infant, may make leases of infant's land, 40.
    Of infant, may surrender lease belonging to him, 74.

HABENDUM—
    Office of the, in a deed, 337.
    May restrict the words of conveyance, 338.
    In a lease, 354.
    In a mortgage-deed, 368.
HEIR—
    Who is, 1.
    Word "heirs" originally synonymous with issue, 22.
    Extension of meaning of word, *ib.*
    Consent of, at one time necessary for the alienation of a fee, 23.
    Consent of, to alienation become unnecessary, *ib.*

HEREDITAMENTS—
    Derivation of word, 1.
    Are corporeal or incorporeal, *ib.*
    Definition of corporeal, 2.
    Definition of incorporeal, *ib.*

HERIOT—
    In villein tenure corresponded to relief in other tenures, 19.
    Custom, origin of, 167.
    Custom, distinguished from heriot service, *ib.*
    When lord can claim a, 168.

HOLDING OVER—
    By tenant, penalty for, 72.

HOMAGE—
    Characteristic of fees, 8.
    Mode of doing, *ib.*
    Consequences of, to lord and tenant, 9.
    Could be enforced by process of law, *ib.*
    Sometimes done by socage tenant, 10.
    Tenants at customary court called the homage, 20.
    Tenure by, abolished, 21.

INDEX. 441

HUSBAND—
When entitled to an estate by curtesy, 87.
Estate by curtesy of a, may be barred, 88.
Has a right to profits of wife's terms of years during their joint lives, 234.
May dispose of wife's term during his lifetime, *ib.*
Cannot dispose of wife's term, by will, *ib.*
Rights of a, where wife has an estate for life or in fee, 235.
And wife may alienate wife's real and copyhold estate, *ib.*
Rights of a, to wife's property may be excluded, *ib.*
Estate given to a, and his wife is held by entireties, 238.
On sale of wife's real estate must enter into covenants for title, 340.
Estate for life given to the, by a marriage-settlement, 388.
Proviso in a marriage-settlement for raising portions during the lifetime of the, 396.
Power of, in a marriage-settlement, to jointure a future wife, 397.
Power of, in a marriage-settlement, to charge portions for children of a future marriage, *ib.*
Covenants for title by the, in a marriage-settlement, 399.

IMPROVEMENTS—
Statutory powers of tenants for life to make, 98.

INCOME—
Restrictions on accumulation of, 214.
Tax, covenant to deduct from rent is superfluous, 357.
Of wife, term for securing, 388.

INCORPOREAL HEREDITAMENTS—
Definition of, 2.
No general occupancy of an estate *pur autre vie* in, 91.

INFANT—
Guardian of, may make lease of lands belonging to, 40.
Cannot make a will of real property, 401.

INHERITANCE—
Of an estate in fee simple, 145—153.
Act relating to, *ib.*

INROLMENT—
Of assurance barring an estate tail, 121.
Of deed containing protector's consent to barring an estate tail, 122.
Deed barring a *quasi* estate tail does not require, *ib.*
Deed giving land in mortmain requires, 127.
Deed barring an estate tail in copyholds requires, 157.

INSURANCE—
Lessor's having received money for, does not relieve lessee from liability on covenant to repair, 359.
Covenant in a lease to effect an, 360.

INTERESSE TERMINI—
Meaning of term, 47.
Lessee has only an, until entry, *ib.*

INTEREST—
Tenant for life must keep down, of charges on the inheritance, 97.
Tenant in tail is not bound to keep down, of charges on the inheritance, 113.
Equitable mortgagee is entitled to, at £4 *per cent.*, 281.
Condition of sale as to payment of, by a purchaser, 321.
Doctrine of equity as to proviso in a mortgage deed for raising rate of, 373.

JOINT-TENANCY—
Essentials of a, 226.
Creation of a, 227.
Form of words for creating a, *ib.*
Incidents of a, 227—229.
Release of a, 228.
Severance of a, *ib.*
Estate in, survives, *ib.*
Cannot be disposed of by will, 229.
Partition of estates in, 231—234.

JOINT-TENANT—
May separately put an end to his demise, 228.
Cannot dispose of his estate by will, 229.

JOINTURE—
Meaning of word, 389.
Made in conformity with the provisions of the Statute of Uses bars dower, 390.
Power of distress to secure, *ib.*
Power of entry to secure, 391.
Term for securing, 391, 392.

JUDGMENT—
Estate tail may be seized under a, 123.
Former law of, 131.
Present law of, 133—137.
Registration of, 134.
Entered up after the 28th of July, 1864, does not affect land not actually delivered in execution, 136.
Copyholds may be extended in pursuance of a, 173.

KNIGHT SERVICE—
Definition of, 8.
All fees granted at the Conquest held by, *ib.*
Principal incidents of, were originally fealty and homage, *ib.*
Tenure by, turned into common socage tenure, 21.

LAND—
Has acquired the name of real property, 1.
Alienation of, by will not formerly permitted, 27.
Present power of disposition of, 28.
Estates in, 30.
Restrictions on holding, in mortmain, 127.

LAND—(*continued.*)
  Alien may now hold, like a natural-born British subject, 129.
  Subject to judgments, 131—137.
  Subject to crown debts, 137.
  Owner of, may lose it by bankruptcy, 137.
  Estate in, may be lost under the Statutes of Limitation, 139—144.
  Action to recover, must be brought within twenty years from time when right first accrued, 139.
  Will of, is governed by the law of the country where it is situate, 410.
  A general devise may include, of which the testator is a trustee or mortgagee, 415.

LEASE—
  By tenant in tail, 36.
  By tenant for life, 37.
  Of settled estate under order of the Court of Chancery, 38.
  By married woman, 39.
  By guardian of an infant, 40.
  By committee of a lunatic, *ib.*
  By trustee of a bankrupt, 41.
  By administrator of a convict, *ib.*
  By the Crown, *ib.*
  By ecclesiastical corporation, 42.
  By municipal corporation, 43.
  By estoppel, 44.
  For term greater than three years must be by deed, 46.
  Reserving rent greater than two-thirds of the full improved value of the property demised must be by deed, *ib.*
  For alternative period, option of determining is with lessee, 47.
  Tenant under ordinary, must enter on the property, *ib.*
  Must be surrendered by deed, 73.
  By joint-tenants, may be determined by a joint-tenant separately, 228.
  Formerly required no writing or ceremony for its validity, 287.
  Agreement for a, two kinds of, 343.
  Agreement for a, must, as a rule, be in writing, 344.
  Agreement for a, may be enforced on the ground of part performance, *ib.*
  Express agreement for a, not usually desirable, 345.
  Stipulations to be inserted in an agreement for a, *ib.*
  Agreement for a, should be stated to be such, 346.
  Agreement for a, should contain all the covenants to be inserted in the, 347.
  Usual proper covenants in a, *ib.*
  Agreement for a, may arise by operation of law, 348.
  Intended for a term, may create a yearly tenancy, 351.
  Agent to make a, how must be authorized, 352.
  Component parts of a, *ib.*
  Premises in a, *ib.*
  Parties in a, *ib.*
  Recitals in a, are, generally, unnecessary, *ib.*
  Words of demise in a, 353.
  Parcels in a, importance of accuracy in framing, *ib.*
  General words in a, 354.
  Estate clause, not inserted in a, *ib.*
  Habendum in a, *ib.*

Reddendum in a, 355.
Covenant in a, to pay rent, 356.
Covenant in a, to pay taxes, 357.
Covenant in a, to repair, 358, 359.
Covenant in a, to permit lessor to enter and view the state of repair, 359.
Covenant in a, to insure, 360.
Covenant in a, not to use premises for purposes of trade, 360, 361.
Covenant in a, not to assign or underlet, 360, 361.
Covenant in a, to deliver up the premises in good repair, 362.
Proviso for re-entry in a, *ib*.
Lessor's covenant in a, for quiet enjoyment, 363.
Testatum in a, *ib*.
Of land belonging to a married woman must be acknowledged by her, 364.
Statutory provisions as to leases, *ib*.
Powers to, in a marriage settlement, 398.

LEASE AND RELEASE—
Introduction of, 293.
Mode of conveyance by, *ib*.
Conveyance by, no longer employed, 297.

LEASEHOLDS—
Covenants on sale of, 341.
Forms of mortgage of, 365.
Will of, is governed by the law of England, 410.
A general devise includes a devise of, 412.

LESSEE—
Meaning of word, 28.
Was originally a bailiff, *ib*.
Gradual improvement in position of, *ib*.
Could bring an action of ejectment against his lessor, 29.
Allowed to prove that action against his lessor was fictitious, *ib*.
Does not hold from the lord paramount, *ib*.
Formerly entitled to hold his land without paying any rent if his lessor's estate had been merged or surrendered, 49.
Now bound to pay rent notwithstanding such merger or surrender, *ib*.
Course to be pursued by, if lessor distrains for rent, 50.
Must pay income tax and deduct it from rent, 53.
Taxes payable by, in absence of agreement, *ib*.
May deduct from rent taxes which he was not bound to pay, *ib*.
Cannot recover amount of taxes if he has paid rent without deducting it, 53.
Is bound to keep premises wind and water tight, 54.
Is not bound, except by agreement, to do substantial repairs, *ib*.
Is liable for permissive waste, *ib*.
Is entitled to estovers, *ib*.
Must keep distinct boundaries between his own land and his lessor's, *ib*.
Is under implied covenant to cultivate the premises in a husband-like manner, 55.
Is not entitled to commit waste, *ib*.

LESSEE—*(continued.)*
    Writ of waste against, under old law, 55.
    Present law as to restraining waste by, *ib.*
    Is entitled to emblements, *ib.*
    When may remove trade fixtures, 56.
    Right of, to remove domestic fixtures, *ib.*
    Could not formerly remove agricultural fixtures, 57.
    Present law as to removal of agricultural fixtures by a, *ib.*
    Should remove fixtures during his term, 58.
    May assign his term, unless he has covenanted to the contrary, 63.
    Assigning his term remains liable on the covenants of his lease, *ib.*
    Assigning his term entitled to a covenant of indemnity, 64.
    When may obtain relief against forfeiture, 68, 69, 70.
    May quit without giving notice, when his lease is determined by effluxion of time, 70.
    When liable to a penalty for holding over, 72.
    Should be precluded from investigating lessor's title, 346.

LESSOR—
    Meaning of word, 28.
    Proceedings by, when distraining for rent, 50.
    Right of, to follow tenant's goods for distress, 51.
    Is not bound to repair, unless by agreement, 54.
    Covenanting to repair is entitled to notice of want of repair, *ib.*
    When presumed to have waived his right to a forfeiture, 67.
    Need not, in general, give notice to quit to lessee whose term has come to an end by effluxion of time, 70.
    When presumed to have waived notice to quit, 71.
    When entitled to double value from lessee holding over, 72.
    Statutory power of, to distrain for rent, 73.
    Title of a, law as to showing, 313.
    Lessee should be precluded from investigating the title of his, 346.

LICENCE—
    Former effect of a, by lessor, 60.
    Present law as to a, by lessor, 61.
    Covenant in a lease not to use premises for purposes of trade without, 360, 361.
    Covenant in a lease not to assign or underlet without, 360, 361.

LIMITATION—
    Conditional, before the Statute of Uses, 207.
    By way of use, after the Statute of Uses, 208.
    Not considered an executory interest when it can take effect as a remainder, 211.
    Of an executory interest, when must take effect, 213.
    Doviso without words of, may pass a fee simple, 412.

LIMITATION, STATUTES OF—
    Arrears of rent recoverable under the, 51.
    Time for bringing action to recover rent how limited by the, 52.
    Arrears of dower recoverable under the, 84.
    Time for bringing action to recover land how limited by the, 139—144.
    Acknowledgments under the, 142, 250, 261, 263.

LIMITATION, STATUTES OF—(continued.)
Time for bringing an action to recover interest limited by the, 249.
Time for bringing an action to recover money secured by mortgage limited by the, 250.
Equity of redemption may be barred by the, 255.
Mortgagee's right to land may be barred by the, 261.
Time for suing on covenants for title, under the, 341.

LIVERY OF SEISIN—
Meaning of, 11.
Applied to every tenant by Knight Service or by socage, *ib.*
Various modes of making, *ib.*
Tenant to whom livery had been made became enfeoffed, *ib.*
Usually accompanied by charter or deed, *ib.*
And feoffment, 284.
Was not necessary for an exchange, 287.
Was necessary for a partition, 288.

LODGER—
Course to be pursued by, if goods are seized for distress, 51.

LORD—
Derivation of the word, 5.
Holding by Knight Service liable to performance of military and other duties, 6.
Was guardian of infant tenant by Knight Service, 18.
Not guardian of infant tenant by socage, 19.
Consent of, formerly necessary for the alienation of a fee, 23.
Of customary manor is bound to renew lives, 154.
May exercise prescriptive rights in a reputed manor, 155.
Of a manor may hold Customary Court though no tenant present, *ib.*
Fitness of, to grant estates in copyholds is immaterial, 157.
Of a manor may admit tenant within or without the manor, and without holding any court, 160.
Of a manor is bound to observe the confidence on which an estate is surrendered to him, 161.
Of a manor cannot demand payment of a fine until after the tenant's admittance, 161.
Of a manor is bound to admit the person entitled, *ib.*
Of a manor cannot compel the admittance of a purchaser, 162.
Of a manor may make proclamation on death of a tenant, 163.
Of a manor, when may seize absolutely, or *quousque*, *ib.*
Of a manor cannot seize as against persons under disability, *ib.*
Of a manor, when entitled to quit rents, 167.
Of a manor, when entitled to a heriot, 168.
Of a manor and tenant, rights of, as to timber and minerals, *ib.*
Of a manor not entitled to cut timber or dig for minerals on tenant's land except by custom, 169.

LORD PARAMOUNT—
Meaning of, 11.
Sovereign is, *ib.*
Entitled to oath of fealty from every owner of land, *ib.*

INDEX. 447

LUNATIC—
  Committee of a, may make lease of land belonging to him, 40.

MAINTENANCE—
  Trust for, in a marriage settlement, 395.

MANOR—
  Description of, 7.
  Part of, kept to form the lord's demesne, the remainder distributed amongst his vassals, *ib.*
  New, cannot be created at the present day, 154.
  Quasi, may be created by statute, *ib.*
  Different kinds of, *ib.*
  Customary, *ib.*
  Reputed, *ib.*
  All dealings in a, are regulated by custom, 155.
  Requisites of custom of a, *ib.*
  Estates in a, how to be granted, 156.
  No estate tail in a, except by custom, *ib.*
  Barring estates tail in a, 156.
  Grants of estates in a, must conform to custom, 157.
  Fitness of lord or steward to grant estates in a, is immaterial, *ib.*
  Form of words for granting estates in a, 158.
  Every now tenant of a, must be admitted, 158.
  Tenant of a, selling his estate must surrender it, *ib.*
  No curtesy in a, except by custom, 171.
  Birth of issue not always necessary for curtesy in a, *ib.*
  No freebench in a, except by custom, *ib.*
  Freebench in a, husband may defeat, *ib.*
  Freebench in a, Dower Act does no apply to, *ib.*

MARRIAGE—
  Meaning of term, 16.
  Claims of lords in respect of, *ib.*
  Values and forfeitures for, abolished, 21.
  Revocation of a will by, 416.

MARRIED WOMAN—
  Lease by, under Fines and Recoveries Abolition Act, 39.
  How must bar an estate tail, 121.
  Husband has a right, during their joint lives, to profits of terms belonging to a, 234.
  Husband may, during his lifetime, dispose of terms belonging to a, *ib.*
  Husband cannot dispose by will of terms belonging to a, *ib.*
  Term of a, surviving her husband, becomes her own property, *ib.*
  Estate of a, for life or in fee, cannot be alienated by her husband, 235.
  May, jointly with husband, alienate her real or copyhold estate, *ib.*
  Right of husband to property of a, may be excluded, *ib.*
  May hold property to her separate use, *ib.*
  Power of disposition of a, over her separate estate, 237.
  Separate property of a, liable for fulfilment of her contracts, 238.
  May be liable to support her husband and children, *ib.*
  An estate given to a, and her husband is held by entireties, *ib.*

MARRIED WOMAN—(continued.)
    Term to secure the income of a, 388, 392.
    Jointure of a, meaning of term, 389.
    Power of distress, to secure the jointure of a, 390.
    Power of entry to secure the jointure of a, 391.
    Term to secure the jointure of a, 392.
    Has limited power of making a will, 401.
    May dispose by will of personal property if husband gives his consent, 402.

MESNE LORD—
    Meaning of term, 11.

MILITARY SERVICE—
    Liability to, was at one time an incident of the possession of land, 6.
    A characteristic of tenure by Knight Service, 8.

MINERALS—
    Rights as to, of a lord and tenant of copyholds, 168
    In the absence of custom neither lord nor copyholder can take, 169.
    Trustee may sell, apart from the land, 221.

MINES—
    Tenant for life may work, if they have been opened by a preceding tenant, 93.

MORTGAGE—
    Equity of redemption is inseparable from a, 242.
    Distinction between a, and a sale with proviso for re-purchase, 243.
    By deposit of title-deeds, how viewed in equity, 279.
    By deposit of title-deeds, may secure future advances, ib.
    Equitable mortgagee is entitled to a legal, 280.
    Form of, of freeholds, 365.
    Form of, of leaseholds, ib.
    Form of, of copyholds, 366.
    Of fixtures, when requires registration, 370.

MORTGAGE DEED—
    Introductory part in a, 367.
    Recitals in a, ib.
    Covenant in a, for re-payment of sum lent, 368.
    Operative part in a, 368—371.
    Effect of operative part in a, as to passing fixtures, 368.
    Parcels in a, ib.
    General words, and estate clause in a, ib.
    Habendum in a, ib.
    Covenant in a, for payment of interest, 373.
    Declaration in a, on loan by trustees, 375.
    Covenants by the mortgagor in a, 376, 382.
    Power of sale in a, 377.
    Testatum in a, 383.
    Statutory provisions relating to mortgage deeds, ib.

MORTGAGEE—

Mortgagor may be tenant to his, 245.
May exercise his rights concurrently, 248.
Action by, on mortgagor's covenants for payment, ib.
May lose right of suing mortgagor, 251.
In possession, is bound to take due care of the property, ib.
Rights of, if mortgaged estate is an insufficient security, 252.
In possession, must account for rents, ib.
In possession, may charge mortgagor with reasonable expenses, ib.
In possession, must not unnecessarily increase the value of the estate, 253.
Cannot charge for personal expenses, ib.
May appoint a receiver, ib.
In occupation of mortgaged premises, must pay an occupation rent, ib.
In possession, must account, ib.
In possession, when to account with rests, 254.
Possession of a, may destroy the equity of redemption, 255.
Possession of a, to bar equity of redemption must be adverse, 257.
Acknowledgment of mortgagor's title by a, when one of several trustees, ib.
When may file bill for foreclosure, 258.
May re-open foreclosure by receipt of rent, 259.
May lose his security, under the Statutes of Limitation, 261.
Right of a, to recover land is not barred by his own possession in another capacity, 263.
Rights of a, against tenant of mortgagor, ib.
When entitled to tack, 266—270.
When entitled to consolidate his securities, 271—274.
Assignee of a, may consolidate, 271.
May consolidate against mortgagor's assignee, 272.
Equitable, is entitled to a legal mortgage, 280.
Equitable, may obtain a decree for foreclosure, ib.
Equitable, entitled to interest at £4 per cent., 281.
May be postponed, ib.
Covenant for title to be entered into by a, 340.
Attornment to, by mortgagor, 381.
Statutory powers of a, 383.
A general devise may include land of which the testator is a, 415.

MORTGAGOR—

May be tenant for a term to his mortgagee, 245.
Position of a, when not a tenant, ib.
In occupation, not bound to account for rents and profits, 246.
May act in some cases as owner, ib.
When entitled to redeem, ib.
Covenants by a, in a mortgage deed, 376.
Attornment by a, to mortgagee, 381.

MORTMAIN—

Meaning of term, 126.
Acts relating to, 127.

NOTICE—
  To quit need not be given when a term has come to an end by effluxion of time, 70.
  To quit demised premises, when may be given by parol, 71.
  To quit demised premises must be half a year's notice, *ib.*
  To quit demised premises, when must be served personally on tenant, *ib.*
  To quit given by lessor how waived, *ib.*
  To quit, lessor claiming double value must give in writing, although term has come to end by effluxion of time, 72.

OCCUPANT—
  General, of an estate *pur autre vie*, 90.
  Special, of an estate *pur autre vie*, 91.
  General, could not be of an estate *pur autre vie* in an incorporeal hereditament, *ib.*
  Cannot be a general, now, *ib.*

OPERATIVE PART—
  Of a purchase deed, what is the, 333.
  Receipt clause in the, of a purchase deed, *ib.*
  In a mortgage deed, 368—371.
  In a mortgage deed, effect of, as to passing fixtures, 368.

PARCELS—
  Meaning of term, 334.
  Should, when practicable, be the same as in former title-deeds, 335.
  Description of, by reference to a plan, *ib.*
  May be set out in a schedule, *ib.*
  In a lease, importance of accuracy in framing, 353.
  In a mortgage deed, 368.

PARTICULARS—
  Of property to be sold, rules for framing, 308.
  Maps and plans are subject to same rules as, 309.

PARTIES—
  To a deed, who should be, 330.
  Order of arrangement of, in a deed, *ib.*
  How to be described in a deed, *ib.*
  In a lease, 352.
  To a marriage settlement, 387.

PARTITION—
  Of what estates might be made, 288.
  Livery of seisin was necessary for, *ib.*
  May be made under the Inclosure Acts, 298.

PERPETUITY—
  Object of rule against a, 213.
  Necessity for guarding against the creation of a, *ib.*
  Present rule against the creation of a, *ib.*
  Limitation is void which may create a, 214.

INDEX. 451

PERSONAL PROPERTY—
  Derivation of term, 1.
  A term of years is, 2.

PIN MONEY—
  Meaning of term, 392.
  Wife cannot claim more than one year's arrears of, *ib.*
  Wife's representatives have no claim to arrears of, *ib.*

PORTIONS—
  Term to secure, 393.
  Who entitled to, 394.
  Time for payment of, *ib.*
  Proviso for raising, during the father's life-time, 396.
  Husband's power to charge, for children of a future marriage, 397.

POSSIBILITY—
  Coupled with an interest, alienation of a, 204.

POWERS—
  Of appointment, 216.
  May be particular or general, *ib.*
  Collateral, and not simply collateral, 217.
  Appendant, and in gross, *ib.*
  Creation of, *ib.*
  Exercise of, *ib.*
  May be exercised without being referred to, 218.
  Observance of formalities in exercise of, 219.
  Defective execution of, aided, 220.
  Non-execution of, not aided, 221.
  Trustee having, to sell land, may dispose of minerals separately, *ib.*
  Destruction and alienation of, 222—225.
  Not simply collateral, cannot be destroyed or alienated, 223.
  Simply collateral, may be destroyed or alienated, *ib.*
  Suspension of, *ib.*
  Release of, 225.
  Involuntary alienation of, *ib.*
  Of sale, in a mortgage deed, 377.
  Statutory, conferred on mortgagees, 383.
  Wife's, of distress and entry to secure jointure, 390, 391.
  Of advancement, in a marriage settlement, 396.
  Of general trustees of a marriage settlement, 397.
  Of husband, in a marriage settlement, to jointure future wife, *ib.*
  Of husband, in a marriage settlement, to charge portions for children of a future marriage, *ib.*
  Of leasing, in a marriage settlement, 398.
  Of sale and exchange, in a marriage settlement, *ib.*
  Statutory, of trustees, 399.
  Of appointment may be executed by a general devise, 412.

PREMISES—
  In a purchase deed, what included in the, 329.
  In a lease, 352.

452   INDEX.

PRESCRIPTION—
   Definition of, 170.
   Copyholder's right to common is founded on, *ib.*
   For common must be reasonable, 171.

PRESENTMENT—
   Of surrender of copyholds formerly necessary, 160.
   Of surrender of copyholds not now required, *ib.*

PRIMER SEISIN—
   Meaning of term, 17.
   Abolished, 21.

PRIORITY—
   Where obtainable by a sub-mortgagee, 276—278.

PROCLAMATION—
   For person entitled to copyholds to come in and be admitted, 163.

PROTECTOR—
   Of a settlement creating an estate tail, 119.
   Who to be, of a settlement, *ib.*
   Settlor may appoint a, 120.
   Vacancy in office of, may be filled up, *ib.*
   Surviving, may execute office, *ib.*
   Powers of a, *ib.*
   Not to be subject to any control, 121.
   Cannot revoke consent formally given, *ib.*
   Deed containing consent of a, to barring an estate tail, must be inrolled, 122.

PROVISO—
   For re-entry, in a lease, 362.
   For redemption, in a mortgage deed, 371.
   In a marriage settlement, for raising portions during the husband's lifetime, 396.

PURCHASE DEED—
   Division of an ordinary, 329.
   Parties to a, 330.
   Recitals in a, 330—333.
   When recitals should be inserted in a, 331.
   Operative part of a, 333.
   Words of conveyance to be employed in a, 334.
   Parcels in a, *ib.*
   General words in a, 335.
   Estate clause in a, 337.
   Habendum in a, *ib.*
   Covenant in a, for right to convey, 338.
   Covenant in a, for quiet enjoyment, 338, 339.
   Covenant in a, for freedom from incumbrances, 338, 339.
   Covenant in a, for further assurance, 339.
   Covenants for title in a, who must enter into, *ib.*
   Covenants for title in a, time for suing on, 341.
   Testatum in a, 342.

PURCHASER—
Definition of a, in the Inheritance Act, 147.
Length of title which a, may require, 312.
Should be precluded from investigating title other than as shown by the vendor, 315.
When bound to fulfil contract and take compensation, 318.
When bound to pay interest on his purchase-money, 321.
Condition of sale as to requisitions by a, 325.
May make further requisitions arising out of answers to his first, *ib.*
Is not bound by condition of sale as to requisitions, when vendor has no title, *ib.*

QUIA EMPTORES, STATUTE OF—
Permitted alienation of fees, 24.
Forbad subinfeudation, 25.

QUIT-RENT—
Origin of, 167.
When lord of a manor can claim, *ib.*

REAL PROPERTY—
Is a name given to land, 1.
Derivation of the term, *ib.*
Payment of debts out of, 138, 139.

RECITALS—
Conditions of sale as to, 316.
Made evidence by statute, *ib.*
Narrative, object of, 330.
Narrative, how far should go back, *ib.*
Introductory, object of, 331.
When, should be inserted in a purchase deed, *ib.*
Should, as a rule, be in general terms, 332.
Operation of, by estoppel, 333.
Are not generally used in leases, 352.
In a mortgage deed, 367.

RECOVERY—
Suffering a, 114.
With double voucher, 115.
Effect of suffering a, 116.
Right to suffer a, was inseparable from every estate tail, *ib.*
Fine and, abolished, 118.

REDDENDUM—
In a lease, 355, 356.
In a lease should not state to whom rent is to be paid, 355.

REDEMPTION—
Bill for, when necessary, 247.
Decree under a bill for, *ib.*
Proviso for, in a mortgage deed, 371.

454   INDEX.

RELEASE—
    Form of conveyance by, 288.
    What estates conveyed by, *ib.*

RELIEF—
    When payable, 15.
    Derivation of word, note (*s*), *ib.*
    Became an incident of villein tenure, 19.
    Against forfeiture of lease for non-payment of rent, 68, 69.
    Against forfeiture of lease for breach of covenant to insure, 73.

REMAINDER—
    Definition of a, 36, 193.
    Creation of a, 193.
    Is always created by act of parties, *ib.*
    May be created by deed or will, 194.
    None, in a term of years, *ib.*
    Alienation of a, 195.
    Attornment formerly necessary for the transfer of a, *ib.*
    Determination of a, 196.
    May be vested or contingent, *ib.*
    Vested, example of, *ib.*
    Contingent, example of, 197.
    Rules for the creation of a, 198—204.
    Contingent, rule as to vesting, 202.
    Contingent, destruction of, 205.
    Contingent, trustee to preserve formerly required, *ib.*
    Contingent, not now destroyed by forfeiture, merger, or surrender of the preceding estate, 206.

REMAINDER-MAN—
    Definition of a, 36.
    Not formerly bound by lease made by tenant in tail, *ib.*
    Is now bound by lease made in pursuance of the Fines and Recoveries Abolition Act, 37.

RENT OR RENT SERVICE—
    Definition of, 48.
    How may be paid, *ib.*
    Is incident to the reversion, *ib.*
    Presumed to be equivalent to annual value of the premises demised, *ib.*
    Formerly lost by destruction of the reversion, *ib.*
    Due to lessee from an under-tenant, formerly lost by surrender of the lease, 49.
    Now preserved, notwithstanding merger or surrender of the reversion, *ib.*
    Must be reserved out of corporeal hereditaments, 50.
    Must be reserved to the lessor, *ib.*
    Must be certain, *ib.*
    Distress for, *ib.*
    Time for bringing action to recover, 52.
    Six years' arrears of, recoverable, *ib.*
    Right to, not barred so long as there is a subsisting tenancy, *ib.*
    Lessee's liability to pay, *ib.*
    Acceptance of, may waive lessor's right to a forfeiture, 67.

RENT OR RENT SERVICE—*(continued.)*
  Action for, may waive lessor's right to a forfeiture, 67.
  Common law distress for, waives lessor's right to a forfeiture, *ib*.
  Relief against forfeiture for non-payment of, 68, 69.
  Acceptance of, by lessor, when a waiver of notice to quit, 71.
  Not formerly apportionable on death of tenant for life, 106.
  Statutes relating to apportionment of, 107, 108, 109.
  On lease made by a tenant in tail may be apportioned, 123.
  Covenant in a lease to pay, 356.

REPAIRS—
  Lessee not bound, except by agreement, to do substantial, 54.
  Covenant in a lease to do, 358, 359.
  Covenant in a lease to permit lessor to enter and view state of repair, 359.
  Covenant in a lease to deliver up the premises in good repair, 362.

REQUISITIONS—
  Definition of, 310.
  Condition of sale as to, 325.
  Purchaser may make further, arising out of answers to his first, *ib*.
  Unwillingness of vendor to comply with, *semble* must be reasonable, 327.
  The fact of a purchaser's making, does not entitle a vendor to rescind, *ib*.

RESCINDING CONTRACT—
  Condition of sale as to, 326.
  When vendor has right of, 327.
  Value of condition of sale as to, *ib*.

REVERSION—
  Definition of, 36, 193.
  Rent reserved on a lease for years is incident to the, 48.
  Destruction of a, formerly put an end to rent incident to it, *ib*.
  Assignee of, the, on a lease, now entitled to benefit of all covenants and conditions contained in the lease, 60, 61.
  Creation of a, 193.
  Is always created by operation of law, *ib*.
  Alienation of a, 195.
  Attornment formerly necessary on alienation of a, *ib*.
  Determination of a, 196.

REVERSIONER—
  Definition of a, 36.
  Not formerly bound by lease made by tenant in tail, *ib*.
  Is bound by lease made in pursuance of the Fines and Recoveries Abolition Act, 37.

REVOCATION—
  Of a will, by marriage, 417.
  Of a will, by will or codicil, 419.
  Of a will, by a writing executed like a will, 420.
  Of a will, by destruction, *ib*.
  Cancellation of a will is not, 421.

SALE—
　Of settled estates under order of the Court of Chancery, 98.
　Of settled estates under the Lands Clauses Consolidation Act, 103.
　Instead of foreclosure, when ordered by the Court of Chancery, 260.
　Instead of foreclosure, may be ordered at the suit of a sub-mortgagee, 275.
　Agreement for, of any interest in land must be in writing, 302.
　Agreement for, of land, what must contain, *ib.*
　Agreement for, need not be contained in one document, 304.
　Agreement for, parol evidence when admissible to prove terms of, *ib.*
　Agreement for, when enforced on ground of part performance, 305.
　Agreement for, signature to, 306.
　By auction, conditions as to conduct of, 310.
　By auction, subject to reserve price must be so stated, *ib.*
　By auction, is within the Statute of Frauds, 312.
　Memorandum of, attached to conditions of sale, 328.
　Power of, in a mortgage deed, 377.
　Powers of, in a marriage settlement, 398.

SATISFIED TERMS—
　When attendant on the inheritance, 76.
　Advantage of, 77.
　Disadvantages of, 78.
　Abolition of, 79.
　May still be attendant on the inheritance, 80.

SEISIN—
　Livery of, meaning of term, 11.
　Livery of, how made, *ib.*
　Lessee has not, 29.

SEIZURE—
　Of copyholds absolutely or *quousque*, 163.
　Copyhold tenants under disability protected against, *ib.*

SEPARATE USE—
　Doctrine of, 235.
　Form of words to create, 236.
　Property held to, under Married Women's Property Act, *ib.*
　Property held to, of a married woman is liable for the fulfilment of her contracts, 238.

SETTLED ESTATES—
　Leases of, may be authorized by the Court of Chancery, 38.
　Sale of, by order of the Court of Chancery, 98.
　Sale of, under the Lands Clauses Consolidation Act, 103.

SETTLEMENT—
　Protector of a, creating an estate tail, 119.
　Marriage, object of a, 387.
　Marriage, parties to a, *ib.*
　Marriage, term limited by a, to secure wife's income, 388, 392.
　Marriage, life estate given to the husband by a, *ib.*
　Marriage, term in a, to secure jointure, 391, 392.
　Marriage, term in a, to secure portions, 391, 393.
　Marriage, estate tail created by a, *ib.*

SETTLEMENT—(continued.)
Marriage, hotchpot clause in a, 395.
Marriage, trust in a, for maintenance of younger children, ib.
Marriage, advancement clause in a, 396.
Marriage, proviso in a, for raising portions during the husband's life-time, ib.
Marriage, powers of general trustees of a, 397.
Marriage, powers of husband contained in a, ib.
Marriage, powers of leasing in a, 398.
Marriage, powers of sale and exchange in a, ib.
Marriage, covenants for title in a, 399.

SETTLOR—
Of an estate tail may appoint a protector, 120.
May direct vacancies in protectorship to be filled up, ib.

SHELLEY'S CASE—
Rule in, 112.

SIGNATURE—
To an agreement for sale, what is sufficient, 306.
To conditions of sale, by auctioneer, ib.
To conditions of sale, by auctioneer's clerk, 307.
To a will, 405—409.
By a testator, 406.
On behalf of a testator, 407.
Witnesses to a will must be present at the testator's, ib.
By witnesses to a will, ib.

SOCAGE TENURE—
Had existed in England before the Conquest, 9.
Recognized by Normans, ib.
Derivation of name, 10, note (i).
Characteristics of, ib.
Did not involve military service, ib.
Gradually adopted by Normans themselves, ib.
Incidents of, less burdensome than those of tenure by Knight Service, 18.
Wardship of infant tenant by, belonged to his nearest relation not capable of succeeding by descent, 19.

STATUTES CITED OR REFERRED TO—
Ll. Hen. I., p. 24.
9 Hen. III., c. 32, p. 23.
        c. 36, p. 126.
20 Hen. III., c. 4, p. 171.
52 Hen. III., c. 23, p. 95.
6 Edw. I., c. 5, pp. 55, 95.
7 Edw. I., c. 1, p. 126.
13 Edw. I., c. 1, pp. 26, 156.
        c. 18, pp. 131, 132.
18 Edw. I., stat. 1, p. 24.
        c. 1, pp. 25, 153.
        c. 2, p. 25.
        c. 11, p. 29.
        stat. 4, p. 116.

STATUTES CITED OR REFERRED TO—*(continued.)*
  1 Edw. III., c. 12, p. 24.
  15 Ric. II., c. 5, p. 127.
  11 Hen. VII., c. 20, p. 119.
  27 Hen. VIII., c. 10, pp. 183, 204, 207, 208, 209, 210, 211, 284, 291, 388.
      s. 1, p. 185.
      s. 4, p. 390.
      s. 5, p. 390.
      s. 6, pp. 83, 390.
    c. 16, p. 292.
  31 Hen. VIII., c. 1, p. 231.
  32 Hen. VIII., c. 1, pp. 27, 209, 294.
    c. 28, pp. 36, 37, 82.
      s. 1, p. 42.
      s. 2, p. 42.
    c. 32, p. 232.
    c. 34, pp. 59, 63.
    c. 36, pp. 117, 119.
  33 Hen. VIII., c. 39, p. 123.
  34 & 35 Hen. VIII., c. 5, s. 14, p. 401.
  21 Jac. I., c. 16, p. 256.
  12 Car. II., c. 24, pp. 21, 28, 161, 210, 294.
  29 Car. II., c. 3, pp. 45, 90, 91, 231, 295, 312, 328, 349.
      s. 1, pp. 46, 88, 296, 348, 352.
      s. 2, pp. 296, 348.
      s. 3, pp. 65, 73, 296.
      s. 4, pp. 190, 279, 301, 344, 348.
      s. 7, pp. 190, 296.
      s. 8, p. 296.
      s. 9, p. 190.
      s. 10, p. 131.
      s. 14, p. 131.
      s. 15, pp. 131, 132.
  2 Will. & Mary, c. 5, s. 1, p. 50.
  3 Will. & Mary, c. 14, p. 138.
  4 & 5 Will. & Mary, c. 20, s. 3, p. 133.
  10 & 11 Will. & Mary, c. 22, p. 203.
  6 & 7 Will. III., c. 37, p. 127.
  7 Will. III., c. 12 (Ir.), 302.
  1 Anne, c. 1, s. 5, p. 41.
  4 & 5 Anne, c. 3, s. 9, pp. 195, 297.
      s. 10, p. 195.
      s. 27, p. 227.
  6 Anne, c. 72, s. 1, p. 92.
      s. 5, p. 92.
  8 Anne, c. 18, p. 68.
      s. 6, p. 73.
      s. 7, p. 73.
  11 Anne, c. 2 (Ir.), p. 69.
  9 Geo. I., c. 29, p. 163.
  4 Geo. II., c. 28, s. 1, p. 72.
      s. 2, p. 362.
      s. 4, p. 69.

STATUTES CITED OR REFERRED TO—(continued.)
4 Geo. II., c. 28, s. 5, p. 390.
   s. 6, p. 46.
9 Geo. II., c. 36, s. 1, pp. 44, 127.
   s. 2, p. 44.
11 Geo. II., c. 19, s. 1, pp. 51, 127.
   s. 2, pp. 51, 128.
   s. 3, p. 128.
   s. 8, p. 50.
   s. 11, p. 106.
   s. 15, p. 107.
   s. 18, p. 72.
14 Geo. II., c. 20, p. 91.
   c. 78, s. 83, p. 376.
5 Geo. III., c. 17, pp. 42, 82.
39 & 40 Geo. III., c. 98, s. 1, p. 215.
   s. 2, p. 215.
47 Geo. III., c. 74, p. 138.
55 Geo. III., c. 192, pp. 158, 165, 295, 411.
10 Geo. IV., c. 50, s. 22, p. 41.
   s. 23, p. 41.
   s. 24, p. 41.
   s. 25, p. 41.
   s. 26, p. 41.
   s. 27, p. 41.
   s. 28, p. 41.
   s. 29, p. 41.
   s. 30, p. 41.
   s. 31, p. 41.
   s. 32, p. 41.
   s. 33, p. 41.
11 Geo. IV. & 1 Will. IV., c. 47, p. 139.
   c. 65, s. 5, p. 163.
   s. 6, p. 163.
   s. 7, p. 163.
   s. 9, p. 163.
   s. 12, p. 73.
   s. 16, p. 74.
   s. 17, p. 40.
3 & 4 Will. IV., c. 27, pp. 232, 263, 313.
   s. 1, p. 140.
   s. 2, pp. 139, 261, 262.
   s. 3, pp. 141, 261.
   s. 4, p. 141.
   s. 7, p. 141.
   s. 8, p. 141.
   s. 9, p. 141.
   s. 14, p. 142.
   s. 16, p. 142.
   s. 17, p. 143.
   s. 21, p. 143.
   s. 25, p. 143.
   s. 26, p. 144.
   s. 28, p. 255.

STATUTES CITED OR REFERRED TO—*(continued.)*
3 & 4 Will. IV., c. 27, s. 36, p. 55.
    s. 40, p. 250.
    s. 41, p. 84.
    s. 42, pp. 51, 249.
  c. 42, pp. 52, 341.
    s. 3, p. 249.
    s. 4, pp. 52, 249.
    s. 5, p. 249.
  c. 74, pp. 192, 196, 297.
    s. 2, p. 118.
    s. 14, p. 118.
    s. 15, pp. 36, 118.
    s. 16, p. 119.
    s. 18, p. 88.
    s. 19, p. 119.
    s. 22, p. 119.
    s. 23, p. 119.
    s. 24, p. 119.
    s. 26, p. 119.
    s. 27, p. 120.
    s. 28, p. 120.
    s. 32, p. 120.
    s. 34, p. 120.
    s. 35, p. 120.
    s. 36, p. 121.
    s. 39, p. 121.
    s. 40, pp. 36, 40, 121.
    s. 41, pp. 36, 114, 122.
    s. 42, p. 122.
    s. 44, p. 121.
    s. 46, p. 122.
    s. 50, pp. 157, 174.
    ss. 56—72, p. 122.
    s. 77, pp. 39, 126, 235.
    s. 79, pp. 123, 135.
    s. 80, p. 121.
    s. 90, p. 174.
    s. 91, pp. 121, 126.
  c. 104, p. 139.
  c. 105, pp. 82, 172, 192.
    s. 1, p. 85.
    s. 2, p. 85.
    s. 3, p. 85.
    s. 4, p. 85.
    s. 5, p. 86.
    s. 6, p. 86.
    s. 7, p. 86.
    s. 8, p. 86.
    s. 9, p. 86.
    s. 10, p. 86.
    s. 11, p. 86.
    s. 14, pp. 85, 86.
  c. 106, p. 145.

STATUTES CITED OR REFERRED TO—(*continued.*)
3 & 4 Will. IV., c. 106, s. 1, p. 147.
     s. 2, p. 147.
     s. 6, p. 149.
     s. 7, p. 150.
     s. 8, p. 151.
     s. 9, p. 149.
4 & 5 Will. IV., c. 22, p. 123.
     s. 2, p. 108.
     s. 3, p. 108.
5 & 6 Will. IV., c. 76, s. 94, p. 43.
     s. 96, p. 43.
6 & 7 Will. IV., c. 104, s. 2, p. 43.
7 Will. IV. & 1 Vict., c. 26, s. 2, p. 401.
     s. 3, pp. 28, 91, 105, 159, 174, 205, 295, 401, 410.
     s. 4, p. 165.
     s. 6, pp. 91, 105.
     s. 7, pp. 126, 401.
     s. 8, pp. 126, 401.
     s. 9, pp. 219, 295, 403.
     s. 10, pp. 219, 403.
     s. 11, p. 401.
     s. 15, p. 409.
     s. 16, p. 409.
     s. 17, p. 409.
     s. 18, p. 417.
     s. 19, p. 418.
     s. 20, p. 419.
     s. 21, p. 421.
     s. 22, p. 423.
     s. 23, p. 418.
     s. 24, p. 412.
     s. 25, p. 412.
     s. 26, p. 412.
     s. 28, p. 413.
7 Will. IV. & 1 Vict., c. 28, pp. 262, 263.
1 & 2 Vict., c. 106, s. 28, p. 43.
   c. 110, pp. 123, 267.
     s. 11, pp. 133, 173.
     s. 13, pp. 134, 268.
     s. 19, p. 134.
2 & 3 Vict., c. 11, pp. 123, 267.
     s. 5, p. 134.
     s. 8, p. 137.
3 & 4 Vict., c. 55, p. 98.
   c. 82, p. 135.
4 & 5 Vict., c. 21, p. 207.
   c. 35, s. 1, p. 176.
     s. 2, p. 176.
     s. 13, p. 176.
     s. 14, pp. 176, 177.
     s. 15, p. 177.
     s. 23, p. 177.

STATUTES CITED OR REFERRED TO (*continued.*)
4 & 5 Vict. c. 35, s. 52, p. 177.
    s. 56, p. 177.
    ss. 73—78, p. 178.
    s. 79, p. 178.
    s. 81, p. 178.
    s. 86, p. 155.
    s. 87, p. 160.
    s. 88, p. 160.
    s. 89, p. 160.
    s. 90. p. 161.
5 & 6 Vict., c. 27, p. 42.
   c. 35, s. 73, pp. 53, 357.
   c. 108, p. 182.
    s. 1, p. 42.
    s. 4, p. 42.
    s. 20, p. 42.
6 & 7 Vict., c. 23, s. 13, p. 179.
    s. 16, p. 178.
7 & 8 Vict., c. 55, s. 5, p. 179.
   c. 76, p. 349.
8 & 9 Vict., c. 18, s. 7, p. 103.
    s. 69, p. 103.
    s. 74, p. 103.
   c. 56, s. 3, p. 98.
    s. 4, p. 99.
    s. 5, p. 99.
    s. 6, p. 99.
    s. 8, p. 99.
    s. 9, p. 99.
    s. 10, p. 100.
    s. 11, p. 101.
   c. 106, pp. 46, 49, 231.
    s. 2, p. 298.
    s. 3, pp. 46, 73, 89, 105, 297, 350.
    s. 4, pp. 106, 298.
    s. 5, p. 352.
    s. 6, p. 204.
    s. 8, p. 206.
   c. 112, p. 76.
    s. 1, p. 79.
    s. 2, p. 79.
   c. 118, s. 147, p. 298.
9 & 10 Vict.; c. 101, s. 34, p. 103.
    s. 38, p. 103.
    s. 45, p. 103.
10 & 11 Vict., c. 11, p. 103.
   c. 111, p. 298.
11 & 12 Vict., c. 99, s. 13, pp. 232, 298.
   c. 119, p. 103.
12 & 13 Vict., c. 83, p. 298.
   c. 100, p. 100.
   c. 106, s. 145, p. 66.
13 & 14 Vict., c. 31, p. 103.

STATUTES CITED OR REFERRED TO—(continued.)
14 & 15 Vict., c. 25, s. 1, p. 33.
              s. 3, p. 57.
15 & 16 Vict., c. 24, s. 1, p. 405.
           c. 51, s. 1, p. 180.
              ss. 2—8, p. 180.
              s. 9, p. 180.
              s. 27, p. 180.
              s. 45, p. 180.
              s. 48, p. 181.
           c. 76, s. 210, pp. 69, 363.
              s. 211, p. 69.
              s. 212, p. 69.
           c. 79, p. 298.
           c. 86, s. 48, pp. 260, 275.
16 & 17 Vict., c. 70, p. 74.
              s. 129, p. 40.
              s. 130, p. 40.
              s. 131, p. 40.
              s. 133, p. 40.
              s. 137, p. 128.
17 & 18 Vict., c. 36, s. 1, p. 371.
              s. 7, p. 371.
           c. 97, p. 298.
           c. 125, s. 79, p. 55.
              s. 82, p. 55.
18 & 19 Vict., c. 43, s. 1, pp. 82, 111.
              s. 2, pp. 82, 111.
              s. 4, p. 82.
           c. 124, p. 129.
19 & 20 Vict., c. 9, p. 103.
           c. 97, s. 1, p. 135.
           c. 108, ss. 63—76, p. 50.
           c. 120, pp. 38, 398.
              s. 2, p. 39.
              s. 5, p. 74.
              s. 11, p. 98.
              s. 13, p. 98.
              s. 14, p. 98.
              s. 32, pp. 37, 38, 39.
              s. 33, p. 38.
              s. 35, p. 37.
              s. 36, p. 41.
              s. 44, p. 37.
              s. 46, p. 37.
20 & 21 Vict., c. 31, p. 298.
              s. 7, p. 232.
           c. 85, s. 21, p. 402.
              s. 25, p. 402.
21 & 22 Vict., c. 44, p. 42.
           c. 57, s. 1, p. 42.
           c. 77, pp. 38, 398.
              s. 2, p. 39.
              s. 4, p. 39.

STATUTES CITED OR REFERRED TO—(*continued.*)

21 & 22 Vict., c. 77, s. 5, p. 74.
     s. 8, p. 38.
   c. 94, s. 6, p. 180.
     s. 7, pp. 180, 181.
   c. 108, p. 402.
22 & 23 Vict., c. 35, p. 123.
     s. 1, p. 61.
     s. 2, p. 61.
     s. 3, p. 61.
     s. 8, p. 64.
     s. 12, p. 220.
     s. 13, pp. 96, 221.
     s. 19, p. 147.
     s. 22, p. 137.
     s. 27, p. 65.
   c. 43, p. 298.
23 & 24 Vict., c. 38, p. 267.
     s. 1, p. 135.
   c. 59, p. 42.
   c. 126, s. 1, p. 69.
     s. 2, pp. 69, 70.
   c. 145, p. 217.
     ss. 1—10, p. 399.
     s. 11, pp. 253, 344.
     s. 12, p. 344.
     s. 13, p. 344.
     s. 14, p. 344.
     s. 15, pp. 366, 385.
     s. 16, p. 385.
     ss. 17—24, p. 253.
     ss. 18—23, p. 344.
24 Vict., c. 9, p. 128.
     s. 1, p. 44.
24 & 25 Vict., c. 134, s. 131, p. 66.
25 & 26 Vict., c. 17, p. 128.
   c. 61, s. 9, p. 129.
   c. 89, s. 1, p. 129.
   c. 108, s. 1, p. 221.
     s. 2, p. 222.
27 & 28 Vict., c. 13, p. 128.
   c. 112, pp. 123, 267.
     s. 1, p. 136.
     s. 2, p. 136.
     s. 4, p. 136.
   c. 114, s. 8, p. 100.
     s. 9, p. 100.
     s. 25, p. 100.
     s. 49, p. 101.
     s. 51, p. 101.
     s. 66, p. 101.
     s. 72, p. 102.
     s. 76, p. 102.
     ss. 78—89, p. 102.

STATUTES CITED OR REFERRED TO—(continued.)
28 & 29 Vict., c. 104, p. 123.
    s. 48, p. 137.
29 & 30 Vict., c. 57, s. 1, p. 128.
30 & 31 Vict., c. 48, s. 4, p. 310.
    s. 5, p. 310.
    s. 6, p. 311.
31 & 32 Vict., c. 40, s. 3, p. 232.
    s. 4, p. 232.
    c. 44, pp. 43, 44, 128.
    c. 89, p. 298.
32 & 33 Vict., c. 46, p. 139.
    c. 71, s. 6, p. 137.
    s. 14, p. 137.
    s. 15, pp. 41, 225.
    s. 17, pp. 41, 106.
    s. 23, p. 66.
    s. 24, p. 66.
    s. 25, pp. 106, 122.
    s. 45, p. 138.
33 Vict., c. 14, s. 2, p. 129.,
33 & 34 Vict., c. 23, p. 401.
    s. 1, p. 131.
    s. 12, p. 41.
    c. 34, s. 1, p. 129.
    s. 3, p. 129.
    c. 35, pp. 123, 144.
    s. 2, p. 109.
    s. 5, p. 109.
    c. 56, s. 2, p. 102.
    s. 3, p. 102.
    s. 4, p. 102.
    c. 93, p. 402.
    s. 7, p. 237.
    s. 8, p. 237.
    s. 13, p. 238.
    s. 14, p. 238.
34 & 35 Vict., c. 79, p. 51.
    c. 84, s. 4, p. 102.
36 & 37 Vict., c. 50, p. 337.
    c. 66, p. 74.
    s. 25, sub s. 7, p. 322.
    s. 25, sub s. 11, p. 301.
37 & 38 Vict., c. 57, p. 144.
    s. 1, p. 262.
    s. 7, p. 256.
    s. 8, p. 250.
    s. 9, p. 262.
    s. 10, p. 249.
    s. 12, p. 262.
    c. 78, pp. 271, 301.
    s. 1, p. 312.
    s. 2, pp. 314, 316, 324, 326.
    s. 7. p. 266.
    c. 83, p. 301.

STEWARD—
Of the manor kept the manor roll, 15.
Was judge of the Customary Court, 20.
Entered on the manor roll matters presented at the Customary Court, ib.
Of a manor may hold a Customary Court although no tenant be present, 155.
Fitness of, to make grants in copyholds is immaterial, 157.
Of a manor may admit a new tenant within or without the manor and without holding any court, 160.
Of a manor, when entitled to fees, from tenants, 166.
Of a manor, amount of fee to, must be reasonable, ib.

SUBINFEUDATION—
Definition of, 24.
Forbidden by the statute of *Quia Emptores*, 25.

SUB-MORTGAGEE—
Definition of a, 274.
Rights of a, different from those of a legal mortgagee, ib.
Bill for foreclosure by a, ib.
Has not a right to a sale, 275.
Court of Chancery may allow sale by a, instead of foreclosure, 275.
Right of a, to tack and consolidate, 275—278.
How a, may obtain priority, 276—278.

SURRENDER—
Of a lease, when must be by deed, 73.
Of a lease, when implied, ib.
Of leases belonging to persons under disability, 73, 74.
Of a lease by a married woman, 74.
Of leases made under the Leases and Sales of Settled Estates Acts, ib.
Of an estate for life must be by deed, 105.
Required, when copyholder sells his estate, 158.
And admittance, theory of, ib.
And admittance, enactments relating to, 158—161.
To use of a will, no longer necessary, 158.
May be made within or without the manor, and without holding any court for the purpose, 160.
Of copyholds, to be immediately inrolled, ib.
Of copyholds, is, practically, a mode of conveyance, 161.
Former mode of conveyance by, 289.

SUSPENSION—
Of powers, 223.

TACKING—
Definition of, 265.
Advantages of right of, ib.
Recent change in the law relating to, 266.
Mortgagee claiming right of, must have a legal estate, ib.
Mortgagee claiming right of, must have made his advance on the credit of the mortgaged estate, 267.

TACKING—(continued.)
Mortgagee claiming right of, must hold securities in the same right, 268.
Mortgagee claiming right of, must not have had notice of subsequent incumbrance, ib.
When sub-mortgagee may have right of, 275—278.

TAXES—
What, are payable by lessee in absence of agreement, 53.
Not properly payable by lessee may be deducted from rent, ib.
Lessee paying, when not bound cannot recover amount if he has paid rent without deduction, ib.
Covenant in a lease to pay, 357.

TENANCY AFTER POSSIBILITY OF ISSUE EXTINCT—
Is a legal estate for life, 82.
Definition of a, 83.
Tenant who has a, may commit waste, ib.
Assignee of, is not unimpeachable of waste, 105.

TENANCY FROM YEAR TO YEAR—
Is determinable at end of any year, 71.
What notice requisite to determine a, ib.
May be created by an instrument intended as a lease for a term, 351.

TENANCY IN COMMON—
When a, occurs, 220.
Creation of a, ib.
Form of words for creating a, ib.
Incidents of a, 229, 230.
Alienation of a, 230.
Does not survive, ib.
Partition of estates in, 231—234.

TENANT—
In capite, meaning of term, 11.
Free tenants bound to attend the court baron, 12.
Tenants at the court baron acted as judges, ib.
Customary tenants bound to attend the customary court, 20.
Customary tenants did not act as judges, ib.
By copy of court roll called copyholder, 21.
In capite allowed to alienate his land on payment of a fine to the king, 24.
New, of a manor must be admitted, 158.
Of a manor, selling his estate, must surrender it, ib.
Of a manor, may be admitted within or without the manor and without holding any court, 160.
Of a mortgagor, mortgagee's rights against, 263.

TENANT AT WILL—
Cestui que trust in actual occupation is a, 33.
Not liable for permissive waste, ib.
When entitled to emblements, ib.

TENANT FOR LIFE—

Can make binding leases under the Leases and Sales of Settled Estates Acts, 37.
Remaining in possession after determination of an estate *pur autre vie* is a trespasser, 92.
Is entitled to estovers, 93.
May take stone for repairs, *ib.*
May cut underwood, *ib.*
May work mines opened by a preceding tenant, *ib.*
May fell timber for repairs, *ib.*
May not, ordinarily, commit waste, *ib.*
Cannot charge the expense of improvements on the inheritance, 94.
May be restrained from committing waste, *ib.*
† Is liable at law, though not in equity, for permissive waste, *ib.*
Has special property in timber of buildings which are blown down, 94.
Not allowed to benefit by sale of timber which he has wrongfully severed, *ib.*
Receives income derived from sale of timber cut by order of the Court of Chancery, 95.
May be made unimpeachable of waste, *ib.*
Can have no property in timber until it is actually severed, *ib.*
Must keep down charges carrying interest, 97.
Not bound to pay arrears of interest due from a former tenant, *ib.*
Paying off a charge on the estate is entitled to keep it alive for his own benefit, 98.
Statutory powers of, to make improvements, 98, 99, 100, 101, 102, 103.
May sell the property, under the Lands Clauses Consolidation Act, 103.
Is entitled to custody of title-deeds, 104.
When entitled to remove fixtures, *ib.*
Representatives of a, may remove fixtures within a reasonable time, 105.
Rent is now apportionable on death of a, 107, 108, 109.
Executors or administrators of a, are entitled to emblements, 109.
Covenants for title to be entered into by a, 340.

TENANT IN COMMON—

Is nearly in the same position as an independent tenant, 229.
In fee simple has been restrained from committing waste, 230.

TENANT IN FEE SIMPLE—

Has absolute power over his estate, 130.
May deal at will with fixtures during his lifetime, *ib.*
Right of executor or administrator of a, to fixtures, *ib.*

TENANT IN TAIL—

Lease by a, did not at one time bind his issue, 36.
Provisions of the 32 Hen. VIII., c. 28, as to leases by a, *ib.*
Can make binding leases under the Fines and Recoveries Abolition Act, 37.
May commit any kind of waste, 112.
Cannot be bound by covenant not to commit waste, *ib.*
Is not bound to keep down interest on charges affecting the estate, 113.
Paying off charges, presumed to have done so for the benefit of the inheritance, *ib.*
Is entitled to custody of title-deeds, *ib.*'

TENANT IN TAIL—(continued.)
　May, whilst in possession, remove fixtures put up by himself or by a
　　previous tenant, 113.
　Executor or administrator of a, has a right to remove fixtures, *ib.*
　Can bar the estate tail, 118.
　Restrictions on power of a, to bar estate tail, 119.
　Mode of barring an estate tail by a, when married woman, 121.
　Apportionment Acts apply to leases made by a, 123.
　Executor or administrator of a, is entitled to emblements, 124.

TENURE—
　By the family, 4.
　By Knight Service, 8.
　Socage, 10.
　Villein, 12.
　Villein socage, 13.
　By ancient demesne, 14.
　Burgage, *ib.*
　In frankalmoign, *ib.*
　By Knight Service, abolished, 21.

TERM—
　Of years is personal property, 2.
　Any tenancy of definite duration is a, 35.
　Grant of a, is called a demise, 36.
　Is a chattel real, *ib.*
　Not put an end to by disclaimer of assignee's trustee in bankruptcy,
　　66.
　Determination of a, *ib.*
　Long terms, advantages of, 74.
　Satisfied, when, 76.
　Satisfied, presumed to be attendant on the inheritance, *ib.*
　Satisfied, advantages and disadvantages of, 77, 78.
　Satisfied terms abolished, 79.
　Satisfied when considered as subsisting, 80.
　Of years, no remainder in, 194.
　In a marriage settlement, to secure wife's income, 388, 392.
　In a marriage settlement, to secure jointure, 391, 392.
　In a marriage settlement, to secure portions, 391, 393.

TESTATOR—
　Who may be a, 401.
　Signature by a, 406.
　Signature on behalf of a, 407.
　Acknowledgment by a, *ib.*
　Witnesses to a will must be present at the signature or acknowledg-
　　ment of the, *ib.*
　Witnesses to a will must be able to see the, affix his signature, *ib.*
　Must be able to see witnesses affix their signatures, 408.
　Will to be construed as speaking from moment of death of the, 412.
　General devise may include land of which the, is trustee or mort-
　　gagee, 415.

TESTATUM—
In a purchase deed, 342.
In a lease, 363.
In a mortgage deed, 383.

TIMBER—
Tenant for life may fell, for repairs, 93.
Tenant for life not entitled, as a rule, to cut, *ib.*
If blown down during a tenancy for life should be sold and proceeds invested, 94.
If wrongfully severed, course to be pursued, *ib.*
Application of fund formed by sale of, under order of the Court of Chancery, 95.
Tenant for life can have no property in, until severance, *ib.*
Mistaken appropriation of proceeds of sale of, may be rectified by the Court of Chancery, 96.
Tenant for life cannot cut ornamental, *ib.*
Rights as to, of a lord and tenant of copyholds, 168.
In the absence of custom, neither lord nor copyholder can cut, 169.
Condition of sale as to valuation of, 312.

TITLE—
To be shown, conditions of sale as to, 312—315.
Length of, which a purchaser may require, 312.
Selection of a root of, 313.
Lessor's, law as to showing, *ib.*
Purchaser should be precluded from investigating, other than as shown by the vendor, 315.
Covenants for, in purchase deeds, 338—341.
Covenants for, by husband on sale of wife's real estate, 340.
Covenant for, by trustee, *ib.*
Covenant for, by mortgagee, *ib.*
Covenant for, by executors, *ib.*
Covenants for, by *cestui que trust*, *ib.*
Covenants for, by tenant for life, *ib.*
Crown does not enter into covenants for, 341.
Covenants for, limitation of time for suing on, *ib.*
Lessee should be precluded from investigating lessor's, 346.
Lessor's covenant for, 363.
Covenants for, in a marriage settlement, 399.

TITLE-DEEDS—
Tenant for life is entitled to the custody of, 104.
Tenant in tail is entitled to the custody of, 113.
Mortgage by deposit of, how viewed in equity, 279.
Mortgage by deposit of, may secure future advances, *ib.*
All the, of an estate need not be deposited to make a mortgage, 280.
Condition of sale as to, 324.
Recent enactment as to retention of, by a vendor, *ib.*

TRUSTEE—
Of a bankrupt may disclaim lease, 66.
Of a bankrupt who is tenant in tail, powers of, 122.
To preserve contingent remainders, 204, 205.

TRUSTEE—(*continued.*)
Having power to sell land may dispose of minerals separately, 221.
Acknowledgment of mortgagor's title by one, of several who are mortgagees, 257.
Covenant for title to be entered into by a, 340.
Declaration in a mortgage deed, on loan by trustees, 375.
Powers of the general trustees, in a marriage settlement, 397.
Powers conferred on trustees by statute, 399.
A general devise may include land of which the testator is a, 415.

TRUSTS—
Uses before the Statute of Uses were, 183.
Re-establishment of, after the Statute of Uses, 188.
Executed and executory, distinction between, 191.
Executory, how given effect to, *ib.*
Changes in the law relating to, 295.

USES—
Introduction of, 182.
Definition of, before the Statute of Uses, 183.
At one time not recognized by the Common Law, but always enforced by the Court of Chancery, *ib.*
Not subject to the rules of law, *ib.*
Resulting, 184.
Objections to system of, *ib.*
Statute of Uses, 185.
How recognized by the law, 186.
Rules of law relating to, 186—188.
Limitations by way of, after the Statute of Uses, 208.
Springing, definition of, *ib.*
Shifting, definition of, 209.
Shifting, employment of, in marriage settlements, 388.

VASSAL—
Meaning of the word, 5.
Originally held his land at the pleasure of his lord, *ib.*
Afterwards allowed an estate for life, *ib.*
Subsequently received a fee descendible to his issue, 6.

VENDOR—
Must deliver a perfect abstract, 325.
When entitled to rescind the contract of sale, 326.
Unwillingness of, to answer requisitions, *semble* must be reasonable, *ib.*

VILLEIN—
Meaning of term, 12.
Was at first the property of his lord, 13.
Gradual improvement in the condition of a, 19.
Most villeins free by time of Edward VI., *ib.*

VILLEIN SOCAGE—
Bracton's account of, 13.
Partook of nature of both free and base tenures, 14.
Only found in lands of ancient demesne, *ib.*
Called also tenure by ancient demesne, *ib.*

VILLEIN TENURE—
Origin of, 12.
Was base, *ib.*
Tenant by, could not quit without his lord's permission, 13.
Gradual improvement in, 19.
Change in form of grant of land held by, *ib.*
Incidents of, *ib.*
Lands granted in, came to be held by the custom of the manor, 20.
Privileges of tenants by, *ib.*

WAIVER—
Of forfeiture of a lease, when presumed, 67.
Of forfeiture of a lease, lessor's acts which are not, *ib.*
By lessor, of notice to quit, when presumed, 71.

WARDSHIP—
Origin of, 16.
Lord had, of infant tenant by Knight Service, *ib.*
Duration of, *ib.*
Abolished, 21.

WARRANTY—
Vouching to, 115.
By tenant in tail, after the 31st of December 1833, is void against issue in tail and remainder-men, 118.

WASTE—
Permissive, what is, 33.
Tenant at will is not liable for permissive, *ib.*
Tenant for years is liable for permissive, 54.
Definition of, 55.
Lessee may not commit, *ib.*
Writ of, under old law, *ib.*
How restrained, *ib.*
Tenant for life may not, ordinarily, commit, 93.
Tenant for life liable at law, though not in equity, for permissive, 94.
Tenant for life may be made unimpeachable of, 95.
Equitable, definition of, 96.
Tenant for life cannot, in any case, commit equitable, *ib.*
Principle of Court of Chancery as to equitable, 97.
Tenant in tail may commit any kind of, 112.
Tenant in common in fee simple has been restrained from committing, 230.

WIDOW—
Cannot claim more than six years' arrears of dower, 84.
Right of a, to dower may be barred by husband, 85.
Married since the Dower Act is not barred of dower by old form of conveyance to bar dower, 87.

WIFE.—See MARRIED WOMAN.

WILL—
Alienation of land by, formerly unknown, 27.
Permitted by statute of Henry VIII., ib.
Extended by statute of Victoria, 28.
Surrender of copyholds to use of a, no longer necessary, 158.
Changes in the law relating to wills, 294.
Who may make a, 401.
Infant cannot make a, of real property, ib.
Of a married woman, ib.
Execution and attestation of a, 402.
Need not necessarily be in ink, 403.
Alterations in a, 404.
Interlineation in a, 405.
Signature to a, ib.
Signature to a, on behalf of the testator, 406.
Acknowledgment of a, by the testator, 407.
Witnesses must be present at signature or acknowledgment of a, ib.
Signature by witnesses to a, ib.
Attestation of a, 408.
Selection of witnesses to a, 409.
Of land, is governed by the law of the country where it is situated, 410.
Of English leaseholds, must be made in conformity with the law of England, ib.
What property may be disposed of by, ib.
Of copyholds does not pass the legal estate until the devisee is admitted, 412.
To be construed as speaking from moment of testator's death, ib.
Residuary devise in a, to include lapsed and void devises, ib.
General devise in a, to include copyholds and leaseholds, ib.
Power of appointment may be exercised by a general devise in a, ib.
Devise in a, without words of limitation may pass a fee simple, ib.
General devise in a, may include land of which the testator is trustee or mortgagee, 415.
Revocation of a, by marriage, 417.
Revocation of a, by will or codicil, 419.
Revocation of a, by a writing executed like a will, 420.
Revocation of a, by destruction, 420, 421.
Cancellation of a, is not revocation, 421.
Revival of a, 423.
Destroyed, cannot be revived, 424.

WILLIAM THE CONQUEROR—
Grants of lands by, after the Conquest, 7.
Probably founded villein socage tenure, 14.

INDEX.

WITNESS—
To a will may sign it on behalf of the testator, 407.
To a will must be present when it is signed or acknowledged by the testator, *ib.*
To a will must be able to see the testator sign it, *ib.*
To a will, signature of a, *ib.*
To a will must attest it, 408.
Selection of witnesses to a will, 409.
To a will cannot take any benefit under it, *ib.*

WORDS OF CONVEYANCE—
Office of the, in a deed, 334.
Appropriate, in a purchase deed, *ib.*

THE END.

JOHN CHILDS AND SON, PRINTERS.

www.ingramcontent.com/pod-product-compliance
Lightning Source LLC
Chambersburg PA
CBHW021415300426
44114CB00010B/507